D0858848

Best Wishes & Keep the
faith—

Ron Bailey

WILDERNESS PATROL

Memoirs of a Federal Agent...
Thirty-six Years Behind the Badge

By Ron Bailey

Lightnin' Ridge Books

Box 22
Bolivar • MO 65613
417-777-5227

First Edition
First Printing

WILDERNESS PATROL

Memoirs of a Federal Agent...
Thirty-six Years Behind the Badge

Copyright 2009 by Ron Bailey

Published by:
Lightnin Ridge Books
Box 22
Bolivar, Missouri 65613
USA

Cover Design and Layout • Dorothy Loges

ISBN - 978-0-9673975-6-6
Library of Congress Catalog Number - 2009921287

Dedicated

To a Court Clerk, The Love of my Life....

A beautiful girl with a crooked smile,
Who went far beyond the extra mile.

In her eyes, heart, and soul lived
    love and commitment.

As she journeyed with me to places
    far distant.

On a destined quest ending much too soon,
I owe all to her, my wife Shirley June.

Blessings
Shirley June Bailey

And their work is concerned with "fish and game management, preservation, propagation and protection, outdoor and nature activities, public fishing and hunting areas, and flora and fauna preservation."

In realization that "The ownership of and the title to all wild animals in this state, not legally confined or held in private ownership legally acquired, is in the state, which holds such title in trust for the benefit of all the people." (Ohio Statute)

IN REMEMBRANCE

Of a beloved son of Ohio and dedicated Wildlife Warrior; State Game Protector Pete Andre, fallen in the line of duty at a poacher's hand, in the wilds of Scioto County. September, 1952.

ACKNOWLEDGMENTS

To those I worked for and with, who nurtured, taught, led, and otherwise influenced me in a positive way, I give tribute and recognition in the text. To my parents, Fred and Frances, my siblings, children, grandchildren and extended family; thanks for your encouragement and "all" you mean to me. To a grand and great lady - a stalwart champion and the love of my life, Shirley June Bailey, who edited and arranged my scribblings so they made sense, I give due credit and heartfelt thanks. To Vernell McCormick, Mary Surratt, and my beloved granddaughter Leah Haupt, thanks for relieving some of the editing pressure off my Shirley June.

To publisher Larry Dablemont, thanks for your patience and advice. To publishing layout specialist Dorothy Loges, your "finishing touches" made it all worthwhile.

I must, in all honesty, give my greatest acknowledgment to a big game warden from California, who during an hour long phone call on his dime, motivated Shirley and I to do this work. His words awoke my professional pride - asleep since retirement. He mustered the "gumption" within that caused my hand to grasp the pen and begin.

For all this, we offer our everlasting thanks to a great game warden and very special, Special Agent - Terry Grosz.

About the Author

Ron Bailey entered this life November 23, 1934 at Columbus, Ohio. That same year a federal law, The Migratory Bird Hunting and Conservation Stamp Act was enacted. Later, it became known as the "Duck Stamp Act." Among its provisions it required those sixteen years of age and older to purchase an annual Federal Duck Stamp prior to hunting and taking migratory waterfowl. Thus, funding in part, our National Wildlife Refuge System. Twenty-one years later Ron began a long career enforcing this Act along with many state, federal wildlife and other natural resource laws.

Born and raised a mid-westerner, Ron's law enforcement career as an Ohio State Game Warden, Colorado State Game Warden, Park Ranger, Project Park Manager and Area Park Manager for the Louisville and Portland Districts of the U.S. Army Corps of Engineers, Special Agent for the National Marine Fisheries Service and Special Agent for the U.S. Fish and Wildlife Service took him the length and breadth of the nation. As Ron comments, "I've seen the sun rise in Maine and set in California. I've seen it rise again in Washington and set in Florida. Throw in Georges Bank and the North Atlantic–I couldn't ask for more." A recipient of numerous Outstanding Achievement Awards, his wildlife management career spanned almost forty years. Of these, thirty-six involved and / or were devoted to law enforcement.

He was aware of what his life-long profession would be at an early age due to a Game Warden experience. After high school graduation, his career began in 1953 as a ninety day temporary hire, making ninety six cents an hour at the Ohio Division of Wildlife's Olentangy Wildlife Research Station at Delaware. Of his time at Delaware, Ron states, "My training and experience at the Olentangy Wildlife Research Station was never equaled." Before retirement, he held the position of Senior Resident Agent in charge of North and South Carolina for the U.S. Fish and Wildlife Service's Law Enforcement Division in Raleigh. As a wildlife professional, he is the product of in-service training, schooling and work experience. An avid student of wildlife management authors, Aldo Leopold, Reuben E. Trippensee, Durwood L. Allen, Ira N. Gabrielson and Edward H. Graham; he also took specialized - career oriented studies at Ohio University, the University of Kentucky and the University of Montana at Missoula.

As told in "Wilderness Patrol," his sometimes heart warming, sometimes comical, sometimes dangerous true-life stories are always adventuresome.

Now, with Shirley June, a retired Para Legal and Court Clerk, and his steadfast helpmate and wife for over four decades, both enjoy their retirement years residing near the Blue Ridge Parkway in Virginia. They have six children, twelve grandchildren and ten great grandchildren. Their church, family, and natural resource oriented retirement activities and "projects" are many.

Preface

Of my profession and career, I've said many times, "I've never worked a day in my life." For me it was never work. It was an early and continuing love – a calling – a privilege – and yes, an obsession. I admit it, I even liked most of my adversaries, the violators. Like it or not, without them the profession wouldn't exist.

It would be nice to say, "No apologies – no regrets," but I can't say that. There are apologies to make and I do have regrets. My apologies go to my family – each and every member. I'm certain they all know how deeply I love them. I'm also certain they each recall all too many times when I placed the job first and them second.

I regret there were times during certain life experiences, I suffered under the illusion my work – my mission – was all I had – all I could rely on. It was most certainly an illusion, although during those times I accomplished some of my best work.

I've been blessed with the privilege of working with many wildlife and other resource management professionals. I am convinced they were as deeply motivated as I was to protect our resources. By the same token, I've had to tolerate all too many, at both the state and federal levels, who should never have gone into wildlife law enforcement. Everything from a State Game Warden so worthless his own sons petitioned the State Wildlife Agency he worked for to get rid of him, as he'd become a "laughing stock" in his assigned duty area; to an intimidated backup Federal Agent who abandoned me in what he perceived to be a dangerous situation in a Florida swamp. There were too many of the unmotivated, inexperienced, political, untested and self serving who sucked and politicked their way into supervisory positions where they plagued and hindered the performance of good officers. As a darn good federal agent assigned to a southern state commented of a certain individual, "He doesn't understand our world so he's trying to cram his world down our throats." By and large, I had no time for these people. I simply did my best to get around them and dismiss them from my thoughts. However, my contempt for them remains today as it will until I pass from this earth. They were a putrid sacrilege who contaminated the cause and did little more than occupy space.

Another "thorn in my flesh" were the cheap, cheesy politicians. As a Wildlife Enforcement Agent with the Ohio Division of Wildlife, part of my duties included doing background investigations on applicants for the Game Protector Training School. I completed an investigation of an applicant who lied on his application about college credits and prior arrests. Before I finished writing his background investigation report, I learned he was hired, wearing a badge and assigned to a duty station – fresh off the street with no training school and no prior experience. His only "qualification" was the fact he was a member of the "Young Republican's Club of Ohio."

How vividly I recall in my fourteenth year with the Ohio Division of Wildlife, I was summoned to the Columbus Office where I was interviewed for a District Law Enforcement Supervisor's position. My interview went well as the Chief of the Division of Wildlife reviewed my entire personnel file and case record. As a Wildlife Enforcement Agent, I stayed in the top five each year with arrests and convictions. At the end of the interview, almost as I walked out the door, reluctantly he stated, "You'll need to go back to your home county or the county you live in now and get an endorsement from the County Republican Chairman." I walked towards the door. I didn't turn around or say a word – just left. Outside the door I paused and leaned back against the door. I was stunned – fourteen years of service, a perfect work record and I had to get a political endorsement from a County Republican Chairman. I don't know who that person is in either county, I thought.

Back in Williams County where I lived, my wife Shirley was the County Court Clerk. She told me who the County Republican Chairman was – a downtown realtor. I thought, I'll play this thing out and see where it goes. I went to see this realtor/County Republican Chairman. I didn't ask for the endorsement, I simply questioned him as to the "why" of the practice and told him how I thought it "contaminated" state service. With that, he puffed up like a toad and the true political hack he was, came out. "Well, I've never heard of you doing anything for the Republican Party here or anywhere else," he chortled. I ended my visit with that statement, excused myself and left his office, seething with rage.

Less than a year later, I was recruited from the Federal Civil Service Mid-Level Register by the U.S. Army Corps of Engineers, Louisville, Kentucky District to fill a Park Ranger's position. This would pay much more per year than I was making plus overtime. I accepted the job.

Just before I left for my new federal duty station in Indiana, I went to see the County Republican Chairman again. What I said to him isn't fit to print. I enraged him so much he followed me out of his office onto the street, exactly where I wanted him. "You think going with the damned Feds is going to save your ass, don't you Bailey?" the red faced political hack stated. "Well, let me tell you something – there's a big wind coming and you'd better find a big oak tree to hang on to," he continued.

"If that big wind you're talking about gets me, you'd better hope it doesn't blow me back here because you're the first one I'll come looking for," I responded. I headed for him but didn't catch him as he ran for his office door and got inside before I got to him. I turned around to see a City Police cruiser pull over and park on the other side of the street and decided to "cool off" and go home.

From making one mistake after another during an entire night catching poachers as a young commissioned Game Protector at age 23; to employing the use of regressive hypnosis to put the finishing touch on a successful after-the-fact investigation, involving a Michigan based deer poaching ring operating in Ohio, as a Wildlife Enforcement Agent, my career with the Ohio Division of Wildlife ended.

Later, as a Federal Park Ranger with the Army Corps of Engineers assigned to Mansfield (now C.M. Harden) Lake, a flood control reservoir in Indiana, an Indianapolis millionaire and big Democrat swore he'd have my job. I had given him a time frame to remove an elaborate encroachment on government property that replaced and destroyed a section of shoreline wildlife habitat. He ignored the notice, as he had many times before my arrival at Mansfield. With a Corps wrecking crew, we ripped out every board and masonry that constituted his illegal encroachment. Soon he phoned me, belligerent and threatening. I calmed him down by telling him, "I thought the way I handled this was better than hauling you into court. If there is a next time, you will be in court."

The State of Indiana maintained a State Park at Mansfield Lake under a Corps out-grant. Shortly thereafter I entered the State Park Manager's Office. The Park Manager (a political appointee) was a little Democrat who butchered the English language. "You'd better pack your bags," he stuttered. He went on to tell me the Indianapolis millionaire Democrat who furnished the building in Indianapolis for the State Democratic Convention each year, had just left his office after bragging to everyone present he was going to have my job.

After learning the millionaire was at his home on the lake, I decided to pay him a visit. The little "politico" State Park Manager assured me I shouldn't do this as the big shot from Indianapolis was "Italian", "hot headed" and "knew how to get things done." Shortly, the "hot headed"

Italian answered my knock on his front door. As he stepped outside and shut the door, I stated. "They tell me over at the State Park you're going to have my job. If that's true, you're in essence threatening the welfare of my family. It looks like you and I have something to settle and now is a good time to get it done." He immediately denied the statements he made at the State Park Office and waffled all over the place, claiming he didn't want any trouble with me or the Army Corps of Engineers. I wasn't worried anyway as my "big boss" in the Louisville Office, Fred Huelson, had phoned and congratulated me on getting rid of the encroachment.

I'll say here and now there was never a time during my tenure with the Army Corps of Engineers working as a Park Ranger, Project Park Manager and Area Park Manager in both the Louisville, Kentucky and Portland, Oregon Districts that I wasn't backed to the hilt by the "powers that be" as I enforced Title 36, Chapter 111 of the Federal Code that governs the public use of Corps Projects and the various easement, wildlife and parks lease and out-grant provisions between the Corps and other contracting parties. I'll freely admit some of the actions I took to accomplish the mission were "controversial."

In 1987, two members of the North Carolina Wildlife Resources Commission (the governing body over the N.C. State Fish and Game Agency), one a Democrat, the other a Republican tried, through congressional appeal, to have a Federal Wildlife Agent (and pilot) transferred. Their claim was the agent was deliberately "frustrating hunters and frightening ducks with his airplane." Specifically, the hunters and duck hunting clubs in Currituck County, where one of the complainants resided and was closely associated with a big duck hunting club.

The Agent/Pilot in question was one of the best Game Wardens who ever drew breath. He not only found their grain baited areas, he landed and caught them and provided every Federal Agent working in Currituck with all he could catch illegally hunting waterfowl over bait. I was the Agent in Charge of the Carolinas where six Federal Agents were assigned. We caught every duck hunting club in Currituck County, some several times. We were always "breathing down their necks" and they couldn't stand it. On one opening day of the season, not a single club gunned because they thought a "Fed" was behind every myrtle bush – a rumor fostered among themselves. I changed motel rooms three times that night to dodge club operators (three at the door of my first location when I got there) and their phone calls. They asked why I was harassing them so badly and how long I was going to have Currituck "saturated" with Feds.

When interviewed by the press concerning the transfer of the Agent/Pilot, I stated the complaints were baseless and what the real motive behind the transfer requests were; any attempt to transfer the Agent would wind up in U.S. District Court. Then I lit into the two Wildlife Commission members -- it was pretty bad. "Ron, I'm not going to print that for your own good – I'll consider it off the record," the reporter (whom I knew) said.

I decided this was a good opportunity to find out what the folks in Currituck County really thought about us and the way we did our jobs. I conducted thirty two phone interviews. I talked with every hunting club operator (except the complainants) and every guide I knew – we busted all of them. I was surprised – not one complained about the Feds or the way we operated. Several complained we didn't stop in and socialize as some agents in the past had done – have a cup of coffee, etc. One club operator stated, "Don't think for one minute the Wildlife Commissioner from this County speaks for all of us. We know why your plane is up there – you caught us fair and square – keep on doing your jobs." From that time on I had a respect for the folks in Currituck County I never had before, even though I'm sure I know where I could go this next duck season and make a baiting case.

Actually, there were two Agent/Pilots who flew Currituck bait patrols. Ted Curtis was the one they went after. The other thorn in their flesh was Jerry Sommers, a great Game Warden, who also landed his aircraft and busted them as well as provide the rest of us on the ground with all we could catch.

Agent Tom Bennett, the principal agent assigned to Currituck, directed most of our operations there. Tom cut a swath through Currituck they'll remember the rest of their days.

Agents Garland Swain and George Hines assigned to South Carolina, were two of the best and toughest Game Wardens God ever made. They periodically came to Currituck, caught who they were assigned to catch and more. In one situation, Garland and assisting Agent Pat McIntosh, lay hidden in the marsh while corn was thrown all over them as the club "baited up" for the next days hunt. Currituck was "old hat" to Agent George Hines. His father, Agent/Pilot Tommy Hines, thirty years earlier, was transferred due to a congressional appeal because he "frustrated hunters and frightened ducks," when in truth he cut a swath in Currituck, and other coastal counties, never forgotten.

Agent Jack Baker arrived late in my tenure. I soon saw he was a darn good Game Warden. During subsequent years, he proved the fact. In 2006 he won the National Fish and Wildlife Foundation's Guy

Bradley Award – one of the highest awards a Wildlife Officer can receive.

Special Agents Dave Cartwright, Billy Mellor and Charles Bazemore, were a part of the "Carolina's crew" for relatively short periods of time, before going on to serve as outstanding Agents in other duty stations. They more than proved their worth as routine field patrol "catch dogs", superb after-the-fact investigators and undercover operatives.

I was blessed with good agents. I regarded them all as "sent from on high." We had our differences but after we got through "disagreeing", we once again jelled as a unit and got the job done – not just field patrol – run and catch type operations but also major, after the fact, and covert undercover operations. For a decade as field agents, we were tops nationwide in covert operations working and bringing to justice, the worst and most dangerous of all wildlife law violators – those engaged in illegal wildlife commercialization.

I wrote a complete report, highlighting my thirty two Currituck interviews, concerning the whole issue and sent it to my SAC (Special Agent in Charge) Dan Searcy in Atlanta. He supported us every way he could. For some reason a report from the Senior Resident Agent in Charge wasn't good enough. The next thing I knew the matter was being investigated by a Fish and Wildlife Service Agent assigned to a western state. I wasn't allowed to meet with him, pick him up at the airport, furnish him a vehicle – nothing – no contact. I guess he completed his investigation – I was never given a copy of it even when I requested one. I don't blame the investigating agent – he did what he was assigned to do. I regard the whole approach as underhanded and no way professional. It sticks in my craw yet today. I'll always believe there was an "element" in the Washington D.C. Office, for whatever reason, had a "thing" about the southeast region. I've heard a rumor as to why this situation existed; however, I'll leave it at that – a rumor. I do know our boss in Atlanta, Dan Searcy, put all the Carolina Agents in for the "Honor" award. However, the "powers that be" in the Washington Office chose to give the award to an agent who completed a case that didn't begin to approach the magnitude of our "Operation Rock", a covert investigation into the illegal commercialization of strippers or "rock fish" in North Carolina, Virginia and reached to the seagoing luxury liners in the Atlantic. There is more to this story but I'll stop at this point.

From out of the blue, came a letter from former U.S. Fish and Wildlife Service Director, Lynn Greenwalt, in full support of the North Carolina agents. It was a scorching document that "set the hair" on this same Currituck "faction," who during Mr. Greenwalt's Directorship, pressured him politically and incessantly to transfer certain agents in North Carolina who did their jobs. Director Greenwalt, in spite of it all, supported his troops who worked Currituck then as he was now supporting Agent Ted Curtis and the rest of us. He sent copies of his letter to "all" concerned. His letter was unexpected and hit the "faction" square between the eyes. I hope he realizes how much it meant and the lasting results he accomplished.

As it all turned out to his everlasting credit, North Carolina Congressman, Walter Jones, Chairman of the Merchant Marine and Fisheries Committee, whose Fish and Wildlife Sub-Committee had "oversight jurisdiction" over the Fish and Wildlife Service (and to whom the two N.C. State Wildlife Commissioners complained) supported my agents and me 100%. Floyd Lupton, the Congressman's Chief Administrative Aid, a former N.C. Wildlife Officer and superb wildlife undercover operative, called me and stated, "Ron, you and your troops are doing a good job down there – keep up the good work. As far as the Congressman is concerned, it's a dead issue." I might add, Floyd Lupton is a brother to Warren Lupton, who was a Fish and Wildlife Service Agent in Charge of North Carolina. Agent Lupton preceded Senior Resident Agent, John Minick whom I replaced. The Congressman, Floyd and Warren Lupton, helped me on several occasions when ridiculous budget cuts prevented us from putting our aircraft in the air (a fixed wing and a helicopter), our patrol cars on the road and our boats in the water. I contacted the Congressman through Floyd and/or Warren only when I had to, but when I did, the aircraft went up, the patrol cars went on the road and we launched the boats. Congressman Jones won the highest award the National Wildlife Federation presents. Both his and Floyd's framed photo hang in my home today. They are two exceptions to my "cheap cheesy politician rule."

With the mention of wrong training priorities, poor goal absent program management, non-prioritized budget constraints, worn out, inadequate and out dated equipment that continually plagued the profession in that day and time; I'll stop writing about the negative side of it all.

Now my thoughts return to the beginning – to a childhood dream and fantasy that came true – back to my beloved Ohio where as a youth, I found and came to know my Creator. Not in a church, synagogue, tabernacle or temple, but under Ohio skies in his magnificent, sanctified wilderness with its woodlands, hills, prairies, wetlands, creeks and rivers and among his wild creatures therein.

I've heard war veterans who experienced and survived many of the worst battles say, "There are no atheists in battle." Some go into battle believing they are atheists but soon become "believers" when the chips are down and they know they may soon "belong to the ages."

I never met a good Game Warden or Park Ranger worth his salt who was an atheist. It's not just the dangers of the profession – all he (or anyone) has to do is look at God's wilderness – the wild places and "up" to the heavens, to know he is real. If, after witnessing his creation, you come away a non-believer, I can only say, "May He have mercy on your soul."

My stories in the text, I consider career highlights. More are un-written. Of those, some untold. Of those untold, some will so remain. However, I am by nature, a story teller and a would-be poet. Perhaps someday - - - - .

Lord willing, if one or more issue of this publication sells, any financial gain due the author will prayerfully find its way to those in need through Franklin Graham's Samaritan's Purse.

Now dear reader come with me, as based on true-life experi-ences past, I tell of a destined crusade long ago -- battling those who would pillage, destroy and lay waste our God given wildlife legacy.

Table of Contents

1
Where and When
It All Began

I was born and raised in rural central Ohio – the eastern edge of the great Midwest – the bread basket of the world – farm country. We lived in a small typical Midwestern farm community named Ostrander, situated in Delaware County north of Columbus, within the rich fertile Scioto and Olentangy River watersheds.

It almost goes without saying, next to farming, school, and church, hunting, fishing and trapping was a very important part of our lives. A part of our culture. We enjoyed very good pheasant and rabbit hunting. Quail and doves were plentiful but hunting them was prohibited by an early and ill conceived Ohio law. Waterfowl hunting was certainly there and available; however, very few of us actually participated. That great hunting experience was left to the "sports" of Columbus who frequently duck and goose hunted the vast grain producing Scioto and Olentangy River bottoms. Deer were almost nonexistent. If someone told you he saw one, you pretty well assumed he was telling a lie. Coon hunting was all important; it seemed like everyone kept hounds. If you didn't hunt those masked rascals you were almost a social outcast. Lord knows I loved night hunting and those wonderful hounds; I still do. I developed an in-depth and working knowledge of the bloodlines and breeds; the Blueticks, Walkers, Redbones, Black & Tans, Plotts and English. Little did I realize someday my knowledge of the hounds would serve the resource well, when I performed as an undercover operative and case agent in charge of one the greatest cases I ever worked for the U.S. Fish & Wildlife Service.

Trapping was an important part of our lives. As a young boy I enjoyed trapping. It was on one occasion while I was setting traps I had my first encounter with a Game Warden. It was 1947 -- I was twelve years old. Clyde Lansdowne and Frank Taylor, whose grandson Dale is my best friend,

1

were the absolute best and dominate trappers in that neck of the woods. They mainly trapped Mill Creek and its connecting wetlands, a tributary of the Scioto. They trapped portions of the Scioto. By and large, they left the little tributary streams of Mill Creek and others to the younger trappers. Blues Creek is one of those streams. It meanders through Ostrander and Jacktown, a community yet smaller and a suburb of Ostrander. Needless to say, the competition to trap Blues Creek, especially within walking, hiking or bicycle distance of Ostrander was keen among the young trappers of the community.

It was mid October and several of us young trappers had checked Blues Creek. It was loaded – we observed a lot of sign i.e. muskrat dens and slides, coon and opossum tracks galore, mink and fox sign. We knew trapping would be good that fall and winter.

Jimmie Roush was one of my good buddies. We decided to trap together. We had eight traps between us. Two Blake and Lambs and six Victors. We decided to "get the jump" on everyone else and "stake our claim" by setting our traps from the Jacktown bridge downstream until we ran out of traps. It was two weeks ahead of the Ohio 1947- 48 trapping season. We arrived at Blues Creek early in the morning and made five sets for muskrat and two for coon. We completed making our last complicated set for mink; Jimmie had to hang from an undercut tree root in order to gently place the trap where it needed to be. We congratulated each other on the completion of our trap setting task. We were estimating the money we would make from the sale of our furs to Mr. Cody, the fur dealer at Marysville. After all, a muskrat pelt was worth about $2.25--$2.75, coon about $3.00, opossum $1.50, mink $40.00 -- WOW!, and a fox about $20.00 plus the $5.00 bounty you could collect from the county clerk for turning in its paws. We would have money for more traps, school clothes, a pair of high top boots, etc.

We sat on the banks of Blues Creek, warming in the early morning sun, musing over our forthcoming success and wealth. It was about 9:00 a.m. when I saw him walking straight toward us -- a tall, slender man wearing the most striking forest green uniform I've ever seen. A broad brimmed Stetson hat with a shiny black leather band around the base; a silver hat badge centered in the front; an olive drab shirt with black tie showed beneath a forest green Eisenhower coat. Over his coat he wore a shined black leather Sam Brown gun belt and shoulder strap with a holstered revolver on his right hip. His trousers flared slightly between the waist and knees, somewhat like riding britches. He wore side buckled black leather boots that rose to just below his knees and a big silver badge on his chest that looked huge. I was in absolute awe of this man even before he got to us.

"Who in the world is that?" I whispered to Jimmie.

"He's a Game Warden, I think he must be Guy Dennis. I think Dad knows him. If he's been watching us, we're caught," replied Jimmie.

"Good morning gentlemen, my name is Ollie Neimeyer. I am an Ohio State Game Protector, and it looks like you and I have a few things to talk about. Climb up on the big rock behind you and get comfortable." His greeting and demeanor was warm and friendly, yet authoritative and somewhat parental. The big rock lay partially in and out of the creek. Around the water side was a favorite fishing hole. We had a trap set downstream within ten feet of it.

"You've just finished setting a trap line during the closed season," the officer said. He went on to explain what we were doing was illegal and wrong, and why it was illegal and wrong.

Later, remembering the incident, I realized Officer Neimeyer, in terms a kid my age could understand, explained both the biological and sociological reasons behind the open and closed seasons. He explained the totally democratic manner in which Ohio's game and fish regulations were established each year. I received my first lesson in wildlife management that fall morning so long ago, and I was fascinated. Moreover, he told us we were "cheating on our peers."

"Do you think trapping before season is fair to the Fink boys who live up across the bridge? How about the Herriot and Smart boys?" How did he know their names? I'd never heard any of those guys talk about knowing a Game Warden. Never, for that matter, heard anyone in Ostrander talk about a Game Warden, I thought.

"Now gentlemen, you're going to pull your traps. After you've finished I have something to show you," Officer Neimeyer continued.

I felt defeated and ashamed as we started downstream to pull our so carefully set traps. One by one we pulled each trap, tripped it and handed it to the Officer. After pulling the seventh set, only the mink set was left. With our heads down Jimmie and I glanced at each other. An unspoken message, let's try to save this one, passed between us. "Well, I guess that's it," Jimmie said.

"Huh-uh fellows, you have another one a little further down the creek – the one up under the cut out bank, let's go get it," Officer Neimeyer responded. Heck, he's watched us set every trap, I thought. We arrived at the site of the eighth (mink) set. Jimmie reluctantly retrieved the trap, tripped it and handed it to Mr. Neimeyer.

"Okay, my young friends, now let's go to the road where my car is parked," the Officer stated. We went, single file with the Officer in the rear carrying our traps. There it was, a black Ford parked in plain view on the road above the area we set our traps. All we had to do was look up and we could have seen him perhaps before he spotted us. Obviously we were so engrossed in our illegal activity we didn't think about or see anything else.

Officer Neimeyer opened the trunk of his car. It was chock-full of bundles of steel leg-hold traps. There were several dead coons and muskrats, some wet and still in traps. The traps in each bundle were fastened together through their chain rings with a wire and attached oil cloth tag. The word "EVIDENCE" was printed in bold black letters on one side of the tag. The Officer secured and tagged our meager bundle of traps in the same manner as all the rest. On the back of the evidence tag, he wrote our names, the date, the township and county we were in and "Blues Creek." Then he put our traps in the trunk of his car along with all the others.

He continued what was obviously a routine procedure by recording our names, addresses, birth dates along with our parent's names and phone numbers on a page in a pocket sized tablet. He told us what we saw in his car trunk was the results of confiscations he made all over Delaware and Marion Counties.

"As you can see gentlemen, you're not alone. I hope and trust your experience with me here this morning will serve you in a good way. Don't ever violate the game laws again. You've lost your traps. You and your parents could be brought to court for your offenses but that's not going to happen due to policy and your age. I'm not your full time Game Protector – I'm the full time Officer in Marion County. Your Game Protector is Guy Dennis. When you report this incident to your parents, tell them Mr. Dennis will be in touch with them." With that parting statement, Officer Neimeyer drove off on his next quest and Ron Bailey was never the same again.

Jimmie and I spoke very little as we trudged home. "Gonna tell your folks?" Jimmie inquired.

"Oh yeah, maybe tomorrow," I responded.

"Gonna get your butt beat?" Jimmie asked.

"Oh no, I'm sure I won't, might get something though, don't know – but gotta beat that Game Warden talkin' to them. How about you – gonna get your butt beat?" I asked.

"Nah, but I'm like you – gonna tell the folks before that Game Warden does," Jim agreed. We parted, agreeing our trapping was over until the season opened and we got some more traps.

By the time I arrived home, I knew someday I would be a Game Warden. For some strange reason I didn't question it, I knew I would become a Game Warden. The thought raised goose bumps. I was thrilled with my decision. Somehow it seemed to offset what happened that morning and I began to realize, even at that young age, the day's events would somehow be one of the best things that ever happened to me.

At home, I told my mother of the morning's events and my decision to become a Game Warden. Dad was a long distance truck driver and gone "on the road," a fact that kind of relieved me because I knew by the time he got home, the whole issue would be "softened." I told Mother I was pretty sure she, Dad or I would not have to go to court or jail, and told her of the pending contact by Guy Dennis, the Delaware County Game Protector, which never happened. Neither family ever heard from Mr. Dennis.

Mother's reaction to my "chosen profession" was typical, I suppose. Uh-huh, tomorrow he'll want to be a pilot. "Sounds good Honey, with your love of nature, hunting and fishing and all," she quietly commented. I'm certain Mother always wanted at least one or all of her five sons to become ministers, preachers of the Gospel. "I hope each of my sons follow their innermost and heartfelt calling," she continued. Later, Dad's reaction was, "Good way to

4

get shot. Well, we'll see won't we?" My wonderful parents neither sanctioned nor disapproved of my career decision, but took the loving position any good parent should.

Jimmie and I didn't trap together that season or any other. Oddly, I can't recall us ever speaking of our experience that fall morning on Blues Creek again. Jimmie went on to become a carpenter and builder – one of the best. He married one of the prettiest girls in town, Mary Sampson and was a great husband and father. He became a well known conservationist, sportsman and community leader, respected and loved throughout his beloved Delaware County and beyond. He knew and supported every wildlife officer assigned to Delaware County during his life time. He sure supported me, when years later I was named Game Protector in Union County, the neighboring county west of Delaware. At our first meeting following my appointment, Jimmie took his hat off, did a pretense head scratch, chuckled as only he could and stated, "Ya potlicker, ya made it – now be the best Game Warden Union County ever had." Jimmie left for Heaven December 2002. Over six hundred souls who knew and loved him attended his funeral. I'll sure enough see him again.

It's said in each of our personal, professional and spiritual lives, at least five "pivotal" people will influence each of us in a positive way. Persons who will turn us around when we're headed in the wrong direction and cause us to make a right decision rather than a wrong one. Officer Ollie Neimeyer was the first "pivotal" in my professional life. During ensuing years I saw him frequently on a Columbus based TV show called, "The Outdoors with Don Mack" where he answered questions on wildlife management along with the game and fish laws, and as he did his entire professional life, preach the gospel of wildlife preservation through sound management. I heard of the talks he gave in the school systems, sportsmen and other civic groups in many counties. As always, delivering the same conservation message.

Soon after my appointment as Union County Game Protector, I put on my dress uniform and went to see Ollie, then retired, at his home in Prospect, Ohio on the banks of the Scioto River. Of course, my purpose was to make a statement, "Look Ollie, look at me. I made it, thanks to you and that great talk you gave me on the banks of Blues Creek so long ago." Ollie was in good health and hunted pheasants about every day of the season behind his two perfectly trained Irish Setters. He really didn't remember Jimmie or me – he caught so many during this thirty years as a wildlife officer. We were just two statistics, I suppose, somewhere in his files. I told Ollie (hoping he would remember) of the incident in 1947 on Blues Creek.

"Well, it's good to know I helped you. You couldn't have chosen a finer profession. It's one of the highest callings a man can receive – you're privileged – do the best job you know how to do so you'll know when it's all over you did your best," he advised.

On that note we shook hands and I headed for my patrol car and almost teared up as I waved goodbye to Ollie, who I'll swear for an instant, was

5

once again wearing that striking green uniform. Suck it up Bailey and get back to work, I thought as I headed down the Scioto, then up Mill Creek checking fishing licenses as I traveled home. It was the last time I saw Ohio State Game Protector Ollie Neimeyer. Who he was, what he stood for – his legacy, stands yet today. The conservation seed he sowed still brings forth beneficial fruit for Ohio Sportsmen and many others who will never know his name.

2
Delaware

About the middle of my senior year, at Scioto Valley High School in Ostrander, Ohio, quite by chance (because it wasn't publicized), I saw a notice on the bulletin board outside the principal's office. It announced night school classes available at Central High School in Columbus.

The requirements were you had to be a second semester senior within a certain number of credits toward graduation. Upon successful completion, you could graduate at Columbus Central or your credits could be transferred to your home school, and you could graduate there. It looked good to me. I did a quick calculation, was pretty sure I qualified, went to the principal's office to be sure, and found out I did.

"You don't want to do that," boomed Principal Ray Aldridge as he returned my credit record to the file.

Later, I learned this program wasn't publicized because funding was on a per student basis, and the schools didn't want to lose students. The various schools were required to post the notice by the State Board of Education. The program was designed to allow students to take full-time jobs to earn money for college.

I didn't respond to Mr. Aldridge's statement. At the beginning of my second semester, I headed for Columbus Central and enrolled. This program allowed me to get a full-time job and start making the money I needed to attend Ohio State University. We had very close family friends (my Godparents you might say), who lived in Franklin County, between Columbus and Westerville. I was invited to stay with them. My school schedule worked out to three nights a week. The schooling was intensified, i.e. no study halls,

7

sports, social activities, etc. I finished three weeks before my classmates at Scioto Valley. I elected to have my credits returned there and graduated with my old classmates in 1953.

There was little I didn't know about the dry cleaning business. My Dad went into that business and worked at it for several years. I worked with him part time. Before and after graduation, I worked for Ohio Curtis Dry Cleaners in Columbus, running a retail pickup and delivery route throughout the Ohio State University student housing sector, Grandview Heights, Dublin, Worthington and Upper Arlington. It was lucrative; I made good money for a kid my age in that time. However, I only worked there a short time. As fate, but I chose to believe The Almighty would have it, one of my dry cleaning customers, Don Warren, worked for U.S. Geological Survey. One evening while delivering his dry cleaning, we struck up a conversation. We talked about his work with USGS. During the conversation I expressed my desire to become a Game Warden.

Immediately Don stated, "You should see 'Chic' Marion, the Director of the State Department of Natural Resources. I know him; he's one great guy, and I'm sure he'd be glad to give you some advice." Don winked, "There's one thing sure, he's in the position to put you to work if he's so inclined." Don's last statement hit me square between the eyes.

At the time I didn't realize Chic Marion was the DNR Director over the Divisions of Wildlife, Forestry, Parks, and four other Divisions who answered only to the Governor. Don gave me directions to Mr. Marion's office in downtown Columbus. The following morning I entered his office at nine a.m. I was greeted by a very gracious receptionist.

"May we help you?" she inquired.

"I'd like to see Mr. Marion," I replied.

"Your name?" she asked. I told her; she pressed her intercom button. "Mr. Marion, there's a young man here to see you . . . a James Bailey, are you available?" she asked.

"What does he want to see me about?" Mr. Marion inquired. She looked up at me for a response to his question.

"I'd like to talk to him about becoming a Game Warden," I answered. "He wants to be a Game Warden," she stated.

"Oh – ho, he does . . . send him in," Mr. Marion replied.

I entered his office and shook hands with what seemed to be a very jovial "Chic" Marion. He sensed my nervousness, and put me at ease immediately. I recalled Don Warren's words, "He's one great guy," and told Mr. Marion of my conversation with Don.

"So you want to be a Game Warden – we call them Game Protectors in Ohio, how old are you?" he asked.

"Eighteen, sir," I replied.

"Have you graduated from high school?" he inquired.

"Yes, sir," I replied.

"You're young, you must be at least twenty-one before you can be a commissioned Game Protector in Ohio; you also have to graduate from a training school. Some pretty rough training for several months, think you could do that?" he asked.

"Yes sir, I sure will if I get the chance," I replied.

"Do you realize there are hundreds of young men in Ohio who would like to become Game Protectors?" he asked.

"No sir, I didn't realize it but I can sure understand it, it's been my dream for a long time," I answered.

"For a long time – how long? What pointed you in this direction?" he inquired.

"Got caught by a Game Protector when I was twelve years old, sir. I'll never forget him or the incident; that's when I knew . . ." I didn't finish, he cut me off.

"Who caught you?" he asked.

"Officer Ollie Neimeyer sir," I answered.

"Ah-ha, the old master himself. That tells me you're from Marion County," Chic concluded.

"No sir, it all happened in Delaware County," I said.

"Okay. Are you willing to start at the bottom? I mean the very bottom?" Chic asked.

I answered, "Yes sir!" I couldn't believe what I thought he was inferring – a job?

Mr. Marion picked up his phone and dialed, "Charlie? How's business over there? . . . Charlie, I'm sending a young man over there from Delaware County. He's got some high aspirations. Let's see what we can do for him, okay. . . okay" Chic hung up the phone.

He picked up a yellow lead pencil and pointed it at me. "No promises, understand? No promises at all. If they've got a place for you in the Wildlife Division, it will be at the very bottom; but a start if you want to take advantage of it. Dr. Charles Danbach is Chief of the Division of Wildlife. He's waiting to see you. The Wildlife Offices are at 1500 Dublin Road. Do you know how to get there?" Chic inquired.

"Yes sir, I do," I responded (I drove by it every day on my dry cleaning route). I left A. W. "Chic" Marion's office and never saw him again. Later, A. W. Marion State Park near Circleville, Ohio, would be named in his honor.

At my arrival, Dr. Danbach rose from his desk, greeted me and shook my hand. Although cordial, he spent very little time talking to me. He escorted me to John Pelton's office, head of the Fish Management Section. Mr. Pelton offered me a temporary laborer's job at a fish hatchery near Lake St. Marys, in the western part of the state.

"Don't make up your mind yet until we see what 'Doc' Martin might have," Mr. Pelton advised.

He took me down the hall and introduced me to "Doc" (I never knew his actual name) Martin, head of the Game Management Section; a man of few words and not too friendly. He sort of glared at me and stated, "Got a temporary laborer's job for you at the Olentangy Wildlife Research Station at Delaware Dam in Delaware County – you want it?" (Right next to home)

"Yes sir!" I replied almost without thinking.

"Report to Rod Smith up there at the pheasant pens at eight in the morning, know how to get there?" Doc asked.

"Not exactly sir, but I'll find it, it's very close to my home," I responded.

"You're not done here yet, you're supposed to go down and talk to Les Bailey in Law Enforcement," he stated as he pointed to Bailey's Office.

I went to the Law Enforcement Office and introduced myself to Les Bailey, head of the L E Section – what a character! After discussing the Game Protector qualification requirements, training school, etc., Bailey relaxed and we engaged in a somewhat lengthy discussion of our ancestry to see if we were related, finally determining "perhaps." He was full of Bailey family jokes. He told me that all of the Ohio Baileys with thick hair were Republicans, and all those with thin hair or bald were Democrats. To this day, if I meet another Bailey, the first thing I look at is his hair.

"If you're a Bailey you've got Game Warden blood in you," he joked. "They're putting me out to pasture (retirement) shortly and I won't be here to see if you make it or not, but good luck!" he said as we parted company.

I made a quick, but friendly, departure from my employment at Ohio Curtis Cleaners. Cliff Curtis was a big hunter and fisherman, and wished me "all the luck in the world." I headed home to Delaware County, and my new job with the Ohio Division of Wildlife. I was the happiest 18 year-old, riding on cloud nine, in the Buckeye State.

"Delaware Dam" as Doc Martin called it, is a U.S. Army Corps of Engineers flood control project, consisting of eight thousand plus acres. It includes a fluctuating pool reservoir of about three thousand acres. At that time, there were fifty-five small water impoundments (or ponds), that had been constructed by the Ohio Division of Wildlife since the Dam's construction at the close of World War II. The entire project, excluding the Dam and its' operation, which is controlled by the Corps of Engineers, is under out-grant to the Ohio Division of Wildlife and the Ohio Division of Parks. The entire project is the ultimate in upland game, forest game, and migratory bird habitat development. The lake and ponds support an excellent fishery for all warm water species native, and introduced to Ohio. An excellent gun and archery range is located there. The entire project is heavily utilized by many hunters, fishermen, campers and other outdoor lovers.

An extensive research project was underway to determine the effects of farming practices on farm game species, particularly cotton tail rabbit and ring neck pheasant. The project utilized two, forty acre enclosed land tracts, each subdivided into numerous smaller tracts, on which all Ohio grain and hay crops were grown, treated, and harvested, by customary Ohio farm practices. The "pens" as they were known, were stocked with brailed (flightless) pheasants and cotton tail rabbits. Avian (raptor) predator control was effected through the use of elevated leg hold (pole) traps, with heavily cushioned jaws so as not to injure the bird. Ground predators were controlled as much as possible, by the use of box traps and the deadly gun.

Rod Smith supervised operations at the "pens" where two other temporary hires and I reported for work. Earl Wallace, Labor Foreman, was my boss – a man I developed great respect for. (He was an ex-Iwo Jima Marine and Police Officer. He was at Delaware "biding his time" so to speak, until the next Game Protector Training School was scheduled to begin. He would serve as Game Protector in Butler and Pickaway Counties, Wildlife Patrolman and Assistant Chief of Law Enforcement. During his tenure in Pickaway County, he ended a state-wide man hunt by capturing a kidnapper who had beaten and raped an Ohio State Co-ed while traveling around central Ohio in a van. For this act of bravery, he received the Dept. of Natural Resources "Valor" award and a second "Valor" award from the County Sheriff's Department.)

Also headquartered at the Research Station, was the State Upland Game Biologist (Bill Edwards), Migratory Game Bird Biologist (Delmar Handley), Forest Game Biologist (Frank Haller), and Special Projects Biologist (Carl Mosley – who retired as Chief of the Division of Wildlife). A statistics and tabulations unit that compiled all the Division's game, fish and associated surveys for publication, was housed there. Other biologists, and Ohio State University Wildlife Management students, doing post graduate work, came and went during my tenure there.

Next door to the Research Station was the headquarters for the Delaware Reservoir Wildlife Management area. It was staffed by Manager, Rod Swagler and Assistants, Ed Harrison (who retired as Area Manager), and Richard "Whitey" Reece (who retired as a Wildlife Enforcement Agent). They and seasonal hires were responsible for all the work associated with managing and operating the rest of the "Delaware Dam Area," excluding Delaware State Park, for public hunting and fishing. Others, whom I had a very short exposure to at Delaware, was Tim Hood and Eddie Shanks. Tim ultimately held Wildlife Officer positions in Ohio, Michigan, and Washington States. He carried the badge for forty years. He definitely was one of the most outstanding Wildlife Officers I ever knew or worked with. Eddie (a schoolmate from Ostrander) worked for Biologist, Delmar Handley, ultimately leaving the Ohio Division of Wildlife seeking other endeavors.

I was privileged to work under and with all of those mentioned. I traveled throughout the state, assisting the biologists with all manner of established and experimental upland game, migratory waterfowl, deer, and respective habitat surveys. I did everything from man hunter checking stations, to plant trees and shrubs. Of all the personnel at Delaware, ex-Ohio State football star (with a trip to the Rose Bowl under his belt), and Upland Game Biologist "Big" Bill Edwards was my most influential mentor, benefactor, teacher and friend. At his urging, I read (devoured) and studied all the books on wildlife management available at the time – books authored by Aldo Leopold, Reuben Trippensee, Durwood Allen (3 times), Ira Gabrielson and Edward Graham. We hunted, fished, and trained beagles together. There was no end to the patience he had with me. No one could have been more ignorant. I knew a lot about hounds but nothing about other hunting breeds. One day in Bill's office, I asked him in all seriousness, "Does an English Setter set down when it finds a bird, and does a pointer somehow point at the bird when it finds one?" Bill was busy at his desk with his back to me. He froze for a second or two, then turned his chair around and looked past me across the room to Delmar Handley who was busy at his desk.

"Get a load of this kid will ya? Did you hear what he just said?" he asked Delmar. Delmar never looked up and kept writing whatever he was working on.

"Yes, I heard him – tragic isn't it," he replied. Bill looked at me and saw I was serious. Then he explained all the inherent hunting traits of both pointing breeds, adding, "We're gonna have to get you behind a couple of good bird dogs one of these days – they'll teach you more than I can tell you." I felt dumb as a clam on that occasion.

On another occasion, I experienced some of his "dry" sense of humor. The spring, large mouth bass run was on in Whetstone Creek. We were fishing not far upstream from the Whetstone's confluence with the reservoir. Spinning tackle was just coming into its own. I managed to buy one of the cheapest spinning outfits the Heddon Tackle Co. of Dowagiac, Michigan sold. I also managed to afford several Heddon spinner baits. I was using this tackle trying to catch large mouth bass, but for the life of me, all I could catch was horny creek chubs. Meanwhile, Bill, using a fine Herters "kit" rod and beautiful, smooth running "Bache" spinning reel, with a locally made Grubes Lucky Strike Minnow on the end of his line, was catching and releasing large mouth bass right and left. Every time I looked downstream he had one on. Finally, upstream he came, he couldn't resist it.

"Ronnie, you should write the Heddon Company a letter congratulating them on their Super Duper Creek Chub killer," he smugly said.

"To heck with you, you should let me use one of those Grube baits if you have an extra one," I retorted.

"No such luck," Bill responded and kept on catching and releasing bass. As it grew dark, nearly time to quit, Bill handed me a Grube Lucky Strike Minnow – the extra he had all the time.

"Here Tiger – go get 'em," he said grinning. I hurried as fast as I could putting the Grube bait on my line, and managed to catch and release two bass before we called it a day. At our vehicles, I removed the Grube bait and tried to hand it to Bill.

"You keep it," he said, "and don't forget to write that letter to the Heddon Company."

Bill told me about a Wildlife Area Manager's position opening soon at the Spring Valley Wildlife Management Area in District Six (Southwestern Ohio). He said if I was interested, he would speak to Dale Whitesell, the Game Management Supervisor in that District, adding, "If I didn't think you were ready for this Ronnie, I wouldn't be telling you about the job." Naturally, I responded in the affirmative. Soon thereafter, I was summoned to Bill's office, where I met Dale Whitesell, absolutely one of the most dynamic personalities I would ever know. (Dale later became Chief of the Division of Wildlife and retired as Executive Director of Ducks Unlimited.) I learned in short order he was a committed law enforcement and game management professional. I noticed he wore a badge. (At that time, all game management and fish management personnel with the job title Game Production Foreman or Fish Production Foreman and above were commissioned Game Protectors. They were expected to perform law enforcement duties, especially at the openings of hunting seasons and/or peak fishing periods. Those who went into counties as full time Game Protectors or Wildlife Patrolmen, later called Wildlife Enforcement Agents, had to complete the training school previously mentioned.) He described the Spring Valley Area in some detail, and outlined what was expected of the Area Manager. He told me the Area Manager is commissioned, and expected to perform law enforcement duties as needed on the area and on special assignments off the area. He indicated an "untrained" (in law enforcement) manager is assigned to a Wildlife Patrolman for training and would be expected to "make cases" only when approval to "fly on your own," was given by the District Office.

Last but not least he stated, "You've got the job thanks to Bill and your performance here – we'll see how good you do in District Six." After given a date to report for work at the District Headquarters in Xenia, Ohio, I was politely dismissed. I was busting at the seams, and at the same time somewhat saddened to leave the Olentangy Research Station – a place I visit yet today when I go "up home."

Bill Edwards left Ohio, and went to work as a Professional Scientist with full Professorship for the Illinois Natural History Survey. I saw him once after that, spending the night at his home in Homer, Illinois, on my way west. Recently he weighed heavily on my mind, and I phoned him.

"Ronnie, I'm dying" was his first statement. In response to my inquiry, he told me of his illness and how long he expected to live. He asked where I'd been and what I'd done. I gave him a quick resume of my career after Ohio, and told him I was retired.

"You more than reached your goals, didn't you? You reached a very important position – I'm proud of you," he weakly said.

We spoke our good byes and I hung up the phone. I couldn't contain the tears on that one. I hurriedly wrote him a letter expressing what I couldn't say on the phone. In July of 2003, my wife Shirley and I stopped by Bill's home in Homer on our way home from being with our sick daughter, Connie, at the Mayo Clinic in Minnesota. Marian, Bill's wife, informed us of Bill's passing in June. She thanked me for the letter I wrote him stating, "It certainly meant a lot to him." Thank God he got it before passing. I look forward to seeing him again – I'm sure by then I'll have another dumb question to ask him.

The good Lord, in his infinite wisdom, could not have placed me in a better place for learning, training and experience, in the vast and wonderful field of Wildlife Management, than the Olentangy Wildlife Research Station. I've experienced no training its equal since.

At the young age I left Delaware (21), a core conviction, belief, or philosophy, if you will, began its growth within my innermost being. It would hone and refine as time passed.

> *Always know it's the welfare of our God-created resource – His wild creatures and their environs, that's the important priority. Your employer is a tool or means only. Focus not on it. Endure the negative forces you're bound to encounter. Keep your heart, loyalty and focus on the resource. Forever the resource.*

Dr. William "Bill" R. Edwards, Wildlife Research Biologist.
My mentor, teacher and friend.
7/8/26 to 6/3/03

(Center) Earl Wallace, my first Supervisor at Delaware, receiving the Ohio Department of Natural Resources Valor Award for Bravery, while serving as Game Protector in Pickaway County.

(Left) Dale Roach, Law Enforcement chief, Ohio Division of Wildlife, whom I succeeded as Spring Valley Wildlife Area Manager.

(Right) Dick Francis, Chief Ohio Division of Wildlife, whom I succeeded as Game Protector in Union County.

Three Ohio Wildlife Professionals who have my utmost respect.

Tim Hood – A Delaware protégé. He carried the badge for over 40 years, serving as a Wildlife Officer in Ohio, Michigan and Washington. Here (close to retirement) he released a nuisance bear near the Washington State -Canadian Border. He was one of the best Game Wardens I ever knew or worked with. A superb after-the-fact investigator and interviewer.

3
A Formative Time

It was spring, 1957. I was settled at my new duty station, the Spring Valley Wildlife Management Area in Greene and Warren Counties. My salary was around $250.00 per month. My wife, two kids and I lived in a state owned house – a beautiful big old hard to heat farm house. My rent (deducted from my salary) was $12.50 each month. I was allowed to raise fifty chickens, two hogs and one beef calf at state expense. At the time, a pretty good deal. We were able to buy a 1955, 2 door, Studebaker Champion automobile.

The headquarters complex consisted of my residence; a two car garage with upstairs and side room; a coop and fenced area for chickens; a workshop building; and a huge two floor (typical Midwestern) barn. Equipment included a new Massey Ferguson tractor, plow, disc, bush hog, corn and small grain planters. The workshop was well equipped with the usual hand and power tools and a chainsaw you couldn't keep running no matter how hard you tried.

For the first time I was issued a uniform (field uniform only – no dress uniform) and a badge. At 21 years of age, I was a commissioned Game Protector for the State of Ohio.

I was notified midweek by the District Office I would be working the following weekend with Wildlife Patrolman Vern Bare, my training officer. I was to be ready to go before daylight. On Saturday morning Vern arrived at my home and we met for the first time. He was a big six foot square built gentleman. Quite jovial, smiled a lot, smoked R.G. Dunn cigars and an occasional cigarette. An ex-Navy UDT (underwater demolition team --frogman) World War II Veteran.

17

Sometime earlier, I'd heard a passing remark while at the District Office in Xenia, that "Bare broke two punks up for trying to take his blackberries." Later in the day I asked Vern about this remark, he chuckled and said, "Nobody takes my blackberries." The event took place the previous summer. Vern loved to pick blackberries and take them home to his wife Mary, who as Vern put it, "Makes the best blackberry pie and cobbler on earth." Fortunately, a little later on I was able to confirm this. Vern, while on patrol in Montgomery County, stopped by a favorite berry picking spot (berries like the end of your thumb as he put it), took his uniform shirt off, stuffed it and his gun in a duffel and went on his way picking berries. Vern said it took no time at all to fill his pail with the big berries and he headed back to his car. At that time Game Protectors and Patrolman used their personal vehicles and were paid mileage. Vern drove a Chevrolet station wagon that had civilian plates. Upon arrival at his vehicle, he found another vehicle had him blocked. Leaning against the second vehicle were two "thugs in leather from Dayton" as Vern put it. The two "thugs in leather" thought it would be a good idea for Vern to give them his wallet and while he was at it, "Just give us those blackberries too – they sure do look good." It will suffice to say the "thugs in leather" made a mistake. Vern broke both their collar bones and kicked them screaming into a ditch. The keys were still in their vehicle. Vern backed it up and drove it down an embankment, ramming it into a thicket and "parked" it. Returning to his two "thugs in leather" he loaded both screaming in his patrol car and transported them to the nearest hospital emergency entrance. He dragged them out of his patrol car explaining, "My billfold is one thing xo#x but you don't take my blackberries. Now you're on your own." He left them hobbling toward the hospital's emergency entrance. Vern really had a "thing" for blackberries.

"We're gonna put in a good full day," Vern commented as we headed for Cowan Lake in Clinton County. We got somewhat acquainted while we traveled to our destination. Although a jovial individual, I sensed he would be a "tough" instructor; I was right. I knew I liked him.

We arrived at the first bank fishermen access point at Cowan Lake well after daylight. "This lake gets heavy use by fishermen from Cincinnati who have a habit of not appearing in court if you issue them a citation. It's bad to have to go to Cincinnati and serve warrants for failure to appear. So we'll probably be taking several violators to Wilmington (Clinton County Seat) to post bond. If we have to do this often it will cut into our patrol time but it's what we've got to live with," Vern explained.

Vern parked at a location where we could observe a group of six black bank fishermen fishing in an inlet off the main body of the lake. "You watch your fishermen until you see each one handle a pole. Just because he's there doesn't mean he's fishing. You have to see an overt act such as handling his rod and reel – better still it's good to witness him bait his hook or catch a fish. Each fisherman is allowed two fishing rigs, that is two units consisting of rod and reel or two hand lines or one of each," Vern instructed as we observed the fishermen through binoculars.

Satisfied all our fishermen were "fishing" Vern stated, "Okay let's go check them." After exiting the car, I slammed the door, walked to the front of the vehicle and found Vern firmly planted with both hands on his sides. "Game Wardens don't slam car doors, Bailey." My instructor was no longer jovial – he was dead serious. "We're a quiet, sneaking sort – we don't slam car doors, we don't sneeze, belch, or cough – we watch, observe and approach quietly! Now go check your fishermen – start with the lady down there!" he ordered. Somewhat shaken after Vern's butt chewing, I approached the lady fisherwoman. She was a black lady – at least 300 lbs. She was seated on a board that spanned the opening of a galvanized wash tub with bricks under it to heighten it. She was catching small bluegills and catfish. As she landed one she would take it off the hook and drop it between the board she was seated on and the edge of the tub containing about 10 inches of water. "May I see your fishing license Ma'm?" I asked. Vern was checking a male companion fisherman. He heard me ask the lady for her license and was shaking his head in disapproval as he conversed with the fisherman he was checking.

Now what have I done wrong? I wondered, as my lady angler asked, "What is I ain't got one?"

"Are you telling me you don't have a fishing license Ma'm?" I asked. "No," she responded. "What is I ain't got one?" she asked again.

"May I ask where you're from, Ma'm?" I asked.

"Cincinnati," she replied.

"Well Ma'm, I'll have to give you a citation to appear in court. You'll have to go with me to Wilmington to post an appearance bond that will guarantee you will appear in court. If you don't appear in accordance with the citation, your bond will be forfeited and that's the last you'll see of your money – the case will be closed," I replied, proud of the mouthful I'd just uttered.

"What is I don't wanna go to Wilmington – is you gonna move me?" she asked.

I was sweating it, I can't move this big woman – we're sure as heck not going to arrest, handcuff the lady and take her to jail for fishing without a license, a misdemeanor. What do I do now? I thought, as I looked up to see Vern walking toward us. "Maybelle, show this kid your fishing license," Vern stated as he leaned down and put his arm around Maybelle's shoulders. "Yes sir, Mr. Bare," she said as she opened her tackle box, retrieved her license and handed it to me chuckling. All six fishermen broke up laughing. They all knew Mr. Bare, who had checked or visited with them many times before and whom he'd recruited as "training officers" for one embarrassed young Game Warden. Before we departed Maybelle advised me, "You be all right honey, all you gotta do is listen to Mr. Bare."

After we got in his patrol car and headed to our next check, Vern stated, "That was a good exercise and you didn't do too bad – not too good understand, but not too bad. One big mistake though – don't ever ask, "May I see your fishing license?" You don't have to ask people to do your job. Simply say, "I'll take a look at your fishing license." When you ask "May I?" you're like a puppy dog. When you say, "I'll look at your fishing license or I'll take a look at your fishing license," you're in command. In every situation, always remember take and stay in command. It's interesting Vern never did tell me how to move a 300 lb. lady who says, "I'm not going." I never asked.

We patrolled Lake Cowan the rest of the a.m. and wrote seven citations for fishing without a license. (Ohio was one of the first States to liberalize fishing, that is to say, no closed season, no bag limits, no possession limits, etc. About the only fishing laws a person could violate was the manner in which fish were taken, i.e. seining (use of a big net), trapping, dynamite, quick lime (an explosive), etc. were prohibited. Fish could be taken only by "angling" as defined by law.) We had a late lunch in Wilmington and headed west on Route 73 towards Waynesville in Warren County.

"You need to get familiar with the geography around the Spring Valley Area," Vern stated. "There's a lot of illegal activity going on near Waynesville, north on the Little Miami River and into Greene County. It will be handy for you to work this area," Vern stated. He went on to tell me about the "Waynesville Net", a group of seiners in and around the Waynesville area who reportedly "posted a gun" (meaning a lookout with a rifle) at a vantage point when the seiners were illegally operating their net in order to ward off Game Wardens or any other kind of law. Later, I would spend many hours working on the "Waynesville Net." Finally, a trusted confidential informant told me the "Net" was no more, due to the fact a big Game Warden (Vern Bare) and Harold Brant, the Warren County Game Protector "made it too hot" for them. To my knowledge, the "Waynesville Net" gang was never apprehended. According to my informant, the "Net" operated for many years providing primarily channel catfish for many a social function in Waynesville. "It wasn't just the Game Wardens," my informant told me. "Those guys (the violators) got too old and burned the net."

Vern told me to be on the lookout for two individuals who trapped catfish in this vicinity on the Little Miami River. They used one trap made of heavy duty-one inch mesh chicken wire formed in approximately a four foot long cylinder about 15 inches in diameter. It had a funnel made of chicken wire in one end. The other end had a wire hinged door permitting them to dump their catch quickly. The trap would probably be baited with chicken entrails or some similar "pungent" bait. It would have a thin rope or cord attached used to tie the trap to a sapling on the river bank. The cord would not be visible as they covered it with leaves and other river bank debris. They set their trap in the eddies formed below the riffles found at the upstream end of a sizable pool. The trap would be carefully placed (and anchored if necessary) at a point where the "swirl" of the eddy entered the slower moving water below the pool. This kind of set was effective with or without bait. If seen on the river bank, they would be carrying a tackle box and bait casting rod and reels. They carried their illegal catch, usually channel catfish, on wire clip stringers – not in a sack. They may be carrying a container of bait; thus, giving the appearance of perfectly legal anglers. They set and tended their trap no more than two days and nights midweek. Then they pulled it and set it elsewhere, hoping to go undetected by the law. Another thing to look for was "cherry red noses" on the illegally taken catfish. The red noses were the result of the fish once trapped, rubbing their nose raw against the galvanized chicken wire trap trying to escape. I spent many hours on the Little Miami trying to apprehend the fish poachers. As fate would have it, Vern caught and arrested both, seized their catch (nine red nosed channel catfish) and their funnel trap on a Wednesday during a week I was on vacation "up home" in Delaware County. Both poachers plead guilty to unlawfully taking fish with an illegal device. They were fined $100.00 each and the court ordered their trap destroyed.

As we worked our way north on the Little Miami River, we checked a good many fishermen but apprehended and cited only one for fishing without a license. He was fishing alone with two poles in front of him. He was surprised, totally unaware of any Game Warden's presence. When Vern stated he would take a look at his license, the gentleman said he wasn't fishing. The two bait casting outfits in front of him belonged to "Louie." When asked where Louie was, the angler stated, "He went up the river for something and asked me to watch his poles until he got back." That statement alone was good enough to write a citation as he admitted fishing. The law didn't require ownership of the fishing poles be established. However, Vern wanted to have some fun and asked, "Why don't you run up there and see if you can find Louie?" Our fisherman took off upstream yelling, "Hey Louie, hey Louie, the Game Warden's down here and wants to look at your license." After awhile he returned, "Can't seem to locate him," he stated. "Why don't you try going that way and see if you can find him?" Vern asked motioning downstream. The guy took off downstream, once again hollering for Louie. Shortly he returned.

Vern stated, "I guess we'll have to take these two fishing poles – sure are nice ones – they look brand new."

"They are new," the fisherman blurted before thinking. "Did Louie buy them for you?" Vern asked. Everyone started chuckling.

"No, Louie didn't buy them – heck fellows it was worth a try," our angler stated.

Vern asked for and received the gentleman's driver's license and issued him a citation. He subsequently forfeited a $20.00 bond in Justice of the Peace Court in Waynesville.

We returned to the Spring Valley Wildlife Area after dark. "We won't start out as early tomorrow (Sunday), gotta give them time to get out of church," Vern stated. "We've had a pretty good day – you did okay. I'll see you in the morning about 10:30. We're going to check boat fishermen tomorrow," Vern told me as he departed for home. It had been a good day. We apprehended eight violators and I loved every minute of it. Even the butt chewing.

By 1:00 p.m. the next day we were back at Cowan Lake in a 16 foot

Aluma Craft boat equipped with a 65 h.p. Johnson outboard, checking boat fishermen. The fishing pressure was light compared to the previous day. We probably should have checked boat fisherman on Saturday instead of Sunday but that schedule wouldn't quite fit with the training exercise I experienced with "Maybelle." However, we did write two citations for fishing without a license and one for fishing with a license issued to another, a rather comical event. We checked and departed from three fishermen, doing rather well catching crappies. Vern suddenly turned the boat around stating, "We need to look at one dude's license again – something's not quite right." As we pulled alongside, he addressed a black gentleman seated in the center of the boat. "Ill take a look at your fishing license and your driver's license again sir." The gentleman immediately handed him both. The documents listed the name "Lester Jones" and the physical descriptions matched the fisherman.

Vern examined both documents carefully, looked at the fisherman and stated, "Tell me your real name and don't lie to me."

"Napoleon Cook," the gentleman nervously blurted out.

"Why are you using Mr. Jones' fishing license and why do you have his driver's license? Do you also have his wallet?" Vern inquired.

"Yes sir, I got his whole billfold. He's been drunk a few days and he's still drunk. His billfold was just laying there on the table and I decided I'd use it," Napoleon replied.

"Did you use his money too?" Vern asked.

"Yes sir, a little of it," Napoleon answered. As instructed, the fishermen followed us to the boat ramp where our patrol vehicle was parked. Napoleon accompanied us to the Sheriff's Department in Wilmington where he posted a $50.00 bond for fishing with a license issued to another and fishing without a license – probably with Lester's money. After filing both affidavits charging Napoleon, we returned him to his fishing party who wasn't too happy with him

"Enjoy the boat ride – you're through fishing until you get a license," Vern told him as they departed the ramp.

"Don't worry, he's done fishing today – he took two hours away from our fishing time," one of Napoleon's boat companions complained.

"How did you know?" I asked Vern.

"The vibes just weren't right. After you've checked a couple thousand, you'll get the same way. I can't explain it – just call it Game Warden intuition," Vern explained. It was late afternoon, Vern decided we should head back to Spring Valley, after eating lunch in Wilmington. The Napoleon Cook case certainly wasn't a significant case but it was one I never forgot. That "Game Warden intuition" thing mystified me. I hoped someday I'd be blessed with the same gift -- a few years later I realized I was.

We returned to Spring Valley Wildlife Area and my residence well after dark. As I got out of Vern's patrol car, I glanced south towards the lake. (About 150 acres of lake and marsh, of which about 80 acres were open water.) For an instant I was certain I saw a light go on and off. I told Vern of my observation. Vern exited the car and began scanning the lake and marsh area with his binoculars from our elevated position at the headquarters complex. "It looks like we've got frog hunters – at least two," Vern exclaimed. The frog season was closed. (The Ohio frog season at that time was closed only during a short time in the spring to offer the critters protection during their egg laying period. The Spring Valley Area was previously owned by Mr. Emerson Sinclair, whose family owned the controlling interest in Sinclair Oil Company. Sinclair raised and experimented with the development of varying color strains of muskrats that were harvested for the fur market. The lake was used for commercial carp production. Sinclair harvested and sold carp in the Chicago market. He stocked the lake with bullfrogs he imported from Louisiana. The frogs at Spring Valley were the largest I've ever seen and presented a continuing temptation to both legal and illegal frog hunters. Their nightly "chorus" was almost deafening especially this time of the year.)

As Vern continued his observations he muttered, "Those darn bullfrogs make too much noise. They can pull a poacher from twenty miles away." Ba-rooom, Ba-room, I'm big, I'm big, they seemed to say. Immediately we departed the headquarter's area, turned right on Roxanna – New Burlington road, then right on Pence Jones road, then right on Collett road into the public parking area at Spring Valley Lake. There were no vehicles in the parking lot which meant our illegal frog hunters had to hike or walk some distance to get to the lake. This fact indicated they knew they were violating the law. We left the parking area and crept north on an old railroad grade that ran parallel with the lake and marsh. After going a short distance, we stopped and observed two lights go on and off. They were coming parallel to the lake levee toward us. Vern, smoking one of his R.G. Dunn cigars and holding it cupped in his hand so the violators wouldn't see the lit end, put his hat in front of his face, took one big puff, bent down, "tuffed" it out on a rock and placed it in his shirt pocket. "Not gonna throw that away – just lit it," he grumbled. I focused my binoculars on both outlaws. Each were carrying and using frog spears or "gigs" as they were called – a multi tined barbed metal fork like spear mounted on the end of a four to five foot pole. As I watched I saw one poacher "gig" a huge bullfrog, lift it from the water's edge on the end of his gig, remove it and place it in a "gunny" sack that tightened and closed with a draw string. The sack was tied to his right ankle at the end of a three or four foot cord. The other poacher was rigged the same way. No more than two minutes later, I observed him repeat the first outlaw's performance taking a bullfrog about the same size. They were both wading without boots at the water's edge. These two guys are poaching frogs within a stone's throw of my house – of all the nerve! I thought as I continued my observations, getting more and more ticked off by the second.

"We've got to let them come to us – those gunny sacks aren't tied to their legs for nothing. They'll cut them loose and kick them in the lake the very second they think they've been detected," Vern predicted. About twenty minutes later and three more gigged frogs, they were in front of us about fifteen feet away. Vern whispered, "Now." We sprang over the levee and literally pounced on our prey. I was ticked off and suddenly chesty as all get out. I landed in the water between them. They were shocked and off balance. Vern grabbed their gigs while blinding them with his flashlight. I had both sacks containing their illegal frog catch off their ankles and thrown on top of the levee before they knew what happened. We didn't announce "Game Warden" or anything else. By then they knew who we were. With our poachers and evidence secured, we marched our pre-season frog poachers to the parking lot and Vern's patrol car where we cited them to appear in court.

As it turned out our poachers parked their vehicle a considerable distance away, down a lane off Pence Jones road and hiked to the lake to carry out their illegal night hunting activities. We cited both to appear in Justice of the Peace Court in Waynesville. They were both from the nearby Village of Spring Valley. They admitted they knew the frog season was closed and claimed their illegal frog hunt at the lake was an "annual event" to get their share of the big frogs before the froggers from Dayton arrived when season opened. They had seventeen frogs between them, three shy of a legal bag limit of ten each had the season been open.

When Vern and I finally got back to the area headquarters, we tagged and secured our evidence. Before placing the two sacks full of frogs in the freezer we took a look at them. They were all eighteen inches long or better.

Both our frog poachers plead guilty before Squire Eddelman, the Justice of the Peace in Waynesville. They were each fined $100.00 and their gigs ordered destroyed.

My weekend of training with my Training Officer, Wildlife Patrolman Vern Bare, will never be forgotten. Although my training with him as my instructor was by no means over, these first two days stand out in my memory. Vern ultimately became the District Supervisor in Wildlife District Six. His hobby was wood working. My favorite picture of Christ is the old antique lithograph of Him holding a lamb in his right arm, a shepherd's staff in his left hand with the rest of the flock behind and beside Him. Vern, observing my old picture needed re-framed, took it to his shop and returned it in a beautiful handmade frame. It hangs in my home today – a piece I'll never part with. When I look at it, I not only see Christ, the Son of God and my Savior, I also think of my teacher, Vern Bare. Vern passed from this earth before retiring because of cancer, the dreaded disease that claims so many. However, he remains with me in loving memory – a champion for wildlife to the end. I look forward to our next meeting.

Wildlife Patrolman, Vern Bare

4
A Busy Night on Anderson's Fork

It was October, 1958. I was in my second year as Manager of the Spring Valley Wildlife Management Area in District Six. I had been on my own, doing law enforcement duties at Spring Valley for some time; my training under Wildlife Patrolman, Vern Bare was completed. My Supervisor, Dale Whitesell, after consulting with Eldon Sturgeon, the District Law Enforcement Supervisor, gave me the green light to go ahead and make cases on my own. Emphasizing, my first responsibility was my game management duties on the Spring Valley Area. I worked with Vern in Greene, Montgomery, Clinton, Warren and on a couple occasions, Butler Counties. We made a lot of cases together. Everything from fishing without a license on the Great Miami River in downtown Dayton, Ohio, where we checked fishermen at night by street light, to closed season hunting in Greene and Clinton Counties. I'd been to court a good many times. I knew the court procedures -- writing and filing affidavits (charges), testifying, search warrant procurement, etc. I was ready to go in that department.

Ohio didn't furnish its Game Protectors with weapons in those days. If you carried a side arm, you bought it yourself. There were no firearm qualification requirements – you were on your own in that category, also.

What firearms training I had was given me by Officer Bare or self initiated. I managed to scrape up enough money ($25.00) to purchase a World War I British military issued .38 cal. revolver. It had a non-glare parkerized finish. Biologist, Clyde Simmerer (a gun enthusiast) once observed, "Looks like it's been drug over half of Malaysia on the end of a lanyard." However, it was tight and shot accurately. I was comforted on more than one occasion

27

knowing I had it.

Squirrel season was winding down. There was very little hunting pressure. Earlier, I observed an older model Dodge automobile pulled well back a lane on the management area. This woodland experienced heavy hunting pressure at the first of the season. I doubted the hunter driving the Dodge would have much luck. However, while going about my duties, I heard the crack of a .22 rifle in his vicinity on three occasions. I decided to check him at the conclusion of his hunt. At 11:30 a.m., I observed him standing in the lane behind his vehicle. I went to his location and found a black gentleman enjoying lunch. He was quite cordial. Two gray squirrels shot through their heads were laying end to end beside his right rear tire. This indicated he was a very good shot in view of the fact he was hunting with a .22 single shot rifle with open sights – no scope.

A good shot, I thought, but I heard three shots.

"Did you miss one?" I asked.

"No sir, I usually get what I shoot at," he replied.

I realized I might have something – three shots – two squirrels – a good shot – what did he bag with the third shot?

"I'll check your hunting license and let you get back to your hunt and lunch," I stated. The bag limit for squirrels was four. Even though I was surprised he'd killed two as heavily as the area was hunted, he certainly had the right to continue hunting.

Ohio law required the hunter carry and display his/her hunting license in the center of his/her back on the outer garment. He removed his hunting license from a front coat pocket and handed it to me. I told him of the license carry and display law. He responded by telling me he saw me coming and wanted to make it easier to check his license. For that reason he removed it from his back and put it in his front pocket.

I noticed during our entire contact he seemed to purposely keep his front towards me. I grasped his right shoulder, turned him around and saw the game pocket on the back of his hunting coat was bulged.

"Let's see what we have here," I stated as I thrust my hand into his game pocket and retrieved a very neatly wrapped (in a white cloth sack) mature red tail hawk. (Ohio law protected raptors or birds of prey long before they received Federal protection under the Migratory Bird Treaty Act in 1972). The red tail, like the gray squirrels, was shot through the head.

"It's obvious you know it's illegal to kill a bird of this species, or you wouldn't have taken this effort to hide it. Can you tell me what kind of bird this is?" I asked.

"It's a eatin' bird," he replied.

"Have you shot and eaten many of these?" I inquired.

"Yes sir," he answered.

(Earlier, my best friend, Dale Taylor, came for a visit. Dale told me a joke about a Game Warden who had just apprehended a violator for shooting a "chicken hawk." The Game Warden asked the violator what a chicken hawk tasted like and the violator responded, "bout like an owl.")

I couldn't resist it – I asked my violator, "What does one of these eatin' birds' taste like?"

"Much like a young goat," he replied.

I guess that makes almost as much sense as an owl, I thought as I issued him a citation to appear in court at Xenia. I told him I was seizing the hawk and rifle as evidence. I bid him farewell, went to the Area Headquarters, filled out and placed evidence tags on the "eatin bird" and the .22 rifle, put the bird in the freezer, secured the rifle and went about my duties. My "eatin bird" violator plead guilty in County Court and paid a $75.00 fine plus court costs. His rifle was returned to him.

After dinner that evening as it grew dark, my coon dog, "Nap" (short for Napoleon and the best I ever owned) came to the end of his chain and let out a bawl, then a chop (bark) telling me, "It's a good night to hunt – they're down and running." Coon hunters who own or have owned a good broke coon dog will tell you this phenomenon is true. The good broke coon dogs know when it's a good night to go hunting.

The coon season didn't open until sometime in November. I received reports from several local coon hunters complaining a coon hunting trio from Dayton, Ohio, in a red Dodge pickup truck were "summer hunting" the nearby Ceasers Creek and Andersons Fork vicinity and killing every coon they treed. The locals were up in arms about this; however, even at my urging, no one got the pickup's license number.

With the "signal" Nap gave me, I couldn't sit still. Somehow I knew I needed to get to a particular location on Andersons Fork and get there quick. Call it what you will, the instincts of a young Game Warden, whatever, I knew I had to get to this location ASAP. I strapped on my trusty .38, got in my International pickup truck and headed for Andersons Fork. It was about 9:00 p.m. I proceeded through New Burlington, turned north on a gravel road across the Clinton-Greene County line and over a single lane bridge that crossed Andersons Fork. Here, the road followed parallel to Andersons Fork a short distance, then went due north as the creek continued northeast (upstream).

It was parked beside the road – the red Dodge pickup! I drove past it to the first farm lane, turned around and traveled "blackout" (lights off) past the pickup to the paved Lumberton-New Burlington Road, turned around again and drove back to where the red pickup was parked, eased up behind it and parked my truck.

As I turned the ignition key off and opened my door, I heard several hounds treed and the crack of a .22 rifle. I hurriedly exited, locked my truck, wrote down the pickup's license number, and took off on a dead run in the direction of the treed hounds. By then I could hear the coon squalling its death cry and the yelping/growling sounds hounds make when they're finishing a kill.

Running across a cattle inhabited pasture, without turning my 5-cell flashlight on for fear my violators would see me, I managed to step, slide and fall in a big pile of cow manure – fresh, I might add. It was all over the outer side of my right pant leg, my holstered .38 revolver and bottom of my coat. In addition, my binoculars hanging around my neck on a strap, flopped up and down hitting me in the chin and nose causing a slight nosebleed before I managed to stuff them inside my coat.

My hat was gone, departing my head somewhere near the pile of cow crap. Any hope of contacting my violators – giving the appearance of a professional uniformed Game Protector for the State of Ohio – vanished. There I was – a third covered with cow crap, hat missing and a bloody nose, once again running towards the scene of the crime.

I came to a flood control levee that ran parallel to the creek, flopped down on its sloping bank, crawled to its crest and realized, by hearing their conversation, my violators were directly in front of me on the opposite side of the creek. I fumbled for my binoculars, rolled over on my back, put them to my eyes, looked through them at the stars (a trick I'd read about to adjust your eyes for night vision through binoculars) and saw absolutely nothing. I waited a few seconds and tried it again – coal black, nothing. I finally did an inspection and found the black plastic protective covers on the big end of the lens were still in place. After correcting this problem, placing the lens covers in my coat pocket and feeling I was at last ready to do business, I peered over the crest of the levee to discover my violators were very close to me – no more than twenty yards. Illuminated by lantern light, I could see one was holding a rifle while two others were creek side skinning a coon. I decided to relax and let them finish skinning the coon before making the arrest.

As I continued to lay belly down on the levee, a big redbone hound found me and decided he liked me (perhaps because somehow he knew I was a coon hunter). He checked me out smelling my body and the cow manure smeared on my right side. He moved forward licking my face. Then, as he heisted his left hind leg, I realized he was going to pee on my head. What next? I thought as I rolled away from him at the same time slugging him in the rib cage. I dearly love hounds but that big redbone was going too far.

He let out one long bawl. One of my violators said, "ol Jeb's struck (meaning he'd found a coon track) – hear him – he's right over yonder." "Ol Jeb" started to return to his owner. I grabbed his collar and pulled him down next to me. "It's okay ol buddy, stay here – stay," I whispered in his stinking ear. He relaxed and laid up against my left side deciding again I was his buddy. I didn't want him to return to my violators. I wanted them to think he had in fact "struck." That old hound stunk reeking with that "doggie" smell most hounds seem to have. But what the heck, my right side stunk – may as well have a stinking left side to match.

I continued watching as the two chaps creekside finished skinning the coon. One "skinner" carefully folded and rolled the pelt up fur side out and placed it in a plastic bag. He continued holding the bag as the other "skinner" field dressed the carcass and washed the body cavity out in the creek. It was obvious they intended to take the hide and carcass home.

I decided it was time to move. I eased downstream along side the levee, went over it and crossed the creek. The redbone hound stayed with me. I crept up to the edge of the lantern light, then "ol Jeb" and I stepped into the light. "Good evening gentlemen, my name is Bailey, I'm a State Game Protector and you're under arrest," I proclaimed. All three went into action. The one with the rifle grabbed it by the barrel and threw it into the darkness as he ran into the darkness himself. The "skinner" holding the packaged coon pelt, threw it and ran in another direction disappearing into the darkness. The third did the same after throwing the carcass.

Two hounds (blueticks) "checked in" as this was going on and were milling around the site. I noticed a leash laying on the ground with a dual snap end on it. I grabbed it and fastened one snap on ol Jeb's collar. I caught one of the blueticks and hooked him to the other snap. If nothing else, I had two of their dogs. If there's one thing a coon hunter will go to ground for, it's his dog and I knew I could use these hounds to get my fleeing coon hunters to return.

I spoke to the darkness, "Okay boys, here's how it stacks up. Number one – I've got two good coon hounds on a leash. I'm a coon hunter and have been for a long time. These potlickers look good to me. In fact, good enough to tie to my bedpost (a phrase used by houndsmen meaning he's got a real good dog) and eat my feed for the rest of their days. Number two – I've got your trucks' license number. Number three – Three Sheriff's Deputies are waiting at your truck (a bluff). Number four – I'll have this place saturated with law enforcement officers. Come daylight, we'll find the rifle, coon hide and carcass. Now it's time for you to come back here to me and ol Jeb and we'll see what we can work out."

(Back then, the Ohio Game Law required night hunters carry a "continuous white light" visible for 360 degrees. A standard kerosene lantern conveniently met this requirement; it was what most coon hunters or coon hunting parties carried. Outlaws as a rule, didn't conform with this regulation for obvious reasons. This is why I was surprised to see this hunting party with a kerosene lantern. Later, my violators admitted they carried a lantern but only lit it when they had a coon to skin and clean. They told me they sold their coon carcasses in Dayton. Under Ohio law the raccoon, along with certain other animals i.e. beaver, muskrat, mink, etc. was classified as fur bearing animals. Legally taken fur bearers, taken in season by trap or gun and dog, could be bought and sold.)

One by one my coon hunting violators returned to the lantern lit area where ol Jeb, the redbone, a bluetick and I waited. All three were wearing valid Ohio hunting licenses on their backs which I removed, checked against their driver's license and placed in my coat pocket. I filled out citation tickets on all three but didn't issue them – I wasn't ready for that yet.

"Okay boys, let's go back to the tree where I saw your dogs treed and saw you shoot the coon out," I said (a bluff). Like obedient puppies, one picked up the lantern and we proceeded upstream with me in the rear, to a big sycamore tree near the creek's bank.

A raccoon will rarely climb a sycamore, only when it's really pushed by the hounds. I thought they were calling my bluff or their hounds could darn sure push a coon, but there it was, blood stains on the tree trunk where the wounded animal "walked" down the tree. There was blood stained leaves and hair on the ground under the tree. I spread my big blue handkerchief on the ground and carefully picked up several of the blood stained leaves along with some hair samples, placed them on the handkerchief, folded it up and put it in my coat pocket.

I detained my violators a good while – questioning them, trying to get them admit guilt. We even engaged in some lively coon hunter talk about hounds and hunting but my violators wouldn't admit anything.

As one stated, "You're darn sure a coon hunter and I wouldn't mind hunting with you and your dog, but if you think I'm gonna admit anything, you're crazy – go ahead and take me to court." The other two agreed with his "go ahead and take me to court" statement and wouldn't admit anything.

They sure weren't about to help me go downstream and search for the rifle, coon pelt and carcass I'd made up my mind to find; thus, cinching my case. I accompanied my trio back to their truck, helped them catch and load their hounds and returned their hunting licenses.

"Where's those Deputy Sheriff's?" one asked.

"Fooled you didn't I," I responded. "I'll see all of you in Dayton in a couple of days," I told them.

Just before their departure, one asked, "What have you got all over you – you smell like cow manure."

"That's what I've got all over me, "I responded. "Had a little mishap on my way to catch you – stinks doesn't it?" I said as my three illegal hunts-men departed.

I was convinced they would return to the scene sometime later, after they thought I was no longer in the area, at least to retrieve the .22 rifle. I followed them to the Lumberton-New Burlington road then right into New Burlington where I turned right hoping they'd think I lived in New Burlington and returned home.

After awhile, I returned to Andersons Fork. I drove past the location my vehicle and theirs were parked to a catawba grove. I parked my truck in a well concealed location, went back to the violation scene to search for my "physical evidence." I knew I had "possession" cases as it was. (An officer witnessing a violation is Prima Facie evidence of guilt.) However, I wanted the physical evidence to go with the charges.

I continued the search for the coon carcass, hide, and the .22 rifle for some time finally finding the hide in the plastic bag. It was past midnight and my 5-cell flashlight was dimming. I carried a small pen or "walking" light when working at night so I wasn't concerned about getting back to my truck with no light to get me through the brush and water. I stepped into the edge of the creek and using some leaves, cleaned the manure off me as best I could.

I was quite successful, by no means presentable for church on Sunday, but sure better than before. I continued my search coming to the corner of a grain "stubble" field. The stubble looked like a somewhat comfortable place to rest and get out of the brush I had been fighting. I laid down in the stubble on my back for a short while and looked at the beautiful starlit sky. I got up and sat down in the folded leg position. I was bone tired, damp and hungry enough to eat the ass out of a skunk. I remembered I put a peanut butter sandwich in the game pocket of my coat before leaving on patrol. After all it had been through it really wasn't fit to eat – I ate it anyway. Other than the faint odor of cow crap, it tasted great.

As I sat there eating my sandwich, I saw two lights spaced about four feet apart, at exactly the same elevation, headed towards me. What's this? I thought. Flying saucer, popped in mind. There was a lot of flying saucer publicity going on at the time. Wright Patterson Air Force Base at Dayton, Ohio was the headquarters for "Project Blue Book," the government's official investigator of UFO's. They were always in the news. Here I was, smack in the middle of nowhere at 1:00 a.m., eating a "tainted" peanut butter sandwich and encountering a UFO that would probably abduct me. I knew I'd stand little chance against them armed only with my .38. Then I realized what it was – an automobile. What's an automobile doing in the middle of a farm stubble field at 1:00 a.m. in the morning? I asked myself. I'd always figured I was kinda "slow," I think is the term. I was a young Game Warden. My Game Warden instincts were not as developed as they would some day be. Sometimes a realization had to sort of smack me up side the head.

Shortly the vehicle stopped. I heard a car door slam. A human male figure carrying a rifle in the upright (barrel pointed toward the sky) position appeared in the light of the vehicle's head lamps. He perched himself on the front fender of the passenger's side with his legs draped over the right head light. Holding the rifle in his right hand, he rested the butt on his right thigh. He raised his left hand and motioned the driver to go forward. The vehicle traveled slowly for a short distance -- the "gunner" raised his left hand again motioning the driver to stop. Immediately the brake light lit up, the vehicle stopped. The gunner took careful aim, fired a single round, jumped off his fender perch and retrieved a still flopping hen pheasant. He disappeared with the bird behind the headlights. I heard the car door slam and the gunner returned to his position perched on the front fender.

My heart was in my throat, Lord, what next, I thought. At the same moment, I sensed these outlaws were dangerous. Perhaps working at night fostered this premonition. The sense I was entering a dangerous situation went all through me.

It was time to move out. My stalk was easy. The cover of darkness was in my favor. Coon hunters were one thing, I understood them and spoke their language but this situation was different -- a first for me. I realized I was scared and at the same time knew what I had to do. I'm proud to admit, I'm a believer in prayer – a sinner – the worst, but nevertheless, a believer. I took a moment and prayed, Lord, I know this is meant to be my life's work. You wouldn't have brought me this far this quick if it wasn't true. You're the only back up I've got here tonight. Give me what it takes to do what I've got to do.

Prayer ended, I began my stalk. While moving toward my target I realized walking in the dew laden stubble was almost noiseless. A sense of "well being" came over me. I knew my "back up" was there. As I approached the vehicle I wondered if there would be more than one individual inside. I realized I was no longer scared, the adrenalin was flowing, all my senses were awake and alert in spite of my lack of sleep. From that point on it was like I was on "automatic pilot."

During my stalk the entire sequence of events unfolded again. This time the killer shot a cotton tail rabbit. I decided I needed to approach the driver's side of the vehicle. Try to determine how many individuals were inside and if they were armed.

The gunner's back was toward me. I hoped to stop them, get the occupants out of the vehicle, on the ground face down as quickly as possible and get any weapons out of reach any way possible. I figured it would take a few seconds for the fender mounted gunner to realize what was taking place. There would be no loud announcement from the darkness "Game Warden, you're under arrest." I knew I needed to be as quiet as possible.

I crept to the passenger's side of the vehicle (an old blue Buick) moving at a snail's pace. I looked at the rear plates illuminated by a single bulb – Kentucky – Damn!

Many people from Eastern Kentucky's coal mining region migrated to all parts of Ohio and other Midwestern states searching for work. They were good honest hard working people. Many would work "up north" all week and return to their beloved Kentucky Mountains on weekends. Unfortunately, many were absolutely lawless when it came to the fish and game laws and they hated Game Wardens. My training officer Vern Bare, told me many "war stories" about dealing with them and could have told a hundred more. It will suffice to say, his dealing with some of these folks was "tough" to say the least. Vern was no man to fool with as many a violator had learned. "You take command immediately and you treat them exactly like they treat you – never let one get behind you," he advised me.

With Vern's advice going through my mind, I got close enough to see only the driver occupied the car. Thank God! The door window next to him was down, obviously so he could hear any verbal commands the gunner gave over the old Buick's noisy and smoky engine. I was right beside him, actually walking at an almost normal pace.

In a loud whisper, I told him, "Game Warden – shut the car off. Hand me the keys and get out of the car." He jerked obviously startled and scared. I could see he was a little person – skinny and long haired. He regained his composure almost instantly. With my pen light in his face, his eyes were glaring at me with all the hate in the world. He put the old Buick in park, removed

34

the keys, handed them to me and exited the car. I did a quick "pat down" search of his person, satisfied he had no weapons, I placed him under arrest. The gunner, now dismounted and standing in the light, looked bewildered not knowing why his driver suddenly stopped.

The little guy in custody yelled, "Game Warden – a Game Warden got me." My outlaw gunner came to attention and slid his finger through the trigger guard resting it on the trigger of the rifle in his hands. Slowly I told him, "Lay the rifle on the ground and step ten paces back – don't leave the light. Yeah, this is a Game Warden speaking. Do as I say right now or ----."

"Or what?" he interrupted. "By juggers, I reckon you don't know who you're dealin' with do you? We're from Pikeville, Kentucky. Game Wardens down in Kentucky don't come in the woods at night – they know better -- we shoot them," he bragged.

That did it. I decided I would kill this man if he gave me half an excuse. I was surprised how calm I was after making that decision. I turned cold blooded as any killer could get and I knew it – it was scary. I realized I hadn't drawn my revolver. I wondered how many cartridges I had in the cartridge pouch on my belt. I drew my gun thinking, Why in thunder didn't you do this sooner? Of course my "head light poacher" saw none of this as I was standing in the dark. My hillbilly outlaw leveled his rifle in my direction but he was at a disadvantage, he was in the light and I was in the dark -- he couldn't see me. Why he didn't make a dive for the protection offered by the darkness I'll never know, plain stupid perhaps. I was sure his rifle was a single shot – no magazine running parallel with the barrel – no clip.

With all the calm in the world I told him, "Okay hotshot, here's how it's gonna be. I'm out here alone and I'm damn sure gonna leave here alive. You're in Ohio now not Kentucky. Things are a little different up here. Game Wardens shoot hillbillies who hunt at night and out of season in Ohio. Let's look at the situation we've got here. You've got one shot – I've got six with at least twelve more to re-load if need be. You can't see me but I can see you – my gun sights are right on your head. If you make one move I don't like, I'll shoot your head off. Now, here's what you're gonna do – you're gonna lay your rifle down, take ten steps backward like I told you and stand absolutely still until I tell you otherwise. If you don't, the first thing I'll do is shoot your buddy. Then I'm going to splatter your brains all over this hay field."

"Do what he says – do what he says or he's gonna kee-ull me," my little companion squealed.

My hillbilly gunner laid his rifle on the ground and stepped backward as I counted in a loud voice, "One, two, three, four, etc." At the count of ten he stood motionless stoop shouldered with his head down – he was sobbing – I couldn't believe it. I knew both my outlaws were whipped – I was in command. I remembered Vern's words, "take command."

I told my little companion to come with me as we went to his hunting partner still motionless where I told him to stand. En route, I picked up his rifle, a single shot bolt action .22, unloaded it, removed the bolt and placed it in my pocket. I searched my second outlaw – clean – no weapons and formally placed him under arrest. He was trying to cover up the fact he'd been bawling, as I asked them for and received their Kentucky driver's licenses. I holstered my revolver and we went to their old Buick where I found two ring neck pheasants (1 cock, 1 hen) and two cotton tail rabbits laying on the rear floor.

Because they were non-residents from Kentucky, I knew I'd have to take them "forthwith" to the county jail to be booked and incarcerated to remain in jail until such time as the court convened or they posted an appearance bond. No citations here as East Kentuckians were famous for simply "going home" never to be seen again. I filled out citations on both for the purpose of obtaining their personal information. I told them the pheasants, rabbits and rifle were seized -- held as evidence. I told them they were going with me to the county jail at the Sheriff's Department in Xenia.

Going with me, hell, I didn't have a vehicle and really wasn't sure where it was from this location. There was no choice but to use their old Buick. I told them we were going to drive their car to my vehicle. I opened their car trunk with its "confiscated" key and placed all my evidence inside. I told the skinny outlaw to do the driving and his partner to ride in the back seat with me.

I told the driver, "We need to get to the first bridge on Andersons Fork this side of New Burlington." I knew if I got to that location, finding my truck (in the catawba grove) would be easy. "Do you know where that is?" I asked. "Yes sir," the driver replied. "Yes sir," I thought, this guy is actually showing some respect. I was glad he knew where to go because at this point, I didn't.

My outlaw seated beside me in the backseat asked, "Can we tell our wives where we're going? – they're back at the house asleep."

"You can call them from the jail," I replied.

"We don't have a phone," he responded.

Darn! I didn't want to go through this but at the same time I knew his request was reasonable. If I were in his shoes I'd certainly want my wife to know where I was going. "Okay, where's the house?" I asked. He pointed west. The driver turned right. We exited the stubble field, went through a pasture, past a barn and stopped in front of a big old farm house.

"Do you own this farm?" I asked, knowing the answer.

"No," one answered. "We rent the house – we're up here huntin' work." "Do you have work yet?" I asked.

"We think so – we'll know soon," the driver answered.

The thought flashed through my mind, if they get in the house without me with them, they could easily get a gun and I'd be in deep trouble again. Even with me going in with them, I wasn't comfortable. I knew we had to go in as near as possible together and I had to make sure they got the lights in the house on ASAP. We went up on the porch. One of my violators stepped toward the door. I was so uncomfortable, I drew my revolver again and held it at my side. "Hold it, we're going through the door together -- where's the light switch once we get inside?" I asked.

"To the left side of the door on the wall," one replied.

"Does it turn on a ceiling light?" I asked.

"Yes sir," one answered.

We must have looked like the three stooges as we literally went through the door together. We were one unit taking little bitty steps – the two of them in front jammed together, with me jammed behind and centered between them with my trusty .38 at my side. Inside, I felt for the light switch and turned on the ceiling light – we were in the kitchen. "Where's your wives?" I inquired.

One pointed to a room off the kitchen. The other said, "In there" and nodded toward another room off the kitchen. They were, for the most part, living in three rooms in the old house to conserve heat.

My "headlight" outlaw started through the first door. "No, huh-uh," I said. "We all three go through together." This doorway was smaller, but we formed "the unit" again and entered taking the same little bitty steps. Inside, my outlaw switched on another ceiling light. There was his wife and three kids sleeping on a full sized mattress on the floor. The mattress, two chairs, a sleeping bag, a woman and three kids – that's it, that's all that was in the room.

"We haven't moved our furniture up here yet," my outlaw explained as he gently shook his wife to awaken her. She woke up all right, sat up in bed, looked at me and started screaming.

"She's in hysterics," I told her husband -- "Smack her!" He looked at me, then smacked his dear wife across her chops. She stopped screaming immediately.

Meanwhile, wife number two, awakened by all the commotion, came to the kitchen with three kids. She was frightened and was crying. Both husbands tried to explain what was going on with little success. I "hushed" both of them, "Ladies – ladies, calm down – I'm a law enforcement officer – a Game Warden – I'm not here to do you any harm. Now listen to what I've got to tell you." Both young women calmed down immediately. I knew when the person they viewed as a "threat" told them who he was and what was actually going on, they would be okay. I told them what had happened and what was going to happen.

With the exception of one burst in which one wife told their men folk, "We told you not to do this but you went ahead - - - - now we're all in trouble. We can't pay for this." She was mad.

Both wives stated they were going to follow their husbands to jail as there would be a phone there and they could call "down home" for the money needed to bail their husbands out of jail. The ladies got their kids dressed and dressed themselves. We exited the old farm house.

The wives and children got in a second "old" vehicle and followed the old Buick my outlaws and I were in. We proceeded south down a long farm lane and came out on the Lumberton-New Burlington road, in Clinton County – not Greene County. Darn! If these violations occurred in Clinton County, we needed to be going to Wilmington, not Xenia -- another problem, I thought. I knew I could sort it out when I got to my truck as I had detailed county maps there.

En route to the truck, I noticed the women and kids in the car following us went straight to New Burlington rather than turn right, as we did, headed for Andersons Fork. Something else was bothering me – why hadn't I heard my mountaineer outlaws shooting while I was dealing with the three coon hunters. I concluded they did their shooting during the time I followed the coon hunters to New Burlington and returned to Andersons Fork. (Later, questioning my two outlaw hunters, I confirmed this theory.)

We arrived at my truck. I handcuffed my two prisoners to each other, using a pair of handcuffs in the glove compartment my Training Officer, Vern Bare, loaned me. I know, they should have been on my gun belt the entire night but they weren't – another boo-boo. I never admitted this to Vern. I checked my county maps – the violations were in Greene County. My outlaws were wondering where their wives went. It was obvious they had a different plan than we did. After removing my evidence from the trunk of the old Buick, placing the rifle behind the truck's seat and the critters in an Army footlocker I had in the bed of the truck, we departed for Xenia.

As we passed through New Burlington, headed north on Rt. 380, the wives in their vehicle fell in behind us. When I looked in my rear view mirror the second time I saw a third vehicle was behind them. The highway was deserted at this early hour in the morning and I realized the third vehicle was part of the procession. Who is this? I wondered.

We arrived at the Greene County Jail and Sheriff's Office. I escorted my prisoners into a reception room that housed the radio dispatcher and served as the room where prisoners where booked for incarceration. I seated my outlaws on a bench against the wall and removed the hand cuffs. I told the duty officer I had arrested two non-residents I needed to jail until they could post bond. I told him I would file charges against the two later that morning with the Court Clerk. The deputy handed me a commitment form explaining, "If there's more than one charge just put down one – what did they do?" he asked.

"Basically they were hunting in closed season," I stated.

"That's fine – put that down," he said.

Suddenly, through the door came the two wives, their children and their landlord in a total rage. "What do you think you're doing Bailey – I've heard about you harassing everyone around Burlington and everywhere else,"---- I cut the landlord off, I sure wasn't in any mood for this – I was getting madder by the second.

"Shut up and take a seat – one more word and I'll" --- he cut me off . "You've got no business on my farm any time day or night – you'd better left these boys alone – just out there trying to get something to eat – xo#x you, if

I ever catch you on my farm again, I'll see that you never go on anyone else's property," he shouted.

That did it, I had him for interfering with an officer and now threatening an officer. I headed for him with the handcuffs I had just removed from his "boys." I was going to arrest him and throw him in jail, when a side door opened opposite the radio complex and booking bench. The Greene County Sheriff came through the door clad in his pajamas and bathrobe. "What is all this darn noise?" he shouted. The land owner began to vent his rage on the Sheriff who didn't acknowledge what the man said.

The Sheriff looked at his desk officer and stated, "Throw this man in a cell. I'll charge him with disturbing the peace and whatever else I can think of in the morning," he told the deputy.

The Sheriff looked at his antagonizer, "You don't come in the Greene County Sheriff's Department at 3:00 a.m. and run your mouth like you've been doing – you're going to jail my friend, and I'm going back to bed." With that, the Sheriff left the room through the door he entered.

The big deputy came around the desk, grabbed the land owner by the scruff of the neck – pumped his left arm halfway up his back and walked him to the cell block entrance door, pressed a red button opening the door and threw him in a cell. During his "arrest" the landowner, shall we say, had a change of heart. He was pleading not to go to jail, apologizing to me, the Sheriff and the Deputy. The last I heard out of him as the cell block door closed was, "Please don't do this to me – I apologize – this is terrible ---."

My mountaineer outlaws and their wives actually began to apologize for the conduct of their landlord. "We went to his house and told him what happened and asked if he could help us," one wife stated. "He told us he would bail our husbands out of jail. He didn't act the least bit mad. If we'd known he was gonna do this we'd never asked him to help," the other wife explained.

I looked at the big Deputy, "You know, with the way these folks have acted compared to their landlord, I hate to see them in jail," I told him.

The big Deputy responded, "I know what you mean – we've got a sort of family room they can stay in for a few hours. Once you get their charges filed and bond is set, who knows, by then someone may post bond for them and they can go home." I thanked the Deputy and headed home. Daylight hadn't arrived.

I traveled south on Rt. 68, stopped at a truck stop near the Village of Spring Valley and ate two eggs over light, hash browns, a double order of bacon, two cups of coffee and a big glass of water. To say I was hungry doesn't get it – I was starved. I arrived home at the Spring Valley Area at first light. I got out of my truck and looked to the east – it's gonna be a beautiful day, I thought. Thank God I'm still here to enjoy it. I tagged the evidence I gathered throughout the night. I placed the critters in the freezer and took the rifle with me as I went inside my home to find my wife, up and in the kitchen.

"Have you been working all night -- do you want breakfast?" she asked. "No, I had breakfast on the way home from Xenia. I'll tell you all about last night when I've had some sleep," I replied. I went to my son, Steve's bed – he was still asleep. I kissed his forehead and thanked God that both he and I were still here. I went to my baby daughter, Betty Jean's bed – she too was sleeping. I kissed her forehead and again thanked God that all my little family and I were okay. I took a shower and crashed.

There's one thing about the bone tired sleep of a Game Warden – it's "intensified." As one old Game Warden I worked with later put it, "I don't sleep long but I sleep fast!" I awoke about two hours later to find a clean uniform with my badge pinned to the shirt along with clean underwear and socks on the bedroom dresser. I "dropped" my filthy (and stinking) clothes in the hall outside the bedroom earlier. My wife removed them to the laundry room, I'm sure on the end of a broom handle.

By 10:00 a.m. I had the "affidavits charging offense" filed with the Court Clerk in Xenia, charging my two Appalachian migrant violators. There were a number of charges I could have filed but "racking up" charges usually didn't fly too well in court. Judge Rudd was one of the best "Wildlife" Courts in District Six and I wanted to keep it that way. Under the Ohio Revised Code each wild bird or animal taken in violation of the law, constituted a separate offense. Judge Rudd was a "cut to the chase -- keep it plain and simple as possible," type Judge. I charged each with two counts of hunting, taking and possessing a wild game bird, to wit: a ring neck pheasant during the closed season; one count of hunting, taking and possessing a protected game bird, to wit: a hen pheasant; and two counts of hunting, taking and possessing a wild game quadruped, to wit: a cotton tail rabbit during the closed season. A total of five charges each – at least four additional charges could have been filed.

Bond was set at $500.00 each according to the bond schedule set by the Court. Later I learned the landlord and the Sheriff "reached an understanding." The Sheriff released him. The landlord in turn posted bond for my two violators and they all went home.

Earlier I called the District Office and reported the night's activities to my supervisor, Dale Whitesell. To his everlasting credit, Dale was every inch as much lawman as he was biologist. He loved to make a good case and hear about a good case. "You've had quite a night – good job – get your crew down there started and get your butt to bed, but stay by the phone for a while. I'm going to have "Sturge" (the District Six LE Supervisor, Eldon Sturgeon) call you. He'll be here shortly"

Soon, Eldon called and I related the night's events to him. "You're making more cases on and around that area (the Spring Valley Wildlife Management Area) down there than half the Game Protectors in this District – good night's work – it's work you'll never forget," Sturge proclaimed. "Do you need help with anything?" Sturge asked. "Yes I do," I answered. "I'm going to Anderson's Fork as soon as I can to find the rifle and the coon carcass the coon hunters threw. Then I've got to go to Dayton and cite them into court. I'd appreciate it if Vern could meet me somewhere near Dayton to help me find them." "You got it," Sturge said. "Vern will contact you – I know he's on duty."

That afternoon around lunch time, Wildlife Patrolman Vern Bare (my training officer) arrived at Spring Valley, entered the kitchen unannounced as he usually did. I was just finishing lunch. "Want some lunch, coffee, or something?" I asked.

"No, just had lunch," he replied. "Well, some Game Wardens have to work long and hard to make a case. Others go out in the boonies, stumble around all night and luck up on one case after another," he said smiling with a R.G. Dun cigar protruding from the corner of his mouth. "Good stroke, kid, now what have we got on deck this afternoon?" he asked. That "good stroke kid" coming from Vern Bare was better than getting an award. I told him what I needed to do and we headed for Andersons Fork.

Arriving at the creek side scene where I first encountered the three coon hunters, Vern asked, "Which direction did he throw the rifle?" I pointed in the direction. Vern looked around, picked up a chunk of a tree limb, "hefted" it a time or two and threw it in the same direction I pointed. "Let's go get it and 'fan out' as we go," Vern instructed. We fanned out as we headed toward the chunk and found the .22 rifle wedged in a blackberry thicket. Vern retrieved the chunk and we returned to the "scene." "Now, which way did the other yo-yo throw the carcass?" I pointed in the direction and we followed the same procedure. There was the coon carcass, covered with mud and leaves laying in the edge of the creek. I washed the carcass off, dropped it in a plastic bag and we returned to Vern's patrol car. "We'll go back to the area and get your truck – you follow me to Bellbrook, then we'll go round up your coon hunters."

At Bellbrook I got in Vern's vehicle and we traveled to Dayton. "You've got your cases all sewed up. You don't need to get them to admit anything – just issue their citations," Vern stated.

"I'd sure like to get them to admit it – especially the one that actually shot the coon," I responded.

"Tenacious, aren't you?" Vern asked chuckling. "You like that don't you?"

"Like what?" I asked.

"Getting these yea-hoos to admit they did it whether you saw them do it or not," Vern stated.

"Well, I hadn't thought much about it but I guess I do," I replied.

Vern knew Dayton and Montgomery County like a cab driver. We soon had our coon hunter's residences located (they all lived close to each other and worked at National Cash Register). I issued all three citations to appear in Greene County Court before Judge Rudd. All three admitted guilt and the "trigger man" told me all about it too.

Vern took me back to Bellbrook. I removed the coon carcass and .22 rifle from his patrol vehicle and placed both in my truck. "Get some rest before you go back at it," Vern admonished.

"Sure will," I answered. I returned to the Spring Valley Area and home. I tagged and secured my latest seizures, the coon carcass and the .22 rifle, enjoyed a good dinner with my family and went to bed.

The next morning I went to the Court Clerk's Office in Xenia and filed affidavits charging each of the three coon hunters with hunting, taking and possessing a wild fur bearing animal, to wit: a raccoon during the closed season. The Clerk advised me the three defendants already posted a $150.00 appearance bond with the Court. She was fairly confident they wouldn't appear (thus forfeiting their bonds). This proved to be the case. Ultimately following phone contact, the chap who owned the rifle came to my residence, I returned his rifle and we swapped a few coon hunter tales.

Later, my Appalachian night hunters, accompanied by their landlord, appeared in night court before Judge Rudd. After hearing the charges, they plead guilty "with extenuating circumstances". They were dressed like paupers even though they had obtained good jobs. Their wives and children were with them dressed in the same manner. Wildlife Patrolman, Vern Bare and Greene County Game Protector, Paul Keckler sat in on the proceedings.

Following the "swearing in" procedure, Judge Rudd asked for my testimony. "If it please the Court your honor -----," I testified to the entire events that took place in the stubble field near Andersons Fork on that "night of nights." I testified only to the actual events surrounding the illegal taking of the pheasants and rabbits, concluded my testimony and sat down.

Judge Rudd looked to the defendants and stated, "All right let's hear your extenuating circumstances."

The landlord rose to his feet, "May I say something, Judge?" "And who might you be sir?" Judge Rudd asked. At this point I knew by looking at Judge Rudd's expression that he knew very well "who" the landlord was. I also knew Judge Rudd was getting ready to "lower the boom." "These folks rent a house from me," the landlord began.

Judge Rudd interrupted, "Oh yes, I've had a talk with our County Sheriff. You're the gentleman who came to our jail the night the defendants were arrested and tried to prevent Officer Bailey from performing his duties. Not satisfied with that, you roused the anger of our Sheriff, who with all justification, threw you in jail. You are that person, am I correct sir? Do you confirm this sir?" Judge Rudd got louder as he concluded his statement and questions to the landlord.

"Well, yes sir, I - - -," the landlord tried to speak.

Judge Rudd interrupted him again. "No sir, you may not address this Court – as a matter of fact, there should be charges filed against you by Officer Bailey and the Sheriff before this Court and the Court may well instruct both officers to file them. Now sir, you will leave this courtroom!" The landlord made a "hurried" departure. Whew! You could have heard a pin drop!

Judge Rudd turned his attention to the defendants, "All right gentlemen, now that the Court has extended you a favor by removing 'an obstruction' that certainly would not have helped your defense, I'll hear what you've got to say."

A shaking mountaineer poacher (the headlight straddler) rose to his feet, "We just wanted to try to get something to eat - - - -," he never got to finish.

"Don't you poor mouth this Court. There are many folks here in Greene County and elsewhere that aren't too well off who don't use their situation as an excuse to violate the game laws. I've heard groundhogs are very good to eat – some say as good as roast beef if properly cooked." With that statement he looked at me, "I believe there is no closed season on groundhogs. True, officer?"

"True, your honor," I replied.

"I don't think there's a bag limit either, is there?" he continued.

"No, your honor," I replied.

"Are there any groundhogs down on Andersons Fork near where you apprehended these two gentlemen?" he asked.

"Yes, your honor, quite a few," I replied.

He turned his attention to the defendants. "You gentlemen know what a ground hog or woodchuck is?"

"Yes sir, we eat 'em," answered my skinny outlaw.

"In other words gentlemen, you had a legal alternative to poaching rabbits and pheasants at night, didn't you?" Judge Rudd asked.

"Yes sir," they both answered almost together.

"I understand you are both gainfully employed in Wilmington, is that correct?" the Judge inquired.

"Yes sir," they answered.

"Is the new car you parked behind the Court the result of your gainful employment?" Judge Rudd further inquired.

"Yes sir," one answered.

"How about you – you got a new vehicle too?" Judge Rudd continued.

"Got a new truck," the other answered.

"Been able to buy clothes and food for your families?" Rudd inquired. "Yes sir," they both replied.

"Then why are both of you and your families dressed as you are here in this Courtroom tonight?" Judge Rudd asked. No answer. "It didn't work gentlemen – it's old hat before every court in the country – you know what I mean don't you?"

"Yes sir," they both answered.

Boy, was the courtroom quiet as Judge Rudd dealt with the two before him – even the "kiddies" hushed. "All right, you have plead guilty to these wildlife charges and the Court finds you guilty. You will pay a penalty of $500.00 each, the amount of your bond. You will not be sentenced to any time in jail. This Court is adjourned," Judge Rudd ruled.

Never before or after this hearing did I see Judge Rudd as angry as he was with those defendants and their landlord. A $500.00 fine was a good one in that day and time. I'll never forget Judge Rudd. Sometime later, I ran into the landlord in New Burlington. He was a perfect gentleman. He stated, "You know Bailey, I got a million dollar education that wasn't worth a dime that night, especially after the Judge got through with me. Don't ever worry about me poppin' off to you again – we need guys like you and I know it."

My "Busy Night on Andersons Fork" adventure, at last came to a close that night in Xenia, Ohio when Judge Rudd adjourned Court. I'd passed a personal test – reached a milestone perhaps. I'd made some significant cases – some significant arrests – alone – as would be the case many times hence for me and as it is for all who wear the wildlife badge and patrol the wilderness. I didn't do real good but not real bad either. In the years to come I would face much worse. There's one thing I know for certain, my God above or my "backup" as I thought of him that night so long ago, was with me -- as he would be the rest of my long journey.

5
Of Mycophagist, Bullfrogs and an Era Ended

During my career I was privileged to work the length and breadth of our great nation, as well as on the "high seas" of the North Atlantic. I know of no other place where mushroom gathering and frog hunting was as popular as it was in Ohio. I presume both these outdoor activities are still popular in the Buckeye State.

Back in the '50s there was a mushroom gathering club known as Mycophagist (fungi eaters) in Dayton, Ohio. Its membership frequented the Spring Valley Wildlife Management Area the year around. Although there are hundreds of different kinds of mushrooms native to the region, there were about fifty different kinds of non-poisonous and/or edible mushrooms available at Spring Valley. Some were available in the spring, others during the summer and others in the fall and winter. There were also about twelve poisonous non-edible kinds that grew on the area. Several mycophagist members told me the area was a veritable "Mecca" for mushrooms of the kinds popular with their membership.

Every year the mycophagist club sponsored, free of charge, a wild game dinner at a location in Dayton, Ohio. I attended two of these and participated in the "feast." It was cafeteria style. The menu offered moose, elk, deer, antelope, pheasant, wild duck and goose with all the trimmings. Naturally, these delicious wild meats were served with all kinds of mushrooms and mushroom sauces imaginable. I loved to attend wild game dinners (some in an undercover capacity). I can truly say the mycophagist dinners were the most delicious of all. I've mushroom hunted all over the U.S. but never found any place as productive as Ohio.

One spring Saturday morning, a group of mycophagist mushroom gatherers showed up at the Headquarters complex. I always enjoyed having these folks come to Spring Valley. They were most interesting to visit with and they taught me more about mushrooms than I've ever learned since. On several occasions, I accompanied them on their quest for the delicious little morsels.

On this occasion, their station wagon had no sooner stopped when a young man jumped out of the car and came running to the kitchen door of my residence. He was dancing on one foot then the other. I sensed an urgent situation existed as I observed him through a window; I answered his knock on the door as quickly as possible.

"Mr. Bailey I need to get to a restroom pronto," he exclaimed. "Right this way," I responded as I led him through the living room into the hallway and the base of the steps leading to the bathroom at the head of the stairs (the only bathroom in the house), all the while noticing his grayish-green complexion. "Oh dear – oh my, I've got to go up those steps, don't I?" he moaned. "If you want to use the bathroom, you sure do," I replied. Up the stairs he bounded, entered the bathroom and shut the door. Immediately came the grastrointestinal sounds associated with an upset stomach emptying its contents and those associated with what many commonly called "the green apple quick step." Thank goodness my wife and kids were visiting relatives; thus, being spared the sounds and odors of this unfortunate happening.

With the upstairs sounds of human discomfort continuing, I went outside to greet the patiently waiting remainder of the mycophagist party. Naturally, I made inquiry about the condition of my upstairs bathroom guest. They were all snickering and chuckling. It seems their fellow mycophagist member, on a dare during the late evening before, partook of some beautifully prepared (by him) mushrooms of "questionable" edibility. The book listed this particular kind of mushroom as non-poisonous. However, the book didn't list them as edible. Although a couple fellow mushroom gatherers present claimed they had eaten this particular kind of mushroom with no ill effects, this obviously wasn't the case with my upstairs guest. Soon he appeared coming through my kitchen doorway, joined his peers and they all left for their day of mushrooming.

As it happened, they chose to begin their search in the woods directly across the road from my residence. I went about my business doing a few Saturday morning chores at the headquarters complex. Periodically, I heard my mycophagist "upstairs guest" barfing while dutifully and bravely pursuing the almighty mushroom. What a glutton for punishment, I thought. This story "points up" the importance of not eating the wrong mushroom. In some instances it could include a trip to the great pad in the sky.

The Mycophagist Club is a good example of groups other than hunters and fishermen who utilize and enjoy the public hunting and fishing lands, game lands, whatever they're called in various states that are bought and paid for by hunters and fishermen. Bird watchers, picnickers, boaters, campers, hikers – this list goes on, all enjoy these public lands and waters paid for by hunters and fishermen.

There are thousands of public owned land and water areas however, where the hunter in particular, may not pursue his favorite outdoor sport. Granted in some instances, hunting is not compatible with certain outdoor recreational pursuits. However, on the vast majority of these acres, usually managed by the various metropolitan, county, state and federal "park" systems, the hunter suffers rank discrimination.

It was spring 1959. I was in my last year as Manager of the Spring Valley Wildlife Management Area. Dale Taylor is my best and lifelong friend. Dale and I, for the most part, grew up together in the small town of Ostrander in Delaware County in Central Ohio. Our families were close. Our fathers both drove trucks for a living – the big long distance rigs. Perhaps the greatest thing Dale and I had in common was the fact we both knew what our life's work or profession would be at a very early age. What we would do in our professional lives was a given.

How vividly I recall, when in Dale's company, whatever activity we were engaged in (usually up to no good) you could call Dale a "captive audience." He was a good and courteous listener with a great sense of humor as he is today. As I said, he was a "captive audience" until an aircraft of any kind flew over us. Then he'd raise his eyes to the sky, stop whatever he was doing, and run after the aircraft, shading his eyes with his hands if necessary until it was completely out of sight. Soon he'd return, "I'll fly those some day," he'd always claim.

Perhaps the fact World War II United States Air Force Four Star General Curtis E. LeMay was his third cousin had something to do with it. Perhaps it was in his genes. Whatever the force that caused him to "raise his eyes to the sky" as a youth, stuck with him. He did in fact "fly one of those someday." He earned his pilot's licenses to fly both helicopter and fixed wing and rose to a high rank in the Ohio Army National Guard. His picture beside his helicopter would some day be on display at the Smithsonian's Commercial Aircraft Exhibit in the National Air and Space Museum. He retired from Bell Helicopter Textron, in Ft. Worth, Texas. Today, in retirement, he is President of Heli/Jet International, Inc., an aircraft sales, brokerage and consulting firm with offices at Orlando Executive Airport, Orlando, Florida – a highly successful and profitable enterprise.

Dale came to Spring Valley for an overnight visit. I'd received reports of pre-season frog hunting activity on the Little Miami River near the Wildlife Management Area. I asked Dale if he'd mind going with me on a short night patrol to see if my pre-season frog hunters were out and about. Naturally, game for anything that came along, Dale said, "Let's go." We got in my truck and traveled the short distance to a tract of state owned land on the Spring Valley Wildlife Area bordering the east side of the river for a considerable distance. We went to a good observation point and began our surveillance. Soon upstream, off state owned property on the river's west bank, we observed a light "operating" -- shining the river bank obviously from a boat hunting frogs during the closed season.

I was familiar with a farm lane that ran from Rt. 42 to the river on the west bank. I had a hunch the frog hunters used this lane to get to the river. It offered an ideal place to launch a small boat. We headed north on the lane where we were "set up" to the Roxanna – New Burlington Road, turned left and drove across the steel bridge over the river to Rt. 42, turned right until we came to the aforementioned lane.

As I turned right on the farm lane, I turned my headlights off as I'd done many times before stalking outlaws. I didn't think to warn Dale I would do this.

"I see you've developed a fondness for driving during pitch dark nights without the benefit of headlights since we last visited each other – perhaps you've acquired the eyes of an owl, I hope, because I can't see a bloomin' thing," Dale uttered dryly, in typical Taylor fashion as we bumped along "blackout" down the farm lane to the river.

"I'm sorry Tater (childhood nickname), I should have said something before I killed the lights – this is a practice Game Wardens use to slip up on violators undetected."

"Don't worry about what you should have told me – what you should do now is turn the cotton pickin' lights on before we get killed – how many Game Wardens survive this practice?" Tater continued as I knew he would. He had me laughing and so was he as was usually the case.

Soon, we came to the edge of a small rise that I thought would be a good observation point. Our frog hunters were en route from the east bank of the river coming toward us and the place at the end of the lane where they'd launched their boat.

"Okay Tater, now is a good time to move," I told my buddy.

"It is, why?" Tater responded playing dumb.

We were both laughing as we exited the truck and went to the river bank to catch our poachers. Dale "entertained" me so much, I left my citation book in the truck – taking only my flashlight. En route we observed an old pickup truck parked to the right of the lane – well back in the "tulles."

Our poachers arrived at the river bank about the same time we did. We waited quietly until both frog hunters got out of their boat and on shore. We continued our wait until they retrieved a burlap sack of frogs, frog gigs, placed both on shore and started to remove their boat from the water.

I turned my flashlight on, "Good evening gentlemen – State Game Protector – we have a problem," I stated.

The apprehension went well – quiet and subdued. I asked for and received their fishing and driver's licenses. Both were "locals" from the Village of Spring Valley. We counted their frogs – 14 in all. I took their sack of frogs, their gigs, went back to my truck and my forgotten citation book.

As I filled out citations on both, I could hear Dale conversing and laughing with them. Soon all three (Dale and his new friends) came up to the truck where I served both froggers with citations to appear before Judge Rudd in Greene County Court. We left our violators and went back to my residence.

En route, Dale chirped, "One of your poachers asked me what Bailey was doing off the reservation (meaning, the Spring Valley Wildlife Management Area) – they must think you're a native American Indian or something." We were both laughing again.

The next morning Dale left for home. It's good the Almighty, in his infinite wisdom didn't call both Dale and I to be Game Wardens. It's better still we didn't wind up as Game Wardens who worked together. We not only wouldn't have survived, we'd have made the comedy teams of Abbott and Costello and Stan Laurel and Oliver Hardy look like amateurs. Dale never accompanied me on another arrest -- thank goodness.

For the male animal of the human race, waking up at 2 a.m. with the uncomfortable urge to answer nature's call, is sometimes a pleasant experience when he can leave his bed, toddle or stumble half asleep through his door into the great outdoors on a warm spring or summer night -- look up at the starlit sky and let it fly – take a whiz, that is. Usually he'll find this a good time to scratch certain vital areas needing scratched.

On one such occasion a few days after my friend Dale's departure, clad only in skivies and slippers, after completing my whizzing and scratching exercise, I took a brief stroll toward the barn. In doing so I glanced toward the lake – there it was – a light working the north end of the levee – pre-season frog hunters again. Those big Spring Valley bullfrogs were at it again -- "Ba-room, ba-room. I'm big, I'm big" -- doing all they could to lure poachers.

I returned to my residence, donned my uniform, badge and trusty .38, returned outside to my truck and proceeded to the lake parking area traveling "blackout" from mid-Collett Road to my destination. This time the culprit's vehicle was parked in plain view. My guess was they thought this was perfectly safe as they chose an early morning hour to violate the law. Certainly no Game Warden would be out and about at this early hour -- surprise, surprise! Making sure my pen light was in my left shirt pocket, I grabbed my five cell flashlight and headed for the railroad grade running parallel (north and south) to the lake. Let me say here – my five cell flashlight I carried on my night patrols was the same one I carried coon hunting. It was a "Ray-O-Vac Sportsman" model made of thinly milled brass and chrome plated. It was a far cry from the sturdily built "Mag-Lights" of today used by law enforcement officers, that are not only designed to illuminate the way, but also "whack" a law breaker who might warrant whacking.

I looked north up the lake levee, observed a single light working and headed my way. I surmised my violator had been at his dirty work for a good while, really having no good reason or indicator this was the case, other than the early morning hour and the fact the many hours of darkness beforehand offered him ample time to take a great many frogs. Having the feeling he had a good number of frogs, I headed towards him in the dark. Shortly I crossed the wet ditch between the railroad grade and levee arriving only a short distance from my poacher. Unknowingly, en route to my frog hunter, I passed his accomplice hunkered down some distance south of his frog poaching buddy who was doing the catching.

I closed the short distance to my prey, illuminated him with my five cell and announced, "State Game Protector – you're under arrest – come up from the water – lay your sack and gig on the ground."

My frog poacher, a big fellow about 280 lbs., complied without a word. I grabbed his gig and sack of frogs making sure the sack was tied off so the frogs couldn't escape. (Even though gigged, many frogs will keep hopping.)

"Give me your fishing license, if you have one and your driver's license. Then we're going to my vehicle at the parking lot," I stated.

"I don't think he'll be giving you his driver's license or fishing license. He won't be going with you to that parking lot," a voice in the darkness behind me announced.

"Easy Mac, he's got a gun," my apprehended poacher said while exhibiting a partially toothless smile.

"Looks like I've made a miscalculation here – stupid on my part," I thought. I knew it was best to stay still. Then I felt it, the tines of a frog gig "tickling" the right cheek of my butt.

"I don't think he'll go for his gun, with what I'm getting ready to stick in his butt, will ya Warden?" the voice in the darkness asked.

Gradually I worked my right hand toward the butt end of my five cell flashlight. Assuming his frog gig was about 3 to 5 feet long, I guessed he was about the same distance behind me. Mentally, I was rehearsing the move I'd have to make to side step the gig and at the same time smash his brains out with the five cell. I intended to hit him with every ounce of strength I had, which at that time in my life was considerable. I didn't consider the gun a possibility – they were watching for that move. Besides, my revolver was holstered on my right side and my flashlight was in my right hand – going for the gun would involve too many moves and take too much time. I knew what I had to do must be instantaneous. I'm not a particularly "fast" person except when scared. I was scared.

Almost without thinking, I jumped to the left at the same time whirling around and smashing my "threat" upside his head. At that same instant the head or lens end of my five cell flew off spewing its batteries into the lake. I don't think, in view of my dismantled flashlight, it actually hit him all that hard. However, my old five cell still did its' job well -- into the lake he went totally off balance. His gig was laying at waters edge, a good 15 feet away from him. He came up from the water with his nose in the muzzle of my trusty old .38. He was wet to his chest and almost immediately began shivering. At gun point, I patted both down to see if I had anything else to worry about.

I addressed the toothless one, "Okay, leave the gigs, pick up the sack, we'll go to the parking lot". I didn't want their gigs in my hands or theirs – they were a potential lethal weapon. At gun point, with me in the rear, I marched them to my truck. En route, both began to apologize for their conduct. I'm the biggest sucker in the world in situations like this – forgive and forget – to me, when it's over, it's over.

"Boys, I accept your apologies, I've sure had enough of this crap for one night and I take it you have to," I responded.

"I sure have," my wet poacher stated. "All I want to do is get to the car, get warm, and get home," he continued.

"Did you gig any of these frogs?" I asked the wet one.

"Yeah – about half. We thought we heard your tires in the gravels when you came down here, but wasn't sure. That's when I took up the lookout place," he continued.

At the truck, I filled out citations on both after receiving their driver's and fishing licenses. I cited them into Squire Eddelman's Court in Waynesville. I toyed with the idea of taking them immediately before the Squire. The Squire was a paraplegic who sat in a wheelchair. He was usually available to hear a case or set bond at any time -- day or night. However, I decided against it. I was too tired and hungry and assumed they were also.

"I could charge each of you with interfering with an officer and threatening an officer while in the line of duty, but since you've changed your attitude, I'm not going to do that," I explained.

"Thank you Warden," they both stated. "We're related and we don't have a lot of money. Every break you can give us will help," the toothless one said.

I explained the bond forfeiture system to them and told them they would have to contact the Squire to find out the amount. I bid them farewell as they left the parking lot for their homes in Dayton.

I dumped the frogs out in the bed of my truck – 19 in all – typical huge Spring Valley Lake frogs. I re-sacked my evidence, filled out an evidence tag and affixed it to the sack. I locked my truck and went back to the west bank of the lake and retrieved the gigs. I labeled them as "Evidence" and put them in my truck. Back at my residence, I secured my evidence and caught another hour's sleep.

After daylight, over a cup of coffee, my wife inquired about my previous night's activities. "I made two good frog hunting cases and had a few problems," I told her. She didn't push the matter further.

The following afternoon I talked with Squire Eddelman by phone. We discussed the night's events and he said he would set their bond at $125.00 each if that sounded okay with me. Later, I filed affidavits charging each frogger for taking frogs during the closed season. My violators ultimately posted and forfeited the $125.00 bond after the Squire granted them a period of time to bring their money to the Court.

During my time at Spring Valley, I wrote many citations resulting in bond forfeitures or guilty verdicts in court. They were what I'll classify as "routine field patrol" type cases that don't warrant a separate story simply because nothing that interesting happened. These citations were for violations such as shooting before and after legal hours, unplugged shotguns while hunting ducks and geese, hunting or fishing without a license or duck stamp, and hunting with an unsigned duck stamp. In unsigned duck stamp instances, provided their hunting and driver's licenses matched, I usually let the hunter sign his stamp in my presence. There were several I'll call "dumb" cases in which an uninformed duck hunter shot a protected species such as a grebe thinking it was a duck.

I'll mention one such case involving the illegal taking and possession of pied-billed grebe by a Private Detective from Dayton, Ohio while duck hunting, only because this case later played an important role in a major "landmark" and highly successful covert investigation of a deer (and other wildlife) poaching ring in Northeastern Ohio.

An undercover investigation engineered by District Three Law Enforcement Supervisor Ben Anderson, who in my opinion, was years ahead of his time. This 1960's undercover probe into the illegal taking and commercialization of Ohio Wildlife would serve me well as a I duplicated many of the techniques used years later in the 1980's, as Senior Resident Agent in charge of the Carolinas for the U.S. Fish & Wildlife Services' Law Enforcement Division. Ben went on to become head of the Statewide Law Enforcement Section and Chief of the Ohio Division of Wildlife, ultimately retiring with Ducks Unlimited. Anderson pioneered many other wildlife enforcement techniques that were "ahead of his time." Such as patrol techniques that maximized the effectiveness of the uniformed officer's presence in new ways -- "To get the biggest bang for the buck." I sometimes visualized Anderson as Chief of the Fish & Wildlife Services Law Enforcement Division and theorized where the federal Law Enforcement Program would be today had he been at the helm. He was a progressive, no nonsense, wildlife law enforcement administrator whose tall charismatic appearance fit the role. At age 86, he remains a committed wildlife professional.

The Spring Valley Wildlife Management Area, small as it was, spawned many wildlife professionals during my tenure with Ohio. Jack Kaman, the first Area Manager, left to assume the Game Management Supervisors' duties in District Five. In 1955, on the opening day of the upland game season, he witnessed the totally unexpected and brutal murder of his patrol partner, Irwin J. Patrick, Fayette County Game Protector and former government trapper for the U.S. Fish & Wildlife Service in Colorado. A totally insane killing by a former Adams County, Ohio Sheriff, George Baldridge, over the illegal taking of two hen pheasants, not by Baldridge but by a companion hunter. After the shooting, Jack put Pat in their patrol car and rushed him to the Fayette Memorial Hospital in Washington Courthouse, Ohio but Pat died before their arrival. Baldridge, age 63 was sentenced to the Ohio State Penitentiary. He was released years later due to poor health and died shortly thereafter. Baldrige, a wealthy man, lost his estate to Pat's widow by subsequent litigation. Jack left Ohio to become Director of the New Hampshire Fish and Game Department ultimately finishing his career with Ducks Unlimited.

Dale Roach my predecessor, went to Hamilton County as Game Protector and became my Law Enforcement Supervisor in District Two. He retired as Chief of the Law Enforcement Section in Columbus. A wildlife professional I have great respect for and view, as I stated at his retirement party, "A friend when I needed a friend."

Bob Ford came to work at Spring Valley; later became Game Protector in Muskingum County, Ohio, and retired as a Wildlife Enforcement Agent with the Washington State Department of Wildlife. He was one of the best Game Wardens I ever knew, especially talented in the art of interview and after-the-fact investigations. Now retired, he lives in Miles City, Montana. We remain friends and fishing partners today. Once when I asked him what his official job title was with the State of Washington, he replied, "Needless to say the key word all those years was 'Game Warden' but quite often one big word, 'fkngame warden' as read on the lips of a thousand fishermen announcing my arrival to their fishing partner whose back was to me."

Tom Brennan who worked at Spring Valley, went to the Indian Creek Wildlife Management Area as Area Manager. He became Game Protector in Shelby County where he passed away at much too young an age and Howard Grable who worked for me at Spring Valley, ultimately became Area Manager and remained there until he retired.

My time at Spring Valley is as much a part of me today as it was then. A nourishing, enlightening and rewarding part of my journey that I thank God for and will cherish the rest of my days.

Bob Ford, one of many Spring Valley Protégés. (Top) a young Ohio Game Protector, Muskingam County (1967). (Bottom) Near retirement, 1992. Washington State Wildlife Officer, U.S. Fish & Wildlife Service Deputy Game Warden, Special Agent Coast Guard Investigative Service, Contract Investigator, Defense Investigative Service and Commissioned Customs Officer.

6
The Killing Fields

Although I made application for the Ohio Division of Wildlife's Game Protector Training School, I wasn't required to attend – a great disappointment. Customarily, before assuming the duties of a County Game Protector, successful completion of the three month training school was required.

Eldon Sturgeon, the District 6 Law Enforcement Supervisor, informed me the Union County Game Protector's position would open soon. He suggested I apply. "Don't be concerned about the training school; sending you through it is a waste of time and money. If you apply, you'll be strongly endorsed by Dan (Atzenhoefer, District 6 Supervisor), Dale (Whitesell, District 6 Game Management Supervisor) and me," he stated. I applied and very shortly received a letter from Hayden W. Olds, Chief of the Ohio Division of Wildlife notifying me I was the new Game Protector in Union County.

In the spring of 1960, I left the Game Manager's position at the Spring Valley Wildlife Area and assumed the duties of Game Protector in Union County at Marysville, Ohio, Wildlife District Six.

I was informed by Eldon Sturgeon (former Union County Game Protector), I would have some "tough shoes to fill", as Dick Francis, my predecessor, was one "power house" of a Game Warden. Later, I found Sturgeon's statement, an understatement. Francis was a "household word" in every nook and corner of Union County. It seemed as though he'd "sacked" half of the population. He kept a clean county.

It's little wonder he was an outstanding Game Warden. He was born to the profession. His father, uncle, and cousin were Game Protectors. Dick (who transferred to District 5), would later rise through the ranks to become

Chief of the Division of Wildlife before retiring and going with Ducks Unlimited. He briefed me well on the game management, fish management, and law enforcement mission in Union County. He gave me a list of confidential informants who performed well for him. "You're no better than the information you get," he advised.

Years earlier, my father bought and operated a dry cleaning business in Marysville, where we lived for a short time. I attended Marysville High School in my freshman year.

During the early fall of 1960, before the opening of the upland game seasons, I was phoned by a major land owner in the county, who held a political office. This gentleman's son was one of my classmates at Marysville High. Consequently, I knew of the gentleman years before meeting him in person. He asked me to meet him at the Union County Sheriff's Department in Marysville. He stated the "business" he wanted to discuss needed to be told "one on one." We held our meeting at the Office of Ed Amrine, the Union County Sheriff, who sat in on the meeting at the gentleman's request.

The gentleman (we'll call him Mr. G.), opened the meeting by telling me, "We're not going to have one piece of game left to hunt this season, on our farm in Liberty Township." He informed me he rented the house to an unmarried woman with two small grade school age children. She worked at Scott Seed Company in Marysville and probably had a hard time making ends meet. For that reason, he found it difficult to ask her to move.

He went on to say, "She's not the problem, the problem is a man who occasionally lives with her. He literally lives off the land. We (Mr. G. and son whom I'll call Mr. K.), have managed to look over most of the acreage, when no one was there. We did this after I received complaints from the neighbors claiming this guy hunts all the time and kills everything he sees.

What we found is upsetting. He's got homemade box traps, made of scrap lumber, set for rabbits. He's got a small wire cage trap, set so it's partially underground. There were quail feathers and other bird feathers in and around it. He baits it with cracked corn. There's another big trap made out of chicken wire baited with cracked and whole kernel corn. We're certain he's used it to trap pheasants. He's got ears of corn, "spiked" to tree trunks, so he can shoot squirrels that come to eat. He's baited the lower end of the pasture, next to the railroad tracks, with cracked corn, wheat, and oats, where he's been shooting morning doves. He's baited a thicket north of the pasture with cracked and whole kernel corn.

The neighbors say they hear him shooting all the while he's visiting the lady. One neighbor says she's sure he's shot wild ducks, across the tracks in the 'low ground', as she saw a duck drop out of the sky just after she heard a shot."

When Mr. G. finished, I asked, "Whew, anything else"?

Sheriff Ed Amrine took the floor. "The man we're talking about is Rudolph Hines. He has prior arrests in Kentucky and West Virginia, for burglary, assault, drunk and disorderly, and drugs. He's a piece of poop. He's under suspicion for breaking and entering at White Sulpher Springs in Delaware County. We almost got a confession out of him for that offense, but at the last minute, he clammed up. We've had him in jail three times for assault and battery. He shacks up with the woman who lives on Mr. G's farm, and two others, one at Plain City, and another at Milford Center. All these women had him arrested for beating them up, usually when he's drunk or high on marijuana.

All three times, we've had to knock the tar out of him before we could cuff him and get him to jail. When one woman has him locked up, the other two will come to the jail, slobber and fight over him. They bring him cigarettes, candy, and whatever. He's never had a job that we know of. On every occasion we've had him in jail, he sweet talked the complainant into dropping the charges. Mr. G. is concerned he'll burn his property. He's crazy and vindictive. He must not know who turned him in."

"Do his two other lady friends live on farms?" I asked.

"No, they live in town," Sheriff Amrine replied.

Mr. G. took the floor. "The Sheriff's right, our identities must remain confidential. We don't want the farm leveled," he admonished.

"Okay, I understand your fears, and the position you're in. It looks like I can establish probable cause for a search warrant, based on my personal observations of the evidence you say is on the property. When did you make this inspection you've told me about?" I asked.

"Two days ago," Mr. G. replied.

At my request, Mr. K. drew a map of their farm showing the evidence locations, outbuildings, house, and a railroad track transecting the property, north and south. He showed me the farms' location on a Union County map.

I thanked both complainants for their report and their concern for the wildlife on their property. I assured them I would take care of the Rudolph Hines matter.

I knew I needed to inspect Mr. G's farm as soon as possible. Leaving Marysville, I drove to the farm on Dog Leg Road, did a drive by, then went north to my home in Raymond. I changed into hunting clothes, grabbed my .22 rifle, some plastic bags, and my camera, dismantled the radio antenna on my vehicle, and returned to the G. farm.

I pulled in the driveway, went to the door and knocked. No one was home, it was a week day. I guessed the kids would be in school and mom at work. What about Rudolph? Apparently he wasn't there either. If someone had been home, I planned to pose as a ground hog hunter seeking permission to hunt.

I left the residence, traveled south on Dog Leg Road to Lee Road, turned right, and traveled the short distance to the railroad grade, that crossed Mr. G.'s farm. I parked at the railroad track. With rifle in hand, posing as a legal groundhog hunter, I hiked the distance to the backside of the G. farm and began my inspection. Everything was as Mr. G. and Mr. K. stated. Everything except the traps, where were the traps? I found one box trap (for rabbits) upside down, and tripped. I found the place I was certain the quail trap had been, evidenced by a depression dug in the ground, with quail plumage around it.

It dawned on me, the traps are gone because Rudolph wasn't there to tend to them. He (or someone) removed them yesterday. They're stashed somewhere. It was getting late in the afternoon. I decided not to look for the traps in the outbuildings then as someone was likely to return home. I was right, I saw a school bus headed south on Dog Leg Road. It stopped at the residence, and two children exited. I surmised their mother would be home soon. Time was of the essence. I didn't need to be discovered while completing my inspection.

I went to the wooded area on the farm's north boundary, and the baited thicket my complainant described. Both offered the concealment needed to continue my inspection. En route, I crossed a ditch, a tributary of Otter Run, a small creek to the south. There it was, a location Rudolph cleaned some of his illegally taken game. More evidence than I needed. There were cock and hen pheasant plumage and heads, quail plumage and heads, wood duck and mallard plumage and heads, cottontail rabbit heads and fur, two fox squirrel hides with heads and tail attached. Not many entrails as scavengers always consume them first. Some of the evidence appeared fresh, some older. There were footprints in the soft earth in the ditch.

At the woods and thicket areas, I found ears of corn mounted on driven spikes (with the nail head cut off), on several maple, oak, and hickory trees. Some eaten to the cob. I found spent .22 rifle casings under nearly all the "baited" trees.

At the thicket, there was still considerable bait all around. I proceeded to the lower pasture field (the elevation was such I couldn't be seen) adjacent to the railroad tracks. I found numerous spent shotgun shells. There was dove plumage from dead or wounded birds. I collected, bagged, labeled evidence samples, and photographed all the sites.

Inspection completed, I "groundhog hunted" south on the railroad grade to my patrol car and returned home. I phoned adjoining Game Protectors, Loyd Hughes (Logan County) and Jim Donahue (Champaign County) and asked them to be on "stand by" in case I needed them the following day to execute a search warrant. Both said they would be available.

As the new Union County Game Protector, I hadn't "tested" my County Prosecutor, Bob Hamilton or my County Court Judge, Robert Evans, yet. I was sure I had sufficient probable cause for a search warrant. I delivered my evidence film to a photography studio for developing as soon as possible. By 1:00 p.m. I had the photos I took the day before of the killing fields and wildlife carnage on the G. property. By 2:30 p.m. I was armed with a search warrant approved by the County Prosecutor and the County Court Judge, for the residence, outbuildings and premises on the G. farm.

I planned to execute my search warrant later that evening when Mr. G.'s tenant was home. I wanted to interview her, and try to get a statement incriminating Hines. If she cooperated, I had no intention of charging her with illegal possession of any protected wildlife (or parts) found in her home. If she didn't cooperate, she would be charged. I surmised this might be a good time of day to find Hines present. He was the one I wanted on the "taking" charges.

Marysville Police Officers carried Deputy Sheriff Commissions. At the Police Department I briefed Chief, Dick Simpson, on my investigation and planned raid on the G. farm that afternoon.

I didn't have to ask for Dick's help. "Don't worry with dragging your officers over here. I've talked to Ed Amrine about this Hines character. Bill McNamara and I will help with your search. Pick us up when you're ready to go," Dick stated. Two big, tough as nails, Irish cops, ready and willing to help – I couldn't ask for more. I radioed my District Office in Xenia and had the dispatcher notify both Game Protectors to cancel as I had "local help."

About 4:00 p.m. I picked up Police Officers, Bill McNamara and Dick Simpson -- we proceeded to the G. farm. Upon arrival, we observed two vehicles in the driveway – a good chance Hines was there. "If he's there, he'll probably run when he sees our uniforms," I stated.

"I'll cover the back door," McNamara stated as he exited the patrol car. Dick Simpson and I went to the front door. I knocked – the lady of the house answered the door. I told her who we were, why we were there, and handed her a copy of the Search Warrant.

Officer Simpson went around me and up the stairs leading to the upper level in about three bounds. He searched every closet and room upstairs looking for Hines. I asked her if Hines was there.

"No, Rudy left two days ago," she replied.

"When will he be back?" I asked.

"He won't. I don't want him to ever come back, I asked him to leave," she answered. This sounded good, I thought; she'll give me the statement I want.

The second car in the driveway proved to be the lady's visiting sister and three kids. This made two women and five noisy kids. I told the lady I needed to interview her in a quiet place and made arrangements to meet with her at the Sheriff's Department the following day after she left work. All this noise and commotion wasn't the right atmosphere to interview her.

"Do you have any wild game in the house?" I asked.

"Yes, there's some in the freezer of the refrigerator, and in the old freezer on the porch," she replied.

"Anywhere else," I asked.

"No," she replied.

Simpson removed two dressed fox squirrels in a pan of salt water, from the bottom of the refrigerator. In the freezer compartment, we found two ring neck pheasant carcasses, three bob white quail carcasses, and four morning dove carcasses. In the freezer on the porch, we found three cottontail rabbit carcasses, one groundhog carcass (legal, if Hines had a hunting license), one mallard, two wood duck carcasses. "This certainly isn't all the wild game

Rudy, killed is it?" I asked.

"Oh no, he killed lots more, he hunted all the time. We ate all he got except what you've found. He got a lot of those young pheasants last summer – they were especially good," she answered.

"Did he use traps to catch some of the game," I asked

"Yes, he had rabbit traps and two cages he caught pheasants and quail in," she replied.

"Where are the traps?" I asked.

"They should be back in the field," she replied.

"They're not there – would he have stored them in one of the out-buildings?" I asked.

"I guess he would have, I don't know," she replied.

Officer McNamara came through the back door stating, "No one ex-ited the back door--nothing in the outside buildings but there's something you should look at behind the barn."

"No wire traps or rabbit traps in any of the outbuildings?" I in-quired.

"No, none," Bill answered. I went with McNamara to the location behind the barn. There was another pile of pheasant plumage along with blood on the ground. I collected a sample of the plumage and photographed this site.

We returned to the house. "Are Rudy's guns in your house?" I asked the lady.

"No, he took them with him," she replied. Search completed, I made an inventory of the illegal wildlife seized, along with one wooden rabbit trap (I later retrieved from a field behind the house), and gave her a copy.

En route to the Marysville Police Station, Dick Simpson suggested I get a warrant for Hines arrest as soon as possible and get the warrant filed with the Sheriff's Department. "That way every badge in the county will be on the lookout for him in the event he shows up," Dick stated.

I agreed. "I'll file charges against him with the court after the pros-ecutor's approval, and ask for a bench warrant when he doesn't appear." I replied.

"You need every badge in the county looking for him. We're in a posi-tion to pick him up, probably quicker than you," McNamara stated.The next day at 4:45 p.m., I met with Mr. G. and the lady tenant at the Sheriff's Office. She gave an incriminating statement concerning Rudolph Hines' poaching ac-tivity during the past year on the G. and surrounding properties. I informed her she may have to testify in court against Hines.

The following day I prepared eighteen affidavits charging Hines with the offenses of taking during the closed season; fox squirrels (2 counts); ring necked pheasant (2 counts); bob white quail (3 counts); cottontail rabbit (3 counts); wood duck (2 counts); mallard duck (1 count); taking groundhog without a valid hunting license (1 count) (to be dropped if he produced a hunt-ing license); and taking a protected non-game bird, morning dove, (4 counts

– doves weren't classified as game birds in Ohio at the time).

I delivered eighteen affidavits to County Prosecutor, Bob Hamilton. After reviewing the affidavits, physical evidence, photos, and the lady's statement, he approved all charges against Hines for prosecution.

Later that day, I filed all eighteen affidavits charging Hines, with the County Court Clerk. Rudolph Hines' court date was set for the following week on Thursday at 9:00 a.m.

On Thursday, Prosecutor Bob Hamilton and I appeared in County Court in Marysville before Judge Evans. As expected, Defendant Hines didn't appear. I was called to the stand by Prosecutor Hamilton. After being sworn, I testified as to the results of my inspection of the G. farm; the results of the executed search warrant; and the statement taken from the lady tenant. Judge Evans issued a bench warrant, listing the counts against Hines. The warrant was issued to "Any Law Enforcement Officer." Following Court, I delivered a copy of the warrant to Ed Amrine, County Sheriff, and kept a copy.

"680 from Xenia," came the radio call from my District Headquarters.

"680, go ahead," I replied.

"You're to proceed to Milford Center. Sheriff Amrine will meet you at the bridge on Darby Creek. His Department has located a subject you have a warrant for," Xenia advised.

"Q-22 Xenia ... ETA twenty minutes," I responded. Shortly, I met with Sheriff Amrine.

It was June, 1961, about eight months after the issuance of the warrant for Hines, the Sheriff's Department found him. Sheriff Amrine was 95% certain Hines was at the home of his "Milford Center concubine" as we spoke. "Since this is a wildlife warrant, I suggest you go to the front door . . announce . . and call him out. I'll stand at the side of the house so I can go either way, when and if he comes out. My deputy will cover the back door . . in times past, he's always broke for the outside of the house . . if he shows with a gun, take cover and shoot him. We'll have trouble with him, we always have," Sheriff Amrine advised. Sheriff Amrine had no use for Hines, and it wouldn't take much for the Sheriff to hurt this guy.

We proceeded to the residence in Milford Center in both vehicles. The Sheriff's patrol vehicle drove in the driveway. I parked in front of the house on the street. We all went to our pre-determined positions.

I pounded on the front door and announced, "State Game Protector. I have a warrant for the arrest of Rudolph Hines . . come out now!" Immediately I heard rustling and footsteps . . he was headed for the back door. I jumped off the porch and yelled, "He's coming out the back door." Sheriff Amrine was in front of me, as we rounded the corner at the rear of the house, to find the young deputy with all he could handle. The deputy managed to get Hines' left arm behind his back in an attempt to handcuff him. However, Hines was kicking the deputy unmercifully in the shins, while at the same time, trying to turn around and "elbow" him. I arrived and "snap kicked"

61

Hines in the groin. At the same instant, Sheriff Amrine "whacked" him on the right side of his head with a blackjack.

Hines went down and doubled up in the fetal position. He was hurting -- trying to hold and protect his testicles from another "snap kick." The deputy and I handcuffed him, got him to his feet, and "loaded" him in the Sheriff's patrol vehicle.

Following the arrest, we rested for a short time, and discussed the situation. "How's the shins?" I asked the young deputy. He raised his pant legs for inspection. "Bruised, hurts, but no broken skin," he stated.

"There won't be any girlfriend to come in and drop charges on him this time," Sheriff Amrine stated.

"Do you suppose his girl friends will pay his fine?" I inquired.

"I wouldn't be surprised if they did," Amrine answered. The Sheriff continued, "You've got a look at him. Can you figure out why a decent looking, hard working, woman would have anything to do with something like that?"

"Beats me," I replied.

Hines stood over 6' -- was skinny, had long red, uncombed, hair that looked like a thatched roof. He had gray/green watery eyes, and a "pocked" face complexion. He and his clothes were dirty. To top it off, he stunk . . a weird odor that made you think it was a matter of body chemistry as well as personal hygiene. I didn't envy the two officers who transported him to the Union County Jail. That afternoon, I notified the County Prosecutor and the Court Clerk Hines was in custody. The Clerk set his court date the following week on a regular scheduled court day.

The following Thursday, I met County Prosecutor Hamilton. We went to the Union County Court, Judge Robert E. Evans presiding. Following the Courts opening procedure, Hines, who was not represented, stood handcuffed before the Judge. After Judge Evans explained his right to be represented by an attorney, either retained or appointed, Hines answered, "No." Following the lengthy reading of the charges, Judge Evans asked Hines if he understood the charges.

Hines replied, "Yes."

Judge Evans explained the three "pleas" Hines could plead to the charges. Following this explanation, Judge Evans asked Hines how he plead.

Hines replied, "No contest."

I was called to the stand by Prosecutor Hamilton and sworn by the Clerk. Responding to the Prosecutor's questions, I testified to the results of my inspection of the G. farm, the executed search, and the statement given by the lady tenant. During my testimony, the Prosecutor introduced, as various exhibits, all the wildlife seized during the search, as well as the physical evidence, and photos I had gathered during my inspection of the G. property.

Before sentencing, Judge Evans asked Hines if he had anything to say in his defense.

"Nothing," Hines replied, unconcerned.

"Very well, in view of the testimony given, evidence presented, and your plea, the Court finds you guilty. For the purpose of sentencing, the Court imposes a fine of $1800.00 and six months in jail. In view of your apparent indigent circumstances, and in view of the fact you will place a burden on the tax payers of Union County, the Court suspends $900.00 of your fine and the six months jail sentence. In the event you appear before this Court again, on any charge, both your suspended penalties will be imposed. The Court orders your incarceration in the County Jail, where you will serve and perform work at the discretion of the County Sheriff. Your fine will expire at the rate of $3.00 per day until paid. If, at any time subsequent to this date, you are able to pay the penalty imposed, you may do so. The penalty amount will be minus the days served at $3.00 per day," the Judge sentenced.

Hines, or someone on his behalf, ultimately paid about $500.00 of his fine, as best I recall. He didn't serve his entire sentence. Sometime later, I received a call from the County Sheriff. He asked if I had a problem with the Sheriff's Department petitioning the Court for an "indigent and banning" order concerning Hines. This would enable the Sheriff to transport Hines over the county line and release him, with the order to never enter Union County again. "He stinks the jail up so bad, we can't take it any more," Sheriff Amrine stated.

I was laughing, "Is it really that bad Ed?" I asked.

"It's that bad. Five minutes after he's out of the shower, he stinks as bad as ever. It's something in his makeup, he's got to go," Ed replied.

"No, I have no objection. I considered the case closed some time ago," I replied. A short time later, Rudolph Hines was transported across the Union/Franklin County line and set out. To my knowledge, he never appeared in Union County again.

The damage a single poacher like Rudolph Hines does to a given wildlife population on a given unit of land, is almost impossible to calculate. The voided niche or unit of land, completely or heavily depleted of its wildlife, will eventually re-populate by populations from surrounding areas. However, filling the "carrying capacity" once again, of this poacher emptied unit of land, takes time. With some wild game species, a long time.

Two years later, I ran into Mr. G. at the Ohio State Fair. He claimed the pheasant population on his farm in Union County, the farm Hines ravaged with his "Killing Field Techniques," had not recovered to date.

The evildoers, the out-of-season "Killing Field" practitioners, must never be allowed to function. Hopefully, the thin-green-line of wildlife officers, the public and other law enforcement officers (as in this case) throughout our great nation, will see to it they don't.

63

7

Coons by the Tubs Full

"They brought them here in two galvanized washtubs," stated (I'll call him) C.D.,a licensed fur dealer near Bellepoint, Ohio in Delaware County.

He summoned me to his place of business the night before. It was shortly after the opening of the Ohio 1960 coon hunting and trapping season.

He pointed to a pile of dead raccoons covered with mud and blood, laying on the floor of his skinning room, 27 in all. "They claimed these coons were caught by several members of their coon hunting club at Byhalia, during the past several nights. They're liars. I've been in this business a long time. I know a fresh caught coon when I see one. These coons were all killed the night before last and brought here yesterday. Most of them shot between the eyes, or somewhere around the head. Not one has signs of being mauled by a hound. There is no coon hunters club at Byhalia and I'm familiar with every club in Central Ohio," C. D. stated.

"How were these coon killed?" I asked.

By jack-lighting. The same as you would a deer, except jack-lighting a coon is easier," C.D. answered.

Ohio law prohibited taking any wildlife, covered by Ohio law, with an artificial light, from a motor driven conveyance, while having firearms in possession. Coon could only be taken with gun and dog or trapping.

"The night before last was a good coon night. It was warm, rainy-- the tile ditches were full of water. The corn fields and bottoms were full of coon. There's where they killed them. That's why they're covered with mud," C.D. explained.

I knew C.D. long before becoming a Game Protector. I sold my furs to

65

him years before. I knew C. D. knew what he was talking about.

"A lot of coon came in yesterday from legal hunters. Most had two or three. One had his limit (4). Over there are the coon they brought in. You can see the difference between those taken with gun and dog, and this pile taken with a spotlight and gun. We purposefully didn't start skinning, so I could show you the difference," C. D. explained.

"May I see the invoices you filled out when you paid them?" I asked. C. D. had them handy. He'd written the vehicle description the subjects drove, and its license number on the back of one of the invoices. He made out two invoices, recording half payment to each subject and their names.

"I need to take these invoices. I'll return copies of them to you," I stated.

"Go ahead," C. D. responded.

"Have you seen or done business with these two before?" I asked.

"Yeah, they were in last year and sold a few coons. They complained their dog wasn't very good. They've figured out an easier way to kill coon," C. D. stated. "Should I continue buying coon from them?" C.D. asked.

"By all means, and call me when you do," I replied. I asked for and received physical descriptions of both subjects. "Thanks for giving me this report, C. D. Rest assured, I'll do something about it. I'll take photos of the 27 coons," I told him.

"You should also take photos after I've cleaned them up. Then you can show they're shot between the eyes or near the head," C. D. stated.

"Good idea, I'll photograph some legal coon to show the difference between a jack-lighted coon, and one taken with gun and dog," I stated. I retrieved my camera from my patrol car and photographed the 27 mud and blood covered coon.

As I was leaving, C. D. stated, "Come back about 1:00 p.m., I'll have them cleaned up so you can get your comparison pictures."

"See you later," I said and left.

I radioed Xenia and ran a license check on the vehicle my outlaw coon hunters used. It came back to (I'll call him) Marvin W., Rt. 1, Byhalia, Ohio on a 1957 Ford pickup. I radioed Don Mycko, the Wildlife Patrolman assigned to Union, Logan, Champaign and Shelby Counties and told him I'd phone him at his residence that night.

I found the Marvin W. residence, a farm near Byhalia with the 1957 green Ford pickup parked in the driveway. I was sure (I'll call him) Ted S., Marvin's fellow outlaw lived near Raymond, Ohio.

At 1:00 p.m. I returned to C. D.'s. I completed photographing the cleaned legally and illegally taken coon. C. D. informed another coon hunter came in with two coons during my absence. The hunter told him Marvin W. and Ted S. were jack-lighting coon in Marion and Hardin Counties. C. D. surmised the pair sold coon to the fur buyers in those counties.

Before I left, C. D. said, "I have more information. They'll have an old dog with them. This dog isn't worth anything -- can't tree a coon. He's an alibi dog they use. They'll claim they caught their coon with him. They'll have a lantern and a couple 5-cell flashlights. They'll have a big spotlight they actually use to shine coon. This information is from the same coon hunter who was here a bit ago, who knows both."

After leaving C. D.'s, I radioed the Game Protectors in Marion and Hardin Counties. I informed each of the descriptive information I had concerning my two jack-lighters. I asked each officer check with their fur buyers and ascertain if my two subjects sold them coon. If so, obtain copies of the sales invoices, inspect any fresh coons bought from my two violators and solicit the fur dealer's opinion as to whether the coon were legally or illegally taken. No record of Marvin or Ted selling coon was found in the two counties.

I figured catching my two outlaws would be easy. I coon hunted alone and with a good friend, George Miller. I had one of the best coon dogs in the country – ol "Nap." He was easily controlled -- never had to leash him. When ready to quit hunting, all I had to do was call him. Unless he was treed or on a red hot track, he would come in, fall in ahead of me, and we went to the truck.

I planned to hunt in areas conducive to shining with plenty of coon. With a dog as easily controlled as Nap, it would be simple; when they jack-lighted the area I was hunting, I'd quickly load Nap and catch them. A good plan, I thought. Wrong!

Night and after night I hunted in areas meeting the aforementioned criteria. Between these hunts, on good nights, Wildlife Patrolman, Don Myco and I patrolled and set up at good surveillance locations. We never found these two jack-lighting during our patrols; however, we wrote several citations for hunting without a license and three for taking over the legal limit.

During the time the night patrolling took place, C. D. phoned twice. Both times I went to his place of business and inspected coons brought in as usual, in a wash tub, swimming in mud and blood, by my two outlaws. On one occasion, 10 coons; 13 on another. I dutifully obtained copies of the sales invoices and photographed the animals. The same story – they were shot between the eyes or in and around the head. Where were they hunting? This is getting old, I thought.

Finally it happened. It was a warm and rainy night. I loaded Nap and headed for a big section with picked corn fields and small wood lots near the Hardin County line. I parked my vehicle in a graveled lane next to a fence row, and covered it with Army surplus camouflage netting. Nap and I headed across a corn field to a small wood lot. Nap struck a track. In less than ten minutes he was treed in the edge of the woods. I shot the coon out and Nap finished it off.

While Nap and I were still at the tree, a pickup abruptly stopped on the county road I'd traveled, before parking and concealing my patrol car. I could hear the bellow of the truck's exhaust pipes, that evidenced a "souped up" engine. I knew the spotlight would be next. I grabbed Nap by the collar. "Stay close to me, ol buddy," I whispered in his ear as we hunkered down.

Quickly the spotlight, hand held out the passengers window, began its deadly search. It illuminated the entire corn field and woods. I pulled Nap closer. He seemed to know what was happening; stayed still as a mouse, as the second "sweep" of the light went over us. Slowly, my night bandits proceeded west past the fence row where my vehicle was concealed to the adjoining corn field. I was excited. At last I've got them, I thought. I sensed another kill and I don't mean a coon. Nap and I moved swiftly to my patrol vehicle, which I'm sad to say was a State owned Ford Falcon station wagon. I had almost forgotten I no longer patrolled in my privately owned 1958 Ford Fairlane 500, with its Thunderbird V/8 engine, a vehicle that moved out like lightening and could catch anything on the road.

My outlaws were still shining the adjacent corn field as I uncovered my sickening little green Game Warden car and loaded Nap. I took off my hunting coat and put on my uniform winter coat. I "killed" the rear brake and back up light switches and drove onto the county road, traveling "blackout" behind my outlaws. As they continued to shine, I slowly closed the distance between vehicles. I didn't dare get too close, for fear of being seen in the illumination of their brake lights.

They continued driving slow, shining as they went. I got close enough to read their license plate and the fact it was a green Ford. They were my coon shining outlaws alright. I hoped they'd shine and kill a coon in their usual illegal manner. No such luck. They were headed for Rt. 31, a major highway. The road we were on dead ended at Rt. 31. They had to go north or south. I knew I'd have to discontinue traveling blackout on Rt. 31. If they would only bag a coon, I thought. At the same time, realizing the coon I had in my hunting coat would probably be theirs and they would be mine, if Nap and I hadn't bagged the coon. We were getting closer to Rt. 31. If I made the stop and they had a rifle in possession, or any "implement for hunting," I had a case. I reasoned they had taken some coons that were in their possession. It was too good a night.

I realized how hard it had been to get this close to catching them. It may be ages before this happens again. I decided to "go for it," and get them stopped before they got to Rt. 31. It started raining. I turned my headlights on. I flipped on my red, rotary, partial hooded, dash mounted light. I veered to the left side of the road, with intentions of going around them, blocking the road, and making the stop.

What a joke! The green Ford pickup "squatted", its exhaust pipes bellowed, and it walked away from me like I was sitting still. Darn this state owned piece of crap. If I only had my Ford Fairlane 500 with its big V/8," I thought as I floored my green Ford Falcon "Game Warden car".

When my outlaws got to Rt. 31, they turned north. I expected them to turn south. As I turned north on 31, my green machine "fish tailed" on the rain soaked pavement for what seemed like a quarter of a mile. Just after crossing the Union/Hardin County line, I glanced at my speedometer, I was doing 90 mph and the Ford pickup was fading in the fog and mist ahead of me. I grabbed the radio mike and tried to call the Hardin County Game Protector. No answer. I realized the state owned vehicle I was driving was unstable at this high speed. My continued attempt to catch my violators was futile. I felt like parking the thing, getting out and shooting it between the headlights, but I needed it to get home. I continued traveling north on Rt. 31, to Kenton, hoping the Highway Patrol had my violators stopped for speeding. No such luck.

I went to the Marvin W. home and maintained surveillance until daylight. He didn't return home. I knew he wouldn't. If he did, there would be no evidence of their illegal activity the night before. It would be disposed of. Even though I was "ticked off" at my little Ford Falcon, it may have saved my life. If I had continued in "hot pursuit," given the conditions of the road, I would probably have wound up in a ditch, with my head in my butt. Lord knows what would have happened to ol Nap. I went home tired and defeated. I fed ol Nap, had breakfast, and hit the sack.

About 11:00 a.m. the phone rang. It was the Union County Sheriff's Department. "There's a Detective Sgt. Clyde Mann, from the Franklin County Sheriff's Department, who would like to meet with you," the dispatcher said.

I told him, "I'm on my way," got dressed and headed for the Sheriff's Office in Marysville. En route, the name, Detective Sgt. Clyde Mann, rang a bell. Detective Mann was quite famous. He was hailed as the cop who single handedly, solved more homicide cases than any cop in the state. Many of the murders he solved were associated with organized crime. Franklin County (Columbus and vicinity) was his beat. I'd read about him in the newspapers and detective magazines. I'd seen him on TV news. Why would this famous detective want to meet with me? I wondered.

At the Sheriff's Department, I was ushered into Sheriff Ed Amrine's Office where I was introduced to the famous Detective. I was somewhat surprised to see he wasn't as big as he appeared on T.V. He was immaculately dressed in a dark blue business suit, wore patent leather shoes, and a tweed hat. He wore a neatly trimmed mustache. He took the trouble to show me his credentials; as if he thought I didn't recognize him, and he wanted me to be sure he was a police officer.

Detective Mann informed me he had pretty well completed a case in Franklin County. His investigation involved a subject who committed a number of burglaries, armed robberies, and ultimately a murder. This subject confessed to breaking and entering a bait and sporting goods store in Marysville. During this B & E, the subject stole a box containing $1500.00 the store took in from the sale of fishing licenses. Detective Mann wanted to know where this money should be sent following the suspects' trial. I told him to deliver the money to the Chief, Ohio Division of Wildlife, 1500 Dublin Road, Columbus, Ohio.

With our business taken care of, I invited Detective Mann to lunch. He accepted my invitation. At lunch, he told me he was an avid deer and grouse hunter and solicited any "tips" I might have, concerning good places to hunt in southeastern Ohio. I told him several good locations I was familiar with.

I considered it quite a privilege to be in the company of this famous Detective. Consequently, I was somewhat surprised when he asked me to tell him about my duties as a Game Warden. I've never been at a loss for words when it came to talking about the profession I love so much. I'd given him a pretty good "overview" of what Game Wardens were all about. Without thinking, I found myself telling him about the Marvin W. and Ted S. case, and my frustration in trying to catch them.

"Wait a second and back up, tell me again about your fur dealer witness, and the evidence you documented, he showed you," Detective Mann inquired.

I answered his inquiry in detail.

"Have you talked to your Prosecutor about qualifying your fur dealer as an expert witness relative to his examination leading to his conclusion the coons were killed illegally? He sounds like he may be your first witness," Mann asked and opined.

"No sir, I haven't," I meekly replied.

"Have you interviewed any of the hunters who gave the fur dealer the information he passed on to you?" Detective Mann asked.

"No sir," I replied.

"Has it occurred to you one or more of these hunters may be an eye witness?" he inquired.

At this point, I realized I was about to get some darn good instruction and advice from this famous Detective.

"No sir, I hadn't considered it," I replied.

"Have you knocked on any doors in their (violators) areas of operation to ascertain if you have any additional witnesses?" he asked.

"No sir," I replied.

"You may come up with additional evidence if you pursue these two avenues," he advised.

"May I ask why you're killing yourself with these night patrols, when it seems you don't have any information that pin-points where they might be operating?" Mann asked.

"Well, I did get close to them on one occasion," I replied.

"One occasion out of how many patrols, and how many hours expended?" he asked.

"I get your point, sir. That's the way we do it," I stated.

"I don't want to insult your agency and certainly not you, but your organization seems to be suffering under the same dilemma as the Highway Patrol. On the highways, they're no more than traffic cops. They have no authority beyond highway traffic. However, on state owned property, they have full police powers, and frankly, they don't know how to use it. They think their officers have to witness a violation in order to do anything about it. They aren't trained in conducting after-the-fact investigations, interviewing, and all the rest that goes with investigative police work," Mann stated. Does your agency give its officers this kind of training?" the Detective asked.

"No sir, all we enforce are misdemeanors. Would we have all that authority? I have taken statements associated with the execution of a search warrant," I responded.

"The authority to question an individual concerning an after-the-fact violation of a misdemeanor is 'implied' under the law. Besides, there is nothing in the law prohibiting you from inviting your suspect to have a talk with you. There is no law that prohibits you from taking his statement, sworn or otherwise," Mann advised.

I thanked Detective Mann for his information and advice. I realized this Detective from Franklin County opened a new world for me. I immediately went to see C. D. at his place of business. "Do you mind sharing with me, the names of the coon hunters who complained about Marvin W. and Ted S.?" I asked.

"Not at all," C. D. replied. He gave me the names of six coon hunters who complained about my two violators. I thanked him for the additional information and returned home. I found all six hunters in the phone directory, phoned them, and made arrangements to interview each the next evening.

The first two coon hunters on my list were Delmer Raye and Floyd Argo, who lived near Raymond, Ohio where I lived. According to C. D., they hunted together for many years. I met with both at the same time. As soon as I told them what I wanted to talk to them about, I didn't think they were going to stop talking. They told me they encountered Marvin W. and Ted S. the same night the two outlaws killed the 27 coons they sold to C. D.

"We were hunting northeast of here, near the Hardin County line. We had Delmer's two English hounds and my old red bone. We'd hunted a good stretch of timber and caught two coons. We came to the south edge of the timber. We saw them shining the corn fields and feeder lots between us and the road. They were actually shining both sides of the road and were coming in our direction. They were using a powerful light. We caught our dogs, afraid they would shine their eyes and shoot them. We'd come to a fence row. We were leading our dogs south, down the fence row towards the road, when they lit up the whole field we were in. I reckon they didn't see us in the fence row because they shined and shot a big coon in the same field. Ted S. held the light and Marvin W. got out of the truck. He was wearing a bump hat with a light on it. He shot the coon; Ted S. ran out in the field, grabbed the coon and took it to the truck. We'd parked our truck in Frank M.'s barn lot, a field away. We hurried, got to the truck, and loaded the dogs. Frank M. came out of his house and asked if we had seen that darn light. He was mad and said it would only be a matter of time until they shot some livestock. We headed toward Rt. 31 to try to catch them. As we got there, we saw them head north towards Mt. Victory. Immediately, Delmer was close behind them. They pulled into the truck stop at Mt. Victory. We parked parallel to them, but some distance away. I hunkered down and Delmer followed them inside. The plan was for Delmer to keep them inside and talking while I looked in their truck. There were two tubs full of coons, covered with blood. The worst mess you ever saw in the bed of their truck. That old dog of their's, that can't tree a coon, was shivering in his box. Their big spotlight and a .22 rifle were on the front seat. I thought, to heck with this and went to a pay phone in the parking lot. I called the Hardin County Sheriff and told them to get a Deputy Sheriff or a Game Warden down here right away. There were two guys here with way over their limit of coons. I went inside where Delmer and the shiners were eating hamburgers and drinking coffee. I ordered the same. Delmer and I tried to stall them as long as we could. No Deputy Sheriff or Game Warden came. Finally, Marvin and Ted said they had to go. We all paid for our food and went outside. Still no Deputy Sheriff or Game Warden. They left and went north on Rt. 31. I told Delmer what I saw in their truck. I told him I called the law and gave them a description of the truck. 'Maybe they'll get them before daylight,' Delmer said. We were both mad. It never occurred to us to make a citizens arrest or we would have," Floyd stated, finally finishing the story.

"Are both of you gentlemen willing to testify to all this in court?" I asked. Both stated, they would.

"I don't think you'll have to worry about catching them, Warden," Delmer stated.

"Oh?" I responded.

"A bunch of us sorta took matters in our own hands," he continued.

"How's that?" I inquired.

"We paid them a visit. We let them know we turned them in and it wasn't only the law they needed to worry about, it was us. Let me put it this way. Big Ben Smart from Magnetic, told them he would break their arms. That way, Marvin wouldn't be able to drive or shoot and Ted wouldn't be able to shine or shoot. In other words, Warden, their shining days are over, they know it, and we mean it. We're all good shots. We let Marvin know when we got through with his pretty green Ford, it would make a good fish net," Delmer continued.

"It hasn't been that many years ago when we didn't have any coons. We all helped ol Eldon Sturgeon and Bill Kirby (Ex Union County Wardens) stock coons from the state coon farm. We put the critters in the county where we thought they'd take hold. They were the most beautiful coons you ever saw, big ones from Minnesota brood stock. They took hold and today we've got good coon hunting and we're going to keep it that way. Those young snots never went through any of that. We love our hounds and we love our sport. Not them or no one else is gonna ruin what we've got now," Floyd stated.

Both of my witnesses finally finished. One, a farmer, the other, a heavy equipment operator; both in their late 50's. I felt the calluses as I shook their hands and thanked them for the help they'd given me. I looked at their weathered faces that spoke of hard work and many nights following their beloved hounds. They made me proud of my membership in the great coon hunting fraternity.

I spent the rest of the evening interviewing the remaining four coon hunters. Big Ben Smart, who lived near Magnetic Springs, was the only one who had actually encountered the coon shiners while hunting. He also witnessed the illegal taking of a coon by both individuals off the county line road south of Magnetic Springs. "I should have called you, but C. D. said he would. I figured if I ran into them again, I'd take care of them. If you've talked to Delmer and Floyd, I guess you know we did take care of it," Ben stated.

"Are you willing to testify in court as to what you've told me about your encounter with these two?" I asked.

"Ain't much wantin' to go to court against anyone, but I will if I have to. Don't think you're gonna find them out jack-lightin' since we paid them our visit. I know most of the boys who hunt the north end of Union County, and the southern half of Hardin County. I also know most of the farmers. No one's seen a light operating since we had our little talk with Marvin W. and Ted S.," Ben said.

I thanked Ben for his time and information. "I'm sure you boys have broken this case wide open. Tell Delmer and Floyd I said that. Now, I'm going to do everything I can to get these two before the judge," I told him before leaving. I was privileged to shake his hand.

By the time I got home, it was snowing. No patrol tonight. I hit the sack and slept like a baby. I was satisfied with my days work. I knew what I would be doing tomorrow.

The gravely sound of a snow plow scraping the road in front of my house, woke me about 8:00 a.m. After breakfast, I headed for the Hardin County line to take care of some unfinished business. About noon, I headed south on Rt 31 en route to Marysville. It was still snowing, Rt. 31 was being plowed for the second time. I pulled up behind a DOT snow plow mounted, salt truck, clipping along, throwing a wall of snow to the right berm of the highway. I followed the truck through the small town of Byhalia where I saw Marvin W.'s green Ford pickup parked, among some other "red neck" pickups in front of a beer joint and pool hall. I'd been cautioned by Sheriff Amrine about this red neck joint. He said it was the main hangout in northern Union County for ner-do-wells, bikers, and other trouble makers. He told me they'd answered several "loud and disturbing the peace" type complaints there, and never sent an officer in alone.

However, I was young and feeling "chesty". I could smell two more "kills." I thought winding this case up at the end of the coon season, in a snow storm, seemed appropriate. I turned my pathetic, state owned Ford Falcon station wagon, around and went back to the pool hall.

I stepped inside the door, with wind and snow following me. "State Game Protector, I'm looking for Marvin W.," I announced. A sizable red neck (who I later learned owned the joint) took about three steps from the first of four pool tables in the room, and planted himself, straddle legged, about four steps in front of me. He had changed ends on his pool que and was holding it in front of him, "port-of-arms," in a threatening manner.

"What you want with him?" he asked.

73

I hooked the corner of my parka behind the butt of my revolver (no longer my .38; I replaced it with a new S & W .38 special). As I unsnapped the keeper, I asked "Are you Marvin W.?"

"No," he replied.

"Then make yourself comfortable on the little stool to your left, unless you have something else in mind," I stated. I took two steps towards him placing us almost nose to nose. He stepped aside and leaned against the wall. He "righted" the position he was holding the pool que. I didn't like him; perhaps because he was a dead ringer for a screwball I grew up with I didn't like.

Again, I announced, "I'm looking for Marvin W."

A big sandy haired chap at the third table put his hand up, almost child-like, and stated, "That's me."

"Marvin, you'll see a green Ford station wagon, with car top carriers, parked out front. Get in it," I ordered. Marvin walked past me and out the front door. Before following him, I looked at my "receptionist." He was glaring at me, "big time."

"Got something else to say?" I asked.

"Nope!" he replied.

Talk about taking command; I was so darn chesty I wondered if the door was big enough to permit my exit.

I slid behind the wheel and pulled onto Rt. 31, headed south.

"Where we goin'?" Marvin asked.

"The Sheriff's Department, unless you would like to talk somewhere else. You notice I said "talk," Marvin. It's time for you to talk. You know why I'm here. You can tell me all about it or I'll tell you. It's far better if you tell me. Then you put me in a position to, perhaps, help you out a little. Then we can both make the world a little better place to live," I told my nervous passenger, whose hands were trembling. I thought, This guy is scared to death, he's all mine. Did I have this effect on him or was it those coon hunters?" I decided "both."

"I wanna talk here, I don't wanna go to town," he stated. I turned around at the next crossroad and returned to the pool hall parking lot. I knew it was risky but this guy was coming my way and I knew it.

"How's this?" I asked as I parked.

"Better," he answered.

"Okay, Marvin, we're going to put all this down on paper. You're going to tell it and I'm going to write it. We're both going to read it and you're going to sign it," I told him.

"Yes, sir," he stated.

(This was before the 1966 Miranda decision).

"Are you the Game Warden who chased us the other night to Mt. Victory?" he asked.

"You got that right; out ran me, didn't you? How big is the engine in your truck?" I asked.

"A big V/8 and a little hopped up," he replied.

"How many coons did you have in the back you killed with your spotlight?" I asked.

"Six," he answered.

"Where did you and Ted S. go after you out ran me?" I asked.

"To Ted's grandma's place," he answered.

"You left the coon, your rifle and your spotlight there, didn't you?" I asked.

"No, sir, just the coon and spotlight," he replied.

"Then, where did you go? Wherever it was, you spent the night, didn't you?" I asked.

"Yes, sir, we went to Ted's place," he answered.

"Are those coons up there in a freezer? Skinned? Or whole?" I asked.

"They're unskinned in a freezer in her woodshed," he answered.

It was time to start writing. I wrote a narrative of what was just spoken. The facts and circumstances surrounding the illegal taking of the 27 coons sold to C. D. and all subsequent takings and sales. Marvin claimed they had sold only to C.D. Naturally, his statement thoroughly incriminated Ted. His statement filled two pages. I read it to Marvin and had him read it. He signed it and I witnessed his signature.

"I've got to have those six coons you left in Hardin County. Go get them and I'll pick them up at your home tomorrow at 9:00 a.m.," I told Marvin.

"Yes, sir," he replied.

"I'll bring this matter before the County Prosecutor regarding court action. You'll be notified," I told Marvin as I left.

"Yes, sir," he replied.

I headed for the Ted S. residence as fast as the bad road conditions would allow. Upon arrival, I waded through snow halfway to my knees to a screened in porch. Entering the porch, I saw eight live quail in a pen. I knew Ted didn't have a permit of any kind. I picked up the cage full of quail, took them to my vehicle, placed an evidence tag on the cage, and put the fluttering little critters in the back of my car.

I returned to the house and knocked. Ted answered. After a short introduction, I stated, "Want you to tell me about the quail?" as I sat down and placed my citation pad on an end table.

"They were covered up out back under the snow. We caught them with a net," he stated.

"What did you intend to do with them?" I asked.

"Eat-um," he answered.

He was nervous as all get out, much worse than Marvin.

"Give me your driver's license," I ordered. He complied, I issued him a citation to appear the following Thursday before Judge Evans in Marysville for illegal taking and possession of the quail.

"Now that the quail business is taken care of, let's talk about jack-lightening coon," I told Ted.

"I don't know . . ," he started.

I interrupted, "I'm not going to give you a chance to lie. You're in too much trouble already, be quiet. I've got something to read to you," I told him. I removed Marvin W.'s folded statement from my inside coat pocket. I read the complete statement to him.

"Is what I've read to you the truth?" I asked.

"Yes, sir," Ted replied with his head down.

"Those coon hunters who came here scared us to death. Now you're here. We don't need - - -" his wife started to say, but I interrupted.

"No, you don't need to start any trouble; look at your husband, he's in enough trouble as it is. Now's the time for you to support him and help him," I told her.

"Yeah, shut up," Ted told her. She complied.

I wrote a brief statement acknowledging everything written in the Marvin W. statement was true and correct. The statement included a Consent to Search concerning the quail. I handed it to Ted S. to read. "Is this true concerning Marvin's statement and do you understand the Consent to Search clause?" I asked.

"Yes, it's the truth and I understand the search line," he replied. I handed him my pen and told him to sign it and I would witness his signature. He signed the statement. I told him the same as I told Marvin regarding the County Prosecutor, court, and left.

I delivered the quail to a licensed "Raise and Release" permit holder, at her farm north of Marysville. She accepted the little critters to take care of and release to the wild as soon as the weather permitted. Subsequently, she released them and didn't lose a single bird.

The next day at 9:00 a.m., I arrived at Marvin W.'s residence and picked up the six frozen coons I told him to have for me. I went home and wrote a brief investigation report, tying the entire coon shining case together, for the benefit of Bob Hamilton, the County Prosecutor. That afternoon, I met him. After going over my report and engaging in minimal discussion, he approved prosecution of Marvin W. and Ted S. "Figure the value of the coon pelts they sold, divide it in half and add a $200.00 penalty to each. That's what I'll ask the clerk to set their bond at, if it's okay with you," he stated.

"It's fine with me," I replied. The value of the illegally taken coon pelts plus the $200.00 fine, set each defendant's bond at $358.00. I contacted both subjects later that evening and cited both into court on the regularly scheduled court date two weeks later.

On the following Thursday, Ted S. appeared in Union County Court before Judge Evans and plead guilty to the charge of illegally taking and possessing eight quail. Judge Evans fined him a token fine of $50.00 because the quail weren't killed. Both Marvin and Ted subsequently forfeited a $358.00 bond in Union County Court. So ended my "coons by the tubs full" case.

This case opened a new investigative world for me, thanks to a famous homicide detective. The art of "after-the-fact investigation and interview" would, from now on, be an important part of my work. I realized I didn't have to see them commit the violation in order to catch them. This new world excited me. I sensed the many victories to come in the years ahead.

I also witnessed a magnificent example of "hunter peer pressure," as those wonderful old time coon hunters made it clear to the young outlaws, "It's not just the law you've got to fear, it's also us." My two coon shiners sure got the message. I don't advocate vigilante action or taking the law into your own hands. However, if all the hunting factions, i.e. deer hunters, duck hunters, etc. policed their own in some manner, as those tough and proud Union County coon hunters did so long ago, what an improved world for wildlife our world would be.

MELVIN T. WEIS
Ohio State Game Protector & Federal U.S. Deputy Game Warden
Assigned to Williams County, Ohio in 1957 – retired in 1988
"The most unforgettable character I ever met
and the best Game Warden I ever knew."

8
Weis

"Bailey, how are you going to tell them about Melvin?" asked retiring Washington State Game Warden, Tim Hood, who is also an ex-Michigan and ex-Ohio State Game Warden. He carried the badge for over forty years. He is a "book" in and of himself, having achieved "Legend" status in his own time.

"Gosh Tim, I don't know. Like it is – like he is – like it was; as best I can," I answered, waning and drifting in thought over my "Weis dilemma" even as we spoke on the phone.

"They're not gonna believe you, you know that don't you Bailey?" Tim spoke, his voice snapping me to.

"I'll just have to give it my best shot," I answered.

"Yeah, I guess," Tim replied.

Sometime ago, at dinner with my wife, Shirley, who knew Mel Weis far longer than I, again I drifted in thought over the Weis dilemma. "Whew, Lord, Lord," I spoke aloud without realizing it.

"What?" Shirley asked.

"I've reached the point where I've got to start writing about Mel and I don't know where to begin," I told her.

"Start with the first time you heard of him, and go with it," she stated in her usual matter of fact way.

Here goes. I'll go back about two years before I officially met Melvin T. Weis. I was still the Game Protector in Union County. I often worked with Don Mycko, the Wildlife Patrolman assigned to a four county area including Union.

District 2 (Northwestern Ohio), where Mel worked as the Game Protector in Williams County, was in much turmoil. The what and why of this, I don't know – probably more politics than anything else. In any event, Don Mycko told me about it. The District 2 Supervisor, Howard Langstaff retired. Walter McGilliard from District 6 replaced him. Several Wildlife Patrolmen and Game Protectors had transferred or resigned. There was one Game Protector they call "Moose Weis" who they didn't get – he got them," Mycko stated.

"What do you mean, he got them?" I asked.

"They hauled him into the Columbus Office several times for some type of infraction and tried to can him. It didn't work. Instead of them getting him, he got them. I don't know how, but he turned the tables on them. The word is they won't touch him with a ten foot pole. The District 2 guy I talked to said he's one heck of a good Game Warden, but sort of follows his own agenda," Mycko continued.

It's interesting to note while working on temporary assignments in Districts 4 and 5, I heard similar stories about "Moose" Weis. He was always referred to as "Moose". Later, after I went to work in District 2, I never heard him referred to by that nickname.

I heard stories about how rough Williams County was before Weis's assignment there. Eight years before, a Game Warden named Bruno "Pop" Folmer who worked his entire career in Williams County, retired. He was a big German -- a tough Game Warden who had the reputation of "ruling with an iron fist." He kept a clean county.

Following Folmer's retirement, Williams County "went to pot". During the interim eight years between Folmer and Weis, poaching ran rampant. The Game Protector assigned to Williams County during that period spent more time in college than he did protecting the wildlife resource in the county.

The word was, when Weis graduated from the Training School and went to Williams County, he walked into a "hornets nest." As one senior Game Protector told me, "It took a big man to clean up Williams County. Weis was darn sure the man for the job."

Another story was told to me by Everett Beals, a Police Officer in Bryan, Ohio, the county seat of Williams County. The story was later verified by Weis.

Weis arrived in Williams County as Game Protector on December 11, 1957; three days before the opening of deer season. Only three deer were killed legally in the county that season. Weis moved Judy, his wife, and family to the county on the 20th – Christmas tree and all.

On Christmas Eve, the 24th, Weis came home from work about 5:00 p.m. Judy needed milk so Mel walked two blocks to the store, stopping at the Police Station on the corner of the Courthouse square to check for calls. The Police Department was taking Weis's calls -- he didn't have a phone in his home yet. Assistant Police Chief, Everett Beals, invited Weis to go to nearby Sutter's Steak House for a Christmas drink. As they approached Sutter's, they observed a county bully named "Dominic" beating the tar out of the Steak House owner's son. Dominic had him down on the sidewalk in front of the Steak House, kicking the lad in the head.

Weis and Beals ran to the scene. Weis arrived first and "smashed" Dominic in the face. Dominic fell back against an adjoining jewelry store window and bounced off as Weis hit him again. There was blood and vomit everywhere. Dominic swung at Weis and missed, hitting Beals in the face, breaking his glasses. Weis grabbed Dominic's arm and cranked it up behind his back. From behind, Weis grabbed Dominic by the testicles and began marching him across the street to a police cruiser.

Even with the pain Dominic had to be experiencing, he bucked and kicked until Weis almost lost his grip. However, Weis spun Dominic around, forced him down onto the double yellow line in the street and dropped on Dominic with both knees in his face.

Another Police Officer, Floyd Zehr, came running across the street from the courthouse to help, Dominic's brother came up behind Weis and hit him in the head. The newly arrived Police Officer grabbed the second Dominic by the neck and with an arm lock, took him to a police cruiser.

Officer Zehr got Dominic No. 2 seated in the front seat of the cruiser but was having trouble getting him cuffed.

Weis finally got Dominic No. 1 to the cruiser, threw him in the back where the third cop, Officer Lindsay who weighed 300 pounds, sat on him.

As this was happening, Dominic No. 2 broke loose, got out of the cruiser and swung at Weis – he missed. Weis hit him in the face with all he had. Blood popped out of his nose and ears. "I thought Weis killed him. But this wasn't the case. The guy kept trying to fight. Weis hit him three more times and he finally went down. As it happened, Officer Zehr was behind the guy picking him up and letting him fall as fast as Weis hit him," Beals stated.

Weis, with the three police officers, all splattered with blood, finally subdued the Dominics and took them to the county jail.

Dan Zuver, County Sheriff, put Dominic No. 1 in a jail cell called the "Planks." It had only planks to sleep on. The second Dominic went into a regular cell. Dominic No. 1 continued to raise cane, calling Weis a furry capped s-o-b. Weis told Sheriff Zuver to "let me in there a minute." The Sheriff told Weis, "I can't do that." Instead, the Sheriff entered Dominic's cell. Dominic called the Sheriff a name and he hit Dominic. Dominic went down for good.

The day after Christmas, Weis got a radio call to go to the Police Station in Bryan. There, he was told the County Auditor wanted him to come to his office in the courthouse. When Mel arrived, the Auditor stated he wanted to meet the Game Warden who put on the show in front of the courthouse on Christmas Eve. He told Weis he'd done a great job and was glad Mel was assigned to Williams County. "Now maybe things will change as not much had been done in the past," the Auditor told Weis.

In January 1958, Weis was scheduled to give a wildlife talk at a Father and Son Banquet at the Methodist Church in Bryan. Supposedly about 75 people were to attend. Over 300 showed up wanting to meet the Game Warden who took care of the two biggest bullies in the county.

"I was scared when I saw that crowd, but I managed to get through the talk," Weis stated. When Mel concluded his talk, the crowd rose in standing applause.

The County Auditor presented Weis with a new pair of baseball shoes.

"I appreciated them. I was asked to play with the Church League," Weis stated.

"The crowd cheered and welcomed Weis to Williams County that night. Not only because he gave a good talk, but because at last, we knew we had a Game Warden who was going to clean up Williams County, and he sure did that," the Auditor stated.

Now let me digress and set the stage leading to my assignment to District 2 as a Wildlife Enforcement Agent.

Near the close of my tenure in Union County, I endured a period of great turmoil. My first marriage ended. Of that, I'll say she gave me a son, Mark, and two daughters, Betty and Anita, to her everlasting credit. Enough said.

I was promoted to a Wildlife Enforcement Agent position in District 4 (Athens, Ohio) and worked in that position a short while. Earlier through avenues opened by Wayne Knisley, the Delaware County Game Protector, both he and I went to Denver, Colorado. We took Colorado's Civil Service Exam for Wildlife Conservation Officer (WCO). We were hired -- Wayne Went to Durango, Colorado where he remained the rest of his career. I went to Walden, Colorado as a WCO. I accepted the job in Colorado only after discussing it with my ex-wife. Believing we had patched things up, and she and my kids would follow, I went West. After finding a beautiful place to live, I received a "Dear John" letter. There I sat with three children back in Ohio.

I managed to work Colorado's big game season. Due to my family situation, I had to contact Dale Whitesell, my old boss in District 6, now Chief of the Ohio Division of Wildlife and ask for my old job back – a humbling experience.

Dale, to whom I'll always be indebted, by phone and subsequent letter, stated, "Come on back, I can use you in District 2. Dale Roach is the Law Enforcement Supervisor there and you're his newest Wildlife Enforcement Agent." My retirement was still in tact -- back to Ohio I went. I abandoned a "western dream" but needed to be closer to my kids.

After a brief visit with Dale and Ben Anderson, Chief of Law Enforcement in the Columbus Office, I went to District 2 at Findlay, Ohio. I took residence in Napoleon.

Now, back to "Weis."

"Findlay 296," Weis radioed the District 2 Office.

"Findlay, go ahead 296."

"Tell, ah, tell Roach, ah-251, I've got a little deer thing up here – out of season and all that. I could use some help from one of those Agents or Patrol-men, or whatever they call them -- you know -- need a little help to solve the case -- it's a toughie, go ahead."

"Q-22, 296, will do," Eloise, the radio dispatcher stated, ending the radio traffic exchange between her and Mel Weis. Traffic Dale Roach, my new boss and I heard while in the radio room finishing a coffee break.

"Tell him 255 is on his way – he'll be in mobile contact," Roach told Eloise just before he and I went upstairs to his office. "You can initiate the paper work to start your first investigation and head up to Williams County," Roach told me, chuckling. "I'm not going to tell you much about Mel Weis, except to say he's a little unorthodox. You'll learn about him soon enough because he's in your work area. He doesn't need any help on this deer case – he's up to something. He's heard you were coming – he may want to meet you. At least that's what it would be nice to think. But, with him you never know. He's got poor old "Mac" (District Supervisor, Walter McGilliard) talk-ing to himself. Incidentally, he's one of the best Game Wardens you'll ever work with, but don't tell him I said that," Dale stated.

I left Findlay headed for Williams County. "296 from 255," I radioed Weis.

"296, go ahead," Weis answered.

"I'm at the Henry-Williams County Line on Rt. 6. Where do you want to meet," I asked.

"State Highway garage, Rt. 20-A, east side of Montpelier," he an-swered. Shortly I arrived there. Standing in the doorway, in winter uniform, was a big German, Mel Weis. He was barrel chested and had no neck – built much like Babe Ruth. He'd pass for a pro-wrestler or pro-football player. Based on his overall appearance, I expected to see cauliflower ears, but this wasn't the case.

I exited my patrol car and walked toward him. At an appropriate distance, I extended my right hand. "Ron Bailey, glad to meet you," I stated. I can only compare the "sizing up" way Weis looked at me with the actor George C. Scott in the movie "Patton," when an Army Chaplain inquired of him about his regularity in reading the Bible. Patton replied, "Every God damned day" with what I evaluated as a "don't try to suck up" expression on his face. So it was with Weis.

"Yeah, what-a-ya say, dynamite," was Weis' return greeting as he shook my right hand and crushed it. "The deer biz is west of town, get in," he said. Trying to hide my mangled right hand, I opened the passenger's side door of his patrol vehicle with my left hand -- we headed west. I dropped my right hand out of sight, beside the seat. I shook it violently trying to restore some feeling (other than pain) in it. I seriously wondered if my hand was not only mashed but broken. My overall welfare, along with my crushed hand, was becoming all important. It was beginning to concern me as much (or a little more) than the "deer biz" investigation we were about to begin.

Thinking, I don't dare let him touch my left hand or I'll be permanently disabled, Weis turned left off the highway and down a fence row on totally frozen ground. Abruptly, he stopped. "It's over there," he said pointing to the left. We exited the patrol car in 3 inches of snow. At the "scene" was a fresh deer gut pile. There were four deer feet cut off at the knee, much hair and blood, no hide. It was the remains of a yearling. Three sets of human tracks were evident. We established where the deer was shot and field dressed. The three sets of human tracks, dragging the yearling carcass, headed toward a farm house.

"Think you can solve this one Agent Bailey?" Weis questioned.

I recalled Roach's words, "He's up to something." This case is so obvious, he just wants me up here to meet me, I concluded.

Weis stood there in the frozen field, beside the deer gut pile, looking at me with a half grin. A grin I would witness many times hence. "A tough one – huh, dynamite?" he asked.

I thought, now what? Do I go ahead and proceed with normal and legal investigative procedures or see what he's got in mind. I decided to go ahead with the normal procedures. "Well, we need to get some photos of the scene and collect some evidence samples. We've obviously got more than enough probable cause for a search warrant. We'll need to go to the county seat and get one as soon as possible - - -." I didn't get to finish, Weis interrupted.

"Don't know how to fill those out," Weis stated.

"What?" I asked.

"That warrant you're talking about – can't fill one out – don't use them," Weis replied.

Oh boy, whew! -- Here we go, I thought.

"How about getting some photos and collecting some samples of the physical evidence here, where they field dressed the deer?" I asked.

"Don't have a camera," Weis commented.

"I do, back in my car," I responded.

"Why didn't you bring it?" Weis asked.

"I thought you'd have one," I answered.

"Haven't got one – no good at using one – all those buttons, clicks and such," Weis responded.

"Don't want any of that bloody stuff in my car," was Weis's reaction to the collection and preservation of the physical evidence at the scene. "O-O-O-Kay, now that you've seemingly cut off every avenue of correct investigative procedure, what do you have in mind?" I asked Melvin.

"What I've got in mind is goin' and gettin' those little devils who did it, Mr. 'B'. I'll call you 'B' from now on," Weis proclaimed.

Most nicknames sort of evolve. Not the case with Weis. "I'll call you 'B' from now on," was the way he handled it. In less than a year the entire District was calling me "Mr. B" or just "B".

"It's your call Melvin, let's go," I said exasperated.

"Atta boy, tiger, hop in, let's clean this one up. It's already taken too much of my time – got other 'biz' to take care of," Weis stated as he drove his patrol car north across the frozen field directly toward the farm house, where three sets of human tracks and deer "drag" tracks ended. There (I'll call it the Wycal farm), Weis parked in front of the house.

"Let's go 'B'", he said as we exited his patrol car. On the front porch we went. Weis knocked on the front door with the side of his fist. It was a screened outer door covered or insulated with clear plastic. The bottom of the door popped in and out as Weis knocked.

"Who's out there?" came a male voice from inside.

"Weis!" Mel answered with one word.

The door opened. In the doorway stood farmer Wycal, "What do you want?" he asked.

"What do I want? You know darn well what I want and why I'm here. Get me the little deer your two boys and Tom Riley shot early this morning – now. I haven't got all day," Weis stated.

"We don't know nuthin' about no deer. . . ," Wycal said, intending to continue - -

Weis interrupted as he elevated his nose, 'sniffing' the air. 'B', they're eatin' the deer right now – come on," Melvin stated as we went across the front door threshold, past Wycal to the dinning room. I followed thinking, No search warrant, no consent to search – no – oh boy.

Seated around a big oblong table sat six people, with one empty place (that of farmer Wycal). It was clear they were enjoying dinner when Mel knocked on their front door. Placed in the center of the table were mashed potatoes, gravy, green peas, steamed carrots, homemade bread, fresh farm butter and a big platter of meat cut in small pieces. The aroma from all this coupled with fresh perked coffee was absolutely tantalizing. I knew there had to be some apple pie somewhere.

Weis plucked a piece of meat from a young lady's plate – ate it and proclaimed, "Yep, venison, someone's a good cook. Nothin' better than a young yearling," he stated.

At this point, the thought struck me, He's gonna order plates and we're gonna eat with these folks. Being a believer in prayer, concerning the rest of our investigation, I silently prayed, Lord, thy will be done!

Continuing to savor the venison, Weis told farmer Wycal, "Get the rest of the deer meat."

"All right Mel," Wycal replied. He went into the kitchen, returning shortly with a porcelain dishpan half full of venison cut in small sized servings, the same as the cooked venison on the table.

As though no one was in the room except us, Mel spoke directly to me.

"You see what I've got to put up with 'B'?" Weis asked. "I run the fish and game biz in Williams County. Folks know I don't allow this. Yet, some have to stray – dumb – dumb – dumb," he stated.

Mel motioned farmer Wycal and me to the front porch. "Take this evidence to the car," Weis stated handing me the pan of venison.

Weis addressed Wycal, "Have your two oldest boys at Reuben's Thursday morning at 9:00."

"All right Mel, you know the little deer just popped up in front of the boys while they were rabbit hunting across the road. You know how boys are." Wycal explained.

"I know all about that business. They were out there hunting before hours. (Legal upland game hunting hours were 9 a.m. to 5 p.m.) You could've had deer for breakfast – probably did, didn't you?" Mel asked.

"Yes, we did," Wycal answered.

"Riley ate some for breakfast too, didn't he?" Weis asked.

"Matter of fact, he did," Wycal replied.

"Boy-oh-boy, out of season deer for breakfast, huntin' early, uh-uh-uh," Weis complained.

"I'm gonna forget the early huntin' business. We're going to town to get Riley. Don't you call him and tell him we're comin' – you got that? If you do, I'll be back – I'm sure you don't want that – right?" Weis asked.

"No, we won't call him Mel," Wycal stated.

En route to Montpelier, I asked "Do you fill out citations to appear in court?"

"You mean a ticket?" Weis asked.

"Yeah, whatever you want to call it – you know – the form the State gives us to fill out and give to a violator. It has his name, address, date of birth and physical description on it. It tells him what he's charged with and when and where to appear in court," I answered.

"Don't fool with those – only if the violator is from off somewhere like Toledo, then they get a ticket," Weis stated.

"Who is Reuben?" I asked.

"Judge Reuben Hayward," Weis answered.

"County Court Judge?" I asked.

"Northern half of the county," Mel replied.

"Good Court?" I asked.

"You'll see," Weis replied.

"What about this Tom Riley? How did you know he's involved?" I asked.

"Because he was out there this morning running around in his Ford station wagon with all that fireworks crap painted all over it. He's in the fireworks biz. A lot of folks saw him out there – stuck out like a sore thumb – he's thick with the Wycals. Didn't you see those good lookin' Wycal girls?" Weis replied.

"He's in the fireworks business?" I asked.

"Yep, about half legal and half illegal. He stays in trouble with the Sheriff and the Patrol – in and out of court and jail," Weis replied.

"How about the Wycal boys. Do you know their first names and ages?" I asked.

"They were the two nervous ones sittin' at the table – the two oldest. We'll get their names when they come in to see Rube. They're both keepers (meaning 18 or older). They know they did it and so does old man Wycal. He'll have the right ones in court. He knows you can't deceive Rube and get away with it," Weis replied.

"I have the impression you pretty well had this case figured out and "solved" before I got here. Any particular reason you asked for my help – you obviously didn't need it," I stated.

"Heard you were coming. Wanted to see if you knew how to do biz – you don't. Most of the biz in these four counties is here. We've got two state lines – all state lines are hot. You'll be spending most of your time in Williams County. Figured you and I may as well understand each other," Weis stated.

"Well, I hope we can," I replied.

"Hope we can what?" Weis asked.

"Understand each other," I replied.

"Oh, don't worry – we'll understand each other Mr. B.," Weis stated in a tone that somewhat disturbed me.

I was almost dreading our next contact – Tom Riley, as we parked on the street in front of his house in Montpelier. We exited the patrol car and went up on the front porch. Weis knocked on the door with the side of his fist, just as he did at the Wycal residence. Garnett, Riley's wife, opened the door.

"Mel Weis. Here to talk to Tom," Weis stated.

"He's taking a nap," Garnett stated.

"Get him up and get him out here," Weis told her.

"It will be a minute," she advised closing the door.

Shortly, the door opened with Tom Riley standing in the doorway. "What-a-you want, Weis?" Riley asked.

"Get in the car," Weis ordered.

"It's cold, I'll get a jacket," Riley stated.

"Huh-uh, no jacket, get in the car, it's got a heater," Weis stated.

We went to the patrol car. Weis seated behind the wheel, Riley in the front passenger's seat, and me in the back.

"What do you guys want?" Riley asked.

"Dumb question, Riley. You know why we're here. Now's your chance, and only chance, to tell us about the deer you and the Wycals shot this morning. The one you ate part of for breakfast," Weis told Riley.

"I'm not gonna tell you a thing, Weis. If I killed a deer, you prove it. You've come here, got me out of bed and bullied me around. You've tried to question me – I've got certain rights. You go straight to xo#x and take that one in the back seat with you," Riley ranted.

"No sense foolin' with you. As far as your rights are concerned – you don't have any. You lost them when you killed the little deer out of season. You be at Reuben's Thursday morning at 9:00. Now get out of the car," Weis stated.

"I'll be there Weis, with my attorney," Riley stated.

"Bring a good one – you'll need it," Weis responded.

We left Riley's residence en route to the State Highway Garage and my patrol car.

"Does the fact Riley says he'll have an attorney concern you?" I asked.

"No" Weis replied.

"In view of the fact this violation wasn't committed in your presence and the fact Defendant Riley will probably be represented, I assume you'll want to get your County Prosecutor to approve the charges and have him present to represent the State," I stated.

"Don't need to have him present – he'd get in the way. As far as the Prosecutor's approval of the charges - - - you might say I have 'blanket approval' for all my cases in Williams County," Weis responded.

Weis told me to plan on spending the next day (Wednesday) with him in Williams County. "We'll file the deer charges with Reuben first thing, then I'll show you some geography – places you'll need to know about because that's where the biz is. Meet me at the horse barns at the County Fair Grounds about 8:00 in the morning," Weis said.

The next morning I arose early. I had breakfast at a truck stop north of Napoleon and proceeded to Williams County. A warm front had moved in overnight -- It was a good day to be out and about. I arrived at the horse barns before the appointed time. Weis owned, trained, and raced harness horses. He had one or more stabled at the Fairgrounds as did other owners and drivers. I noticed him seated on a buggy behind a big handsome horse going full tilt around the track. Shortly he exited the track and came to the barn as steam rose from the horse's body and streaks of steam blew from its nostrils.

"Nice looking animal," I stated, not knowing what else to say as I knew nothing about race horses or horse racing.

"He'll do," Weis stated.

After making arrangements with another driver to "cool out" and stable his horse, Weis removed an outer jacket revealing his uniform. "Ready to go, B?" he asked.

"Sure enough," I answered as we got in his patrol vehicle and headed downtown to the County Court on Main Street in Montpelier. Arriving, I expected to see a Justice of the Peace style courtroom. To the contrary, what I found was a sizable modern courtroom complete with Judge's podium, Clerks, Defendant's and Plaintiff's tables and courtroom seating. The Clerk's office and Judge's chambers were down a hall just outside the two entrances to the courtroom.

We proceeded to the Clerk's office. Seated at her desk was Court Clerk, Shirley McCrea. Weis ascertained the correct names of the two Wycal defendants sometime the night before. We filed four affidavits charging Gregory Wycal, Timothy Wycal, and Thomas Riley with one count each of taking and possessing a white tail deer during the closed season. Farmer Wycal was charged with "unlawful possession."

After swearing to the charges before the Clerk, Weis addressed the Clerk, "Mr. B, I'd like you to meet Shirley McCrea, the best lookin' gal in Williams County - - - Shirley, this is Ron Bailey, my new partner."

"Oh, Melvin, you're too much. Mr. Bailey, I'm glad to meet you," the beautiful Clerk stated.

I couldn't help but take further notice of this beautiful Court Clerk. She had auburn hair. She was dressed in a very conservative manner. Her white blouse was buttoned to the top. She wore a pleated gray skirt, seamless hose, and maroon loafers. It was obvious she was "well endowed" above the waist – a female trait I've always been attracted to (as is most of the male population). Her eyes sparkled as did her beautiful white teeth exposed by the cutest little crooked smile I'd ever seen. Her figure and legs were perfect. Her overall appearance could best be described as "librarian" or "conservative", and sexy as all get out. Looking back all those years, I realize I was "smitten" with the lady the first time I saw her.

We left the Court and headed for the eastern part of Williams County. Entering the small community of Stryker, we noticed a Sheriff's patrol car parked in front of a country store. "I need to see him," Weis stated as he parked beside the Sheriff's cruiser.

We went inside to find a Deputy Sheriff busy investigating a breaking and entering. Store merchandise and cash was stolen. Present were the store owner, Deputy Sheriff, and a young man employed by the store owner.

As the Deputy finished his inventory of missing items, he asked the store owner, "Do you have any idea who may have done this?"

"No idea at all," the store owner replied.

"He did it," Weis stated abruptly and unexpectedly.

"What?" the Deputy asked.

"He did it – the kid standing over there," Weis stated nodding toward the young male employee.

"What are you talking about, Weis? I've known that boy and his folks all their lives. There's no way that fine young man broke into my store," the angered store owner stated.

Weis walked to the very nervous young man and stated, "Let's you and I take a little walk." Weis and the lad left the store.

The Deputy Sheriff looked dumbfounded. He finally stated, "This is my case – he's the Game Warden." The store owner continued to rant and rave about the lad's innocence . . . , "Where does that xo#x Weis get off!"

Shortly Weis returned escorting a very tearful and sorry young man. "He's sorry he did it – he'll take you to your stolen stuff. He says he didn't spend any of the money, you'll get it back," Weis stated while escorting the lad to the Deputy Sheriff, now chuckling.

"I'll be a monkey's uncle. Weis comes in here and solves my case before I've even got my report turned in," he stated as he threw his pencil on the counter.

"Son, did you rob my store?" the owner asked.

"Yes sir, I did -- I'm sorry – I'll return all I took. The Game Warden said you wouldn't be too hard on me," the lad tearfully stated.

"I owe you an apology, Mel," the store owner stated.

"No you don't. Anybody who would apologize to a Game Warden is dumb. I'll probably sack you or one of your relatives come deer season. We'll see if you want to apologize then," Weis stated with his half upper lip raised grin.

"How did you know he did it," I asked as we headed north in Weis's patrol car.

"Anyone could tell. All you had to do was look at him with his neck stretched out listening to every word being said. He was listening because he wanted to know how safe he was not getting' caught," Weis stated.

"Well, I guess I missed all that," I responded. I thought, No Mel, not just anyone could tell.

This was my first "inkling" Weis possessed a natural insight into human nature and behavior far beyond the average person. In the years to come, I would see this insight exercised time and again. It's said William Shakespeare had an insight into human nature such as none before him or since. There's is an exception – Mel Weis.

We went north, touching a portion of the Tiffin River. As we traveled, Weis pointed out different locations where he'd made arrests. "Took two illegal deer out of that barn" -- "got a road shooter here" -- "five Michigan coon hunters in closed season in that woods" -- etc.

"I believe the reason you stopped at the store in Stryker was to see the Deputy about something. You didn't do that?" I asked.

"Wrong Deputy – it'll keep," Weis replied.

We traveled through West Unity, Alvordton, and Pioneer to County Road "S", the first east-west road in Ohio on the Michigan State line. "This is the hottest spot in the county – you'll make more good cases here than anywhere else. Got a federal badge?" Weis asked. (Meaning a U.S. Deputy Game Warden's Commission issued by the U.S. Fish and Wildlife Service. Among several authorizations, it authorizes the enforcement of the Lacey Act that covers the interstate movement of illegal wildlife.)

"Yes," I answered.

"You'll need it," Weis responded.

We found ourselves behind a school bus traveling west. We slowed as the bus stopped at nearly every farm letting kids out who scampered to their homes. Some of them played, throwing wet snowballs at each other, as they romped their way to their homes. This and similar scenarios play out every afternoon in rural America. Every scene fit for a "Norman Rockwell" original.

At one stop, two pre-teen age boys exited the bus. As they looked back at Weis's patrol car, they recognized it. As we slowly passed their home, the ornery little snots saw fit to pelt our car with wet snowballs.

Immediately following the snowball barrage, they each inserted their thumbs in both ears, stuck their tongues out, and wagged their fingers at us.

This "often seen" gesture is repulsive and prompted Weis to comment, "Little farts are asking for it again."

Past their house, Weis stopped the patrol car. With the engine running, he exited the vehicle and walked in the middle of the road to a position in front of the "little farts" house. There, before the Almighty and the occupants of another vehicle headed west and stopped east of us, Weis inserted his thumbs in both ears, wagged his fingers and stuck his tongue out "back at the kiddies."

As Weis, in full uniform, "performed", the two young lads, at their mother's beckoning, scampered to their house. With her arms fanned out in a gathering gesture, she herded her offspring through the front door. Before entering herself, she leaned forward, thus "protruding" her butt towards Weis. Looking back over her shoulder with a look of contempt, she wagged her hind end at Weis. Then she went in the house and closed the door.

Weis tipped his big furry issued "Alcan" hat to the vehicle occupants behind us, who were very amused with the entire episode. He returned to the patrol car and we proceeded on.

"What in heavens name was that all about?" I asked totally amused.

"Had to take a pet coon – no permit, you know – away from them last summer. Little snots robbed a den. Mean little devils – tried to pee on me. When they see me on this road, they run out and make faces at me. Sometimes they wag their butts at me like their mother did," Weis replied.

"And you stop and do likewise – right?" I asked.

"Yep, sure do, turn about is fair play," Weis responded.

"Do you wag your butt at them also?" I asked.

"Usually do, but they got in the house to quick this time," Weis replied.

"Unusual," I stated.

"I'll probably give them a Raise to Release Permit so they can take care of some of the orphan coon I get every spring. They don't understand who runs the Fish and Game biz in Williams County yet. Both those ornery little rascals would make good Game Wardens," Weis opined.

We continued west, stopping at Nettle Lake; then south along the Indiana State line.

"Hear you split the sheets with your old lady," Weis stated.

"Sure did. Something I don't care to talk about," I responded.

"Any kids," Weis asked.

"Three," I answered.

"Have you met any interesting women yet?" Weis asked.

"What?" I asked.

"Are you dating anyone? Weis continued.

"That's a private matter Weis," I stated.

"Well, I'll tell you what B. You're not the quickest guy in the world. My guess is, when it comes to women, you probably fumble it most of the time," Weis opined. He continued, "Tell you what I'm gonna do B. I'm gonna fix you up with a good woman. One you ought to marry if she'll have you, which I doubt – being as slow as you seem to be."

Boy oh boy, is there any end to this guy, I thought. "Okay, let's cut to the chase. Who is she?" I asked.

"Reuben's Clerk – you met her this morning. She got to you, didn't she B.? She's a widow with three kids. Hasn't had it easy since her husband passed on. Good woman – lots of character. If you could get her B, she'd stick with you – not run for cover like your first one did. Shirley's got the word "commitment" written all over her. I can read people B," Weis commented.

"What do you mean, she got to me? How do you know the first one ran for cover?" I asked.

"Your first question – it was written all over you. You were gawking all over the little Court Clerk. Second question – all I'll say is, the word gets out," Weis replied.

"Okay sharpie, fix me up with the Court Clerk if you can. You're right, I was impressed with her – didn't realize it showed. Must be slipping," I stated.

"You done slipped," Weis responded.

It was getting late. Half way down the Indiana State line, we turned east for Montpelier and my vehicle at the Fairgrounds.

"See you at Reuben's tomorrow at 9:00," Weis stated as I exited his patrol car and went to mine.

As I drove to my apartment in Napoleon I thought about Weis, this character that I'd spent a day and a half with. We, or I should say, Weis completed an after-the-fact deer in closed season investigation. An investigation during which we made a "debatable" search. (Weis, in a later discussion, would claim we had "implied" consent. Heck, one man's word against another.) For physical evidence, we had a dishpan half full of venison. Lord, I forgot all about that – where is the dishpan of venison? Did Weis take it home and eat it? We had three defendants coming to court who were not issued citations. One who stated he would be represented by an attorney. We had no County Prosecutor's approval for any of the charges already filed with the court. Nor would we have the Prosecutor in court to represent the State of Ohio. With all these "variables", Weis didn't seem to be the least bit concerned about the outcome of these cases.

Earlier that day, he solved a breaking and entering investigation for the Sheriff's Department in a matter of minutes. He stopped in the middle of a county road and made "faces" at two little boys and their mother. Then he was fixing me up with a woman. "Have I left anything out, I wondered. Whew! I need supper and some sleep," I thought.

Having experienced a "troubled night" as far as sleep was concerned, I arose next morning, took care of the usual personal chores and went to breakfast.

En route to Montpelier, I remembered something I noticed in Judge Reuben Hayward's courtroom. It was a plaque on the wall centered over the

Judge's podium. It read, "Judge Roy Bean, The Hanging Judge." A plaque, I would later learn, he received from a resident of a western state who appeared before him on a Highway Patrol (Turnpike) charge and got "hammered" so to speak. A plaque the Judge was quite proud of and treasured a great deal. He considered it "complimentary."

With this in mind, I looked out of my patrol car window at the flat prairie countryside. Had I stepped back in time? The happenings of the two previous days were surreal. Was I in another time dimension – one from the old west? Was I actually headed for Judge Roy Beans' Court? What I experienced during my short working tenure with Mel Weis and the little I'd seen of Williams County made me wonder.

I arrived at the court and entered carrying my briefcase containing the Ohio Revised Code, a set of Wildlife Council Orders, some forms, etc. --- nothing that pertained to the cases about to be heard. I thought I might as well try to look professional. I felt uneasy and out of place.

Shirley McCrea, the Court Clerk, was busy placing and arranging documents on her desk and the Judge's podium. I glanced up – it was still there – the Judge Roy Bean plaque. Seated in the courtroom were Tom Riley, a young well dressed gentleman (Riley's attorney), Farmer Wycal, and his two sons.

From outside -- down the hall, all heard "Ho-ho-ho, where's my good lookin' Court Clerk" – it was Weis, who entered the courtroom carrying nothing. He looked around and stated, "I see everyone's here – good." Looking at Riley's attorney, Weis stated, "I suppose you're representing Firecracker." The attorney looked at Weis, smiled, and said nothing.

"All rise," Shirley McCrea, the Court Clerk hailed as Judge Reuben Haywood entered the courtroom and seated himself behind the bench.

"Sit down," he stated. He was short, slender with gray hair. He wore horn rimmed glasses. He was impeccably dressed in a blue three piece suit, white shirt, and black bow tie. He read the documents before him and stated, "Everybody here, name yourselves."

"Mel Weis, State Game Protector," Weis stated and nodded to me.

"Ron Bailey, State Game Protector," I stated.

All the rest present did the same with Riley's counsel emphasizing "Attorney at Law, Toledo, Ohio, your honor."

"Hello Tom, back again, huh," Judge Hayward said to Riley.

"Yeah," Riley responded. With the tone of this exchange, I sensed what was to come.

Silence – Judge Hayward continued to read the documents (and I assume charges against the defendants).

Suddenly Judge Hayward stated, "Well boys, what have you got to say for yourselves – why did you kill this deer?"

The young attorney jumped to his feet, "Your honor – you haven't read the charges to my client. No one has been sworn. I haven't plead my client one way or the other – I plead him not guilty."

"I don't have to read the charges to them – they know what they did. Don't worry about that pleading business – I found your client and the Wycals guilty. You calling our Game Protector, Mr. Weis, a liar?" Judge Hayward stated.

"No sir, but you haven't followed correct court procedure. I can't believe this – we'll appeal this ruling," the young attorney protested.

"Shut up," Judge Hayward ordered.

"I won't shut up, your honor, I won't let this happen. You haven't heard the last of this," the young attorney proclaimed.

"You will shut up. One more peep – one more peep – do you hear me? I'll find you in contempt of this court and you'll take a trip to Bryan to the old cold and stoney. Do you understand me?" Judge Hayward asked.

"Yes sir," the young attorney stated as he sat down.

"I told you not to make him mad," Riley told his attorney.

"Mel, who's the new officer you have with you?" Judge Hayward asked Weis, oblivious to all present in the courtroom.

"His name is Ron Bailey, Rube. He's not a new officer. They transferred him here from the middle of the state," Weis replied.

"Welcome to the north country Officer Bailey. I hope you're half the officer Mel Weis is – Mel could use a little help – we've still got a lot of cleaning up to do here," Judge Haywood stated.

"Thank you, your Honor, it's my privilege to meet you," I stated.

"That will be $800.00 and costs. I don't care how you four split it up – just see my Clerk here, Mrs. McCrea gets the money – court is adjourned," Rube stated.

Tom Riley, his attorney, and the Wycals conferred with each other for a short time. Riley came to the clerk's table and paid the entire fine and costs. The defendants and Riley's attorney left the courtroom but remained milling around out in the hall. Riley's attorney could be heard getting progressively louder, continuing to complain about what happened.

Judge Hayward addressed Weis, "Yank him back in here." That was all Weis needed. He went into the hall and returned with the attorney by the "scruff" of the neck. "Here he is Rube," Weis stated.

"You just can't get the message, can you boy?" Judge Hayward asked the attorney.

"Judge, I've been manhandled here. I certainly have the right to talk to my client in or outside this courtroom," the young attorney stated.

"You weren't just talking to your client, you were insulting the court. I heard you. Now understand this, if you can. This courtroom's jurisdiction includes the hallway out into the middle of the street. Now, the best thing you can do is get back to Toledo. I've got some forms down here in my right hand drawer. They're called commitment forms. If I fill one of them out, you're charged with contempt of this court and on your way to jail. I'm opening the drawer and getting a commitment form now . . . ," Reuben stated.

"I'm gone sir, I'm gone, I'm on my way to Toledo," the attorney stated and exited pronto. Thus ending the whole matter, I hoped.

Judge Hayward invited us to his chambers and offered us a drink – of whiskey – that is. We both declined with the "on duty" excuse. Judge Hayward opened a lower (deep) left hand desk drawer containing several bottles of whiskey of various brands. "The Highway Patrol confiscated this stuff on the Turnpike – it's usually associated with a case they have before me. I have to seize the stuff. The law says I'm supposed to pour it down the drain which I'm about to do," he stated as he took a healthy snort. We exchanged amenities with the Judge and returned to the courtroom.

The Clerk, Shirley McCrea, was still at her table in the courtroom quite busy. "Time to make your move B," Weis stated as we both walked to Shirley's work table. For the first time that morning, I noticed what she was wearing and again, how beautiful she was. She wore a red plaid jumper with a white long sleeved blouse closed tight at the neck. Seamless hose and the same maroon loafers.

"Okay B., stand there with your thumb in your ear – Shirley, my partner here would like a date," Weis stated.

Shirley looked up at both of us with a horrified look on her face. Hurriedly, she gathered her papers and exited the courtroom. She ran down the hall to her office. I stepped into the hall and watched her kick up her cute little heels as her little feet, moving ever so fast, carried her around the corner and into her office. As I once again visualize that "running down the hall" scene, I realize at that moment, I "fell" for the lady.

I followed her to her office and entered. She wouldn't look up. "Do you ever go out," I asked.

"Sometimes," she replied.

I remembered Weis telling me about her dating a Highway Patrolman. One Weis didn't like. I thought, She might still be dating this guy. I asked anyway, "Would you go out with me – to dinner perhaps?"

"Yes," she stated still not looking at me.

"That's great. I have to go home for Thanksgiving but when I get back, we'll make it definite," I stated.

"Okay," she stated finally looking up at me with her beautiful little crooked smile – her smile really got to me.

I worked the 1964 Thanksgiving holiday weekend in Henry County. The Henry County Game Protector's position was vacant. I didn't know the geography, but managed to apprehend two hen pheasant poachers near the Henry / Wood County line. They both forfeited $200.00 bonds in County Court in Napoleon. I spent some time on an assigned and unusual investigation. It involved a lady who reportedly was shooting pheasants from the road during the closed season in Henry and Wood Counties. All I was able to accomplish was locating where the lady lived. She was not at home – apparently gone for the holiday.

On Thanksgiving Day, I managed to get to my folks' home in Delaware County and spend some quality time with them and my kids. The following day, I returned to Williams County. Weis was developing information on the greatest case he and I would work together – a Michigan based deer poaching ring operating in Ohio, Michigan and Indiana.

Weis told me Shirley, the Court Clerk -- my future date, was in a car accident over the holiday. She was in the hospital at Montpelier. "The accident happened while she was riding with a Highway Patrolman and his wife going to a baby shower. If you're smart B, you'll visit her in the hospital," Weis commented.

I went to the Montpelier Hospital to find she was transferred to the Bryan Hospital. I went there and ascertained her room number. I went to the men's room where I checked my appearance to make sure I looked as "swave and deboner" as possible.

We had a good visit together, we both learned a little about each other. This was Monday. On the following Saturday we had our first date – dinner at Sutter's Steak House in Bryan and a movie.

I met the love of my life thanks to Mel Weis. When Judge Hayward heard his Clerk and I were dating, he called me into his chambers. "You know Officer Bailey, she's the same as my daughter. Officer Weis tells me you're seeing her quite a bit," Judge Hayward stated.

"Yes, your Honor, we are going together," I stated.

"I hope your intentions are honorable. If things work out for both of you, don't ever mistreat her. If you do, there's a second thing you'd better do," Judge Hayward stated.

"What's that, your Honor?" I asked.

"Don't let me or Mel Weis find out about it. If we hear of such a thing, you're in deep trouble," Judge Hayward admonished.

"I'm sure that's true, your Honor," I responded.

Not long after, I proposed by asking her, "Do you suppose we could see each other on a regular basis?"

She said, "Yes."

"How about for the rest of our lives?" I asked.

She hesitated, looked at me with her beautiful eyes and asked, "Are you asking me to marry you?"

"Yes," I answered. "I guess we'd better make it soon as I'm probably going to be transferred to Athens, Ohio."

"We could do that," she responded.

The rest is history. On March 5, 1965 we were married in St. John's Lutheran Church in Montpelier, Ohio. Pastor Bob Lepien performed the ceremony. Mel and Judy Weis stood with us during the ceremony. I kissed my new bride after Pastor Lepien pronounced us husband and wife. Weis kissed the bride and did a better job of it than I did. He picked Shirley up and carried her out of the church and down the front steps while Judy and I looked on. "Did Mel and Shirley get married or did you and Shirley get married?" laughingly, Judy asked. We all went to Angola, Indiana for our "honeymoon dinner." En route back to Williams County, Judy stated, "I guess we could go to our house and play cards."

"Go to our house and play cards, absolutely not. I've got to have my rest. Xo#x, Judy these two just got married. They've got other biz to take care of when they get home," Weis bellowed.

"Just like a man," Judy quietly commented.

With my marriage to Shirley June and her gift of three step-children, David, Steve and Connie, I'll end this story I simply titled "Weis."

Mel Weis served as Ohio State Game Protector in Williams County and became Senior Game Protector in charge of Henry, Fulton, Defiance, and Williams Counties. His award winning career began in 1957 and ended in 1988.

The "Hanging Judge" (Ex Justice of Peace) Courts of Williams County changed with the establishment of a county wide Municipal Court system in 1968. Weis changed with the times and kept on doing biz. He cultivated the new attorney judges the same as he did the old JP's. It continued – biz as usual.

He organized an informal Wildlife Officer's District. It consisted of state line wildlife officers in Ohio, Indiana and Michigan. It fostered good information exchanges and working relationships between states. It brought about the arrests and convictions of many interstate violators.

At his heavily attended retirement party, a dignitary speaker stated, "Williams County can go back to the state law. The legendary 'Weis law' era has ended as the legend himself has retired."

Mel was asked to run for Sheriff of Williams County after he retired. He declined by stating, "Yep, I'll accept the nomination. It's time for the county to have at least two houses of "ill-repute". One in the north, the other in the south. I'll bring in slot machines from Indiana. It's about time we get this county on the map." Needless to say, he didn't hear any more about running for Sheriff.

I was only exposed to Mel Weis for three short years – what an adventure. I've often thought, "What was his other twenty seven years like?" even though I heard of his exploits long after I left Ohio.

He not only brought about the biggest and best change in my life – he's one of my best friends and the best Game Warden I ever knew or worked with. There will never be another quite like him.

9
Quarterline
Deer Poacher

"This will leak 'B'. All we have to do is sit on it for a while," Mel Weis stated. He was speaking to me, using the nickname "B" he hung on me earlier.

It was the opening day of Ohio's upland game season in mid November, 1964. We were witnessing the ultimate in wildlife carnage and waste as we examined the whole carcasses of two trophy sized eight point white tail deer killed during the closed season. We'd been summoned to the scene by radio from our District Office in Findlay, who was notified of the violation by the Williams County Sheriff's Department. The Sheriff's Department received the report of the two deer from two opening day pheasant hunters who discovered the carcasses while hunting earlier that day.

Both bucks were shot through the heart. Both were laying on their right sides facing each other. The deer "rutting" season was in full swing. Both animals were heavy necked and showed signs of engaged battle. The vegetation and brush was mashed down around them indicating they were doing battle when shot. They were lying in a thicket within easy gunshot of a county road named the Quarterline Road. The only Williams County road with no homes and thus, possible witnesses. It was the ideal location to commit this heinous and despicable crime.

The eight point racks on both animals were perfectly symmetrical. They were thick at the base and "trophy" in every aspect. The meat of both deer was spoiled, wasting about 320 lbs. of good venison. We estimated they were illegally shot and killed during the closed season about four days earlier.

"Both well placed shots were near the back of the heart," Justice "Sonny" Bashore stated as he wrapped two .22 magnum bullets in cotton and dropped them in two separate plastic "coin" tubes and screwed the lids on.

Sonny Bashore was a Commissioned Game Protector who worked in Fishery Management. As all Commissioned Fish and Game Management folks, he was on duty checking hunters on the opening day of small game season. He was working in nearby Defiance County when I summoned him (and his wench equipped truck) by radio, to the scene. He was adept at tracing and removing bullets from shot animals. In this instance, he completed his task quickly and efficiently as was always the case.

"In my opinion, you have a single shooter. The bullet paths in both deer went straight in. I'd bet the shooter was in a vehicle on the Quarterline Road," Sonny stated. I photographed the animals where they laid and the surrounding scene. We winched both deer into the bed of Sonny's truck and he hauled them to the tankage company. I asked him to remove and preserve the two trophy racks to have mounted for state office displays and hold for future evidentiary purposes. Sonny stated he would take care of both. The racks would be at Oxbow Lake Headquarters if and when needed.

"What makes you think this whole thing will leak?" I asked Weis.

"Because he or they didn't field dress the deer or make any attempt to take them home. They let them lay here to rot. They didn't try to collect two darn good trophy racks. Why? Because he's running scared. He shot these deer while they were fighting. I would say in broad daylight – not with a light at night. He thinks someone may have seen him. He's afraid to come near the deer. He knows he's killed two trophy bucks. I read him as a dumb head who will brag about it sooner or later. When he does, we're gonna get the word. All we've got to do is hang in there and stay quiet," Weis concluded.

Weis's theory made sense and I agreed with it. I learned Weis had a way of pretty well ascertaining how a violation, after-the-fact or unseen, happened. I knew he had the best informant network I'd ever seen even to this day.

With no homes on the Quarterline Road, there wasn't a door to knock on in search of a witness. This left a "happen along" witness as a possibility. Although I'd been able to ferret out a few of these in the past (and did in the future), I agreed with Weis. To pursue this avenue of investigation would make "too much noise." We needed to stay quiet.

"Staying quiet" was hard for me to do. I wanted to seek out and interview the two pheasant hunters who made the initial complaint. I wanted to seek out and find that "happen along" witness if he or she existed. Doing these kind of things during an investigation was pure joy for me. However, I knew Weis knew his people and how to get things done in Williams County. I impatiently bided my time.

Mel sensed all this and shortly thereafter told me, "Okay, when it does break tiger, it's all yours. If you get the information first, go get him. If I get it first, I'll give it to you and you can still go get him. In the meantime hold

– just hold."

I'll have to say this case taught me there were times you "just hold." Over the next few months I revisited the scene several times looking for any clue we may have missed. It was all I could do to keep from knocking on doors the next road over to the north and south of the Quarterline Road. One of them may have been traveling the Quarterline Road and observed something – a vehicle, a license number, anything.

Naturally, there were plenty of other cases to work on. My assigned case load in Henry, Fulton and Defiance Counties had grown. Weis and I were getting into a much bigger deer investigation.

Finally, it happened. A certain male resident of Montpelier, whom we'll call L.B., participated in an ice fishing trip to Houghton Lake, Michigan in January 1965. Those who went on this expedition all worked for a local gas company. The head of this gas company, whom we'll call W.B. had a strong dislike for Game Wardens, thanks to Weis who busted him on two occasions – a factor that helped greatly in the successful conclusion of this case.

While on this trip, L.B. began drinking and boasted about shooting two trophy buck deer from the Quarterline Road in early November of 1964. A Weis informant, also participating in this ice fishing trip, heard all this and passed the information on to Mel. However, he didn't give this information to Weis until later in July of 1965. Nevertheless, as Weis predicted, "it leaked."

Mel called me at home. He gave me all the information on L.B. and his bragging (admissions) about killing the two deer the preceding November. "You've been darn patient on this one, Mr. B – it's all yours. Go get him," Weis stated. He was chuckling as he gave me my assignment.

Immediately after the poaching scene investigation, I delivered the two .22 magnum bullets, removed from the deer by Sonny Bashore, to BCI (Bureau of Criminal Investigation) Lab at London, Ohio. I had a BCI report stating both bullets were fired from the same rifle, along with chain-of-custody receipts.

I thought for a while about how I was going to go about apprehending L.B. Soon a plan developed in my mind. I phoned W.B. -- L.B.'s boss who hated Game Wardens. W.B. answered the phone.

"My name in Ron Bailey, I'm a State Game Protector and I work with Mel Weis. Do you have a L.B. working for you?" I asked.

"Yes, L.B. does work here and he's a mighty fine man. What the xo#x do you want with him?" W.B. asked.

"Never mind, I'm confirming his residence and his place of employment. Thank you." I hung up listening to W.B. yell "What the xo#x do you want with him – xo#x you - - - - Bailey."

I gave W.B. nine days to do what I knew he would do. I "reasoned" it would put L.B. in the right frame of mind for my forthcoming interview with him. It worked like a charm. I chose a Saturday when I knew L.B. was not working. I arrived at his home at 8:00 a.m. sharp. I parked my patrol car in front of his home, went to the front door and knocked. He answered the door.

He'd just finished his breakfast.

"Good morning L_ _. My name is Ron Bailey. I'm a Wildlife Enforcement Agent for the State of Ohio. I'm here to talk to you about the two buck deer you shot and killed out of season, off the Quarterline Road on or about November 1, 1964. Go in the house and get your .22 magnum rifle. The one you used to kill the deer. I'll wait here on the porch," I stated.

"Yes, sir," he responded. He was trembling. I knew he was "all mine" and W.B. had done his job well. Shortly he returned with his rifle.

"I'll take the rifle," I stated. He handed it to me.

"Now we'll go to my car," I stated. We went to my patrol vehicle. "Be careful, don't bump your head," I stated as I opened the door on the passengers side and pointed to the seat. He got in and I slammed the door (on purpose). He jerked – he was scared and I knew it.

"The first item we'll get out of the way is your rifle. I'm going to give you a receipt for it. I'll take it to the Ohio Bureau of Criminal Investigation at London, Ohio for test firing. I'm sure the test bullet fired from it will match the two .22 magnum bullets taken from the two deer by one of our experts," I stated.

Now, he was really nervous – on the verge of tears. "May I get my wife? I'd like her to be here with me," he asked.

Somehow, I can't explain it, I knew his wife's presence would be to my advantage. "By all means, get her, and try to calm down. You're a nervous wreck," I stated.

He went in his house and returned with his wife. She was a nice looking girl who weighed at least 280 lbs. As she seated herself in the back seat of the passenger's side of my Plymouth patrol car, it sank a good three inches.

As soon as L.B. seated himself in the front passenger's seat, his wife stated, "You little xo#xo#ox, you tell him the truth. We've had to live with this thing for almost a year and I'm sick of it. Do you understand me?" she stated in no uncertain terms.

"Alright honey, I'll tell him the truth," L.B. Stated.

It was obvious I had a willing ally in Mrs. L.B. as well as an unwilling ally in W.B. "Your wife is a very wise woman – she has your welfare at heart. I'll take your statement in writing," I informed him. I took a sworn and signed statement from L.B. that substantially told the following story.

He (L.B.) participated in a "fox drive" between Bryan, Ohio and the Defiance County line. At that time, a legal method of taking fox during which many hunters surround a section of land. They walk to the center and shoot the fox therein. He carried a .12 gauge shotgun on the fox drive and had his .22 Magnum rifle in his car. At the conclusion of the fox drive, while returning home, L.B. drove several county roads, including the Quarterline Road, hunting something to shoot. On the Quarterline Road traveling west, he saw the two buck deer fighting. He shot both in the heart. Then an interesting thing happened. The deer kept on fighting for a short time after they were shot, before dropping dead. Another car came along behind him and he fled the scene. He didn't know what the occupants of the car may have seen. He (and his wife) worried about the whole affair since.

"You caused about 320 lbs. of venison to go to waste. You kept two legal hunters from getting a trophy buck – do you realize that?" I asked.

"Yes, sir, I fully realize it. I'll never do anything like it again," L.B. stated.

I cited L.B. to appear in Judge Reuben Hayward's Court the following week. I advised L.B. of the maximum fine he was facing -- $200.00 for each deer. I also advised him of the bond posting and forfeiture procedure. Shortly thereafter, Ohio increased the maximum penalty for illegal deer violations to $500.00

Subsequently, I test fired L.B.'s Magnum rifle and took the bullet to BCI for comparisons. The resulting BCI report stated the bullet fired from L.B.'s rifle matched the two bullets removed from the deer "to the exclusion of all others." Thus, cinching my case.

L.B. later posted and forfeited a $400.00 bond. I returned his rifle to him after he signed a receipt for same.

This case exemplified a typical poaching scenario in many respects. One in which the illegal killing of a game animal results in the total waste of that animal. In this case, 320 lbs. of venison went to a tankage company. The trophy racks of both deer now hang on a state office wall rather than in a proud hunter's trophy room, where they could bring back many memories of a legal and successful hunt.

It took nine months, but Officer Weis was right, "It leaked."

10
She Shot a
Buffalo

During my tenure as a Wildlife Enforcement Agent, Ohio Division of Wildlife's District 2, I often received temporary duty assignments outside my regular duty area -- Williams, Fulton, Henry, and Defiance Counties – all located in the extreme northwest corner of Ohio. Some of these assignments carried full case agent responsibilities. The designation "case agent" meant the agent was in charge of and responsible for the case investigation from beginning to end.

To close a case, the case agent's report had to show;
1. A violation did or did not exist.
2. A progressive case narrative.
3. Every investigative lead was pursued.
4. Recommendation to close or re-open the case pending new leads.
5. Prosecutor approval or denial of charges.
6. Criminal or civil litigation results.

Other temporary duty assignments included routine field patrol work and/or assisting another assigned "Case Agent."

"Haney's got a good investigation going in Erie County. He's asked for your help; particularly, your interviewing and investigative skills," Dale Roach, my Supervisor stated by phone. Dale was a master at "whetting a subordinate's poacher catching appetite" with statements like, "Haney's got a good investigation going in Erie County." Followed by a challenging and flattering statement, "We need your interviewing and investigative skills."

Roach was sharp. He knew what made his agents tick. He knew his statements would "ready" me to get to Erie County and help.

"How about an overview?" I asked.

"Two principals – buyer and seller. The buyer is a black gentleman reselling to the black community. The seller heads a close-knit organization that is killing game in and out of season. Security guards at NASA (National Aeronautics and Space Administration) near Sandusky are implicated. There's good cooperation with the Sheriff's Department who won a conviction against the seller for statutory rape. Haney believes it should be worked overt rather than covert as there's good intelligence," Roach replied.

"What species?" I asked.

"Everything – game birds, deer, rabbits, fur bearers and a buffalo. It's a good one Mr. B. Haney will give you all the details at our agent's meeting on Monday," Roach replied.

"Buffalo?" I asked.

"Haney will tell you all about it," Roach responded.

"Sounds good, "I stated..

"Another thing. You've got free lodging and breakfast at the Erie County Jail or free lodging at the Holiday Inn, if you're willing to do a little night security work," Roach said.

"We'll see," I stated.

All this occurred in the late fall of 1965. My assignment as the Wildlife Enforcement Agent in Williams, Fulton, Henry, and Defiance Counties was recent. I had a significant case load in my assigned area. However, it was obvious my boss considered the Erie County investigation a priority. It sounded like a good one. I wished I was the assigned case agent rather than going to help the case agent, Dale Haney.

I didn't know Haney. I heard he was a good investigator. I heard he made a year old deer case. (Meaning it was one year from the time the deer was poached until Haney nailed the violator.) I wondered why Haney's year old deer case got so much publicity within the Division of Wildlife, when Mel Weis made cases like it for years. One thing was certain, I would soon find out how good he and his Erie County investigation was.

Haney and I met the following Monday at the District 2 Office in Findlay. Prior to our meeting, I had a very brief talk with another agent I knew well. This agent described Haney as a good investigator but "quite political." "Quite political" Game Wardens didn't impress me. As a matter of fact, in most instances, I didn't like them. However, I learned there were basically two types: Some, although political, used their politics in a positive way to accomplish good for the resource. Granted, they were rare, but a few existed then and undoubtedly still do. However, most of them used their political connections in the wrong way and were totally self-serving. I'd have to make up my mind about Haney.

"Erie County Sheriff, Al Hess, has the ring leader of a poaching tribe in jail waiting sentencing on a statutory rape charge. He's also got him for theft, possession of stolen property and dope," Haney stated and continued. "He is in his late twenties, has a wife and kid, but likes under aged girls. His name is (we'll call him) Teddy Tigart. Tigart's old lady split, doesn't condone the young girls. She's rat-finking on Teddy – good for intelligence only because of the 'wife can't testify' thing. Hess has good informants in Erie County. He's a retired Detective from Sandusky P.D. They say he was a good cop and brought a full sea bag to the Sheriff's Department. One of his informants broke the theft, possession and dope case. This same informant told Hess about the wildlife violations -- Hess contacted me. The informant will only talk to Hess. we have to go through Al to get our info. However, I think, I've got the picture.

Tigart sang like a canary on the theft and dope charges. At this point, Tigart won't talk about wildlife violations. Hess thinks we can change this when the timing's right. I pay attention to Hess, he's good at what he does.

Tigart was running with two completely different casts of characters. One -- the theft group, the other -- the wildlife poaching group. Both completely different.

Seems he didn't want the left hand to know what the right hand was doing. The theft group is history. Al's got good cases on all of them, and most have been convicted.

The wildlife group. We'll start with (we'll call him) Luther Johnson. Johnson is an elderly black gentleman who lives in Sandusky's black community. He bought illegal game from Tigart and resold it. Luther and Al Hess go way back. Al says Luther won't be a problem when the time comes. Al will pave the way with Luther. Al says when it's time to interview Luther, he'll play sick, in bed, the whole nine yards. He thinks he'll get sympathy this way – he always plays sick.

(We'll call them) Pat and Tom Smith. Pat is the daughter of (we'll call him) Lute Gowaslki, a duck hunting guide and outlaw for years. Lute went to jail last year on duck hunting violations and went bananas. He couldn't handle jail. It worked – they let him out. Says he'll never kill another illegal duck.

Pat and Tom jack-lighted game with Tigart. Tigart sold to Luther and split the money with Pat and Tom.

A guy called the "Yawner." His name is (we'll call him) Clyde London. He was questioned by Deputy Webb Beyer -- no results. Beyer says Clyde yawns and stretches incessantly during questioning – a sign he's telling a lie. Same M.O. as the Smith's with Tigart and Luther Johnson.

An under aged female (we'll call her) Jennifer Trulove. Jennifer accompanied Tigart on many jack-lighting escapades, periodically having sex with Teddy in the backseat. Usually, they went by a captive buffalo herd at Castalia Farms and shot a large bull buffalo with a .22 rifle. Ultimately, the old buffalo died of lead poisoning. The hired help buried him. The owner had him exhumed to determine the cause of death. They got a lot of .22 slugs out of him which they gave to Al Hess and I now have. Maybe we'll come up with the gun and make a case for Al on the buffalo. (Buffalo were extinct in Ohio for hundreds of years and were not covered under the Ohio Game Laws.)

When Jennifer found out Tigart was married, she went bonkers, had a nervous breakdown and turned suicidal. Her mother had her committed to a mental hospital in Fremont.

"Meeve, (Eloise Evans) Al's female deputy is on top of this. Meeve says Jennifer's shrink says it's okay to interview her. How about you taking that assignment?"

"Will do," I answered Haney.

Haney continued, "Under aged female number two. (We'll call her) Betty Bluenote. Betty traveled with Tigart on his night jack-lighting escapades. Tigart also had sex with her in the backseat. Unknown of course, to Jennifer Trulove. When Trulove found out about Bluenote and Bluenote found out about Trulove, they went at each other. Bluenote is another one of Trulove's problems. Another reason Trulove is in the nut house. Bluenote shot the buffalo while night hunting with Teddy. Tigart gave Betty the .22 rifle and said, 'here honey, shoot the big bull.' This really turned Bluenote on, but Tigart stopped her when she wanted to shoot the old buffalo's testicles. Meeve is on top of this one too. She says Bluenote will give a statement whenever we want."

Haney continued, "Under aged female number three. (We'll call her) Loretta Lovejoy. Loretta jack-lighted game at night with Tigart, and periodically 'romped' with Teddy in the backseat. Loretta, witnessed Tigart buy deer from two security guards at NASA. She witnessed Teddy and 'The Yawner' shoot game and the buffalo. She wouldn't shoot the buffalo claiming, 'The poor thing is in a pen.' We don't know if she can identify the NASA guards. Meeve talked to Loretta and says questioning her and getting a statement should not be a problem. The under aged females received no money from the sale of wildlife. Their only reward was a romp in the backseat with Teddy. In Loretta's case, Teddy and the Yawner.

Deputy Sheriff, Web Beyer has the cooperation of the Chief of Security at NASA. We need to get the names of the security guards selling to Tigart. Hopefully we'll find out who they are from Tigart and/or his under aged concubine, Loretta Lovejoy.

The Erie County Prosecutor's Office thinks we should get parental approval before we question the three under aged females. They couldn't come up with a statute for this. However, we're going to have to play by their rules. They must approve the charges we bring against the adults.

That's it, Bailey. When can you come to Erie County?" Haney asked.

"I've got business to take care of in Fulton County tomorrow. I'll meet you at the Erie County Sheriff's Office at 1:00 p.m. on Wednesday," I replied. The following Wednesday I met Haney at the Sheriff's Office. I was introduced to Sheriff Al Hess. At Al's suggestion, we toured the Sheriff's Department facility. I was shown my new sleeping quarters. A very neat and clean jail cell near and outside the cell block.

"You can have breakfast here every morning, compliments of Erie County, if you like," Sheriff Hess stated smiling.

"If you're smart, Bailey, you'll eat breakfast here. It's the best in town," Haney suggested. As the tour continued, Sheriff Hess introduced me to Deputy Sheriff Eloise Evans, nicknamed "Meeve" -- a middle aged, tall blonde and pretty woman. I would soon learn she was a good cop with a very quiet demeanor and resolve.

I was introduced to Deputy Sheriff, Webb Beyer. He had blonde hair, slender and short of stature. A good looking gentleman from West Virginia who loved to return home and engage in West Virginia's fine trout fishing.

According to Haney, Beyer was a good cop, quick, smart with a lot of moxie. Haney's description of Beyer proved true. I noticed Beyer wore no belt in his uniform trousers. They fit so perfectly, they were supported by his gun belt which, of course, didn't pass through his belt loops.

All during the tour and introductions, I couldn't help notice how immaculately clean everything was. The windows were spotless. The air had a definite clean, mild Lysol odor. I observed aerosol spray containers of Lysol at "key" locations. Periodically, Sheriff Hess removed a Lysol container from its appointed place and lightly sprayed the air. He placed the container back in its exact location, making sure the label faced one's view. The floors were clean enough to eat from, waxed and polished. The cell block was as clean and neat as the administrative part of the complex.

Meeve, observing me looking about, whispered, "Al's a cleanliness freak."

Al, hearing Meeve, stated, "She's right, I am."

Both chuckled as the tour ended and we entered Sheriff Hess's Office. We sat down and Meeve poured coffee. It was the best I ever had. It obviously wasn't grocery store coffee and it sure wasn't the proverbial "jail house" coffee.

"I've briefed Bailey on the wildlife investigation," Haney stated.

"Okay, let's talk about a plan of attack. I have a few suggestions. Oh, Officer Bailey, did Dale tell you I'm a retired Detective from the Sandusky Police Department?" Sheriff Hess asked.

"Yes, he did. Congratulations on your completed Police career. I'm sure you've 'been there and done that,'" I responded.

"Yes, I have. Would you like to see my retirement badge?" he asked.

"By all means," I replied.

Sheriff Hess reached inside his coat pocket. He retrieved a tooled wine colored leather credentials wallet, opened it and handed it to me. Beautifully displayed on a blue velvet background, was a gold Sandusky Police Department shield labeled "Detective." Its outer perimeter was inlaid with diamonds and rubies.

"Beautiful, isn't it?" Sheriff Hess asked.

"It certainly is. Did the City of Sandusky have it so beautifully customized?" I asked.

"No, I had all the trimmings put on it," Hess replied. For a second, before returning his credentials wallet to his coat pocket, Al admired his jewel studded retirement badge. He smiled and seemed to "coo" as he closed the wallet and returned it to his pocket. At this point, let me say I'm convinced the modern day "Monk" TV Detective series was inspired by Sheriff Al Hess.

"The weakest link in the chain is Jennifer Truelove. Meeve says her doctor at the mental hospital says she's safe to interview," Hess stated, breaking the ecstasy surrounding the badge inspection interlude.

"Go from the weakest link to weakest link until you get to Tigart. Right now he's not talking. But if you nip off his cohorts, one by one, he'll break down. We'll help you with this, of course. Let us know what you need," Sheriff Hess stated.

"There may be another possibility. We cracked Tigart on the theft ring by making him crazy mad. A version of the good guy – bad guy routine. He lets things slip when he's mad. You might try it. It worked for us," Hess continued.

"Sounds like it's worth a try," I responded.

"Which one of you is best at making a bad boy mad?" Hess asked.

Haney looked at me and grinned, "I'll nominate Bailey." he answered. Not knowing me well at all, I assumed Haney was dodging the assignment.

"Okay, I'll try him this evening if it's possible and okay with the Sheriff," I stated. I knew playing "bad guy" during an interview wasn't my style. I always got more with honey than poop.

"I tried to interview him once and got nowhere," Haney stated.

"I'll have him moved to an isolated cell. Talk to him through the bars – no interview room – he gets too mad. If he slips and gives you information, I'll try the good guy thing in the morning," Hess stated.

At 5:00 p.m., Deputy Sheriff Beyer escorted me to a jail cell occupied by Tigart. A single stool was on the aisle side of the bars.

"Ron Bailey, State Game Warden," I stated, introducing myself to Tigart as I sat down on the stool.

"I was wondering why they brought me to this cell again. I figured some xo#xo#x wanted to question me again and I see it's another Creek Dick." (From this point on, the conversation "deteriorated". For openers, Tigart inferred Agent Haney and I were the worst kinds of sexual deviates, interested in seducing him. Finishing his filthy and lengthy dialogue by stating, "You may as well get some kind of pleasure while you're here because I'm not going to talk to you about any poaching, which I haven't done anyway.")

Tigart looked like Conway Twitty. It was easy to see why his under aged concubines fell for him.

With the pile of filth he laid on me, I found I was the one getting mad. "Control it, Bailey," I said to myself.

"Well, well," I began. "You're real tough, aren't you Teddy. Tough granted, but not smart. I'm on this side of the bars and you're on that side for stealing stuff and seducing little girls." (I continued being abusive by inferring he had sexual desires for juveniles of both sexes and animals. I told him what happened to deplorables like him in the State Penitentiary. I called him the worst of names. I named the most sickening and abnormal sexual acts known to mankind – then stated he was a participant. I insulted his wife, sister and mother in the worst imaginable way.)

I accomplished part of my assignment. Teddy was raging mad. He lunged at the bars like a caged animal, grabbed them, his knuckles turning white. "If I could get to you, you Creek Dick xo#xo#x, I'd yank your tongue out," he stated as he yanked and pulled at the bars.

"That's just it Teddy, you can't get at me. You're like the Castalia Farms buffalo you shot – you're in the cage. You're like the deer you bought from the NASA guards. They were in a cage behind the NASA fence. But what if you could get to me Teddy? Do you think I'd stand here and let you yank my tongue out? No such luck, Teddy. I'd drive your nose bone up through you're rotten filth infested brain. Then shoot your testicles off like your little girlfriend wanted to do to the buffalo," I continued.

Tigart ran to the far corner of the cell. Standing there, he began snuffing, hacking, and snorting. Hacking up a big "greenie" from the remote regions of his sinuses and throat. Having succeeded, he balanced the snot cased greenie on his palate as he once again charged the bars and blew the whole disgusting, sickening mass directly at me.

My memory of this incident automatically goes into slow motion. I watched his tongue thrust outside his oval shaped mouth as it shoved added momentum to the blow propelled snot encased goober headed my way. As it cleared the bars, I stepped aside to see it pass me just below eye level. It traveled the width of the cell block aisle, splattered on the wall, oozed down onto the floor, making it appear twice the size I observed as it passed by me. The "goober", green gray portion of the mass remained centered and intact, giving the appearance of an opened rotten egg of a small non species bird – a horror movie creation.

"Oh, oh, now you've done it, Teddy. You've made a mess on the floor of Sheriff Hess's jail. I'm going to tell the Sheriff on you. You know he won't like what you've done, Teddy," I stated, in much the same manner as a tattle-tell child.

"Don't tell Hess, Bailey; don't tell Hess!" Tigart begged.

"Why not, Teddy? You just made a heck of a mess," I replied.

"Do you know how he is? He'll make me scrub the whole jail on my hands and knees. He makes us use a hand scrub brush and water loaded with chemicals. No gloves – my hands get raw and sore," Teddy pleaded.

"Teddy, we've said some nasty things to each other. We'll let bygones be bygones. I won't tell Sheriff Hess about the putrid mess you made on his floor if you talk to me about your wildlife poaching ring. How about it, Teddy?" I asked.

"Xo#x you Bailey! I'm not telling you a thing," Tigart yelled.

"Suit yourself Teddy," I responded.

I rose from the stool and headed toward the cell block door. My visit with Tigart lasted a half hour.

"Don't tell Hess, Bailey!" Tigart continued yelling.

"Sorry Teddy, you had your chance. Now it looks like it's the old scrub bucket for you," I stated and signaled for the duty officer to open the cell block door.

I told Haney about my interview with Tigart. "Al left for the day, but asked me to call him and let him know the outcome," Haney stated. As Haney hung up the phone following his report to Sheriff Hess, he stated, "Al's not happy about the spitting incident. I'd say Tigart will pay dearly for that tomorrow morning, probably before breakfast."

We called it a day. Haney left for home; I checked into my new lodging quarters – the only jail cell with a full bathroom. I visited a while with the duty officer, then went to a restaurant he suggested for dinner. I returned to my new temporary home with a newspaper. After a hot shower, I retired for the night. It was a long day; my interview with Tigart was not my style of interviewing bad guys. It took its toll – I was exhausted.

I woke the next morning refreshed. I took care of the personal morning chores; put on a clean uniform ready for the day. Soon I was served a great breakfast I thoroughly enjoyed. About 7:00 a.m. Sheriff Hess arrived. He asked me to "hang tight" until I completed the task of showing and telling him about the previous afternoon's spitting incident. As I told him of the incident and interview with Tigart, he summoned (by radio) two on-duty Deputies to the office.

Upon their arrival, we went to a utility closet where the deputies got a bucket, scrub brush, bottle of Clorox, and a box of laundry soap. We proceeded to the spitting scene. From this point on, the spitting incident took the complexion of a crime scene investigation. Sheriff Hess asked me to stand in the exact location Tigart was positioned when he "spat" the fatal wad. At the Sheriff's request, I assumed the position I held when the despicable spittle wad passed by me hitting the wall.

Sheriff Hess inspected the now dried greenie/goober pile on the floor along with the dried and fragmented streak down the wall.

"My, my," he stated as he whipped out a palmed and heretofore unseen miniature spray can of Lysol and sprayed the entire spittle landing zone. He ordered his deputies to go into the cell and make an inspection to determine if there were any additional "unpleasant things" caused by Teddy Tigart.

At Sheriff Hess's orders, the bucket was filled with hot water and placed in the center of the aisle outside the cell. A quantity of Clorox and soap was put in the bucket. Then the Sheriff ordered a rinse bucket brought to the scene. It was filled with hot water and placed beside bucket number one.

As Sheriff Hess strummed the fingers of his left hand against the lapel of his suit coat, he stated, "Fetch Mr. Tigart."

"He's probably having breakfast," a Deputy stated.

"No, he's not having breakfast, he'll have breakfast later. Fetch Mr. Tigart," Sheriff Hess reiterated.

I excused myself as I was sure Haney arrived and I had no desire to see Teddy suffer due to the error of his ways. I thought Hess might use the incident to get Tigart to talk about his wildlife violations. But this wasn't the case. Later, we learned Tigart scrubbed the entire cell block aisle. Wisely, Hess decided it wasn't the right time to "lay the deal" on Tigart that would trigger his cooperation with our wildlife investigation and break it wide open.

On Thursday morning, Haney and I met with the Erie County Prosecutor. We received his sanction to question juveniles, Jennifer Trulove, Betty Bluenote, and Loretta Lovejoy. At my request, we spent the afternoon looking over the geography. I learned the hard way, it always paid to know everything about the terrain where violations took place. The time spent engaged in this activity was always worthwhile.

During the evening, we contacted the parents of our three under aged females. All were cooperative and gave their consent to question the girls, take written statements from them and use them in court as witnesses. They all loathed Teddy Tigart and the Lovejoy's loathed Clyde London.

We decided on Friday, I would interview Jennifer Trulove at her domicile in the mental facility at Fremont, Ohio. Deputy Sheriff, Meeve Evans, arranged this with a phone call to Trulove's custodian. Meeve offered (I accepted) to assist me with the interview. However, she was unable to, due to an unexpected assignment.

Meeve's absence made me uncomfortable with the Trulove assignment. Interviewing a young girl with mental problems due to being raped was a first for me. But, what the heck. You don't get your feet wet by standing on the bank, I thought.

9:00 a.m. Friday morning found me entering the mental facility at Fremont. I met Clair Trembly, Jennifer's Counselor. After brief discussion of what I planned to question Jennifer about, she was brought to the room. I introduced myself and stated the nature of my business. She agreed to answer my questions truthfully. Her counselor remained in the room.

I'll sum up the Trulove interview and subsequent five page statement. She related approximate dates and times of the day and night she witnessed Tigart shoot and collect cottontail rabbits, raccoons, pheasants, wild ducks and geese, and muskrats. All qualified by the statement, "As best I can remember." In view of the fact the preamble on all affidavits charging a wildlife violation stated, "On or about," I was comfortable with the Trulove statement. Her story of wildlife slaughter was sickening.

Jennifer also admitted taking part in the violations by occasionally trying to shoot some of the game. She added, "But I usually missed." Her statement assured her participation was heavily encouraged by Tigart.

She stated Clyde London accompanied her and Tigart on at least two occasions. She claimed she witnessed London kill and collect a rabbit, raccoon, and Canadian goose. The statement was witnessed by her Counselor, Clair Trembly.

I began to question her about shooting the buffalo at Castalia Farms. Immediately, her Counselor asked to speak to me in private. We adjourned to another room.

"Did she actually shoot a real live buffalo?" her Counselor asked.

"Yes, our information is she did. The animal was part of a captive confined buffalo herd at Castalia Farms," I told her.

"That's the only reason she's still in this institution. She continually talks about shooting a buffalo. We checked and found buffalo have been extinct in Ohio for a long time. She never told us the buffalo was in a pen," the Counselor explained.

"You didn't ask her if the buffalo was in a pen?" I asked.

"No, we didn't," she replied.

"Jennifer and others who associated with Ted Tigart periodically, while illegally hunting with a spotlight at night, drove by the buffalo pen at Castalia Farms and shot a bull buffalo with a .22 rifle. He finally died of lead poisoning," I further informed the Counselor.

"I'll notify her mother to take her home. Thanks for enlightening us. I'm sure glad you came by," the Counselor stated.

We returned to Jennifer's interview room where I resumed questioning about the buffalo shooting. She described occasions during which Tigart went to Castalia Farms to shoot the buffalo. This occured following a night of jack lighting game. She admitted shooting the buffalo and being a willing participant. She claimed only one .22 rifle was used; it belonged to Tigart. She didn't know the make or model. Her description of the gun indicated a pump action. She knew nothing about deer bought by Tigart from the guards at NASA or the sale of wildlife to Luther Johnson.

I took a separate statement from Trulove regarding the buffalo. This statement was witnessed by Counselor Trembly. I concluded my interview with Trulove and went home to Williams County. I talked to Williams County Game Protector, Mel Weis, the night before by phone. "This Camden, Michigan deer thing is breaking fast "B". We need to get on it no later than Saturday. Polish your Federal badge – you're gonna need it," Weis stated. I briefed Haney by radio on the Williams County situation, the successful Trulove interview, and said I would see him in Erie County next week.

"Q-22, go get 'em Hoss and tell the big guy in Williams County I said "hey", Haney replied.

Mel Weis and I worked on the deer poaching ring composed of outlaws from the Camden, Michigan area on Saturday, Sunday, and Monday.

On Tuesday, I returned to Erie County and met with Agent Haney at the Sheriff's Department in Sandusky. We decided to proceed with the interviews of juveniles, Betty Bluenote and Loretta Lovejoy. Deputy Sheriff, Meeve Evans arranged both interviews. The Bluenote interview took place at 3:00 p.m. at the Sheriff's Department with her parents present. The Lovejoy interview took place at the her home at 6:30 p.m. with her parents present.

"Your interview with the girls shouldn't be too awkward. You'll talk to them about wildlife. I talked to them about sex," Meeve stated. It's interesting to note, of the three sets of parents, only the parents of Jennifer

Trulove were interested in prosecuting Tigart for statutory rape. The other two wanted to get it over with. However, with or without parental support, the state could still prosecute Tigart and London for statutory rape. This gave Sheriff Hess a good "bargaining chip" when the time came to break Tigart and London down on the wildlife offenses.

At 3:00 p.m. Sharp, the Bluenotes arrived at the Sheriff's Office. Deputy Sheriff, Meeve Evans conducted the introductory amenities. Following an explanation of our investigation and assuring the Bluenotes we were not interested in prosecuting their daughter, the Bluenotes proved very cooperative. Betty's father instructed her to be truthful and cooperate with us. The Bluenotes signed a brief statement giving their consent to question their daughter.

I began questioning by reassuring the young lady we were not going to prosecute her for any wildlife violations. We wanted her written statement regarding what she saw, participated in and heard. Bluenote talked faster than I could write. Agent Haney had information (via Al Hess informant) on specific dates and times. He questioned her extensively. She recalled "as best she could", the answers to Haney's questions.

She told a second sickening story of wildlife slaughter involving day and night closed season hunting with a "big light". Her story told of the unlawful shooting of six deer by Tigart who left them lay to retrieve later with the help of Clyde London and his pickup truck. She told about Tigart killing many rabbits, wild ducks, wild geese, pheasants, raccoons, opossums shot at night and muskrats stolen from legal trappers. She admitted participating in and witnessing the shooting of the bull buffalo at Castalia Farms. She got excited and seemed to light up as she told of shooting the buffalo. We didn't question her about her reported desire to shoot the buffalo's testicles. She claimed to know nothing about Luther Johnson or the sale of wildlife, although she wondered what Tigart and London did with all the meat. The length of her signed statement was about the same as Jennifer Trulove's. We took two statements from Bluenote. One relating to the wildlife violations and one relating to the buffalo shooting.

At the conclusion of Bluenote's statement signing, both were witnessed by her parents and the officers present. We thanked them for their cooperation.

At 6:30 p.m. Deputy Sheriff, Meeve Evans and I arrived at the Lovejoy residence in Sandusky. Haney met with a CI (confidential informant) on another unrelated case. Following introduction by Officer Evans and a statement by me as to the nature of our business, the Lovejoy's invited us to sit down. I told the Lovejoy's I was interested in questioning their daughter about wildlife law violations only. I asked them to sign a brief statement stating they approved of the questioning. They did without hesitation after receiving my assurance their daughter would not be prosecuted for any wildlife violations.

In response to my questions, Loretta Lovejoy answered as I recorded the information on sworn statement forms. Like Trulove and Bluenote, she qualified her answers with this statement, "to the best of my memory."

She related another sickening story of illegal wildlife slaughter. She told of witnessing Tigart and London killing and collecting wild cottontail rabbits, raccoon, opossum, muskrats and pheasants. She claimed to know nothing about the sale of these animals. When I brought up the subject of deer – BINGO! She told of witnessing Tigart buy field dressed deer from (we'll call them) Oliver Shagnasty and Lester Neredowell. Both security guards (in uniform at the time of sale) at NASA. "Teddy paid Oliver and Lester $25.00 each for the deer – cash – no checks," she stated. She witnessed the purchase of eight deer by Tigart and London on three occasions. She stated Tigart told her they "had a buyer" for the deer. She didn't witness the delivery or resale of the deer to Luther Johnson or anyone else.

She told of visiting Castalia Farms at night in the company of Tigart and London. She witnessed Tigart and London shoot the bull buffalo "in front of a big light." She stated she shammed both men and would not shoot the buffalo because it was "penned up."

As with Trulove and Bluenote, I took two statements from Lovejoy. One concerning the wildlife violations and one concerning the buffalo shooting. Loretta's parents, Meeve Evans, and I witnessed Lovejoy sign both statements with our signatures.

Spending another night in jail, I enjoyed another Erie County jail house breakfast the following morning. At 7:00 a.m., Sheriff Hess arrived. I was privileged to observe another "Hess ritual".

Meeve, already on duty early as always, appeared carrying a small bowl of fresh whole fruit cradled inside the bowl on a white napkin. She placed the bowl on Al's desk near his left hand. Then she poured Al a cup of that wonderful jail house coffee and placed the saucered cup on Al's desk near his right hand.

"Has the fruit been scrubbed, Meeve?" Al inquired quietly, not diverting his attention from the stack of papers on his desk in front of him.

"Yes Al, it's been washed," Meeve quietly answered.

"Did you witness them scrub the fruit, Meeve?" Al asked.

"Yes, I did Al," Meeve replied.

"Thanks Meeve," Al stated in the same quiet tone.

"You're welcome Al, good morning! Enjoy your coffee," Meeve answered as she departed Al's office and entered the reception and radio room where I sat writing some investigative notes in my shirt pocket sized notebook.

Assuming I observed and heard all or most of the fruit and coffee ritual, Meeve glanced at me, rolled her eyes, and nodding backward towards Al's office stated, "We have to see Al gets started every day on the right foot."

"I heard that Meeve," came Al's voice from his office in that same quiet monotone voice heard throughout the entire fruit and coffee ritual.

Agent Haney arrived; we went to his patrol vehicle for a short conference. "I talked with Dale Roach last night. He thinks we're at a juncture where he might want to approach Hess about laying Hess's deal on Tigart. Roach believes if we can get Tigart to roll over now, it will shorten the investigative time and we can get on with other things. What do you think?" Haney asked.

"He's right. But we need to play this thing according to Al's agenda. He's the big gun here, especially as far as Tigart is concerned. Tigart's down on one statutory rape count and that's heavy. He's facing two possible other rape charges. If he's got any brains at all, he would be ready to deal anyway possible. Hess assures us the statutory rape sentence has got Tigart worried – it sure should. We've got good evidence from the three weakest links in the chain. We know the six remaining links aren't going to be easy. With Tigart down, the remaining five should be a piece of cake," I replied.

"Okay, makes sense. Let's lay it on Al," Haney stated. We were able to get Al's closed door attention at 10:00 a.m.

I read Hess the Jennifer Trulove and the Loretta Lovejoy statements and Haney read the Bluenote statements.

"Those are good statements. It looks like I've got my buffalo case – we'll cinch it when we get the pump action rifle. I agree with Mr. Roach, now is the time to deal with Tigart," Hess stated. He picked up the phone and dialed. "Freddie? Good morning. How about coming over here about 2:00 p.m. We're going to question your client," Hess told Tigart's Attorney, a Public Defender.

"Wildlife law violations. There are two Wildlife Officers here to question him. I'm prepared to throw you a pork chop if your client wants to cooperate (- - - - - Freddie obviously talking). I don't care what you told him. We're questioning him at 2:00 p.m. Get over here." Al proclaimed as he hung up the phone.

"That was Tigart's attorney. He'll have to be here and he will be. No worry here, I've known him all his life. Not worth a dime as an attorney. He's no problem. Each of you ask Tigart a couple of insignificant questions. He'll tell Tigart not to answer. It will make it look like he's doing his job. Don't sweat Freddie, he'll make a deal anytime day or night," Hess stated.

Hess continued, "Okay, here's what I'll offer Teddy if he cooperates. I'll tell him I'll intercede with the court on his behalf concerning his statutory rape sentence. Nothing more – nothing less. No promises on the other two statutory rape possibilities, although we can play with him a little on these two possible charges. I'll open the proceedings, then turn the questioning over to you. I may interject from time to time. If I do, follow my lead – it will be obvious. I'm going to have Teddy served a T-bone steak dinner at noon. Sometimes a good meal puts these xo#x in the right frame of mind. Okay, we're all set. See you at 2:00 p.m.," Sheriff Hess stated as we thanked him again for his help and exited his office.

"Short and to the point (referring to Hess)," I stated as we seated ourselves in Haney's patrol vehicle.

"Wanna make a bet?" Haney asked.

"What?" I answered.

"Tigart goes down this afternoon. I've witnessed Hess interview once

– he's unreal – he's good. Takes absolute command. I watched him out-fox a good attorney," Haney stated.

"I won't take your bet. The guy's sure got the right vibes," I stated.

"We need to contact Web and tell him we've got the names of the two NASA security guards, so he can get the NASA security chief on line," Haney stated as he started to pick up the mike on his Sheriff's Department radio.

"Let's hold on that until after the Tigart interview. Then, hopefully we'll have two eye witnesses rather than one," I stated.

"Yeah, I'm smelling blood and getting anxious," Haney responded.

"Me too, let's grab some coffee and lunch, then do a drive-by at the Luther Johnson residence. I need to pick up some vibes on Johnson. I've never interviewed a black guy playing sick before," I requested.

After lunch and the Johnson tour, we arrived at Al Hess's office at 1:45. "Freddie's in the cell block talking to Tigart. He's telling his client to cooperate. Tigart's going to roll over, gentlemen. If he stalls, I've got an ace in the hole that will chill the xo#x in him," Hess stated.

"Like what?" Haney asked.

"Confidential for the time being, gentlemen – let's go," Hess responded as we exited his office headed for the interview room.

"After your introduction Al, I'd like to lead off and get the air cleared concerning the verbal exchange Teddy and I had the other day," I asked.

"Sure thing, Bailey. Eat humble pie if you think it's necessary," Hess responded.

We entered the interview room. It was not a typical interview room with bright overhead lamp hanging at the end of a cord. No small table in the center of the room with hard chairs. It was more like a lounge. Tigart and his attorney were seated at the table. I noticed two uniformed Deputy Sheriff's seated in different corners of the room. Outside the room was an inmate busy washing windows – windows elevated and near the ceiling level on one side of the room.

"Sheriff Hess began with quick introductions. Addressing Freddie, Tigart's attorney, Hess stated, "Counselor, make a note on your tablet of the fact our Wildlife Officers attempted to interview your client on two occasions without counsel present. A moot point in view of the fact that your client admitted nothing. Nevertheless, something you should be aware of."

As Freddie made the notes suggested by Hess, Al continued, "Now, Mr. Tigart and Counsel, I'll tell you what I'm prepared to do if you, Mr. Tigart, cooperate to the fullest with our Wildlife Officers. I don't have to tell you the charge of statutory rape you, Mr. Tigart, stand convicted of, is serious. You haven't been sentenced for that offense. Frankly, Mr. Tigart, with respect to your sentence, you need any and all the help you can get. If you cooperate with the two Wildlife Officers, I'll intercede on your behalf with the court. I'll make the court aware, in great detail, of your cooperation. That's it gentlemen, that's our offer. No guarantees, only the fact that I will intercede on your behalf with the court. Counselor, I believe you know I'm a man of my word."

"Yes, I do know that, Al. My client will cooperate," Freddie responded.

"Fine, I'm going to turn the rest of this meeting over to State Wildlife Officers, Dale Haney and Ron Bailey. I believe Officer Bailey has a beginning statement to make," Sheriff Hess stated as he turned the floor over to me.

"Ted, I owe you an apology for the manner in which I spoke to you the other day. Even though your greeting wasn't very cordial, my response was inexcusable. I insulted you and your family. My conduct was a disgrace to the State of Ohio and definitely unbecoming a professional Wildlife Law Enforcement Officer. I ask your forgiveness at the same time I congratulate you for being man enough now to stand up and be truthful. Your cooperation with us will not go unnoticed by the Ohio Division of Wildlife ---- thank you," I stated.

"It's okay man, I was way out of line too," Tigart responded.

"Whew!, with that over with, I started to turn the initial questioning over to Haney only to read a note he slipped to me that said, "You're doing fine, keep going."

I continued, "Ted, I'm going to read a series of signed and sworn statements. They are somewhat lengthy but bear with me. At the conclusion of each reading, I'll ask you one simple question; is the statement true or untrue? I began reading the Jennifer Trulove statements. At the conclusion, I carried the Trulove statements around the table to Tigart and let him and his Counsel see the Truelove signatures, her custodians and my witness signatures. Are the Trulove statements true?" I asked.

"They're true," Tigart replied.

During the reading of the Trulove statements, Hess paid acute attention to the inmate washing the windows. The inmate completed washing the first window and started on the second. Al went to the first window and tapped on it. He motioned the inmate back to the first window; pointed to two smudges or streaks the inmate missed cleaning. Of course, the inmate immediately corrected his mistake and Al returned to the table and sat down. Haney looked at me and grinned.

I began reading Betty Bluenote's statements. At the conclusion of both statements (one concerning the wildlife violations and one concerning the buffalo shooting, the same as Trulove), I carried both statements to Tigart and his Counsel and showed them the Bluenote signature along with the witness signatures of her parents, mine, Dale Haney's and Meeve Evans'. "Are the Bluenote statements true?" I asked.

"Yes, they're true," Tigart replied.

I looked up from showing the signatures to Tigart and Counsel, to see Sheriff Hess was tapping on a window. Again, he pointed out spots and smudges the inmate missed. Again, the inmate corrected his mistakes. I looked at Haney, nodded toward Hess and grinned. Haney looked at me and grinned. The two Deputies and Freddie were grinning. All were amused by

Al and his inmates' performance. A performance punctuated by everyone's knowledge of the fact Al was a cleanliness nut.

Next, I read both the Lovejoy statements. Again, I carried both statements around the table to them. As before, I showed them the Lovejoy signature along with her parent's, Meeve's, and my witness signatures.

"Are these statements true?" I asked.

"Yes, they're true," Tigart answered.

Again, Al Hess was at a window correcting the cleaning method of his inmate window washer. This time everyone in the room was grinning, including Tigart who was shaking his head and chuckling. Then it dawned on me, Hess wasn't just picking at a window cleaner's performance. He broke the tension between both parties. We all were quietly laughing at Hess and his idiosyncrasies. I thought, You old fox.

At the conclusion of my statement readings, Haney assumed the questioning. This was the first time I witnessed Haney conduct a lengthy interview. He was a master. His delivery was quick, monotone, and concise. He smiled as he questioned Tigart. His line of questioning had to do with the details of times, events, and places not covered in the three girl's statements. More important, he was receiving the right information. I was writing Tigart's statement and continually asked Haney to slow down in order to get it written. With a few questions I had concerning Luther Johnson, the Tigart interview and statement concluded.

I asked Tigart and Counsel to read the statement I had completed. They did and stated it was accurate. I added wording to the Tigart statement stating that he (Tigart) acknowledged the Trulove, Bluenote, and Lovejoy statements were true. I asked Tigart to sign the statement which he did following Counsel's approval. All present witnessed his signature. We were over the hump! We'd busted the Erie County investigation wide open! The rest was almost a matter of procedure.

In his sworn and signed statement, Tigart confessed to the following illegal taking and sale of legally protected wildlife. The wildlife was taken mainly at night by shooting in closed season, with the aid of an artificial light from a motor vehicle, and from a public road. Each "taking" constituted five separate law violations.

The purchase of eleven deer from two NASA security guards at $25.00 each. He resold the deer in field dressed condition to Luther Johnson for $75.00 each. The sale of six additional illegally taken deer to Johnson for $75.00 each -- field dressed.

Concerning the numbers of small game birds and animals, he gave estimates; 40-50 cottontail rabbits sold to Johnson for $3.50 each, 20 wild ducks and geese sold to Johnson for $3.00 each, 25-30 ring necked pheasants sold to Johnson for $3.00 each, 35-40 raccoons sold to Johnson for $8.00-$12.00 each, 35 muskrats sold to Johnson for $6.00-$8.00 each, 40-45 opossums sold to Johnson for $5.00 each, and 15 quail (illegally taken in Seneca County) sold to Johnson for $2.00 each. Total about $2700.00 in illegal wildlife sales, amounts and totals we considered conservative.

Tigart claimed all his poaching and illegal wildlife sales took place within a two year time frame. He stated his companion poachers (all previously mentioned in the text) and he hunted primarily during the months of November and December. He admitted shooting the Castalia Farms buffalo. He stated Trulove, Bluenote, London, Pat Smith and Tom Smith also shot the buffalo. He stated all the aforementioned and Lovejoy participated in the illegal taking of the wildlife sold to Johnson. He stated all except Trulove, Bluenote, and Lovejoy shared in the monies received from the wildlife sales.

Interview concluded, Haney, Hess, and I went to Al's office where he poured three cups of hot gourmet coffee. As we all relaxed, I asked, "What's with the window cleaning bit, Al?"

Hess smiled, "No comment."

"Come on Al, it was staged, wasn't it?" I asked.

"It's an old trick – old as the hills. A ploy of any kind to get everyone on common ground. It breaks tension. Everyone has the same thing to laugh at. In this case I used my crazy habit. We dirtied up those windows before the interview. The old inmate was in the know and got a kick out of it," Hess stated.

Haney was grinning from ear to ear. "How about the ace in the hole you said you had – the one that would chill the xo#x in Tigart? Tell us about it," Haney asked.

"Didn't have one. I told you fellows that for the sake of your interview confidence level. Both of you did a fine job. As good a job as I've seen. You're both professionals. It's downhill from here on," Hess stated. We exchanged amenities with Hess and departed his office .

We went to dinner at a local diner and planned our next step. We decided Clyde "the Yawner" London was the next weakest link.

"We'll ask Al to summon London to his office – get him off his home turf," I suggested.

"A good idea. I'll contact Al tonight by phone and run it by him," Haney responded.

"I'm concerned that we've not picked up any physical evidence," I told Haney.

"I am too; however, I've discussed it with the Prosecutor. He says if we never have any more than statements, its fine. He'll prosecute the cases," Haney responded.

We called it a day. It was a good one. I spent another night in the Erie County Jail and enjoyed another jail house breakfast the following morning.

Hess arrived at his office at his usual time. He asked me to come to his office. Meeve had Al's washed fruit ready and waiting. "Care for some," Al stated offering me some of his early morning delight.

"No thanks Al, just finished a great breakfast," I stated as Meeve poured the three of us a cup of coffee.

"Dale called me at home last night regarding your interview with

London. London will be here at 10:00 a.m. Beyer says this guy is a real character – good luck!" Hess stated.

I thanked Sheriff Hess for arranging London's appearance. I retreated to my cell where I stayed busy catching up on paper work until Haney's arrival at 9:00 a.m. Dale asked Hess if we could use his interview room and of course, received the go ahead. We went there and waited. We were both in quite a jovial and relaxed mood as a result of the resounding success of the Tigart interview. We decided to have some fun with London. We wanted to see if his yawning and stretching habit was as bad as Deputy Beyer said it was.

London arrived shortly after 10:00. Meeve escorted him to the interview room. London looked around the room. "I thought the Sheriff wanted to talk to me. Who are you guys? London asked.

"We're State Wildlife Officers and we're going to talk to you about your illegal poaching activities while in the company of Ted Tigart and some others the past two years," Haney stated.

"I sure don't know nothing about any game poaching," London stated. He immediately stretched as though he was trying to reach the ceiling, and displayed a gaping yawn.

From that point on, we asked him about twenty incriminating questions. Every answer he gave was a lie. He yawned and stretched with every lying answer. When Deputy Beyer stated he yawned and stretched incessantly, he was putting it mildly. I've never before or since seen anything like it. He almost put himself to sleep.

After about forty-five minutes of experiencing "the yawner's" crap, Haney looked at me and nodded; it was confrontation time. I opened my briefcase and removed all the statements taken thus far in the investigation. I showed London only the signatures on all the statements except Tigart's.

"It's all here Clyde, my boy. Now I'm going to read you Ted Tigart's confession. It will give you something to yawn about. Oh, incidentally, about that yawning and stretching habit you have. Try to get over that, will you?" I asked.

"What yawning and stretching habit?" he asked.

"The yawning and stretching habit you have when you tell a lie. You're annoying and obvious as xo#x," Haney replied.

I read the Tigart statement in its entirety to London. As I read, you could see London melt – he knew he'd been had. Next, I began reading the Loretta Lovejoy statement. I chose her statement due to the information we had concerning Clyde's romp with Lovejoy in the backseat of Tigart's vehicle. I knew he would be scared to death of a statutory rape charge. London continued to melt slowly but surely.

"It's all true – you don't have to read any more. How much more blood do you want?" he asked.

"We just want the whole story," I replied.

"Tigart just told you the whole story and I'm verifying it, okay?" London stated.

"Okay Clyde, I'm going to prepare a short and simple statement. It will simply acknowledge those parts of the Tigart statement involving you and your activities in this whole mess, is true. Are you willing to sign such a statement of your own volition?" I asked.

"Yes, I will," London replied.

With the completion of the London statement, he signed it after Haney read it to him. Haney and I witnessed his signature. We excused London after thanking him for his cooperation. As Haney shut the interview room door behind London, he stated, "The yawner just went down." With no discussion, Haney and I looked at each other. Almost together we stated, "It's time to interview Luther Johnson." "I'll ask Al to set it up," Haney stated as he knocked on Sheriff Hess's door and disappeared inside at Al's invitation.

Shortly Haney emerged. "Al's got it all set up. We interview Luther at his home at 6:00 p.m. Luther won't come to the Sheriff's Office. When Al finally got past Luther's wife and got him on the phone, Luther told Al he was bed ridden and feeling poorly. However, as a favor to Al, he agreed to talk to us although he couldn't imagine what a Game Warden would want with him. Al wants to talk to both of us in about a half hour," Haney stated.

Shortly, we entered Sheriff Hess's Office and sat down. "Luther won't admit or confess to anything. I had Luther for running a few prostitutes and receiving stolen property when I was with Sandusky P.D. He's a character. He always plays sick when he's under suspicion for something and a cop is trying to interview him. Even though he won't admit anything, regardless of what you throw at him, he'll try to make a deal. You can expect him to try and make a deal at the end of your questioning. How you play that card, of course, is up to you. Good luck!" Hess advised.

At 6:00 p.m. sharp, we knocked on Luther Johnson's door. He lived in a very nice spacious home. Our knock was answered by a very gracious middle aged black lady who told us she was Luther's wife.

"Luther's poorly and sick in bed, but I'll show you to his bedroom. Please try not to upset him and don't stay too long," she stated, her eyes showing all the concern in the world for her sick husband. Lord, what an actress, I thought.

With that, we followed her upstairs. She took us to Luther's bedroom and introduced us to him stating, "I can't remember their names, honey, but here are the two Game Wardens Mr. Hess called about." In bed, propped up on pillows, lay Luther Johnson wearing a two piece set of white satin pajamas. As she admonished again, not to be too long, she exited the bedroom.

Luther invited us to sit down in two chairs each located near the bottom right and left side of his bed. I sat in the chair on the left, Haney sat on the right.

"Now what in world could two fine young Game Wardens like you possibly want with a sick old black man like me?" Luther asked.

Haney gave me the nod. I removed the Tigart statement from my briefcase – Luther watching my every move.

"Mr. Johnson, we appreciate the time you've given us. We understand that you're a little under the weather. May I ask what ails you?" I inquired.

"Lord, Sonny, I got the consumption, assumption, arthritis, and a little hepatitis. Besides that, I'm just plain sick," Luther stated weakly and chuckling. "What's wrong with me, I can't even pronounce. Would you please reach me that glass of water?" he asked. Stepping over what appeared to be a hurriedly exited pair of bib overalls, I went to Luther's bedside table and handed him his glass of water. He drank it all and handed me the empty glass to place back on the table.

"Luther, you've been named as the buyer of a considerable quantity of illegally poached wildlife by a Mr. Ted Tigart and Clyde London." With that introduction, I read the Tigart and London statements (parts that pertained to Luther) to Mr. Johnson.

"Would you care to comment on Mr. Tigart's or Mr. London's statements? Would you say the statements are true or untrue?" Haney asked Luther.

"Lord, gentlemen, them two boys sure has got a wild imagination. Why I'd be crazy to admit to anything like that, wouldn't I?" Luther responded.

"Perhaps," I answered.

"Officer Bailey, would you help me get to my feet. I have to use the bathroom, it's down the hall," Luther asked.

"I'll help you get to your feet but I won't help you go to the bathroom. Perhaps we'd better page Mrs. Johnson," I stated.

"No, I'll be alright as soon as I get on my feet," Luther stated.

I rose and went to his bedside and helped Luther out of bed and on his feet. I hurried ahead of him, returned to my chair and sat down. Just as I sat down, Luther turned to his left, going around his bed post. Immediately, I saw a very large penis broadside and headed for the left side of my head. It obviously had exited the fly of Luther's pajama bottoms as he turned to the left. I jerked backward as it missed my forehead by inches.

"Oh, I'm sorry Officer Bailey. It looks like the old horse kinda got out of the barn there," Luther exclaimed as he grabbed his penis as though it was an uncontrollable snake and stuffed it back inside his pajamas. He toddled to the door and turned right. Haney was breaking up – laughing as hard as he could but trying at the same time to quiet his laughter.

"Looks like you darn near got bashed up side the head with a big ol xo#x, didn't you Mr. B," Haney chirped, near blowing a head gasket as he continued trying to be quiet and suppress his laughter.

"I've had enough of Luther. Confession or not, this interview is over as far as I'm concerned," I stated.

"I agree, Mr. B. You've been through a lot – almost getting whacked up side the head by a xo#x isn't in your job description," Haney blurted out, now out of control and laughing out loud.

We heard a toilet flush. Luther returned to his bedroom and crawled into bed. "Mr. Johnson, we thank you for your time. We're leaving now. We'll see you later in court," I stated as Haney and I both rose to leave – Haney a complete mess trying to keep a straight face.

"Before you go gentlemen, let me ask you something," Luther stated.

I thought, Here comes the deal, as I answered. "What's that, Luther?" Haney still unable to say anything.

"What's the easiest and cheapest way for me to get out of this?" Luther asked.

"You're getting into the court's business, Luther. Your question is very awkward for us to answer. We only investigate these matters. We don't adjudicate them," I answered.

"Mr. Al always gave me good advice along these lines. I don't want to spend a lot of money on attorneys. I've been that route before. All they did for me is run up the cost of everything," Luther stated.

"Well, I guess there's nothing to prevent me from explaining the possible legal procedures involved. One option, of course is to simply plead guilty and throw yourself on the mercy of the court. However, I doubt any good attorney would advise you to do this. A second option is to simply post and forfeit an appearance bond. Bonds are fixed amounts set by the court to assure your appearance in court. If, for any reason you don't appear on the scheduled date, your bond is forfeited to the court and that may end the case. The court still has the option of issuing a warrant for your arrest but in most misdemeanor cases, the court doesn't. That's all I can tell you, Luther," I stated. We departed the Luther Johnson residence. As we entered Haney's patrol car, he began thumping on the steering wheel and laughing for all he was worth.

"That's what I call above and beyond the call of duty. Almost getting whacked up side the head by a big xo#x, that's the high light of this investigation Mr. B," Haney howled.

"That's enough!" I stated.

"Boy, wait until Roach and District 2 hears about this," Haney continued.

"I said, that's enough, xo#x head!" I reiterated.

We returned to the Sheriff's Office. Wouldn't you know it, Al Hess was in his office working late. Haney burst through his office door. "Al, you won't believe what happened to Bailey during the Luther Johnson interview," Haney exclaimed.

"What happened?" Hess asked.

Haney told the entire "xo#x whacking" story, embellishing quite a bit, I add. Hess leaned back in his chair and grinned. "He didn't spray you with anything, did he Bailey?" Hess asked quite amused.

"No Al," I answered.

"Well, you'd better take a good hot shower right away in any event," Hess stated. "Gentlemen, you did okay with Luther. Don't worry, he'll go down like the proverbial fat hog, he always does. He'll plead guilty and beg and plead with the court. It usually works, he gets off relatively easy," Hess stated.

Haney and Hess left for home. I took Hess's advice, took a good hot shower, then dressed in civilian clothes and went to dinner. After dinner, I bought a newspaper, returned to the jail, watched TV for a while and called it a day. Another night of blissful rest in my jail cell.

The next morning, Haney arrived at the Sheriff's Office at 8:00 a.m. I'd had another good jail house breakfast and was ready for the day. "I talked with Webb last night. He's setting up interviews with the two NASA security guards. The NASA Security Chief is still in a cooperative mood," Haney stated. For the next hour, Agent Haney and I went through a pot of coffee and discussed the investigation.

"We're wrapping this case up faster than I thought Mr. B. As soon as we get through with all the interviews, there's no need for you to remain in Erie County. I know you and Weis have a good deer ring going in Williams County and you need to get on it. I'll handle the remaining litigation work on this case. I look for most to go down as guilty pleas and bond forfeitures. I'll contact you if you're needed for any meetings with the prosecutor's office or to testify in court," Haney stated.

"Fine with me, Dale," I responded.

Shortly, Deputy Sheriff, Webb Beyer arrived at the Sheriff's Office. "The security guard interviews are all set up gentlemen. We need to get to NASA as soon as possible. The interviews will take place in the Security Chief's Office; he's cooperating one hundred percent," Deputy Beyer stated. We got in the Deputy's patrol car and departed for NASA.

The NASA security guard motioned us through the security gate. We arrived at NASA Headquarters where we were escorted to the Security Chief's Office. There seated were the Chief, Security Guard, Oliver Shagnasty and Security Guard Lester Neredowell.

Following the customary amenities, the Security Chief took the floor. Speaking to us, he stated. "Gentlemen, I've already told my two guards why you're here. They have admitted to me they shot deer within the NASA compound and sold these deer outside the compound to Mr. Ted Tigart. They know they can also be charged in Federal Court for these offenses. They know they may face disciplinary actions imposed by their employer. They have been told if they cooperate with you, their employing agency's disciplinary actions and Federal Court charges might not be pursued. They have been told if they lie to you and the same is later proven, they're fired. Now, gentlemen, they're yours to question," the Security Chief stated.

What a mouthful – these boys are between a rock and a hard place, I thought.

"Gentlemen, Officer Bailey is going to read to you the signed and sworn statements of Ted Tigart and Loretta Lovejoy. If what you hear and subsequently read is true, we will prepare a very short statement for you to sign that simply states the statements are true. Those present will witness

126

your signature and that will be it for now. Any state charges filed against you must be approved by the Erie County Prosecutor. You will be notified when and where to appear in court," Haney told both guards. I read the parts of the Tigart and Lovejoy statements to both guards.

"Is what I've just read to you the truth to the best of your knowledge?" I asked.

Both answered, "yes!" I prepared two brief statements, one for each guard, stating Tigart and Lovejoy statements were true and correct. Both guards signed their statements. The officers present witnessed their signatures. The Chief of Security asked for a copy of their statements which was later provided to him. We thanked the Security Chief and his two outlaw guards for their cooperation and left.

As we left NASA, a soft Erie County rain began. A refreshing and cleansing rain from on high, I thought as I realized my part in cleaning up the Erie County poaching mess would soon end. For me, all that was left were the Tom and Patricia Smith interviews.

"The Tom and Pat Smith interviews will probably be the most difficult," Haney stated as we sat down in my jail cell, after returning to the Sheriff's Department from NASA and thanking Deputy Beyer for his help. "Pat is the daughter of Lute Gowalski. She grew up in a game outlawing environment. Her dad and brothers have all been sacked at one time or another by State or Federal Game Wardens. Actually, we probably don't really have to interview either of them. We've got enough from Tigart and London to convict them. However, I would like to go for it and put the frosting on the cake," Haney stated. "What's your thoughts on this?" Haney asked.

"Let's go for it," I answered.

That decision made, we spent the rest of the day trying to locate the Smiths. They were not at home as of 10:00 p.m. that night. Haney finally called it a day and went home. I decided to keep the Smith residence under surveillance awhile longer. After Dale delivered me to the Sheriff's Department, I got in my vehicle and returned to the vicinity of the Smith's residence. I maintained a surveillance of their home until 1:00 a.m. Both the Smiths returned home in the same vehicle. I knew now was not the time for the interviews. I surmised they were both employed at the same place. I returned to my jail cell and hit the sack.

The following day, Haney had a commitment in Seneca County. We decided to put the Erie County case on hold until I returned the following Tuesday. Over the weekend, I worked in Williams County with Mel Weis on the still rapidly developing Camden, Michigan deer poaching case. On Sunday, I worked a fisherman checking detail on the Maumee River with Officers Jerry Richardson, Tim Hood, and Marvin Rittenhouse. We made seventeen cases in all for fishing without a license and one for stream littering.

On Monday, I caught up on my paper work at home in Montpelier and talked with Dale Haney by phone. Al Hess had arranged the Tom Smith interview at the Sheriff's Office at 10:20 a.m. on Tuesday. We would be interviewing the Smiths separately.

On Tuesday, I returned to Erie County early and checked in at the jail. I'd grown quite fond of the place. I enjoyed the good breakfasts and the usual early morning jail house rituals. Especially the morning patrol briefings and the small talk as the Deputies went out on their patrols. It was a good and satisfying environment. I knew I would miss it when my part in the Erie County investigation was over. Haney arrived at 10:00 a.m.

"Al set this interview up in a hurry yesterday with no problems, when I reiterated the Smith's game outlawing backgrounds. He suggested we interview them separately. Al says interviewing husband and wife together, when they're both suspects, is never a good idea," Haney stated.

Shortly, Tom Smith arrived and was escorted to the interview room where Haney and I waited. His interview went unexpectedly quick. When confronted with the Tigart statement, he immediately acknowledged it was true.

"We knew this was coming. Ted's family called us and said he had confessed. We knew what that did to us," Smith stated. He signed and we witnessed a short statement stating the Ted Tigart statement was true.

"Can we expect this kind of cooperation from your wife?" I asked Smith.

"Yes, she'll cooperate. We want to get this thing behind us. Can we expect any jail time?" Smith asked.

"I doubt it very much. Perhaps, only if you can't pay the fine," Haney responded.

"We're prepared to pay the fine, even if we have to borrow the money. It's all arranged," Smith stated.

"How about having Patricia phone Sheriff Hess and tell him when she can come in for an interview?" I asked.

"I can answer that. She'll be here tomorrow at 10:00 a.m., the same as me. She'll cooperate with you," Smith reiterated.

We thanked Tom Smith for his cooperation and he left.

"Well Mr. B, I can take care of Patricia's statement and you can get back to Williams County. Hoss, I really appreciate your help. I'll keep you posted," Haney stated as we shook hands.

"It's been a pleasure and try to contain that xo#x bashing incident," I admonished Haney. Immediately, he started laughing again.

I went to Al Hess's Office. I thanked him for the hospitality, especially those good early morning breakfasts and all his invaluable help. "We would never have broken this case without you Al," I stated.

"Yeah, you would have; may have taken a little longer but you'd have nailed them," Al stated. I bid farewell to Web Beyer and thanked him for his help.

"Anytime, my friend, anytime," he responded.

Meeve Evans went with me to my patrol vehicle. "You're one of a kind Meeve. Thanks so much for all your help," I told her.

She kissed my left cheek. "It's been a pleasure working with you, Ron. Come back to Erie County anytime. I'd consider it a privilege to work with you again," she stated.

I left for Williams County knowing I had worked with some mighty fine and professional law enforcement officers. I've never forgotten them. I never will.

Dale Haney steered the cases against Ted Tigart, Clyde London, Luther Johnson, Tom and Patricia Smith, and the two NASA security guards through the entire court litigation process. I don't recall the exact charges actually approved by the Erie County Prosecutor and filed against each defendant. However, I do recall the bottom line. They all plead guilty and/or forfeited appearance bonds. They paid a total of well over $9000.00 in penalties.

Dale obtained the .22 rifle, a Winchester Model .06 slide action, owned by Ted Tigart and used to shoot Castalia Farms buffalo. It was test fired at the Bureau of Criminal Investigation (BCI) at London, Ohio. The test results and resulting report showed the Tigart rifle test bullet and those removed from the buffalo, matched "to the exclusion of all others." Thus, Al Hess's buffalo case was cinched. The owner of Castalia Farms (perhaps the wealthiest man in Ohio) was content knowing the buffalo shooters were caught. He didn't press any charges.

Wildlife Enforcement Agent, Dale Haney was one of the best investigators I ever worked with. He rose through the ranks to become Chief of the Ohio Division of Wildlife. Admittedly, his political connections, right or wrong, contributed greatly to his "rise to power." However, Dale, to the best of my knowledge, always used his political connections for the good of the resource. He was an excellent Chief. Dale left the ODW Chief's position to become CEO of the Woodstream Corporation (the old Animal Trap Company) at Lititz, Pennsylvania.

Dale passed away of a heart attack while the CEO at Woodstream. He was on the phone to Ohio trying to assist ODW Chief, Dick Francis. Dick was under political pressure to transfer wildlife funds to another state agency which he refused to do. Dale was once again, fighting politically for the good of the resource.

The story of Dale's passing was told to me by Charles Cooper, a retired Ohio Wildlife Officer. In his retirement years, Cooper worked for me as a U.S. Deputy Game Warden in an undercover capacity in North Carolina. Dale Haney (and his memory) has my undying respect. He was darn sure another exception to my "cheap, cheesy, politician" rule.

11
Hypnosis, Polygraph and State Line Deer Poachers

"We have two state lines here and all state lines are hot," the Williams County, Ohio State Game Protector, Mel Weis, stated during my first meeting with him. Weis was describing a unique situation in his patrol area, meaning Williams County was bordered on the north by Michigan and on the west by Indiana. To many who operate on the wrong side of our wildlife protection laws, a state line offers a refuge or safety zone. They mistakenly believe if they can get their illegal deer (or whatever) across the state line, they're home free. Thinking the State Game Warden's authority ends at the state line and he can't come any further.

Nothing could be further from the truth. Most State Game Wardens, especially those assigned to patrol areas bordering a state line, carry U.S. Deputy Game Warden commissions. These commissions in the form of a badge and/or I D card are issued by the U.S. Fish and Wildlife Service, under the Department of the Interior. This commission empowers the State Wildlife Officer to enforce all Federal wildlife protection laws including the Lacey Act. This Act prohibits the interstate movement or transport of illegally taken wildlife or parts thereof. This is an example of what's called "the long arm of the law." In other words poacher, getting across the state line won't help you. The man in the green uniform can keep on coming. In many instances, multiple state lines lay between the state where the illegal wildlife is taken and where it is transported to. In these situations, a State Game Warden enlists the aid of the full time agents of the U.S. Fish and Wildlife Service. The Federal Agents track the violator down in the far away state. In most cases, the violator is extended the option of voluntarily settling the matter with the State Game Warden involved or answering to Lacey Act charges in Federal Court. In most cases the violator will opt to settle with the State Game Warden by phone and bond forfeiture or other means of paying the penalty by mail without appearing in State Court. I add, the preceding applies to tribal and international boundaries and borders.

This is why, during an earlier phone conversation I had with him concerning this investigation, Weis stated, "Polish your Federal badge – you'll need it."

This investigation began with a report from one of many Weis' confidential informants. The C.I. reported (I'll call him) Larry Tanner, a used farm implement dealer, of Camden, Michigan was the leader of a deer poaching ring. Tanner and associates were killing 95% of their deer in Bridgewater and Northwest Townships in Williams County, Ohio. The deer were taken during the open and closed season. They were shot at night from a public road with the aid and use of a spotlight. An illegal practice known as jack lighting or fire lighting.

The C.I. named (we'll call them) Randy Bullock, Dick Smith, Tom Turner, and Joe Hines, Michigan residents who lived near the Ohio/Michigan state line, as accomplices. The C.I. stated there were others. A week later, the C.I. reported more state line Michigan residents as Tanner accomplices. (I'll call them) Dean Beyerly, Ted Shrader, Don Jones, and Lonnie Heath. He stated he had information indicating some of the deer this group poached was sold -- some given away.

Shortly thereafter, the C.I. added three names. All state line Michigan residents. He named these three (I'll call them) Fred Snyder, Stanley Taylor, and Len Sparks. He stated there were others -- he would be in touch.

At this point, let me do a little stage setting. In this particular Tri-State region (where Ohio, Indiana, and Michigan come together), the best deer range or habitat in those days lay in northern Bridgewater and Northwest Townships in Ohio. Although there were good state line deer populations in Steuben County, Indiana and Hillsdale County, Michigan, the heaviest concentrations of deer were in the two mentioned townships in Ohio. The reason for this was primarily two very large tracts of land. One, under the ownership of the Boy Scouts, the other known as the Broadbeck Estate. Both of these land holdings offered ideal white tail deer habitat. Both tracts were bordered by very rich agricultural land that further enhanced the wildlife food supply of this almost pristine wilderness. The area was well watered by the West Branch of the St. Joe River, Nettle Creek, and many lakes and ponds. All county access to the area began with Ohio County Road "S" running through the region, east and west and its transecting roads running north and south. There you have it – an ideal deer region, remote, with good road access. A perfect setting for those who seek and use every advantage they can to rape and pillage a public owned resource. In this case, the white tail deer.

Let me add, the Broadbeck Estate today is named the Lake La-Su-Ann Wildlife Management Area. It is owned by the Ohio Division of Wildlife. This productive wildlife area is now open to the public where all can hunt, fish, and enjoy God's great outdoors thanks to Mel Weis and his tireless career-long efforts to bring it all about. In Mel's honor, the Division of Wildlife named a principal body of water "Lake Mel." What a legacy for a Game Warden, now retired, who although a little tired and spent, still fights for the cause as he will until his last breath.

"Let's go to Camden, find Tanner's place of business and see if we can get a look at him," I suggested.

Weis agreed and we headed for Camden, Michigan in civilian clothes. Once we crossed the state line, we would be functioning as Federal Wildlife Officers investigating violations of the Federal Lacey Act. Our authority, of course, was our U.S. Deputy Game Warden commissions. After one inquiry, we soon found Tanner's place of business and his home – a farm on the outskirts of Camden. In the fields beside his house were parked many mechanized and non-mechanized farm implements. Tanner's white Ford pickup bearing a Michigan license plate, that according to the C.I. was Tanners', was parked near a large red barn. Among three persons milling about the farm machinery, one fit the C.I.'s description of Tanner. He was a very diminutive, slight built person about 5' 8", thin, and somewhat effeminate in appearance. Definitely not an imposing figure. A very deceiving appearance as we would soon learn.

"He's a wimp," Weis stated.

"Sure looks like one," I stated. Weis and I looked at each other.

"Let's put the "B" on him – what do you think?" Mel asked.

"Let's do it, maybe we can make short work of this one," I replied.

A stupid decision by two experienced and seasoned Game Wardens who knew better. No thought given to the "weak link" theory we were both familiar with. No ground investigative work completed on the rest of the Tanner associates to determine the weakest link in the chain and thus who to properly begin with. Based on Tanner's physical appearance alone, that of a wimp or weak link, we jumped headfirst into the tank of stupidity.

We drove into Tanner's driveway, exited our patrol vehicle, and approached Tanner. "Larry Tanner?" I asked.

"Yes sir, what can I do for you?" Tanner replied.

"My name is Ron Bailey, my partner is Mel Weis. We're Ohio Game Wardens and Federal U.S. Deputy Game Wardens." We both showed Tanner our Federal badge and I D's.

"We're investigating complaints the States of Ohio and Michigan have received. These complaints and our investigation so far, tell us you and several companions have been and are engaged in deer poaching activity, primarily in Ohio. You and your associates have transported illegal deer across state lines. This is a violation of a federal law known as the Lacey Act. Violating this Act is the primary reason we're here. Now, you'll accompany us to our automobile where we'll discuss this matter further," Weis told Tanner.

Tanner obediently accompanied us to our vehicle. It was obvious he was shaken after hearing Weis's spiel. We asked him to be seated in the front passenger's seat -- he complied. I sat behind the wheel and Weis sat in the back seat.

"You've probably been expecting us, haven't you Larry?" Weis asked.

"No, I haven't been expecting you. I've heard the Sheriff's Department is asking around about some stolen farm machinery I had nothing to do with, but they haven't been here. I've never heard of a Federal Game Warden. Let me see your identification again," Tanner stated.

We showed Tanner our U.S. Deputy Game Warden badges and I D cards again. He scrutinized our federal credentials closely.

"You say you're also Ohio State Wardens?" Tanner asked.

"Yes, we are," I replied.

"Let's see your State I D's," Tanner requested.

We showed him our state badges.

"That federal badge gives you the right to come to Michigan and enforce this Lacey Act, is that right?" Tanner asked.

"We've already explained that to you, Larry. Now let's get on with some more important matters," I told Tanner.

"This is your opportunity to level with us. If you do, we may be able to arrange for you to voluntarily come to Ohio and answer to the state charges as opposed to being tried in federal court in Detroit or Toledo. I'm sure you can understand this is your easiest way out, but it requires your full cooperation with us," Weis told Tanner. Weis laid it on the line – now it was win, lose or draw. Tanner sat silently for what seemed like eternity. He was thinking it over so hard you could almost hear his thoughts.

I broke the silence, "It's not a hard decision, Larry. You've just been offered a deal; a deal you'd better take," I said quietly. Tanner was actually physically sweating on that cool fall day.

"Almost persuaded, you know the right course to take, Larry. Play ball or go down swinging. You know what's right, Larry, you know what's wrong. You're on the wrong side of the law now, Larry. Let's get you on the right side?" I softly continued. Tanner continued remaining silent. I started to speak again -- Tanner interrupted.

"Screw you guys. I'm not going to tell you anything about me or any of the guys I hunt with!" Tanner shouted.

"With that statement you've already told us more than you'll ever know, Larry. You've chosen to do this the hard way. We'll see you and all the others in federal court. Now get out of the car and get ready for one rough ride. You've not seen nothin' yet," Weis loudly told Tanner.

Tanner obliged and we departed. Less than a mile down the road, simultaneously we stated, "We blew that one." Then we both fell into deep thought analyzing what seemed to be a grave investigative error.

Weis broke the silence. "Maybe we blew it and maybe we didn't," he stated. Mel took the words out of my mouth. By now I'd worked with this big

German enough to know a lot about the way his mind worked.

"Okay, come out with it," I stated.

"Tanner is going to tell his cohorts we were there. He may have been cocky at the end of our contact but don't let him fool you, he's scared. He was nervous, shaking, and sweating it. He'll tell his cohorts about the return to Ohio deal we laid on him. There's a lot of them. You can bet all of them won't see this thing the same as Tanner does. We're back to the 'weak link' thing again. There's bound to be one of them that will break. One who knows he's better off to come down and see Reuben rather than go to the big federal court," Weis stated.

"I agree Melvin, we've got to make sure it goes exactly that way. We've got to figure out who's the weakest link and go from there," I stated.

"Oh, we're going to nail every one of these xo#xos, Mr. B – count on it," Weis stated.

I knew when I heard that kind of German determination in Mel Weis's voice, it was good as done. However, little did I realize how long the investigation ahead of us would take.

"I'm ready for a cup of coffee," I stated as we crossed the state line entering Ohio.

"Cup of coffee? I'm ready for a cold beer. We're going to the Eagles," Weis stated. We went to the County Court in Montpelier and parked our state vehicle. We commandeered my wife's car and went to the Eagles Club where we had a beer or two – well, actually we got about half "snockered." During our beer drinking session, Weis stated, "I'll call my C.I. in a couple of days. He'll know how much we stirred things up in Michigan. He's right in the middle of them."

The following Sunday, Weis phoned me at home. "I've talked to my C.I., Tanner has visited everyone of his cohorts. He's telling them the Feds are after them. He's telling them not to talk. We've stirred them up; three of them – Taylor, Snyder, and Sparks are moving to Oregon," Mel related.

"Did your C.I. know if Tanner told them about the voluntary return to Ohio deal?" I asked.

"He didn't say anything about it even when I asked. It's safe to say he didn't hear anything," Weis replied.

"I suggest we return to Michigan and stir things up a little more," I stated.

"Like how?" Weis responded.

"By going door to door around each of their homes. We'll talk to their neighbors about what they may have witnessed each of them do. Like, did you ever see him unloading a deer when the season was closed? – and so on. If we find a good witness or two that's well and good. The main thing is to stir things up more. A good percentage of these people are going straight to our target when we leave. We'll do this, then lay off for awhile. Let nature take its course," I stated.

"A good idea Mr. B – we'll do it. We'll split them down the middle.

We'll work separately. When we get done, we'll let them stew for awhile," Weis replied.

We followed this plan to a "T." We plotted each of our targets residence's on a Hillsdale County map with the aid of a Hillsdale County Census directory. We divided them 50/50 and hit the road. During the subsequent days, we made thirty contacts with neighbors of the suspects including Tanner's. We made most of these "door to door" contacts during the evening hours when we were more likely to find our contacts at home. We left our business cards with our phone number with each contact. We added a little salt and pepper and put the pot on the back burner to simmer.

I was called out of my work area to participate in a take down raid following the close of an undercover investigation in District 3 at Akron, Ohio. Trumbill County, on the Pennsylvania state line, was the principle "theater of operations" for this covert investigation of a deer and waterfowl selling ring. The investigation was brilliantly designed and engineered by Ben Anderson, Chief of the statewide Law Enforcement Section at the time of the raid, District 3 Law Enforcement Supervisor when the investigation started.

At the raid briefing station, I met Tim Hood for the first time since we both worked at Delaware. Tim was the Game Protector assigned to Trumbill County. Later he would transfer to Defiance County where he worked with Mel Weis. What a combination! Still later in 1969, Hood went to work for Michigan State Fish and Game. Of all places, he was assigned to Hillsdale County and was still working next to Mel Weis. Then in 1974 he went to work for Washington State Fish and Game where he remained until retirement.

"This kid (Hood) is one bear-cat of a Game Warden," Lou Grubb, one of the Wildlife Enforcement Agents in District 3 told me.

A raid team consisted of a Wildlife Enforcement Agent and two Game Protectors. At the beginning of the raid briefing session, Ben Anderson gave a presentation on the background intelligence leading to the investigation. Then he presented the undercover operative who worked the case. He was none other than Bill Schroeder, the Private Detective from Dayton, Ohio, I cited into court years earlier for shooting a protected bird during the duck season at the Spring Valley Wildlife Area. Schroeder was contracted by Anderson to do this undercover investigation at the suggestion of Chief, Dale Whitesell. Anderson wanted an individual with a prior wildlife arrest.

Schroeder scanned his audience until he spotted me. He grinned, "Ben told me you'd be here, Ron. Remember me?" he asked.

"Sure do, Bill. You worried about that ticket I gave you keeping you from becoming a Game Warden. Looks like it helped you more than it hindered you," I chuckled.

"You've got that right, Bailey. Thanks for the ticket," Schroeder responded.

With the end of his brief exchange with me, Schroeder plunged head on into the briefing. He gave each raid team detailed information about each target (or subject) of the investigation. A good percentage of the deer illegally taken were actually killed in Pennsylvania. Of particular interest was the fact Schroeder (posing as a contract census taker) ingratiated himself thoroughly with the deer poaching ring leader. This ring leader was, of all things, a school teacher. Schroeder actually moved into the home of this teacher. He witnessed an incestuous relationship between the school teacher and his mother. "Nothing like a close knit family," Schroder noted.

Schroeder's written detailed investigation report covering his entire covert investigation of approximately twenty months was a volume.

Anderson and his Columbus staff completely dismantled the Schroeder report. Every page pertaining to a particular subject was assembled and given to the raid team who would later arrest the subject and bring him to court. Based on the information in the report, the raid teams wrote all the affidavits for search warrants, search warrants and affidavits charging offenses for each subject they were assigned to arrest. Blanket approvals were issued by the court for all search warrants. All charges and search warrants were reviewed and approved by an Assistant Ohio Attorney General, then filed with the court. Any contested cases would be prosecuted by this same Assistant Attorney General. Special arrangements were made with the court to try each defendant soon after his arrest. Judge Dale Williams, Cortland, Ohio presiding. The trials went on day and night with Schroeder testifying hours on end. Most plead guilty.

My raid team had two subjects to arrest and bring before the court. We apprehended one at work and one at home. We had one search to conduct that produced a quantity of venison. We brought both our defendants before the court where they plead guilty to all they were charged with. The venison seized was tagged and placed in a common repository. Both received maximum penalties. All the defendants I saw brought in plead guilty and received maximum penalties.

I never forgot the way Ben Anderson designed and engineered this case, particularly the raid at the close of the investigation. It would be emulated many times in years hence, by my Federal Agents and I, during the 1980's in North and South Carolina.

At the close of the case, Bill Schroeder was assigned as a full time Game Protector. He didn't last in this position long. For some reason he resigned and I never heard from him again.

"255 from 296," Weis radioed. I was north of Wauseon, Ohio, returning to Williams County after my week long assignment in Trumbill County.

"I'll meet you at your house," Weis (296) stated.

"Q-22," I replied. I arrived home and got in Weis's patrol vehicle.

"Your door to door idea worked, Mr. B. The C.I. says they're humming like bees in Michigan. Three of them supposedly moved to Oregon. The C.I. thinks our weakest link is Beyerly. The next weakest is Jones but he's half nuts. It's time to go back to Michigan. We'll put the "B" on Beyerly first," Weis stated.

"Okay, we'll start tomorrow morning. How about the Michigan Game

Warden in Hillsdale County? Isn't it time to bring him in on this thing?" I asked.

"I hate to say this B, but 'no', we can't bring him into it. He's a nice guy, not far from retirement. I know him well and I like him, but he doesn't understand after-the-fact investigating and all that goes with it. He thinks he has to witness a violation to make the case; just can't grasp after-the-fact investigating. I've gone to Hillsdale County many times on this type of investigation, mostly for pheasant and deer violations. I've got all of them to return to Ohio and face charges because they didn't want to go to Alcatraz or Leavenworth (chuckle). I find them; put the 'B' on them and cite them into court in Ohio. They always come to Ohio and usually post and forfeit a bond; case closed. He (the Michigan Warden) knows how I operate. He just looks at me and shakes his head – says he doesn't know how I do it. I won't go into any particular cases that I tried to involve him in. The bottom line is, he won't help us nor will he hurt us. So we'll proceed and brief him when it's all over. If we can throw him a cut and dried pork chop, that's fine," Weis explained.

"What about Indiana?" I asked.

"That's a different story. John Conrad (Supervisor) and his boys will take the ball and run with it. When they've come to Williams County after a poacher, they know I'll not only help, but the bad guy's had it," Weis continued.

Weis and I agreed to meet the next day at his residence and go to Michigan. I went downtown to Judge Rueben Hayward's Court and my Shirley June. Had to get hold of that girl – I'd been gone a week.

The following day, I met Melvin at his home in the early a.m. and we went to Waldron, Michigan. Two of our subjects lived in the vicinity – Dean Beyerly and Don Jones. We located both residences. We called on Mr. Beyerly first. He eagerly agreed to conduct business in our patrol vehicle. He didn't want his spouse to hear anything about his association with Tanner. Beyerly was nervous. He was definitely a weak link and it didn't take long to realize it. He went down like the proverbial "fat hog."

He admitted to involvement in the illegal taking of two deer in Ohio. Upon detailed questioning, we established the exact location and estimated dates of both kills in Ohio. On both occasions, he was in the company of Tanner and Bullock. He admitted he "pulled the trigger" on a big doe and held the light while Bullock shot a spike buck. He admitted both deer were transported to Michigan. He admitted he took and consumed the spike buck. He stated Tanner and Bullock kept the big doe and gave parts of it away.

Oddly, he claimed he didn't know Don Jones who lived nearby. We took a signed statement recording his admissions. It was witnessed by both officers. We mutually agreed on a date and time for Beyerly to meet me at Judge Hayward's Court. He lived up to the agreement and posted a $400.00 appearance bond with the Court Clerk. He didn't appear for court.

Next, we went to the Don Jones residence. Jones proved to be a tenant farmer, originally a native of Kentucky. "(Informant's name) says this guy is half nuts. For some reason he thinks he'll spill the beans," Weis stated before exiting our patrol car. Weis went up the steps to a very large front porch that reached both corners of the house. He knocked and the door was promptly opened by a young woman. For some stupid reason, I lagged behind remaining at the foot of the porch steps. We "badged" the young lady, identifying ourselves as Federal U.S. Deputy Game Wardens.

"We're here to talk to Don Jones," Weis stated. Before Weis could say anything else, the lady slammed the door shut. We both knew something was bad wrong.

"Get down B, something's not right!" Weis stated as he stepped to the right side of the doorway – his back to the side of the house.

I took one step towards the patrol car when the door burst open with Jones half naked, coming through it carrying a shotgun with the business end of the barrel pointed directly at me. Jones didn't know what hit him. In one of the fastest moves I've ever seen, Weis grabbed the fore stock and barrel of Jones' shotgun and twisted it out of Jones' grasp. At the same time, using the gun as a "push pole," he shoved Jones off the porch on his butt. Mel immediately unloaded the shotgun; a 12 gauge Stevens single shot, loaded with .00 buckshot. He placed the cartridge in his pocket, then removed it and threw it into a nearby wooded area. Weis started to wrap Jones' shotgun around a porch pillar, then quickly caught himself and didn't execute the shotgun's destruction. In the meantime, I pounced on Jones and sat on him after executing a single blow up side his head. A blow, I don't believe hurt him as much as it did my fist.

Jones yelled, "My butt hurts, I lit on the tail of my backbone."

I let him up. Not a big man I noticed, but darn sure a dangerous one. I thought, this guy is crazy.

"Looks like we got off on the wrong foot, tiger," Weis told Jones.

"I meant you fellows no harm. I thought you were some kin I'm havin' trouble with," the now quiet and docile Jones stated.

"You knew good and well who we were. We identified ourselves to the lady who answered the door. She told you who we were, didn't she?" I asked.

Jones didn't answer the question. We escorted him to our patrol vehicle and placed him in the passenger's seat. Weis seated himself behind the wheel and I got in the backseat.

Jones was afflicted with stuttering. He started running off the head about planting soybeans, raising hogs, and I can't recall what else. The more he talked (about nothing), the more he stuttered. I heard Weis mumble, "Nuts, he's nuts."

Then Weis shouted, "Shut up, we're here to talk about the deer you and Larry Tanner shot in Ohio, not your crops. How many deer did you shoot?" Weis asked Jones.

"T-T-T-Two," Jones replied.

"How many times did you go to Ohio with Tanner or anyone else jack lighting deer?" I asked.

"T-T-T-Three times," Jones answered.

"On what dates," I asked. I was amazed this nitwit immediately reeled off three separate dates with the two deer killed on consecutive nights.

"You got two deer in three trips, correct?" I asked.

"Y-Y-Y-Yep, two deer, three trips," Jones reiterated.

"You got both deer on consecutive nights. What took place on the third night hunt?" I asked. Did you kill anything that night?" I asked.

"A d-d-d-damned white cat," Jones answered. "Didn't see one d-d-d deer, not one," Jones replied.

"Who actually shot the two deer?" I asked.

"M-M-M-Me. Larry took me so I could get some deer meat," Jones replied.

"Who was with you besides Tanner?" Weis asked.

"R-R-R-Randy Bullock, every time," Jones stuttered. Jones went on to confirm the three hunts were in Tanner's truck with Tanner doing the driving and operating the spotlight part of the time. He claimed Bullock held the light when he (Jones) shot two deer. Upon detailed questioning, he described certain landmarks that firmly established both deer (does) were killed in Ohio. Jones claimed he and family consumed most of both deer but still had some steaks left. We told him to tell the lady of the house (standing on the front porch) to get the deer steaks. She complied. What a mess the steaks were in. Jones obviously processed his own deer. We were convinced the meat was spoiled but we tagged it as evidence and later froze it until after we processed Jones through court. Weis returned Jones' shotgun by laying it, with the action broken open, on Jones' front porch. We didn't take a signed confession from Jones although we should have. All this excitement with Jones was before 9:00 a.m.

"We're clickin', Mr. B, I'm glad he's down – nuts, he's absolutely nuts," Weis proclaimed as we left the Jones farm.

"Gotta keep rollin', Melvin. We'll soon be in the driver's seat. Two down, not a bad morning's work," I stated.

"I'll talk to (C.I.) tomorrow and we'll go from there. So far, we've taken down two dumb ones. You can bet it won't stay that way," Melvin advised.

Jones later went through the same bond forfeiture procedure as Beyerly in Judge Reuben Hayward's Court. Clerk, Shirley June Bailey presiding.

We decided the next step was to check out the three Tanner accomplices that the C.I. informed moved to Oregon -- Stanley Taylor, Len Sparks, and Fred Snyder. They had resided near Frontier, Michigan. According to the C.I., each had poached at least one deer in Ohio while in the company of Tanner and Bullock. We hoped they hadn't moved yet and we could nail the coffin shut on all three.

We went to Frontier, Michigan arriving before 11:00 a.m. All three of our suspect's residences were vacant. Their former neighbors informed us each hurriedly and unexpectedly moved. A check at the Post Office revealed none of the three left a forwarding address. We ran down relatives of two of the three, who would only say they thought they (Taylor and Snyder) had moved to central Oregon and were going to work in the timber industry. We were unable to find any of Len Sparks family members. One of his former neighbors described Sparks as a loner and very odd. We ultimately forwarded all the information we had to the Oregon State Police; the agency that enforces Oregon's Fish and Game Laws. Our report stated they were reported deer poachers wanted in Ohio for questioning for violations of the Lacey Act, Ohio and Michigan wildlife laws.

Weis remained on the lookout for these three outlaws (hoping they'd return) until the day he retired. Although the statute of limitations ran out, I know as sure as I write this, Weis would have nailed them for something if they returned.

I returned home that evening, Shirley told me Lonnie Heath phoned and asked I return his call, regardless of how late it was. I returned his call at 9:00 p.m.

"Mr. Bailey, I'd like to meet with you and get some matters settled," Lonnie stated.

"Like deer matters, Lonnie?" I asked.

"That's right, Mr. Bailey. My neighbor gave me your card. I can't afford to have you up here asking any more questions. I'm rather proud of the reputation my family and I have in the Camden community. I've hurt that reputation and I don't want this issue to go any further," Lonnie stated in a very matter of fact and polite manner.

"I understand, Lonnie, and I stand ready to help you. I believe your situation can be handled very quickly and quietly. Do you know where Judge Reuben Hayward's Court is in Montpelier, Ohio?" I asked.

"Yes sir, I do. Larry Tanner told me where it is," Lonnie responded.

"Who told you?" I asked not believing what I thought I heard.

"Larry Tanner told me," Lonnie replied.

My mind went into high gear. Tanner told him? Should I feel Lonnie out and try to determine if Tanner was ready to talk? Something deep inside me said, back off – not yet.

"That was nice of Larry. He's made a few mistakes but down deep he's a pretty good guy and wants to do the right thing when it's all said and done," I told Lonnie while that small voice inside said, "That's enough – no more!" He'll tell Tanner what I've said, I hoped.

"Okay Lonnie, meet me at Judge Hayward's Court in Montpelier at 9:00 a.m. tomorrow," I stated.

"I'll be there," Lonnie replied.

I phoned Weis and told him about the Heath contact. "That's good B, the ball is in our court. Let's keep on scoring," Weis responded.

At 9:00 a.m. sharp, Lonnie Heath accompanied by an unknown subject, met me at Judge Hayward's Court on Main Street in Montpelier. Following greetings, Lonnie introduced me to none other than Ted Shrader, another target of our now shifting into second gear, investigation.

"Ted wants to talk to you," Lonnie stated.

"That's fine. We'll certainly talk to Ted," I responded as we entered an empty office (arranged by Shirley June) and sat down. I excused myself for a moment -- went to my patrol car and radioed Weis.

"255 -- 296," I transmitted.

"296 go ahead," Weis answered.

"I've got two birds here. Could use your help," I transmitted.

"Be there in five," Weis replied.

I returned to the Court. "Ted, very shortly another officer will be here to talk to you. His name is Mel Weis. With an officer for each of you to talk to, we won't take up much of your time," I stated. We shared a few pleasantries. Shortly Weis arrived and invited Ted Shrader to his patrol vehicle where they could communicate in private.

Upon polite questioning, Lonnie Heath talked freely. He was a farmer with a degree in agriculture. He admitted jack lighting a six point buck in Ohio during the closed season from County Road S. He was in the company of Tanner and Bullock when the incident took place. Tanner drove -- Bullock held the light. They were in Tanner's pickup truck. They transported the buck to Michigan. He estimated this event occurred a year earlier. He had the rack from the buck; the meat was consumed. (He later gave the rack to Weis.) He admitted holding the light on a subsequent occasion while Bullock shot a yearling. He stated the yearling was transported to Michigan. He stated Bullock kept the yearling. I took a signed statement from Heath confirming his admissions. I witnessed Heath's signature with mine. He posted and forfeited a $400.00 bond.

Shortly Weis and Shrader returned to the office. Weis obtained a statement similar to Heath's. The difference being Shrader killed a doe. Tanner drove while Bullock held the light. Shrader claimed he accompanied Tanner and Bullock on one hunt. He pinpointed the date the violation occurred. He gave an exact location in Ohio where the deer was illegally shot. Shrader posted and forfeited a $200.00 bond.

Next, on the advice of Weis's C.I., we turned our attention to Dick Smith. The C.I. felt Smith was the next weakest link in the chain and we had to take his word for it. Our batting average was pretty good so far.

Smith was a big red haired and red faced farm boy from the vicinity of Montgomery, Michigan who worked part time for Tanner. We contacted Smith at home and invited him to accompany us to my patrol car, after identifying ourselves as U.S. Deputy Game Wardens. En route to the vehicle, Smith stopped and yelled, "What's this all about?" A simple and logical question for one in his position, but asked in a very belligerent manner.

"You know good and well what this is about. Get in the car before I shove your head up your xo#x!" Weis stated.

"Said your name was Mel Weis, didn't you? From what I've heard, I guess you could shove my head up my xo#x, but you'd have your hands full," Smith said chuckling.

"Why don't we try and see, tiger," Weis replied taking a step toward Smith. Smith took three steps and entered our car through the front passengers side door I held open. I slid behind the wheel. Weis got in the back seat behind Smith – a seating position we took many times. Weis explained once, "In case you have to give him a rabbit punch."

Before Weis or I could say anything, Smith blurted, "Okay, how many of these pieces of Michigan xo#x came to Ohio and paid the tariff for their deer killing spree?"

Wow! he'd caught me – not off guard, but surprised at this statement out of this Michigan tough guy.

"F-f" I started to say four." "Seven!" Weis interrupted (a lie).

"Well, make me number eight. Now let's talk turkey. I don't want any part of any federal court. You know I work some for Larry. He's told me all about that federal court. Let's deal – how much is this mess going to cost me?" Smith asked.

"According to your cohorts and the evidence we've gathered, you're up to your neck in this thing. It's hard for me to believe you've killed or been involved in killing so many deer in Ohio, not to mention Michigan and Indiana," I told Smith hoping he'd grab the bait and pull the bobber under.

He ran with the bait and pulled the bobber clear out of site replying, "You listen to me, not them. I only killed two illegal deer in Ohio and none in Indiana. What I've killed in Michigan is none of your business. I didn't cross any state line with those. Besides, darn few Michigan deer I've killed were out of season."

"Yes, but what about the big doe – you shot it in Indiana, didn't you?" I asked (a bluff).

"I got that big doe on the Boy Scout Reservation in Ohio. Whoever told you I got it in Indiana is a liar," Smith answered as he pulled the bobber under again.

I pulled my notebook out of my right shirt pocket; leafed through several pages stopping at one page and pretended I was referring to my notes. "Okay, here's another Ohio deer – a big buck - - - -," I trailed the sentence off acting like I was continuing to read.

"I didn't kill no big buck. The second deer I got was another doe – a smaller one than the first," Smith responded as under the bobber went again.

"Okay, let me get this straight. Perhaps we've been given wrong information. You killed two doe deer in Ohio and brought them home to Michigan. Both instances were in December after the rut, correct?" I asked (a bluff).

"That's right, two does. I'm sure it was in December," Smith replied.

"You killed two does after the November rut. It's safe to assume both were pregnant. So in essence, given the quality of the deer range, you actually killed six deer, including at least four fawns the two does would have given birth too. Who was with you besides Tanner and Bullock?" I asked.

"No one. Bullock wasn't there, just me and Larry. I wouldn't hunt with any of those guys Larry ran with. They all talked too much," Smith responded.

Whew! If this statement was true, we had only one witness as far as Smith was concerned – Larry Tanner. However, with the bluff questioning, we had him for two Ohio deer by his own admission.

"You actually shot both does while Larry held the light?" I asked.

"No, Larry held the light on the big doe. I held the light and shot the little doe – just plunked her between the eyes," Smith stated.

"How many times did you and Larry jack light in Ohio?" I asked.

"Probably four or five times. We only saw deer on two nights. I got the does on these two nights. The other times were heavy snow – bitter cold – the deer weren't moving," Smith replied.

"Anything left of the two does?" Weis asked.

"No, we ate the big doe and I gave the little one to some people who needed the meat," Smith replied.

"Noble of you," I stated, deciding we wouldn't push the second deer any further. It meant an illegal possession charge against poor folks who needed the meat. I glanced at Weis in the back seat. He gave me the nod saying, "good enough, let's move on."

Dick, you indicated at the get-go you wanted to come to Ohio and settle this matter with the Ohio Court. We're going to let you do that rather than prosecute you in U.S. District Court," I stated.

"I appreciate it," Smith responded.

"Do you know where the Court is in Montpelier, Ohio?" Weis asked.

"No," Smith replied.

"Okay. you can find the Police Station. Meet Bailey there at 9:00 a.m. tomorrow?" Weis stated.

"I'll be there, how much is this going to cost me?" Smith asked.

"That's up to the Court, I'd suggest you have a thousand available," Weis replied.

"That's too steep, can't we talk about this?" Smith asked.

"Here's where you're confused, Dick. The penalty or bond is not a matter you negotiate with us. This is between you and the Court. Officer Weis suggested an amount you have available just to be safe," I replied.

"Okay, I'll be there in the morning," Smith stated.

I wrote a statement recording all Smith admitted concerning the taking and transport of the two Ohio deer. I read the statement to him; he signed it; Weis and I witnessed his signature. We bid Mr. Smith farewell and departed.

We traveled two miles south of Montgomery on Rt. 49, when Weis stated, "Pull over B." I complied. Weis changed positions from the back seat to the passenger's seat before leaving Dick Smith's. He exited and stood in front of the vehicle. He rolled his pant legs up to just below his knees. He shook one foot then the other, rolled his pant legs down and re-entered the vehicle.

"What was that all about?" I asked.

"Just cleaning all the crap you spread back there off my feet and legs. What a load of crap; it worked B. -- he went down. I saw you were sailing pretty good on that one and decided to keep my mouth shut and let you sail – good job B.," Weis stated.

"All in a days work, Melvin," I responded. We filed affidavits in Judge Reuben Hayward's Court against Smith. He was charged with two separate counts of killing a doe deer during the closed season with the aid and use of an artificial light from a motor vehicle with firearms in possession. We added one additional charge for "attempting to take" during the closed season to cover the unsuccessful hunts. His bond came to $600.00. The following day Smith met us at the Montpelier, Ohio Police Department at 9:00 a.m. We escorted him to Judge Reuben Hayward's Court where he posted a $600.00 bond without hesitation. Court Clerk, Shirley June Bailey presiding.

During this investigation, Weis and I had many other investigations and patrols to work. We worked through a complete cycle of upland game, waterfowl, big game and fishing seasons. I continually left Williams County on investigative and patrol forays in my other assigned counties.

I was plagued with a time consuming and complicated fish kill investigation on the Auglaize River in Defiance County. With the advance of cold winter weather and ice conditions, especially near its confluence with the Maumee River at Defiance, a continuing fish kill occurred under the ice.

Ultimately, I was able to show this unusual fish kill was caused by the beet sugar industry many miles upstream. Several beat sugar companies were responsible. This effluent, although treated and pronounced safe at the source, ultimately caused high BOD's (biological oxygen demands) many miles downstream. Combined with the natural occurrence of cold weather and ice, the fish kill occurred. The dollar damages associated with this fish kill ran into the thousands. I recommended a $60,000.00 penalty pro-rated and assessed the beet sugar processors. The case was submitted for civil litigation. The outcome was still pending when I left Ohio and entered the federal service. I worked several severe fish kill investigations on the Maumee River and tributary streams, obtaining successful prosecutions on all of them. I remember the Auglaize River fish kill investigation as the most difficult.

Another important case involved the Campbell Soup Company at Napoleon, Ohio and their high BOD effluent entering the Maumee River. Following litigation, the company cleaned up their act as the result of an investigation I was a part of. A much cleaner Maumee River today has seen the return of its great walleye runs from Lake Erie as well as the return of other game fish populations.

It's comforting to return to Ohio today and see the results of the Ohio Division of Wildlife's pollution abatement programs of the 1960's, under the leadership of Chief, Dale Whitesell. He completely changed the manner in which pollution investigations causing fish kills were conducted. The investigation procedure prior to Whitesell, had the biological folks in charge of the investigation. The tendency was to "work with" the polluter. It didn't work. Whitesell placed the law enforcement folks (Wildlife Enforcement Agents) in charge of each fish kill investigation. Whitesells' new concept worked. Law enforcement people understood one thing above all else. To put it simple – gather provable evidence and prosecute the polluter in either criminal or civil court, according to the appropriate culpability standards. The biological folks gathered the evidence proving the case and turned their evidence over to the Wildlife Enforcement Agent who litigated it. The program was an overwhelming success. Major polluters all over Ohio "went down", one by one. Ohio waters are far cleaner today than they were when I grew up in the Buckeye State. My favorite stream, the Kokosing – a good small mouth stream in the 50's and 60's is still better today.

Weis and I soon found ourselves in the middle of another state line deer poaching investigation. This time further south and involved the Indiana and Michigan state lines.

"255 from 296," Weis called by radio about 2:00 p.m.

"255, go ahead," I replied.

"A lady called who lives on Rt. 6 near Edgerton. She saw two white males load a doe into a tan Ford pickup, beside the woods across the road from her house this morning. She wrote the license number down -- it's an Indiana plate. I'm coming to Montpelier, I'll fill you in when I get to your headquarters. We need to roll on this one right away," Weis radioed. He soon arrived.

"I've ran the Indiana plate. It checks out to (I'll call him) Jose Alvarez, Elkhart, Indiana on a '62 Ford pickup. I've contacted Indiana Fish and Game; their officer at Goshen, Indiana called me. He'll meet us at the junction of the Turnpike and Rt. 15 northeast of Elkhart. He thinks he knows Alvarez. He says he'll have Alvarez and hopefully the deer located by the time we get there," Weis stated.

We headed west on the Turnpike in my patrol car. Bad weather was setting in – freezing rain. I should state, Mel, although he could drive fast when he had to, could be labeled a conservative driver. He certainly didn't like bad roads and driving conditions, especially with someone else at the wheel. Needless to say traffic on the Turnpike moves at a fast pace. We had ninety miles to travel with road conditions worsening. As the freezing rain hit my windshield, Weis started, "Now, B, watch the road, be careful, oh, ho-ho-ho, I don't know if we should be making this trip or not—xo#x it B – be careful," Weis stated as we watched a snow plow pass us obviously en route from a stand-by location.

Slowed somewhat by the adverse road conditions, we arrived at our appointed location 6:00 p.m. We parked at the place of business designated by Indiana Wildlife Officer, Ray Zeke. Forty-five minutes later, Officer Zeke arrived. We entered his vehicle -- he apologized for being late explaining it took longer than expected to locate Alvarez. He recently moved from Elkhart to Mottville, Michigan. Zeke obtained directions to Alvarez's present residence near Mottville from a former working partner. He ascertained Alvarez was working at a location near Hicksville, Ohio where he stayed during the week and came home on weekends.

Officer Zeke asked, "Do you gentlemen carry U. S. Deputy Game Warden commissions?"

We both answered "yes".

"Good, let's go to Mottville. Hopefully we'll get your Mr. Alvarez and your Ohio deer," he stated.

I went to my vehicle and got two flashlights and my briefcase containing statement, consent to search, and citation forms; then returned to the Indiana Officer's vehicle. Weis got in the back seat, I sat in the front passenger's seat. Off we went to Mottville, Michigan – two Ohio Wildlife Officers and one Indiana Wildlife Officer, now acting under authority of our U.S. Deputy Game Warden Commissions, enforcing the Federal Lacey Act. All indications were, the deer crossed two state lines.

Officer Zeke's driving indicated he competed in the Indianapolis 500. He was a wild man – skidding around curves, going like xo#o down the straight away on the paved and gravel roads. Roads that took us to Mottville, Michigan and Jose Alvarez's home located in a remote area south of Mottville.

During this wild ride on roads in horrible conditions, Melvin T. could be heard loud and clear concerning Officer Zeke's driving. "Oh-ho-ho-ho! Oh boy! We're not gonna make it. Oh xo#o! Look at this curve coming up - - - Whew! Oh no! We made it. Oh-ho-ho! Here we go again – there's no way he's gonna' handle this one – Whew! Oh, boy, made it again. This is bad – real bad, etc." Weis continued the entire trip.

What's his problem?" Zeke whispered.

"Your driving. You've got Weis scared to death. Frankly, you've got me scared to death. If we arrive at our destination in one piece, I hope you've got some toilet paper – we're gonna need it," I answered.

"I'm trying to get us to the deer as soon as possible. As cold as it's been, there's a good possibility they haven't processed it yet. Maybe we can get the deer still whole," Zeke stated.

Immediately Zeke turned right onto a gravel road. We traveled one quarter mile when he suddenly turned left into a short driveway leading to the Alvarez home.

I saw it immediately – a fresh doe head and hide lying beside the steps to the front porch. The tan '62 Ford pickup bearing the reported Indiana license plate was parked in front of us. Daylight long since left. The house was dark – no light visible anywhere. Without speaking a word, we exited Zeke's patrol vehicle with flashlights in hand. Weis went to the bed of the pickup, "It's all here boys – hair and blood," he stated. I went to the front door and knocked, Zeke took a position behind me with his hand on his revolver. Shortly one light then another went on. The front door opened. A tall black haired male stated, "Who are you and what do you want at this time of night."

"Are you Jose Alvarez?" I asked.

"Yes, who wants to know?" Alvarez asked.

I showed Alvarez my federal badge and stated, "Federal Game Wardens – did anyone other than you drive this Ford pickup today?"

"Only me and my son," Alvarez answered.

"How old is your son?" I asked.

"Fifteen, sir," Alvarez answered.

"We'll give you a minute to dress. Then we'll discuss the doe deer you brought here from Ohio. We'll discuss it in our patrol car," I stated.

"Yes sir, did you say you were Federales?" Alvarez asked.

"Yes, we're Deputy Federal Game Wardens," I replied.

"Yes sir, I'll be right out," Alvarez responded.

The gentleman seemed scared. Years later I found out why. Agents of the Fish & Wildlife Service told me about working joint white winged dove hunts with Mexican Federal Game Wardens or "Federales" in Mexico. The Federales checked hunters from a wagon equipped with a machine gun mounted on a tripod. The hunters were ordered to line up with their licenses in hand ready for inspection as a Federale seated himself behind the machine gun. Needless to say, the hunters (American and Mexican) complied.

Alvarez appeared; we escorted him to Officer Zeke's patrol car and seated him in the front passenger's seat. Upon questioning, Alvarez stated he and his son worked near Edgerton, Ohio before their present work location near Hicksville. They noticed many deer while working near Edgerton and decided to take the biggest one home to eat. He admitted the deer head and hide laying near his porch steps came from this deer. The rest of the deer was quartered and hanging in a small building beside his house. We told Mr. Alvarez his deer was seized. We explained his option of voluntarily returning to Ohio and resolving this matter or going to U.S. District Court and answer to Federal Lacey Act charges. He elected to return to Ohio. I prepared a statement recording Alvarez's story. He signed it along with a consent to search form -- all Officers witnessed his signature. I told him he could keep his gun (.22 Magnum). We seized the venison quarters, head and hide, placed all in plastic bags Officer Zeke had in the trunk of his car.

Weis instructed Alvarez to meet me in Montpelier, Ohio at 10:00 a.m. the following day for the purpose of posting an appearance bond. The bond and court appearance procedure was explained to him.

Alvarez stated, "I'll be there."

We loaded our evidence in the trunk of Officer Zeke's patrol car and departed. Again, Officer Zeke drove like a bat out of xo#x the entire distance back to my patrol car.

As before, Officer Melvin T. moaned and groaned about Zeke's driving. Upon arrival at our patrol car, we transferred our bags of evidence to our vehicle. We thanked Officer Zeke for his assistance and headed back to Ohio as a gentle snow fell.

At 9:00 a.m. the next morning, I swore to and filed charges against

Jose Alvarez for illegally taking and possessing a doe white tail deer during the closed season. His bond was set at $400.00 by Judge Reuben Hayward. At 9:45 a.m., Alvarez appeared at the Court. He posted the $400.00 bond and advised Judge Hayward he would not return for his Court hearing. His bond was forfeited; Weis delivered the deer meat to the County Home where processing was completed and it was placed in their freezers for consumption. Case closed.

We turned our attention to the Camden, Michigan deer poaching ring. In particular, subjects Joe Hines and Tom Turner. The fact we saved Randy Bullock and Larry Tanner until last was a given.

After the "exciting" Dick Smith contact, we decided to get Hines and Turner to come to Ohio for questioning. It would be nice to get both off their home turf. I contacted Hines by phone. With little discussion, he agreed to meet me the following day at Judge Hayward's Court where the Judge gave us an interview room. Weis made similar arrangements with Tom Turner. Both showed up at the Court the following day at 5:30 p.m. I interviewed Hines in my patrol vehicle. Weis interviewed Turner in the room provided by the Court. Both Hines and Turner proved to be rather insignificant players. Neither admitted to shooting a deer in Ohio and transporting it back to Michigan. Both clearly admitted to aiding and abetting others (Tanner and Bullock) in the unlawful attempts to take deer in Ohio by the aid and use of a spotlight from a motor driven conveyance on a public road with firearms in possession. Both claimed their assisting efforts didn't result in taking a deer. Both indicated a willingness to plead guilty to an attempt to take charge if we would assure them the matter was over with and they wouldn't have to go to Federal Court. Naturally we gave both the assurances.

Weis said to me in private, "I'll phone Reuben and get him down here -- we'll slide these two through in a hurry."

Shortly, Judge Reuben Haywood arrived at the Court. "Been a while since you called on the Court after hours, Melvin – got a couple of bad characters?" Judge Hayward asked.

"Not too bad, Judge. These two boys would like to plead guilty to these affidavits we've just drawn up," Weis told Judge Hayward as he and the Judge entered his office closing the door. Shortly both emerged carrying the affidavits charging Hines and Turner.

"Call Court to session Officer Bailey," Judge Hayward ordered.

This was a first for me. I had never called Court to session before; however, I gave it my best shot.

"All rise! The Northern District Court for Williams County, Ohio is now in session. The Honorable Judge Reuben Hayward presiding," I announced as the Judge entered the Courtroom and seated himself behind the bench. "You may be seated," I announced.

"It's my understanding from talking with our State Game Protector, Mel Weis, you gentlemen are residents of the State of Michigan. Correct?" Judge Hayward asked the defendants Hines and Turner.

149

"That's correct," both answered.

"I have before me one charge on each of you. You're each charged with attempting to take a white tail deer during the closed season on or about November 15th in Bridgewater Township within Williams County, Ohio. This means you came to Ohio from Michigan and tried to kill a deer illegally but you were not successful. Correct?" Judge Hayward asked.

"That's correct," both answered.

"I'm told by Officer Weis you could also be charged with aiding and abetting others in the unlawful attempt to take deer in Ohio. This charge will not be brought against you because of your cooperation. Do you understand this?" Judge Hayward asked.

"We understand your Honor," both answered.

"I understand you wish to plead guilty to the first offense I've brought to your attention. Correct?" Judge Hayward asked.

"Correct your Honor," both answered.

"Very well, the Court accepts your guilty plea. You're each assessed $200.00 plus Court costs. Are you able to pay your fine at this time?" Judge Hayward asked. Hines and Turner indicated they could pay their fines.

"Court is adjourned!" Judge Hayward stated.

Two more down and two to go (we thought at that time) – Tanner and Bullock. Weis's C.I. stated during an earlier contact, Bullock bragged to his fellow Michigan deer poachers he would kill Mel Weis if he ever came near him. Based on this deadly threat, we decided to go after Tanner and save Bullock until later.

"Larry, I'm sure you know most of your deer poaching accomplices voluntarily returned to Ohio and answered to illegal deer taking charges. Not one forced our hand concerning Federal charges. Now it's your turn – we have a ton of evidence against you. What will it be, State or Federal Court?" I asked Tanner by phone.

"I want to make a deal with Ohio like Dick Smith did. I don't need to go to Federal Court," I wasn't surprised at Tanner's response, but must admit I was relieved. Tanner and I made arrangements to meet the next day at 5:30 p.m. at Judge Hayward's Court in Montpelier. I told Tanner Officer Weis would attend the meeting.

"Reuben's on standby," Weis stated as we met during the after hours of the Court the following day. At 5:30 p.m. sharp, Tanner drove into the parking lot behind the Court. We escorted Tanner to our special interrogation room. I read the signed statements of his deer poaching accomplices. Beyond the statements, we questioned Tanner using our notes containing information received from Tanner's accomplices we didn't take statements from. Tanner cooperated one hundred percent.

"It's all true," he stated. "I'm a business man, it's time to make a deal," he stated.

"Okay Larry, but before we deal, are you willing to give us a signed statement and answer a few more questions?" Weis asked.

"Yes," Tanner replied.

While I began writing a statement that simply acknowledged all the statements from the other principals involved were true, Weis asked, "You aided all the others in the illegal taking of Ohio deer. How many did you actually shoot and take back to Michigan?" Weis asked.

"Only one," Tanner replied. His terse and immediate answer impressed me as being the truth. Not Weis. He continued questioning Tanner concerning how many deer he (personally) actually shot and transported. He remained firm, admitting "only one".

Tanner finally ended this line of questioning by stating "xo#x it, I personally shot one deer – that's it – I can't admit to something I didn't do."

As an after thought and to this day I don't know why, I asked, "Larry, we've discussed (and I named all the subjects of the investigation) – what about the others?"

Tanner replied, "Do you mean Bluegill and But-Cut?"

His response jolted me, "Yeah, I mean Bluegill and But-Cut – you know -- give me their real names?"

"Jimmie Pierce and Andy Thurston," Tanner replied.

"Yeah, those two – they live at - - - (hesitating) - - at - - ," I continued.

"They live in Camden," Tanner responded.

"Yeah, in town," I stated.

"That's right, but Pierce lives in Reading part of the time," Tanner stated.

"What about these two – tell us about your jack lighting forays in Ohio with Jimmie and Andy?" I asked.

"I took these two with me on one occasion each – back when I first started. There were too many trips with too many people – I can't recall anything specific about my trips with Pierce or Thurston," Tanner replied.

"That doesn't help much, Larry. We've got complaints on these two (a lie). Try and remember so we can wrap this whole thing up," I told Tanner.

Tanner continued to claim he couldn't recall the specific events that took place during his hunts with Pierce and Thurston.

"I'm sure we didn't get a deer – I would remember that," he stated. We dropped the Pierce and Thurston matters for the time being.

I continued writing the Tanner statement, adding Pierce and Thurston, plus the fact Tanner had accompanied both on at least one illegal jack lighting trip to Ohio but couldn't recall specific events that took place. (Exactly as Tanner wanted it worded.)

In his statement, Tanner gave information concerning the subjects Stanley Taylor, Fred Snyder and Len Sparks who moved to Oregon. He claimed one, Fred Snyder, killed and transported a deer from Ohio to Michigan with his (Tanner's) assistance. He stated he aided Taylor and Sparks in the attempt to take a deer – neither had killed one.

I completed Tanner's statement. He read it, stated it was true and signed it. Weis and I witnessed his signature.

Next, we negotiated with Tanner on the exact charges he would answer to. It was agreed he would be charged with one count each of aiding and abetting, another in the unlawful attempt to take a white tail deer by the aid and use of an artificial light, during closed season from a motor vehicle with firearms in possession. A total of thirteen attempt to take charges. He would be charged with one count of taking a white tail deer in closed season. We agreed we would recommend a $1500.00 appearance bond set by Judge Hayward.

Weis wrote one "attempt to take" affidavit charging Tanner and ran it through the Court copier twelve times. I wrote one "take" affidavit charging Tanner.

Shortly the Judge arrived. After a short conference with Mel Weis, Judge Hayward set Tanner's bond at the agreed amount of $1500.00. Tanner posted his bond (in cash) and told the Judge he wouldn't appear for trial.

Judge Hayward stated, "The Court will honor your request, your bond is forfeited. This case is closed."

We were left with Randy Bullock and two new suspects – Jim Pierce and Andy Thurston. Our information on Pierce and Thurston was skimpy. We only had Tanner's mention that he hunted with both on one occasion. He claimed he couldn't recall specific information regarding each hunt.

Randy Bullock's time had come. In view of his reported threats on Mel's life, he sure received and got "special" attention. Mel was afraid of no man; however, he was no fool and didn't take threats lightly.

"We're gonna get him processed through one Court or the other, B. After that, I'll deal with him one on one – man to man," Weis stated. (This happened one year after the investigation ended. Mel invited Bullock to meet him at a location on the Broadbeck Estate, later becoming the Lake La-Su-Ann public hunting and fishing area just inside the Ohio State line.

"No weapons, just fist to fist – you and me," was Weis's actual challenge -- Bullock didn't show.)

I was busy cleaning the interior of my patrol vehicle following the close of a very wet and messy deer season when I heard the phone ringing inside the house. "It's all set up Mr. B. The Randy Bullock interview will take place tomorrow evening at 7:00 p.m. at the Hillsdale County (Michigan) Sheriff's Department. The Deputies will pick Bullock up as soon as he's off work and bring him in for questioning. Questioning by you and me if you're available," Weis stated.

"You bet I'm available, Melvin. Don't know how you got this set up but sounds like the way to go," I responded.

"How I got it set up was just a matter of asking. The Hillsdale County Sheriff's Department and Mr. Bullock go way back – they jumped at the opportunity to pick up Bullock. Fish and game or anything else – cooperating one hundred percent. I'll pick you up at five tomorrow," Weis stated.

6:30 p.m. the following day found us at the Hillsdale County Sheriff's Department. At 7:00 p.m. Randy Bullock was ushered into the room where we waited.

"The Sheriff's Department picked me up to talk to you? Why didn't you just come to my house, Weis?" Bullock howled.

"This is the best way to handle it Randy – in view of the threats you've been making. I'll take care of you and your threats later, but now we're here to talk about deer business. You know what I'm talking about, don't you?" Weis asked.

Bullock responded, "Yes."

"All your buddies settled their deer problems with the State of Ohio in Montpelier. They're getting on with their lives. How about you Dynamite? Will it be State or Federal Court -- maybe the Federal Penitentiary? The choice is yours, what will it be?" Weis asked.

"You know the answer, Weis. It's State Court in Montpelier with Judge Hayward," Bullock answered.

Whew! Our big Michigan tough guy was the same as down.

"Tanner says you'll negotiate – I want to negotiate," Bullock stated.

"Slow down Tiger. Yeah, we'll negotiate but we've got a few formalities to go through first. Officer Bailey will read you some hi-lights of a few of the signed confessions your buddies gave us. It's gonna be a little lengthy so light up a cigarette if you smoke. We're interested in your response to the statements, particularly where your involvement is concerned," Weis stated.

"Okay," Bullock stated as he settled back in his chair.

I read the Beyerly statement, excerpts from my notes on the Jones interview, Heath statement, Shroder statement, excerpts from notes on the Hines and Turner interviews and Tanner's statement to Bullock.

"Are the signed statements and other allegations, based on our investigation I've read to you and brought to your attention, true?" I asked.

"Yeah, yeah, it's all true. Let's get on with it. What's the bottom line?" Bullock responded.

"We're not quite to the bottom line yet, Randy. I'm going to write a statement that says the Beyerly, Heath, Schroder and Tanner statements are true. The statement will further state the allegations I read you from my notes on the Jones, Hines and Turner interviews are true. Are you willing to sign this statement?" I asked.

"Write it up," Bullock responded.

I did as quickly as possible. I shoved the statement across the table to Bullock. He read it and signed it. Weis and I witnessed his signature with ours. Time to negotiate.

"Here are the charges we'll file with Judge Hayward," Weis stated. It was clear Melvin already had this matter firm in his mind. "Two charges of taking deer in closed season by jack lighting. Seven charges of attempting to take deer in closed season by aiding another," Weis told Bullock.

"How much?" Bullock asked.

"That will be up to Judge Hayward when you appear before him at 7:00 p.m. tomorrow – be there," Weis stated.

"I'll be there – will he take a check?" Bullock asked.

"Probably, if it bounces, we won't have far to come to get you, will we?" Weis stated.

The following evening at 7:00 p.m., all 280 lbs. of Randy Bullock appeared before Judge Reuben Hayward. The Judge didn't read the affidavits we filed charging Bullock. Judge Hayward told Bullock what the charges were in the same terms used by Weis the day before. The Judge explained the bond forfeiture and trial procedures. He informed Bullock his appearance bond would be $1100.00. Bullock posted his $1100.00 bond and advised Judge Hayward he would not appear for trial.

All the main subjects, except three who moved to Oregon, paid their penalties. But two more names haunted me – Pierce and Thurston. Our information on them was practically nil – only Tanner's vague recollection that he'd been with each, on an illegal "shining" hunt in Ohio.

"Those two are all yours Mr. B., you'll manage to nail them for something – I've got other biz to take care of," Weis stated.

Before I managed to "nail them for something," another adventure for Mel and I happened. We were on a post season jack lighting patrol in northern Williams County. Another patrol unit consisting of Officer Marv Rittenhouse, Fulton County Game Protector and Jerry Richardson, Henry County Game Protector, was on patrol in Fulton County. Around midnight, Rittenhouse and Richardson apprehended two jack lighters in northeastern Fulton County. An hour later, they informed us by radio, they were headed in -- calling it a night. It was a good night with all species of nocturnal wildlife on the move. We continually saw deer, coon, etc. along side and crossing the road. As we neared the Fulton County line, we spotted a light operating. It appeared inside Fulton County. It was visible for miles in the flat prairie terrain. Weis flipped the kill switch off on the brake lights and began working his way towards the light. After crossing the Fulton County line going east, the light was still operating; Weis killed the headlights. We were running black out and had considerable distance to close on the light that finally stopped operating. Traveling on a gravel road we soon became aware we were going through freshly disturbed dust.

Suddenly, less than three tenths of a mile ahead, the lights of a pickup truck came on. The truck apparently stopped beside the road for some reason. We suspected to attend to a freshly killed deer. Traveling west with a light again operating, it scanned each field and woodlot it passed by. Weis closed rapidly on the jack lighter. Just as I said, "Melvin, you're getting too close – he's gonna hit his brake lights and see us," our violator did just that. His brake lights caught the reflection of our darkened headlight lens. Rather than take off as we expected, our violator pulled over on the berm and stopped.

"Move B – move! I'll take the drivers side. You take the passengers side and try to get the gun," Weis ordered as we departed our vehicle and ran towards our violator's stopped vehicle. We both arrived at the same time. I observed a pump action shotgun on the seat beside the driver. I opened the unlocked passenger side door and grabbed the gun. It was a twelve gauge Ithaca slide action loaded with one deer slug in the chamber and two in the magazine. The vehicle was occupied by one male subject. His spotlight was cradled in his lap and plugged into a cigarette lighter. I had his gun outside the truck and unloaded. I heard Weis ask the driver to step outside his vehicle and produce his driver's and hunting license.

"Are you Mel Weis?" the jack lighter asked, still seated in his truck not complying with Weis's order.

"Yes, I am," Mel replied.

"I've heard about you. I'm not getting out of my truck. That other xo#x better give my gun back. You'd better let me go on my way. I'm out here trying to see how many deer we've got left after the season. I own the land on both sides of the road. You're in Fulton County now, Weis – not Williams. Mess with me and I'll sue both of you. I've heard how you smack people around, Weis. Lay your hands on me and see what happens!" our unidentified jack lighter proclaimed.

I went back to our patrol vehicle and placed the Ithaca shotgun in the back seat. I returned to the rear of the jack lighter's vehicle. I was recording the truck license number in my citation pad when I heard Weis respond to our mouthy outlaw.

"First of all Dynamite, you crossed the county line fifty yards back. You don't own the land on both sides of the road here in Williams County; I know who does, not that it makes any difference what county you're in. You were violating the law by using a spotlight to shine deer with a gun in your possession. You admitted you were looking for deer. You and I know you'd have shot one if you saw it. Now, stop mouthing off -- get out of your truck and show me some identification. You're getting a citation to appear in the Williams County Northern District Court before Judge Reuben Hayward."

Our jack lighting outlaw really became unglued. He exited his truck and got in Weis's face. He continued to rant and rave, threatening law suits, etc. Then he started in on Judge Hayward.

"I've heard about that puppet, Judge Hayward, you've got in your hip pocket, Weis. I'll sue him too," he yelled.

I decided to get the ignition keys in our violator's pickup by entering through the unlocked passenger's door, when I heard Weis say, "I told you to give me some identification. Instead you've continued to mouth off and now you've got in my face – too close."

Then it happened. I can only compare it with the sound of a baseball bat hitting a grapefruit. I walked around the front of the pickup to see our belligerent outlaw on one knee, holding his head in his hands, with blood seeping out between the palm of his right hand and his face.

Weis "whacked" him good. Slowly he got to his feet. He was a big man, red haired and stood a head taller than Weis. His "injury" was only a cut lip.

"That hurt," he stated as he worked his jaw from left to right.

"You got too close, Tiger and you shouldn't have swung first – you missed, I didn't. Now get some I D out and give it to Officer Bailey. You're going to court. Any more trouble and you're going to jail in Bryan now and then court," Weis told the now subdued violator.

"I'll have all you own, Weis – all both of you own – count on it," he stated as he removed his wallet from a hip pocket, retrieved his driver's license and handed it to me. As I filled out his citation, I realized his last name was the same as a major restaurant chain. I later heard he was a member of this restaurant family who had significant land holdings in Fulton County. I handed him his citation and ignition keys. I asked for his spotlight which he handed to me.

"Where's my gun," he asked.

"It's in our patrol car. It and your light are held as evidence until after court. We probably should seize your vehicle but we're not going to because we'd have to take you home. If you post and forfeit an appearance bond, both items will be returned to you at the court. If this case goes to trial, you may or may not get them back – it's up to the court," I stated.

"Don't worry, I'll get both of them back along with a piece of you," our violator (I'll call Mr. "F") stated.

"There you go again – threatening. Now here's how it's gonna be. You go ahead and file all these lawsuits you're threatening. If you do, we'll both file charges against you for interfering with and threatening an officer while performing his duties and I'll file another charge against you for attempted assault for swinging at me first. You've got one witness – we've got two. Our additional charges, if you force us to file them, will more than offset your lawsuits. If you think you can win, have at it. Now shut your mouth before you get it again. You xo#x sure better comply with that citation. If not, we'll come after you with a bench warrant. This is the last word. I don't want to hear your mouth again – understand?" Weis told our violator who was now very quiet.

"Yes sir, Mr. Weis!" Mr. F. stated as he entered his pickup truck and left.

It was time to head in and call it a night. What started as an uneventful patrol, ended a very eventful one.

"What do you think he'll do, Melvin?" I asked.

"He'll post and forfeit bond, pick up his gun and spotlight and go home – he's all talk," Weis replied. As it turned out, Weis was right.

Two days before his scheduled court appearance, Mr. F. posted a $200.00 bond in Judge Hayward's Court. He never appeared. Shortly thereafter I met him over a cup of coffee at an Ohio Turnpike restaurant and returned his shotgun and spotlight. A much subdued and apologetic Mr. F. even paid for my coffee.

"You'd have shot one if we hadn't caught you, wouldn't you Bill?" I asked Mr. F.

"Oh yeah, the only reason I was out there was because I didn't get one when the season was in," he responded.

We shook hands and departed each others company. We never heard from or had an encounter with Mr. F. again.

I asked Weis to contact his C.I. again concerning Thurston and Pierce. The C.I. hadn't heard anything about them. I made two more contacts with Tanner. I tried to get enough information concerning his one-time hunts with both subjects to intelligently question them. The results were the same as before.

Although the "Camden deer poachers" were rounded up and processed through court, I wasn't satisfied with Thurston and Pierce still dangling. Nevertheless, I decided to drop them from my investigative thoughts until I read an article in the Montpelier newspaper. It was about the use of hypnosis to stimulate the performance of the local high school football team. The coach solicited and received the services of "Hypnosis Practitioner" Dr. Melvin Wentz who was a Methodist Minister in Montpelier. The coach claimed, "Dr. Wentz's hypnotic treatments of each member of his football team significantly improved their performance on the field."

This news article caused me to remember a book I'd read some years before. It was titled, "The Bridey Murphy Story" -- a book about regressive hypnosis. It claimed a hypnosis practitioner regressed a woman who recalled detailed events of her lifetime and past life times. I recalled reading two articles in professional police publications about regressive hypnosis. In both articles it was applied by a professional practitioner and was used to aid witnesses recall events accurately to help solve crimes. I thought, "why not?"

I contacted Dr. Wentz -- he told me he was familiar with regressive hypnosis. He had applied it many times to cause patients to remember where they misplaced lost articles as well as a host of other situations that required total and accurate recall. He stated he was willing to examine Larry Tanner. He was confident he would invoke Tanner's "total recollection" of his hunts with Pierce and Thurston. He told me his fee. I contacted my District Law Supervisor, Mike Fitzgibbons to approve payment to Dr. Wentz.

"What are you up to now? This has got to be a first in wildlife law enforcement, Bailey. You'll go to any lengths to make a case. Go ahead," Fitzgibbons chuckled as he approved payment of the fee.

I contacted Tanner by phone and laid the regressive hypnosis proposal on him. I anticipated his refusal and decided to seek his cooperation by making it sound like a challenge. At the end of my request and lengthy explanation, I made my request for his cooperation by stating, "I doubt you've got guts enough to try this, Larry."

"Bailey, if you're crazy enough to think of something like this – I'm crazy enough to try it. I can't imagine anyone hypnotizing me. When and where?" Tanner responded.

After contacting Wentz and Tanner, we all met at Wentz's office two days later at 6:30 p.m. I explained what was taking place to Weis and invited him to attend the hypnotic session.

"Xo#x no, Mr. B, that's spooky stuff. I don't want anything to do with that," Weis stated.

On the appointed date and time, Larry Tanner and I met at Dr. Wentz's office. He seated Tanner in front of his desk and I was seated to his right with tape recorder. Dr. Wentz addressed Tanner and gave him a rather lengthy explanation of what regressive hypnosis was all about. As Wentz talked, I noticed his voice graduated into a very rhythmic, relaxing, monotone. I could see it was having an effect on Tanner. I realized then he had actually begun the session.

Wentz asked, "Larry, are you ready to begin?"

Tanner replied, "Yes."

Wentz activated an 18 inch wide black and white spiral wheel situated to the front and center of his desk directly in front of Tanner. He instructed Tanner to concentrate on the wheel and relax.

"In a few moments Larry, I'll count backwards from fifteen to one. At the count of one, you'll be in a complete hypnotic state. You'll recall totally and completely the hunting events that took place during deer hunts you had with James Pierce and Andrew Thurston. I'll ask that you firmly see their images in your mind. Then I'll direct your attention to Officer Bailey who will ask you questions that you'll answer truthfully," Wentz told Tanner. (PAUSE) "Fifteen, fourteen, thirteen, twelve, eleven, ten, nine, eight, seven, six, five, four, three, two, one – do you hear me, Larry?" Wentz asked.

"Yes," came a drowsy answer from Tanner, now with his head bowed and eyes shut.

"I ask you recall James Pierce – do you see him clearly?" Wentz asked.

"Yes," Tanner replied.

"I ask you recall Andrew Thurston – do you see him clearly?"

"Yes, Bluegill and But-Cut?" Tanner replied in the same drowsy tone.

Wentz looked at me, puzzled. I wrote "NICKNAMES" in big letters on a yellow tablet and held it up.

"Those are nicknames for Mr. Pierce and Mr. Thurston. You will not use these nicknames again. You'll use their real names – James Pierce and Andrew Thurston," Wentz ordered.

"Okay," Tanner responded.

"Now I'll turn this inquiry over to Wildlife Officer Ron Bailey. You will answer his questions completely, accurately and truthfully. Do you understand?" Wentz stated.

"Yes," replied Tanner.

Wentz nodded to me to proceed. I was nervous as all get out but I had initiated all this. Now I was right in the middle of it and the spotlight was on me.

"Larry, we'll start with Andrew Thurston. I want you to give me the exact date or dates you and Andrew came to Ohio and jack lighted deer," I asked my hypnotized outlaw turned witness. Tanner was silent for a time.

Then his face contorted, he began to emit a very low guttural animal like growl that seemed to come from deep within his very soul. It scared me to death!

Immediately Wentz took command of the situation. "Larry! Larry! You'll stop that! You'll stop that right now! Don't repeat it! Do you hear me?" Wentz stated in a very raised, almost shouting tone.

"Yes," Tanner replied, now in a very crisp voice – no longer drowsy but alert. The change in his tone of voice was scary.

"All right Larry, now Officer Bailey will resume his questioning," Wentz told Tanner in a very authoritative and commanding tone.

Officer Bailey will resume questioning xo#x! I was scared to death after what I had just witnessed and heard. What in xo#x have I got into here, I thought. I gave Wentz the time out (T) signal. He could see that I was shook up and nodded approval.

He began talking to Tanner, "Larry, I want you to rest for a few seconds. Then we'll proceed," Wentz told Tanner all the while visually evaluating me. Tanner gave no response, only sighed and seemed to settle more in his chair. Shortly I indicated to Dr. Wentz I was okay and ready to proceed.

"Officer Bailey will proceed now with his questions, Larry," Wentz told Tanner.

"Okay," Tanner replied almost cheerfully.

"All right Larry, we'll start with James Pierce - - - ." With that opening, I asked Tanner very specific questions concerning the actual date, time of day, specific places they went and events that took place. He named the actual date of the hunt; the actual time Pierce arrived at his home to go hunting; the fact they used Tanner's truck and light and Pierce's gun. He completely described in detail the routes they took in both Michigan and Ohio – spotting ninety percent of the deer they saw in Ohio.

Tanner shivered, his lips actually turned blue as he vividly described a scene in Bridgewater Township, Ohio where they had six deer in the spotlight. It was the preceding December and was very cold as both he and Pierce exited his pickup and got in the bed of the truck where Tanner held the light while Pierce shot at the deer.

Tanner stated, while shivering almost uncontrollably, "He (Pierce) shot and shot his 30/30. Xo#x! He missed them. No, he's got one crippled. I see blood on its shoulder! They're running west – the deer ran west – we're back in the truck with the heater on. We're going around the section to get another shot. We're there – on the west side of the section – no deer! No wait! There are four of them. We're back in the truck bed. It's colder here than the east side (starts shivering again). He (Pierce) shot and shot! Xo#x, he missed them again I guess, but they had it in high gear. Bluegill can't hit nothin."

"What about the crippled deer – the one Pierce crippled on the east side of the section," I asked.

"Never saw it again. I'm sure it was hit hard. Went back in the day time with no guns but couldn't stay long because of Weis," Tanner replied.

"All right Larry, now we'll talk about Andy Thurston - - - ." I questioned Tanner in much the same manner I questioned him about Pierce.

Again Tanner gave specific dates and times. Twice, not once, as he previously claimed, he picked up Thurston at his residence and went to Ohio jack lighting deer "because Andy wanted a deer to eat." These two hunts took place the preceding December. Again Tanner described the specific routes they took while shining deer in Michigan and Ohio.

"We took Andy's .12 gauge shotgun with deer slugs." He described specific occasions, with the truck windows down, he got cold as Thurston shot at deer. Like Pierce, Thurston never actually killed a deer, only shot at them perhaps crippling a doe – not sure.

When satisfied I had gotten all I could get from Tanner concerning Thurston, I told him I was through questioning him and thanked him. I looked at Wentz. He stated, "Larry the session is over. You did quite well and we thank you for that. Now it's time for your return. At the count of seven, you'll return from the hypnotic state. One, two, three, four, five, six, seven," Wentz stated.

Tanner immediately looked all around the room. "It's all over, right?" he asked.

Tanner looked at my tape recorder. "You said you were going to tape this – I'd like to hear it," he stated.

"Later," I replied. We thanked Dr. Wentz and left his office. I later sent him a check for his services. I told Tanner he could come to Judge Hayward's Court after hours the next day and listen to the tape. He stated he would be there but phoned early the following morning and cancelled. He never heard the tape. He stated, "If the information you got from me lays the dime on Bluegill and But-Cut, I'll help pay their fines."

"That's a nice gesture, Larry. That will be between you and them," I said. I thought about contacting Dr. Wentz concerning what was happening when Tanner "performed" as he did at the beginning of the session. To me, given my religious upbringing, the episode was satanic to say the least. I never re-visited Wentz concerning this matter. I guess I didn't have the guts. I shudder when I recall the episode even now. My hypnotic session with Tanner yielded no Lacey Act cases against Pierce and Thurston. Getting them to answer to "attempt to take" charges in Ohio would be a matter of salesmanship. Based on the Tanner tape, so graciously transcribed by my wife, Shirley June, I prepared statements for both Pierce and Thurston to sign when the time came.

I chose to question Thurston first. I questioned him in my patrol vehicle parked in front of his residence in Camden, Michigan shortly thereafter. When I fired the dates, times and details of his jack lighting hunts in Ohio with Tanner at him, he folded like an accordion. He knew my detailed information came from Tanner. He signed my prepared statement and I witnessed his signature. I went for broke and issued him a citation to appear before Judge Hayward in Montpelier, Ohio on a certain date. I explained the bond forfeiture system to him. He could have torn the citation up and forgot the whole thing. He subsequently forfeited a $200.00 bond (set by Judge Hayward) for two charges of "attempting to take" deer in closed season. Later, through the Weis C.I., we learned Tanner helped Thurston pay the bond.

My next and last quest was Jimmie Pierce. Little did I know what I was in for. After making several attempts to contact Pierce (who was dodging me), I finally made contact with him in Reading, Michigan. I questioned him in my vehicle parked on a downtown street. As I fired the detailed questions (based on Tanner's information) at him, he denied all the allegations one by one, again and again.

Finally in desperation, I told Pierce, "Okay, if all the information I've put before you is untrue and you didn't commit any deer hunting violations in Ohio, you'd be willing to take a polygraph or lie detector test, wouldn't you?"

"Yeah, I'll take one," Pierce stated, much to my surprise.

Using the polygraph was a "first". Not having a form that addressed the matter, I wrote a quick statement stating Pierce was willing to take a polygraph examination and was not coerced in any manner. He signed it, I witnessed his signature. I excused him and left Reading.

I contacted the Williams County Sheriff's Department and ascertained they used the Patton Detective Agency in Toledo, Ohio to do their polygraph work. The examiner was Dick Patton -- the fee $35.00. I called District Law Enforcement Supervisor, Mike Fitzgibbons for approval to pay the polygraph fee.

"Regressive hypnosis, now the polygraph, you never quit do you Bailey? Go ahead, this is probably a first – at least in Ohio wildlife law enforcement," he stated.

I contacted Pierce and Dick Patton in Toledo and scheduled the examination three days later at 10:30 a.m. On the morning of the polygraph, I picked up Pierce at his home in Camden, Michigan. During the sixty mile trip to Toledo, Pierce stared straight ahead. He didn't utter one word even when I tried to invoke conversation. I noticed his eyes hardly blinked. I thought, *He's stoned on something.*

At the Patton Detective Agency, Pierce would hardly acknowledge Dick Patton in any manner. Patton escorted him to the examination room. I observed through a one-way glass window. Patton hooked Pierce to the machine and began questioning. Patton was working from a list of questions I gave him. Forty minutes later, Patton emerged from the examination room. "He's not being truthful but our examination won't show it. The test is inconclusive. This person is "high" on something. Whatever it is, it's affecting his responses in a way quite favorable to him. We're wasting our time."

"Will you give me your report on this examination now or will you mail it to me?" I asked.

"Either way you want it," Patton replied.

"Does Pierce know he beat the test?" I asked.

"No, but if he asks, I'll have to tell him," Patton replied.

"When you bring him out, signal me by nodding or shaking your head so I'll know if you had to tell him the test results," I requested.

"I'll do that," Patton replied. He exited and returned shortly escorting Pierce. I wrote him a check for his services. As I handed it to him, he shook his head slightly from side to side indicating Pierce didn't know the test results.

"Mail your report to me," I stated as Pierce and I departed. All the way back to Camden, it was the same thing. Pierce wouldn't say a word even when I tried to invoke conversation. By the time we got to the Michigan state line I had decided what I would do. I would issue him a citation for "attempting to take a deer in closed season" and advise him of the appearance bond system. What the heck, I had nothing to lose. I could get Tanner subpoenaed if Pierce chose to appear in State Court.

As we arrived at Pierce's residence, he started to get out of the car. "Not yet, stud. I need your driver's license. Hand it over!" I stated.

"What for?" Pierce asked.

"You didn't do too well on your polygraph examination. I'm issuing you a citation to appear in court."

"Xo#x," Pierce stated. That was all, just "xo#x."

I issued Pierce a citation to appear in Judge Hayward's Court one week later. On the offense line, it stated, "Attempting to take a deer during the closed season." On the date of violation line, I wrote the specific date and time ascertained from Tanner. I advised Pierce his bond was $200.00. I excused him and drove off. I watched him in my rear view mirror until a left hand turn precluded same. He remained standing at the curb staring at his citation until out of sight.

The day before Pierce's scheduled court date, I was working in Henry County. "255 from 296," came Weis's radio call.

"255, go ahead," I answered.

"Your buddy, Mr. Pierce, just posted a $200.00 bond with your lady – says he won't be back for court. You pulled it off Mr. B.," Weis reported.

"Q-22, 296 – Thanks, "I responded.

That short radio message ended the Camden deer poaching ring investigation. We broke their backs. We knew it and they knew it. We apprehended eleven out-of-state deer poachers on our terms. All paid stiff penalties. Three fled never to be heard of again. We employed the use of a very unique and unusual law enforcement tool – regressive hypnosis – to nail two violators. Perhaps a first in wildlife law enforcement. We employed the use of another great law enforcement tool, perhaps for the first time in wildlife law enforcement – the polygraph – only to learn it could be beaten.

Our non-resident deer poachers illegally killed eleven Ohio deer and transported a portion of an important Ohio wildlife resource back to their native state. They paid $5400.00 in penalties for the error of their evil ways. The investigation remains vivid in my mind. Not only because it was a good one, but because I was privileged to work it with the best Game Warden I ever knew – Mel Weis.

Addendum:

The Camden deer poaching ring was the last investigation I worked prior to the Miranda Decision in 1966. The Ohio Division of Wildlife's Law Enforcement Section completed training sessions concerning Miranda in late 1966. All commissioned law enforcement personnel received complete schooling on Miranda – the new law of the land.

From that point on, all persons suspected of committing a crime had to be advised of their rights. It was thought this new requirement would seriously hinder criminal investigations. Almost the reverse proved to be true.

I was so concerned over the Miranda Decision, I tape recorded my spiel as I read suspects their rights before questioning. It was my experience (and others) advising a suspect of his/her rights as set forth in Miranda really didn't make any difference. Almost all still consented to questioning.

12
An Illegal Deer and A Crippled Doll

John Staab was one of the best Game Wardens the State of Ohio ever commissioned to enforce its wildlife laws. He was assigned to Lucas County – a nightmarish, high activity beat on the western end of Lake Erie's shoreline. Toledo is the county seat. The Maumee River transects the county from northeast to southwest and forms its southeast boundary. In bygone days (20's and 30's), the Maumee was ranked the number one small mouth stream in the nation. It "choked" annually with great walleye runs from Lake Erie. The post World War II years saw it polluted due to the growth of agricultural, industrial, and human development. The late 1960's saw the beginning restoration or "cleaning up" of this great water course.

I was frequently assigned to work the Maumee and its nearby environs in Lucas County, checking hunters, fishermen, and conducting after-the-fact investigations. These were special assignments in view of the fact Lucas County was outside my official assigned area.

The Ohio Division of Wildlife's case management system within its law enforcement program was basically as follows:

A job titled Game Protector was assigned to each county. His law enforcement duties were classified as routine field patrol, hunter and fishermen checking. His other duties included game management, fishery management and public relations. One Game Protector in each four county area was job titled Senior Game Protector. He functioned as a supervisor in each work unit or four county area.

After-the-fact (violations not committed in an officer's presence) complicated and covert investigations were conducted by those job titled Wildlife

Enforcement Agent. The pay grades for Wildlife Enforcement Agents and Senior Game Protectors were the same.

Agents were assigned to investigations requested by Game Protectors or higher authority. These investigations were requested on a Form W-45 (Request for Investigation). The Agent recorded his investigation results on a Form W-104 (Report of investigation). His W-104 had to show those elements listed in the story, "She Shot a Buffalo."

John Staab submitted a W-45 requesting investigation of two possible out-of-season deer gut piles located on the Maumee State Forest. The W-45 set forth no leads. It had good photos and a detailed map plotting the exact locations of both gut piles. The W-45 was assigned to me for investigation by my District Law Enforcement Supervisor, Mike Fitzgibbons.

"Mike, this W-45 isn't very encouraging. It's well written and the photos and maps attached are nice, but there are no leads. You know and I know if there were any possible leads, John would already be on them. I really don't have time to play around with something like this," I told my Supervisor.

"I know Ron, but you're pretty darn thorough. I've got a feeling you or Palmer might be able to pull something out of the hat on this one. Go on up there and look the site over. If there's no leads, there's no leads, but give it your best shot. If you can't do anything with it, close the case out. I'll honor your recommendation," Fitz responded.

Leaving the Findlay Office, I headed for the Maumee State Forest in Lucas County. I figured I would inspect the scenes, find nothing in the way of leads and close this nuisance case.

Arriving at the gut pile scenes (about ten yards apart), I found the night critters had been there and accomplished their natural cleaning up process. Nevertheless, I probed what was left of the stinking messes in hopes of finding a bullet, slug, buckshot – anything. I found nothing. I found a good tire print in a reasonable proximity to the southern scene. I broke out my homemade plaster cast set, framed the tire track and made a good plaster cast.

I made ever widening circles around both gut piles. The ground cover showed no disturbance. I found another tire track in the soft ground reasonably close to the northern gut pile. It matched the tire print I found at the south scene. It dawned on me – Bailey, what does it take? These gut piles were hauled here and dumped. The deer were actually killed elsewhere.

I continued my inspection of the scenes and their immediate surroundings and found nothing. No nearby homes with possible witnesses; no doors to knock on. I sat on a log for a few minutes thinking perhaps I could pick up some "vibes". Strange as it seems, the vibes practice was one I always engaged in at wildlife crime scenes. I'll never prove a nexus between the vibes I picked up at a crime scene and those same vibes I experienced when I finally got to the violator. I can only say they seemed to exist and work for me. Curiously, during my career, I've met four Wildlife Officers who related similar practices and experiences. I never thought I'd write about this practice or ability but there it is, believe it or not.

It was growing dark. I'd made up my mind to close the investigation to be re-opened only if leads that could be investigated came to light. I entered my patrol car and started the engine, when something white caught my eye. It was in a briar patch and almost concealed by leaf litter. It was within a reasonable proximity of the northern gut pile. I picked up a stick and swished away the leaf litter covering it.

Behold! A crumpled envelope. I flipped it out of the briar patch with my probe stick. Although faded, the front of the empty envelope was addressed to a (I'll call him) Jerry Clifton at Neopolis, Ohio. The return address was not discernible and I got the impression the envelope was there for some time. I examined its back side. It's got poop on it, I thought. Closer inspection revealed it was stained with blood.

I didn't view this lead as a good one. I felt its age or (when placed there) was much older than the gut piles. But what the heck, it was all I had. I returned home and slept on the matter.

The next morning I was more comfortable with my "white envelope lead". I went to the small community of Neopolis and very quickly ascertained the home of Jerry Clifton. I maintained surveillance of the Clifton home. In about fifteen minutes Clifton arrived. I drove the short distance, parked and approached him at a side entrance door to his home.

"Jerry Clifton?" I asked.

"That's me," a very pleasant, sandy haired, medium built gentleman replied.

"Ron Bailey here, State Wildlife Officer. You and I need to talk for a short while. Come with me to my car. I won't take much of your time," I stated.

"Come in the house. I just got off work. I'm famished for a cup of coffee." Mr. Clifton responded.

"My business is official and confidential. I'd prefer we conversed in my patrol car. I don't want to involve anyone else in the house," I stated.

"There's no one in the house, I live alone," Jerry replied.

"Sounds like a winner," I stated as I followed him. I didn't like "in-home" or "on their property" interviews. I knew from experience the farther you get them off their home turf, the better. However, because I didn't feel too strong about my white envelope lead, I wasn't too uncomfortable interviewing Clifton in his home, obviously a bachelor's quarters.

"Married?" I asked.

"No, divorced," Clifton answered.

"I see. While you're fixing coffee, I'll get a few items from my car. I'll be right back," I stated. I retrieved my briefcase. Inside was the white envelope in an official looking plastic bag with a more official looking evidence tag attached to it.

I entered Clifton's house and sat down at his kitchen table. After clearing a space on the table covered with male necessities such as shotgun shells, hunting knives, socks, underwear, etc., I placed the encased white envelope on the table in front of me. As the coffee perked, I asked, "Deer Hunter?" A not too brilliant observation in view of the fact half the twelve gauge shotgun shells on the table were deer slugs (only legal deer ammo in Ohio).

"Yes," he replied as he got two cups from his cupboard placing one in front of me beside the white envelope evidence bag. As he poured both cups and seated himself across the table I realized, I'm getting some good vibes here – scene matching vibes. I was confident I was at the right place. Clifton looked at the evidence envelope.

"Jerry, before we go any further, it's my responsibility to advise you of your constitutional rights," I stated as I ran my right hand into my briefcase and depressed the "on" button on my micro-cassette tape recorder. I removed a Miranda Warning card from my uniform shirt pocket and read it to Clifton.

"Jerry, I've read all that because I'm here investigating a deer hunting violation – a violation in which you're a suspect. Now that you know this and you've heard your rights, are you willing to discuss the matter with me and answer my questions?" I asked.

"I haven't killed an illegal deer," my now nervous suspect answered.

"Did you kill a legal deer during this past season?" I asked.

"Yes – a nice doe," he replied.

"Did you tag it and check it through a deer check station?" I asked.

"Yes, I took it to the checking station at Swanton," he stated. At my request, he told me where the deer check station was located.

"Where did you kill your deer?" I asked.

"About eight miles from here," he replied.

"What county?" I asked.

"Fulton I think, it may have been Lucas County – it was near the county line," Clifton replied.

"Did you hunt alone?" I asked.

"Always do," he replied.

"Where did you field dress your doe?" I asked.

"Here in my yard. It wasn't far to bring her here and a lot more convenient," Clifton replied.

"Where did you put the entrails after you field dressed your deer?" I asked.

"I threw them out a few miles from here," he replied.

"On the Maumee State Forest?" I asked.

"Maybe so," he replied.

I showed Clifton the photos accompanying Officer John Staab's form W-45.

"It looks like the place I dumped the deer guts," he responded.

"I'll take a look at your hunting license. Do you still have your deer tag?" I asked.

"I believe I do," he replied. We went to Mr. Clifton's pickup truck parked in the driveway. After rummaging through the glove compartment and retrieving his orange hunting vest from behind the seat, he showed me his hunting license, deer permit and a numbered bloody deer tag. I recorded the numbers on all documents and made an inspection of the truck's bed. There was deer hair and dried blood still in the truck's bed. I noticed his truck's rear tires matched the plaster cast I made at the scene.

"The deer gut piles I'm investigating aren't far from here. Let's go there and see if where you dumped your doe's entrails and the site I'm checking are the same," I stated.

"No problem," Jerry replied.

We got in my patrol car and went to the scenes on the Maumee State Forest. Clifton verified the southern deer gut pile was his. He indicated an approximate date – the day after the close of the previous deer-gun season as the date he dumped the entrails.

"Let's look at another site," I stated taking Clifton to the second gut pile location.

"I had nothing to do with this," Clifton stated.

"Very well, thanks for your cooperation so far," I stated as we returned to Clifton's home.

"What time of day did you dump you deer's entrails?" I asked.

"It was at night – probably about 10:00 p.m.," he replied.

"I see," I responded.

I hadn't confronted Clifton with the white envelope found closer to the northern gut pile than the southern one. I knew in my "heart of hearts" Clifton was responsible for both and the second pile was from an illegal-closed season deer. I knew I had to get him to admit it. We re-entered Clifton's home. I sat down at his kitchen table and asked, "How about a fresh cup of coffee?" Clifton obliged and poured one for himself.

"This envelope with your name on it was found near the second gut pile I showed you. The back of the envelope is smeared with deer blood (a stab in the dark). I believe somehow this envelope found its way to the ground from your truck the same time you dumped the second gut pile. I have to prove this and rest assured I will, unless you want to tell me about it now. Your cooperation will save the Sportsmen of Ohio a lot of money. It will show your willingness to cooperate in this matter, which I'm sure will favorably impress the Prosecutor and the Court. Do you want to tell me about it?" I asked.

"I didn't kill a second deer. I don't know nuthin' about that other pile of guts," Clifton responded.

"You stated you hunted alone this past season. Do you want to stick with that?" I asked.

"I always hunt alone," he replied ruling out the possibility the second deer gut pile belonged to a companion hunter.

"If all you're telling me is true, I assume you don't have a problem with me preparing a statement for your signature stating the first deer gut pile was from a legal deer you dumped on the Maumee Sate Forest. This statement will render you guilty of dumping on public lands only. Are you willing to sign such a statement?" I asked.

"Yeah, I'll sign it. That's all I'm guilty of – dumping," Clifton responded.

I prepared the statement on the proper form. Clifton signed it; I witnessed his signature. I cited Clifton into Maumee Municipal Court for illegal dumping on the Maumee State Forest. Judge R. McKeanna, presiding. I informed him of the bond posting and forfeiture procedures and showed him the court bond schedule listing his offense at $75.00. The next morning I obtained the City Solicitor's approval of the charge (a little after the fact) before filing it with the Court Clerk. Clifton forfeited bond and never appeared.

Normally I would have closed this investigation satisfied with making a dumping violation case. However, I wasn't satisfied with the investigation's outcome. I decided to "hang on" for a while. My case load was heavy; my court schedule busy, but I knew now was not the time to close this case.

I ran a check on Jerry Clifton's legal-season killed deer through the deer checking station records at the Statistical Section at Delaware. Everything was okay. Clifton checked a doe deer through the station as he stated. The tag and license number checked out okay.

Nine months passed. Then another investigation request from Game Protector Staab. This time it was a case of dumping household trash on the Maumee State Forest. I glanced at the unassigned W-45 on Mike Fitzgibbon's desk at a Monday Agent's meeting. As usual, no easy leads. No names or addresses on discarded mail, prescription pill bottles, etc. -- nothing. Leads, John would already have jumped on had they existed.

"How about assigning that one to me?" I asked my boss, Mike Fitzgibbons.

"Why? It's outside your duty area and you hate these no lead W-45's Staab sends in. Why do you want this one?" Mike asked.

"It's near an old one I haven't closed yet – a deer case. I've got a feeling on this – how about it?" I asked Fitz.

"It's all yours ol buddy," Fitz stated as he wrote my name on the assigned line, signed the approved line and handed the W-45 to me.

"Why in xo#x did I talk Fitz into assigning me to this piece of crap case?" I asked myself as I completed my third inspection of the household trash at my feet and all around me. I found no traceable leads – none. The one fact that fascinated me was this dumps proximity to the old deer gut pile scenes and the resulting Jerry Clifton case. I sat on a stump right in the middle of the whole mess after pouring a cup of black coffee from my thermos. There I sat in the midst of dirty pampers, egg shells, coffee grounds, banana and potato peelings, plastic bags and packing, lots of packing. The kind used by retail stores – plain with no markings. The thought struck me, part of this crap is from someone who has moved! I sat idle, motionless for a while. There they were again – the vibes. I noticed for the second time, a book of matches. A nice crisp new appearing, dry book of matches advertising a nearby truck stop and service station. I went to the match book, picked it up and placed it in my shirt pocket. At the same time, I noticed a toy doll's leg. I picked it up and went to my patrol car. I put the match book and doll's right leg in a plastic bag and threw them in the trunk. Something is better than nothing, I thought. I went home and got a good night's sleep. Sleep filled with dreams and visions of a beautiful toy doll. I woke up and found her laying beside me – my beautiful little Shirley June – my real life "beautiful doll".

Following an early morning breakfast with Shirley June, I traveled to the truck stop advertised on the match book cover. It was situated close to the junction of Route 295 and Route 24 near the Maumee River in Lucas County. I knew the possibility of tracing a customer who picked up the match book while visiting the truck stop was impossible. But what about an employee? A slim possibility, a very slim possibility.

I arrived at the truck stop and soon made contact with the owner/manager. "It's one of our match books," he stated adding, "It's one of the old ones."

"What do you mean, old one?" I asked.

"It's the issue we had made before this one," he answered as he selected a book of matches from a box beside the cash register and handed it to me. Its appearance was altogether different.

"How old is this present issue?" I asked.

"A year old. Why all the interest in one of our book of matches?" he asked.

I told him the book of matches came from the scene of a law violation.

"And you hope to trace someone who obviously picked up a book of matches here or perhaps got them here and gave them to someone else?" he asked.

"That's what I'd hoped to do. I know my chances of doing that are slim to none," I replied.

"Slim to none? It's darn near impossible," he replied.

"I realize this. I know trying to trace a customer is next to impossible; however, how about your employees? Were all the employees you have on board now working when you were giving out the previous issue of match books?" I asked.

He thought for several moments, then stated, "We have quite a turnover in waitresses. I'm sure there's only one working now who was working before we bought the new match books," he stated.

"May I ask her name?" I asked.

"Janet – Janet Thompson. I'm pretty sure she's the only one," he replied.

"Has Janet moved recently that you know of? Does she live near here?" I asked.

"She hasn't moved. She lives in Wood County. I'm not sure where," he replied.

"Is she on duty now?" I asked.

"She doesn't come to work until late this afternoon," he replied.

"How about ex-employees. Did you have one who lived near here and worked here before you got your present match books?" I asked.

"There's one who comes to mind – Norma Baird. She left here and went to work for Campbell Soup Company. I wish I had her back. She was a very good waitress," he replied.

"Do you know if Norma moved recently or if she has a new baby?" I asked.

"Yes, she did move recently – not far from where she did live. I know because I recently phoned her and reached her after calling information. I tried to get her to come back to work here. I found out she moved and went to work for Campbell Soup. As far as the new baby is concerned, Norma doesn't have one but I believe her sister, who lives with her, does," he replied.

"Can you direct me to her house?" I asked.

"I can come pretty close – I can get you in the vicinity," he responded. He gave me directions to her old residence, stating, "I know she moved to a house close by." The location he directed me to lay between the truck stop and Neopolis.

I thanked the truck stop manager for his time and headed for the Norma Baird residence regarding this lead as a pure "stab in the dark." I found her residence in short order and parked my patrol vehicle in the driveway beside her home. I noticed two vehicles parked in front of me; I was sure someone was at home. I went to the front door and knocked. A nice looking blond lady peeked at me through a small glass window in the door and stated, "You'll have to come around back – we're moving furniture around; the front door is blocked."

I went to the back and entered a screened in porch. I started toward the back door when I saw it! A nude toy doll on a shelf beside the door, minus a right leg. I returned to my patrol car, got my evidence doll leg out of the trunk. I returned to the screened in porch to find the blond lady standing beside and outside the door.

"May I help you?" she asked. I picked up the toy doll on the porch shelf. I inserted my toy doll leg into the doll's right leg socket. As it popped into place I stated, "Hi, I'm State Game Protector Ron Bailey, I need to discuss a matter with you. I believe this is the leg missing from your doll. The doll was dark complexioned; the evidence leg was also dark complexioned. The match was perfect.

"Yes, that is the leg missing from my doll. How in heavens name did you get it?" she asked.

I explained the facts and circumstances surrounding my finding the doll leg. I showed her photos of the dump site on the Maumee State Forest and stated, "Norma, before we go any further, I have to read your rights to you." I removed my Miranda Warning card from my shirt pocket and read Miranda to Norma.

"Of course, I'll talk to you. You don't realize how happy I am to get my doll's leg back. She is a very early issue and a valuable collector's item. I've been devastated since her leg came up missing. I could just kiss you. That's my trash alright but I didn't put it there. My boy friend hauled it away after we moved here," she stated.

"May I ask you're boy friend's name?" I asked Norma.

"I hate to get him in trouble but he shouldn't have dumped my trash on the Forest. We go there often hiking and on picnics. I hate the fact he put my trash there. He told me he was taking it to the dump at Neopolis. His name is Jerry Clifton," she replied.

"And he lives in Neopolis," I added.

"Yes, he does. Do you know him?" she asked.

"Yes, we've met over a little deer matter," I stated.

"Oh? Yes I know he's serious about his deer hunting. He got two deer last season and gave us one. We sure appreciated getting the meat," she stated.

Bingo! Case closed on the second deer gut pile – over the limit on deer last season for Mr. Clifton or the second deer was killed during the closed season!. I thought. "Was the deer you received from Jerry a doe?" I asked.

"Yes, I believe he told me it was. He brought it to us all cut up and packaged," Norma replied.

"I'm going to prepare a statement; it will exonerate you concerning your trash illegally dumped on the Maumee State Forest. I'm going to add a few facts concerning the processed doe deer Jerry was kind enough to give you, as this deer answers a few questions concerning when and where the deer was killed. I'll ask you to sign the statement. Would you be kind enough to do that?" I asked.

"I suppose so. Is Jerry in any kind of trouble concerning my deer meat?" Norma asked.

"Norma, the statement exonerates you on the trash. It will give me information I'll need to further investigate the deer," I replied.

"I'll sign it," she stated in a very matter of fact manner and invited me into her kitchen where we sat down at her table. I prepared a statement containing all Norma told me concerning her household trash and the deer she received from Jerry Clifton. She carefully read it, then signed it. I witnessed her signature.

"Norma, do you have any of the deer meat Jerry gave you?" I asked.

"Yes, quite a bit," she replied.

"Where is it?" I asked.

"Over there in the freezer," she replied pointing to a chest freezer.

"I'd like to take a look at the deer meat. However, there's a form I'd like you to sign before I do," I stated. I excused myself, went to my patrol car and got a "Consent to Search" form. I showed it to Norma. As she read it I stated, "That's to protect me. I have no authority to look in your freezer unless you agree to it." "That's no problem Officer Bailey," she stated as she signed the form, handed it to me and opened her freezer. After my inspection I told Norma, "Most of the deer is still here. You haven't consumed much of it, have you?"

"Only a couple of pieces," she replied.

I went to my vehicle and got my camera. I returned to Norma's kitchen and photographed the packaged venison I stacked on a table beside the freezer. I returned the packages to the freezer. I thanked Norma for her cooperation and departed for Jerry Clifton's residence in Neopolis. I knew I could get to him just as he arrived home from work hoping to preclude any phone contact between him and his girl friend, Norma Baird. I got there in time. I waited, parked across the street from his home. Shortly he arrived.

"We meet again Jerry. I'm here to talk to you about the second deer gut pile you dumped on the State Forest. You'll accompany me to my car," I stated as I escorted him to my patrol car and opened the passenger's side door. He entered and sat down. I slid behind the wheel and didn't waste any time. I read Clifton the Miranda Warning. He was nervous as all get out but agreed to questioning. "I'll answer your questions to show you I had nothing to do with the other gut pile," he said nervously.

"I have a statement here I want you to read," I stated as I handed the Baird statement to him. He read it; as he finished and started to hand it back to me, I looked at him and said one word, "GOTCHA".

"Oh no, the deer I gave Norma was the doe I killed, tagged and checked in during the open season," Clifton stated struggling with every word.

"It won't fly, Jerry. Two gut piles, two deer, one in season, one over the limit or one out of season, plus a big pile of Norma's trash you dumped. I've another ace in the hole, Jerry. You should look around a little more before you dump deer guts day or night. A lot of lovers park back in all those lover's lanes in the State Forest. They see things and some of them write down vehicle license numbers and vehicle descriptions. How would you like to lose your vehicle over a deer? I stated. (The lover's statement was a stab in the dark)

"Who saw me!" he exclaimed before thinking.

"Never mind that. You tell me the truth and I mean now! You're going down for taking and possessing an illegal deer, dumping its guts and Norma Baird's trash on a public land. I've got you, Jerry. Now let's hear the truth and I mean now!" I shouted (time to be the bad guy).

"Alright, I did it! I did all of it! You don't have to get so mad," Clifton stated.

"I'm not mad, Jerry. I'm just growing a little impatient with you. If I gave you the impression of being mad, I'm sorry. Please excuse me. (Time to be the good guy.) When did you kill the second deer?" I asked in the most pleasant tone I could muster.

"The day after the season went out. I got her very near where I got the first one," Clifton replied.

"You were kind enough to get the second deer professionally processed and wrapped for Norma. How did you get the locker plant to process the second deer without a tag on it or did you go to a different facility and re-use the tag you used on your first (legal) deer?" I asked answering my own question.

"That's the way it happened," Clifton replied.

"This is the reason you still had the tag in your truck the first time we met. You intended to use it again on a third deer, didn't you? As a matter of fact, you did kill a third (illegal) deer didn't you? You used the tag at still another meat processing facility, didn't you?" I asked.

"No! I didn't kill a third deer. I still have the tag. Don't try to pin something on me that I didn't do!" Clifton responded.

"I think I'd better have that tag. We'll go get it now," I told Clifton. We exited my patrol car and went to Clifton's truck where he removed the old and illegally used deer tag.

"This tag is now the State of Ohio's evidence, Jerry. Your illegal use of it constitutes another violation of the law. You will also answer to this in court," I told Clifton.

"Yes sir," Clifton replied. Now very humbled and ashamed, as we returned to my patrol car. I didn't ask Clifton if he would give me a statement. I got a form out of my brief case and wrote a statement concerning Clifton's illegal acts of dumping (second deer gut pile) on State owned land, taking a doe deer during the closed season, illegal use of his deer tag, and dumping Norma Baird's trash on State owned land, for a total of four separate charges. I read the somewhat lengthy statement to Clifton. At the conclusion of the reading I asked, "Is the statement I just read to you the truth?"

"It is," he responded.

"Sign it, I'll witness your signature," I stated as I handed Clifton the statement attached to a clipboard. As Clifton signed it, I attached an evidence tag to his deer tag and dropped it in a plastic bag.

"I'll see you in a couple of days, Jerry. I have to meet with the Maumee Solicitor concerning the charges against you. After that I'll issue you a citation to appear in the Maumee Municipal Court before Judge McKeanna," I told Clifton. I departed Neopolis and went home.

"Determined, aren't you?" the Assistant Solicitor stated as he finished reading my W-104 (Investigation Report) concerning Jerry Clifton, his statement and four affidavits charging Clifton with four offenses. "And all done through a book of matches. I'll prosecute your cases; file them with the Clerk. Cite Mr. Clifton for a week from Friday. Your work reminds me of John Staab's – you know John I assume?" the Solicitor asked.

"Yes, I know Johnny. Thanks for your time, sir," I told him as I left his office. That evening I called on Jerry Clifton. I cited him to appear in court as instructed by the Solicitor. The citation listed as offenses; two counts of dumping on the Maumee State Forest Area; one count of taking a deer during the closed season; and one count for the illegal use of a deer tag.

Clifton asked, "Can I take care of this like I did before?"

"I assume so Jerry; however, you will have to check with the Court Clerk on that," I replied. I left a saddened Jerry Clifton standing in his driveway and went home to my Shirley June.

On Clifton's appointed day to appear in Court, I arrived early. The Court Clerk told me Clifton posted a $600.00 bond that was set outside the bond schedule by Judge McKeanna and the Solicitor. She stated she was sure Mr. Clifton would not appear. Nevertheless, I waited until 9:00 a.m. when Court convened. Jerry Clifton's name was called and he was not present. His bond was forfeited, thus closing the cases – officially that is, but not altogether. I didn't seize the illegal venison Norma received from Clifton. I would have if the case had gone to trial, but it didn't and I figured Norma could use the meat as well as any institution.

Sometime later, not long before I entered the Federal Service, I ran into Jerry. We enjoyed a very brief visit with each other over a cup of coffee at a Maumee restaurant. Jerry chuckled, "If I decide to violate the law again, I sure hope you're not the one who comes after me. I wouldn't stand a chance," he told me with a big smile.

"You flatter me Jerry," I stated as we shook hands.

"By the way, Jerry, I hope things worked out between you and Norma – she seemed like a great gal," I stated.

"Well, Mr. Bailey, after she got over being mad at me for dumping her trash where I shouldn't have, she married me," Jerry responded with another big smile.

On that happy note we parted company. As I resumed my patrol on the Maumee River, I thought, a nice young couple, I sure hope everything works out okay for them. All's well that ends well.

13
Black Ducks and Mallards

During the history of waterfowl management in the United States, four "flyways" were identified for management purposes. That is, four migration routes the birds travel from the northern tundra to the southern tropics. The flyways are named the Atlantic, Mississippi, Central and Pacific.

Management entities known as "Flyway Councils" evolved and established in each flyway in the late 40's and early 50's. Each council included wildlife professionals, mainly waterfowl biologists from the various states within each flyway. A very important function of the Councils were to determine the number of hunting days the waterfowl resource could withstand each year. Known as a hunting season "framework", it was presented to the U.S. Fish and Wildlife Service for approval and legal enactment.

Each flyway state set their respective annual hunting season dates within each framework. During the 60's Ohio, partially within the Atlantic and Mississippi Flyways, chose to use several of its allotted days for a late season that ran from Christmas through New Year's day. As I recall, the bag limit was four and included only one black duck. This late season was designed to capitalize on the normally late and most abundantly populated flights of black and mallard ducks from the north. This late season clearly hit the target during a late 60's season. At the season's opening, the Lake Erie marshes were frozen. In Lucas County, within Wildlife District Two, the only open water was the main body of Lake Erie and the Maumee River. The season caught the main thrust of this gigantic movement of black ducks and mallards at its highest peak. The Maumee River, open and unfrozen was loaded.

John Staab was the Game Protector assigned to Lucas County. He was one "bearcat" of a Game Warden, definitely one of Ohio's best. His pre-season observations of the massive buildup of black ducks and mallards on the Maumee caused him to proclaim three words to the District Two Law Enforcement Supervisor, Mike Fitzgibbons -- "I need help!"

"296 or 255 from Findlay," broadcast Eloise's voice, the radio operator at the District Two Headquarters in Findlay.

"Go ahead Findlay. This is 296, 255 is with me," Mel Weis, the Senior Game Protector in charge of Williams, Defiance, Henry and Fulton Counties replied. We were working a deer investigation on the Ohio-Michigan state line.

"Call 251 by public service ASAP relative a waterfowl assignment," Findlay advised.

"Will do, Findlay, in about twenty minutes," Weis replied.

We went by my house in Montpelier where we phoned Mike Fitzgibbons (251). "I need your work unit (Officers Marvin Rittenhouse, Fulton County; Jerry Richardson, Henry County; and Tim Hood, Defiance County) and Ron to head for Lucas County tomorrow. You need to be in place early for the opening (Christmas day). Staab needs help big time for the upcoming duck season. Staab says the Maumee is packed full of blacks and mallards. He says he's never seen anything like it. The heaviest concentration of ducks lay between Waterville and the Henry County line. That's where John wants your crew to work – all the islands. With the forecast weather conditions, the ducks will be milling about all day and flying low. The marshes are frozen but a strong warming trend is coming. John looks for the marshes to open up and divert some of the birds from the river, but for now and the opening, the river is where the action is. John expects serious overbagging, bait, late shooting – all of it. John and whoever I can muster to get up there will work the river north and the Lake Erie marshes when and if they open up. Oh, another little goodie -- a well known outdoor writer who can't seem to say anything good about us or the Feds will be hunting on one of the islands. He'll have an entourage with him. They'll gun on more than one island and run their overbags to some shoreline cabins. Staab wants this clown iced down! You guys divide the geography anyway you like – happy hunting!" Fitzgibbon stated.

"The heaviest concentration of ducks lay between Waterville and the Henry County line," as Fitz put it. This piece of geography included twelve meandering miles of river, Granger Island, Missionary Island (360 acres), Indian Island, Otter Island, Otsego Park, Millers Island, Sheets Island, Howard Island, and numerous smaller satellite islands. Most had duck blinds on them. Ninety percent of these blinds were associated with a cabin or home on the main banks of the Maumee River. It was an ideal setup for over bagging. Kill a limit, run them to a house or cabin, go back to the blind and kill some more – a Game Warden's nightmare.

Mel Weis knew more about this section of river than anyone else in our meager crew. On arrival the day before the opening -- seeing the huge number of ducks trading up and down the river, I thought of David and Goliath – us being David.

Each officer had a boat and outboard. I had a canoe, a watercraft I saw wasn't going to be of much use, especially if I had to pursue someone. Using a map of the river, Weis divided each officer's work area as evenly as he could. Rittenhouse and Richardson would work the big islands to the northwest. Hood would work the next section to the southwest including Otsego Park and Otter Island. Hood was the fastest among us. Mel knew this and put Hood where he would be most effective in getting to one of us who needed help. Weis would work Millers Island and a small satellite island southwest of Millers. I would go to Sheets Island, Howard Island, and the smaller islands in between. Not much was expected to happen on Howard Island. We thought Sheets Island would be the hot spot. Weis pointed out two cabins on the south bank he thought was associated with Sheets Island.

Millers Island, in Weis's area, was where our unfriendly outdoor writer had a blind and was expected to hunt. The writer's entourage was expected to hunt Sheets Island and southwest in my area. We each went our separate ways to scout the geography in our work areas and plan for the opening day. Looking over my area, given the fact I had a canoe, I decided to set up with my long range spotting scope and watch the cabins where we suspected overbags would be stashed. The observation point I selected gave me a very good view of the cabins and river. I couldn't see any identifiable blinds on Sheets Island. I could see a single blind on the small island upstream of Sheets Island. I also saw a heavy concentration of ducks on the water and milling around in the air near this little island. I scanned Sheets Island again – it was heavily posted with "No Hunting or Trespassing" signs. Not knowing who owned or controlled Sheets Island, I hoped the blind on the small island was associated with one or both of the cabins I planned to watch. I knew I could get to the small island by canoe in fairly short order. With my big black lab, Biff, in the canoe with me, clad in hunting garb with my Remington pump shotgun, I felt I could get to and check any hunters on the island. My best bet was to stick with the cabin surveillance plan. (Ah, the best laid plans - - .)

I returned to my patrol car, unloaded my canoe, carried it to a location near my planned surveillance location and hid it in a fence row, covering it up with camo netting and brush.

The next day, (Christmas – season opened) owing to a problem with my patrol car, I arrived at my work area too late to work early shooters. As I headed for my pre-determined surveillance location I ran head on into two hunters literally running from the river bank to their vehicle parked nearby. Running away from the hunt to their vehicle this early – they're wrong sure as xo#x, I thought

"Whoa gentlemen, slow up! State Game Protector. You must have limited out early – in a hurry to get home, huh?" I asked as I stopped them. It was barely daylight.

"Yes sir, gotta get to work," one answered.

"On Christmas Day? Let's take a quick look at your ducks. Shotguns, hunting licenses and duck stamps," I stated. I heard all xo#x break loose on the river -- shots everywhere. In the dimness of first light, I could see ducks dropping everywhere on the river and in the adjacent fields. This is an absolute slaughter, I thought as I began checking my two hunters who were in such a hurry. I saw both their game bags were bulging.

"Gentlemen, unload your guns," I ordered. Both complied.

"O.K. Warden, you've got us. We're both over the limit," one stated.

"And you planned to stash your ducks in your car trunk and go back hunting, didn't you?" I asked.

"Yes sir, we did. Are you Gil Palmer?" (Wildlife Enforcement Agent) one asked.

"No, Gil is working north of here. I take it you know Gil," I responded.

"Yeah, he got us last year," one stated.

"For what?" I asked.

"Too many ducks," one responded.

"Let's count them," I stated as I emptied their hunting coat bags in two separate piles. They were four ducks each over the limit. All the ducks they killed were mallards. Both lads were carrying properly plugged guns. Both had proper resident hunting licenses. Both had duck stamps, unsigned as required by law. I handed them my pen and told them to sign their stamps. They were in enough trouble already with eight ducks over the limit.

"C'mon boys, help me get these birds to my car. You're going to lose your legal limit. I'm seizing them to prove to the court you took more than the limit," I stated. I picked up the over bag birds. I had each lad put what would have been his limit in his hunting coat bag and we went to my patrol car. I stacked each hunter's ducks in a separate pile in my car trunk. I cited both into court. I told each of the bond forfeiture system and bid them farewell. I hurriedly placed a copy of each citation on each pile of ducks in my car trunk, shut the lid and hurried towards the river.

I took about five steps when I glanced to my left and saw two hunters hurriedly walking along a fence row leaving the river, headed for their parked vehicle. They were looking back over their shoulders and in every other direction except mine. I returned to the road, got in my patrol car and drove to where their vehicle was parked. I knew if I continued to walk towards them, they would see my uniform. In my state vehicle, they paid no attention to my approach as my patrol car was a black unmarked Plymouth. It had civilian plates on it that I borrowed from a second car I owned – an illegal practice I sometimes participated in to throw the opposition off. I add, a practice not condoned by the Ohio Division of Wildlife and certainly not by the Highway Patrol. Checking both hunters, both had their limits and their guns were unplugged as required by law. I checked their vehicles for additional ducks. I thought their hurried exit from the river may indicate they took a second "limit". Their duck stamps and hunting licenses were in order. One claimed to be late for an appointment, thus the rush.

As I completed citing these two hunters into court, I noticed a tan Ford sedan pull off the road and park behind me. I recognized a Gruman flat stern canoe secured to L.L. Bean car top carriers on the roof. Two gentlemen dressed in camo were seated in the front seat where they remained until I completed filling out citations on my two violators and bid them farewell after explaining some court procedures. I knew both these gentlemen were U.S. Game Management Agents with the U.S. Fish and Wildlife Service (Federal Game Wardens) but I didn't recognize either of them as the agents assigned to Ohio. Both exited their vehicle and introduced themselves as Agent Bill McClure and Bob Meyerding, assigned to Michigan.

"We've worked our way down the river from the north. From Waterville on, we've seen nothing but what looks like all the ducks in Ohio, hunters and State Game Wardens writing tickets. It looks like you boys have got things under control. We've considered going back to Michigan unless you think we can be of some help," Agent McClure stated.

"Got things under control xo#x, you could put fifty Game Wardens on this stretch of river and not have enough. Listen to the war going on down there (motioning towards the Maumee). There's ducks dropping everywhere. I've been trying to get to a surveillance point where I can observe some hunters I know xo#x well are all over bagging and double tripping. Xo#x, triple tripping and I haven't got to them yet for writing tickets. You bet you can be of some help! Have you got a motor for your boat? Have you got any portable radios?" I asked.

Agent McClure answered, "Yes" to both inquiries.

"Good! I need your car, your boat and a portable radio. I need both of you to follow me with a portable radio and spotting scope if you have one. If not, binoculars will do," I stated.

"We've got both," Agent Meyerding stated as they got their equipment out of the back seat of their car.

"I did a quick familiarization with their portable radio. "My call signal is 255 – what's yours?" I asked.

"G-3 and G-4 is fine," McClure responded. As Agent McClure handed me the keys to his vehicle, I gave him the keys to mine. I pointed to a location (down a farm lane) where the Federal Agents could park and hide my vehicle after they covered it with my second camo netting. I showed them the location of my hidden canoe. We walked a short distance down a fence row where I could show them the surveillance point I'd selected -- downstream from the two cabins I felt were associated with the blind on the small island. This location was situated at an elevated curve in the river. It gave the Agents a good view of the front and rear of the cabins as well as several small outbuildings. From this location they would also observe the blind on the small island where two gunners were shellacking the xo#x out of ducks – an island I planned to visit ASAP.

En route back to our vehicles, we crept to the rivers edge. As luck would have it, we observed one subject in a jon boat propelled by less than five horse power outboard, leave the duck blind on the small island and go to the northwest cabin. A Brittany Spaniel was in the front of the boat. He beached, exited the boat, and went inside the cabin carrying nothing. He returned to the boat shortly carrying a small brown paper bag. He entered the boat and returned to the blind. His well trained Brittany Spaniel remained seated on the front seat of the boat during this entire interlude.

This observation made us all feel better as we now knew the hunters in the small island blind were definitely associated with one of the shoreline cabins under surveillance. What occurred prior to our late arrival was anyone's guess.

"Well gentlemen, we don't have the best of situations because we're late. Maybe we can do something with it. If you'll watch the cabins for double tripping, I'll put on my hunting coat and cap, get my shotgun and use your car to get to the other side of the river. I know where there is a little used ramp where I'll put overboard. With my lab in the boat, hopefully they'll think I'm another hunter. I plan to go downstream past them and get on the island with them undetected. Between both our observations, hopefully we'll nail them. I know they're way over the limit. The question will be – where have they stashed the ducks? I'll call you with a radio check as soon as I get overboard," I stated.

"Okay" came an assured response from both Federal Officers. I got my binoculars, hunting coat and cap and shotgun from my patrol car. With my equipment and Labrador Retriever "Biff" loaded in the Federal Agent's vehicle, I departed for the opposite side of the Maumee and the little known boat ramp.

I traveled south and west on Rt. 65 to Grand Rapids, crossed the river from Wood into Lucas County and headed downstream to the boat ramp. I had a heck of a time locating the exact lane I needed to find to get to the ramp and get overboard. I finally selected one that looked right and took it. This is what I get for not scouting out all the geography ahead of time. Xo#x it Bailey, you know better. There it is – lucky me, I thought as I got to the ramp. I happened to pick the right lane.

I unloaded the canoe and slipped it partially into the water. I mounted the little three horsepower outboard I retrieved from the trunk. Now watch, this thing won't start, I thought. Wrong! The first pull after setting the choke, the little outboard started. These Feds take care of their equipment, I thought.

After a radio check with my Federal peers, I donned my hunting garb. Placed my shotgun unloaded and muzzle up where it could be seen, told Biff to sit on the front seat and took off downstream towards my gunning hunters. Soon I approached their small island "honey hole" midstream a good distance from their blind. Passing them, one stood up in the blind and yelled, "Can't you see we're hunting here, you xo#x."

They sure think I'm another hunter – that's good. It's nice to know hunters call each other xo#x. I thought that name was reserved for Game

Wardens. I gave them the "perch" finger. "Both you xo#x go to xo#x -- you don't own this river," I yelled.

"Guess they got you told 255," came a voice over the radio.

"You guys heard all that?" I responded.

"That's affirmative," answered G-3.

This was my big Lab's first exposure to duck hunting. My son and I bought "Biff" and his liter mate "Kip" from a Michigan resident when they were three years old. Their former owner (and trainer) hunted them on pheasants only, mainly in Nebraska. Biff's reaction to all the shooting and ducks dropping all around him was one of surprisingly quiet resolve. He was excited all right, but remained in the boat and seated as I quietly told him to "stay". I was pleased with the way he obeyed. A good Game Warden dog, I thought. I beached the canoe well downstream of my prey, I spotted a crippled black duck about the same time Biff saw it. He looked at me. I quietly said, "Get him Biff." The duck hid itself well in the marsh. Biff caught and retrieved the duck in short order. I put the bird in the boat after relieving its misery. Then Biff did what seemed to me a strange thing. He jumped into the boat and laid quietly on the bird. I headed back upstream toward the little island. My target blind with my two outlaw hunters were situated on the upstream end of the island. The two were still dropping ducks right and left and yelling commands to their little Brittany who was doing his best to retrieve the slaughter. I could see plenty of tree and shrub cover on the island that would conceal my landing on the island's downstream side. I would be in an ideal location to count their drops; I knew they were well over the limit. What I didn't consider was the little Brittany and Biff.

I crept as close and I dared towards the blind. Biff, to my pleasant surprise, stayed quietly beside me to my right. Then it happened. We were upwind. The little Brittany caught our scent and more important, Biff's scent. He came running full tilt, yapping, with every hair on his back standing up. I should state at this point Biff weighed 110 lbs; the Brittany about 40 lbs. The little dog left the ground about six feet in front of Biff headed for the big dog's throat. Biff, seeing the little warrior, who thought he was defending his domain, quietly without as much as a growl, side stepped the little guy and caught him in mid-air just ahead of his left hind leg with his jaws firmly gripped around the little dog's penis and belly. Biff threw the little dog a good five feet in the air somewhat like a frisbee. As the little dog plummeted earthward, Biff caught him in the air and by the throat with his massive jaws and proceeded to choke the life out of the gurgling little Brittany.

I got Biff off the little dog in short order only to look up and see my two xo#x duck hunters charging towards me full tilt as their whimpering little Brittany met them, pride robbed and unhurt.

"It's you again. What the xo#x do you mean coming on this island hunting. We've got this island leased and that xo#x dog of yours – if he's hurt my dog, I'll kill him," the bigger and uglier of the two stated.

By the time he had uttered all this, he was right beside Biff. I had

Biff by his collar and said, "Everything's under control - -" my statement was interrupted as the xo#x drew his foot back to kick Biff.

That gesture did it. All the professional Game Warden in me left. The coon hunter -- "my dog" filled its place, big time! There's certain things you don't do to a coon hunter's dog – you don't mess with him --you don't hurt him – you don't "throw off" on him and you xo#x sure don't steal or shoot him. Even though Biff was a Lab, this xo#x's gesture awoke all the houndsman blood in me and all my blood kin before me who "followed the hounds."

"Go ahead, you xo#xxo#x – kick him and see how long you stay alive!" I stated and meant every word. I had lost it and I knew it. I was raging mad. I removed my hunting coat revealing my uniform, badge and more important, my sidearm that I rested my right hand on.

"He's a xo#x Game Warden, Dick cool it," the not so ugly one stated as he continued petting and consoling the little Brittany. "Well that sure does change things. Now by xo#x, we'll write the Governor and tell him what one of his Game Wardens and his xo#x xo#x dog did to us," stated big and ugly.

"That's right, I'm a xo#x Game Warden. Write the Governor, your Senator, or the President but right now your little duck shooting honeymoon is over. Unload your shotguns and I mean now!" I shouted, still so mad I couldn't see straight with my right hand still resting on my revolver.

"Do as he says Dick. He's mad – we'll do what we have to do later. This thing has gone too far," the sensible and not so ugly hunter stated.

For a reason I can't explain, I glanced down at Biff. His ears were slightly perked up. His big brown eyes looked straight into mine as though he was waiting a command. Here was my big Lab, totally untrained on ducks and doing so well, as though he had been there before, I thought. Biff's big brown eyes brought me to my senses. Why or how he had such a calming effect on me I'll never know.

I checked their shotguns -- unplugged. I suspicioned their guns were plugged but they removed them when they saw the huge numbers of ducks on the river. Later, through their own admissions, this proved to be true. Their hunting licenses (which I temporarily pocketed) were okay. Their duck stamps were valid and signed.

"Now Hot Shots, we'll go to the blind," I stated. I could see both were nervous – far more nervous than mad. Inside the blind in a nice neat row were six mallards and two black ducks – the exact legal limit. I knew there had to be more, many more.

"How many birds have you taken to the shore and hid in or near your cabin?" I asked.

"None," big and ugly stated.

"Not a single one," the other stated.

"Don't lie to me. There's two Federal Game Wardens who've had your cabin under surveillance. I'll check with them by radio shortly, but now I want the truth," I stated.

"We're telling you the truth. We didn't run any ducks ashore – I almost wish we did," big and ugly stated.

"If you did, the Federal Agents saw you (a lie). If that's not the case, you've hidden them somewhere on this island or stomped them in the marsh. Tie or hold your little dog. It's time for my Lab to go to work," I stated.

I wasn't sure what Biff would do. He knew what the command "dead bird" meant. He'd learned the command retrieving countless pheasants for his previous owner. The little Brittany was acting anxious, as though he wanted to patch things up with Biff. The little dog seemed to know what was about to take place.

"Dead bird," I told Biff and pointed to the marshy area in front of the blind. Biff went into action. He began searching the area I pointed to. Suddenly, he threw his head upward sniffing the air and headed to the higher and dryer geography behind the blind. I thought, he's going pheasant hunting, but what can I expect – until today he's never seen a duck let alone retrieve one. He continued working the higher ground behind the blind. All the while the little Brittany was going nuts. It was obvious he wanted to help Biff with his ever widening search. I walked to where the little dog was tied and unsnapped his chain.

"Don't do that – you're gonna start another dog fight," big and ugly stated.

I smiled at the big xo#x, "I don't think so, hot shot. I know dogs and this little guy wants to help find the ducks you've hidden. It's obvious he understands what "dead bird" means. I have a feeling your little dog is pretty good at finding dead and crippled birds," I stated.

"I told you not to turn my dog loose, xo#x it, and you went ahead and did it. If your dog kills him, you're gonna have xo#x to pay, believe me!" big and ugly blurted.

"Yes, and I'm telling you to shut your big mouth," I shouted. I looked up to see Biff coming to me with a big fat hen mallard. The little Brittany ran to greet him – sniffed the mallard in Biff's mouth – licked the big black Lab's nose and took off in a dead run in the exact direction Biff came from. Biff dropped the mallard at my feet. As I sent him back to his search with the "dead bird" command, here came the little Brittany, not to his master but to me, carrying a big black duck. I patted the little guy as I gently took the black duck from his mouth, said "dead bird".

"Good boy, good boy," I stated as the little Brittany, now anxious to please me, took off happy as a lark to find and bring me another bird.

"You can't prove we shot those birds," the hunting companion of big and ugly stated.

"Oh yes I can, shut up!" I stated as I inserted a rectal thermometer in the hen mallard's vent and got my notebook out of my uniform shirt pocket and stood ready to record the thermometer reading. Shortly, I removed the thermometer – held it up and looked at it – then my watch – then recorded the readings in my notebook. I repeated the procedure with each duck as the dogs brought them to me.

Big and ugly snickered, "What do you think you're going to prove with the thermometer bit, Game Warden?"

"You'll find out stupid, when you stand in front of the Federal Court Judge in Toledo," I replied.

"What do you mean, Federal Judge?" not so ugly asked.

"There are two Federal Agents involved in this case. They're ashore where they watched you and your cabin all morning (a lie). The last I talked with them by radio, they reported your last trip to the cabin and the brown paper bag you brought back to the blind (another little truth stretching). What's in the bag – a little booze perhaps? Drinking and hunting perhaps? (Implying another violation.) We can tell when a duck was killed by measuring body temperature loss, given the outside temperature, by taking rectal temperature readings. It's all been pre-researched and charted. When the Federal Agents and I compare their recorded observations of your 'drops' or kills and the temperature data I'm collecting now, it will suffice to say you've been had. (A little gobble-gook). You might be smart enough to see the hand writing on the wall but I doubt it. You killed every one of these ducks the dogs are bringing to me. You know it and I know it. You also know the Federal Agents and I can and will prove it in court. What about it – think you have something you'd like to tell me?" I asked. Both looked at each other, took a few steps aside and conferred briefly. The more pleasant of the two stated, "Alright, the ducks are ours. You should have sixteen by the time the dogs are through. We hid them – we got word before season that you guys would be watching the cabins."

I could see a change of attitude in my two outlaws. I also knew I had full command of the situation as I again recalled Vern Bare, my respected training officer's instruction so many years before, "Always take command."

"Who told you we'd be watching the cabins?" I quickly countered.

"Have you ever heard of (I'll call him) Lee Clower?" big and ugly asked.

"No, I answered (a lie). Clower was the hostile outdoor writer who John Staab, through our District Law Enforcement Supervisor, told us to be on the lookout for. Little did I know at that time that Mel Weis already had Mr. Clower "iced down" with fifteen ducks over the limit along with a close relative for shooting ducks from a boat under power. Mr. Clower didn't run his over limit ducks to a shoreline cabin. Instead he took them to a barn – the same barn Weis used as a surveillance station. If it wasn't for bad luck, Mr. Clower had no luck at all! To put a little frosting on the cake, Weis sacked two more of the Clower entourage by simply putting the "B" on them. Weis didn't witness them do anything, he simply talked them into it. They took Weis to their ill gotten booty (over bags) and told Melvin, "They were sorry they did it and decided to help Weis make the world a little better place to live." Ah! There will never be another Weis! There was no end to that big German!

Within another fifteen minutes, Biff and his little companion had sixteen ducks at my feet. The dogs started milling around the blind, heisting their hind leg and congratulating each other on a job well done. I knew they considered their search concluded – there were no more hidden birds. They proved my two outlaw hunters told me the truth.

"You boys have finally come around and started to act like men instead of poor sportsmen. Because of your change in attitude, I'm going to cite you into State Court in Maumee as opposed to Federal Court in Toledo. I'm going to split the over bag counts down the middle. I explained the bond forfeiture system to them and added – If you decide to go this route it will eliminate the necessity for the Federal Agents to come back to Ohio to testify as they are both assigned to Michigan. Of course, if you want to go to trial, we'll handle that. Realize of course, all this is contingent on the fact the Federal Agents confirm your story claiming you didn't run any ducks ashore," I told them as I completed the next to last rectal temperature procedure.

"I've got no desire to go to trial," the big one stated.

"That goes for me too," the other chimed in.

"I haven't checked with the Federal Agents yet. If you've run ducks ashore you realize they've documented it. Do you still claim you didn't run any ducks to the cabin or anywhere else on shore?" I asked.

"No sir, we absolutely didn't. We planned to take the birds to a boat ramp up the river, hide them and pick them up on our way home to Toledo tonight," one stated. I'll bet it's the same boat ramp I used, I thought.

"Okay, I'll buy that," I responded.

"It's the truth," the other one stated.

I looked at my watch – it was ten minutes to ten. I cited both hunters into Maumee Municipal Court for taking over the limit, taking more black ducks than allowed and hunting with shotgun capable of holding more than three shells (unplugged).

Biff and I returned to the canoe at the downstream side of the island and maneuvered the boat to the upstream side of the island in front of the blind. Using the Federal Agent's bait drag (or basket), I checked the water in front of the blind for bait and found none. Later, I heard the downstream or "lee" side of the island where I originally pulled my boat ashore, was where the bait was. In other words, I missed it. I didn't know much about duck baiting at the time. I didn't know under stream conditions the lee or downstream side of a river island was where bait was usually placed. It was placed at that location for the simple reason there was virtually no current there. Thus the grain would stay in place longer as opposed to being washed away by the current. I would learn much about the "lee" side of river islands years later, while working the famous Susquehanna River in Pennsylvania as a Federal Agent. With the help of my now, not so hostile gunners, I loaded all their ducks into the Sportsman's canoe including their "professed limit" in their blind. After a small amount of discussion concerning the location of the Maumee Municipal Court, I bid my outlaw hunters farewell but not before advising them their hunt was over for the day. I stated, "It's time for you to leave the river so you won't be tempted by the heavy flights overhead."

"G 3 or G 4 from 255," I radioed.

187

"Go ahead 255," G 3 (Agent Bill McClure) replied.

"I've apprehended the two hunters you've been watching. I cited them into State Court for over the limit and unplugged guns. If you would, load my canoe, hop in my car and come around to the ramp where I've left your car," I radioed. (I then gave G 2 and G 3 directions to the ramp.)

En route back to the ramp, Biff sat on the front seat of the boat where I made him stay after he tried to lay down on the pile of evidence ducks on the boat floor, the same as he did on the earlier collected black duck. As we traveled upstream, he would spot ducks (and a few geese) trading, up and down the river. He was so intense watching these flying birds that he would fall off his seat backward as he followed their line of flight from bow to stern. He was definitely a duck dog.

I soon pulled the federal boat ashore at the little known and used boat ramp. I unloaded my gear and evidence on shore. Shortly, Agents McClure and Meyerding arrived. We loaded the Sportsman's canoe on top of the federal patrol car and secured it to the car top carriers after dismounting the little outboard and placing it, their bait drag and their portable radios in the trunk. We lined my sixteen over bag ducks up in a row and I snapped a picture. I snapped a separate photo of the "legal limit ducks" my two outlaws had in a neat row in their blind. We loaded all my gear in my state patrol car excluding the ducks. After the Federal Agents departure, I field dressed my seized ducks of the day and cooled their warm carcasses in the cold waters of the Maumee River. I tagged them as evidence and placed them in a cooler in the trunk of my vehicle. A considerable chore but worth it, as they ultimately went to the needy in two counties.

Before departing, Agent McClure asked if I had any suggestions as to where they should work. I told them I was sure there was no more than one State Officer working the Maumee from the Henry County line to the Indiana State line and I was sure the Lake Erie marshes were "opening up" due to the warming trend. I suggested they take their pick. I'm not certain but I believe they went to the marshes.

Returning to my patrol car and resuming my patrol, I heard two of my fellow warriors (Rittenhouse and Richardson) on the radio calling in prior arrest checks. In subsequent radio conversation, I learned they had a good morning making many early shooting, unplugged guns and over bag cases. Tim Hood, as usually the case, was silent – a certain indicator he had a good morning – that fact was a given. Weis and I had a brief exchange advising each other of our morning results. This was when I first learned Weis had sacked a main target (the outdoor writer) over bagged by fifteen ducks.

As the day wore on, although there were still many birds in the air, the gunning slowed. In my patrol area the gunning seemed heaviest on the Lucas County side of the river. Consequently, that's where I remained. I managed to apprehend three late shooters and picked up two more unplugged gun cases. I finally called it a day long after dark.

The second day you wouldn't know it was the same river. The ducks, for the most part, were gone. The marshes warmed and opened up diffusing the large numbers of blacks and mallards that choked the island section of the Maumee. The hunting pressure was comparatively light as most hunters had gone back to work – the Christmas holiday over.

Biff had a ball finding and retrieving cripples from the previous days slaughter. I put all the cripples out of their misery and distributed them throughout the river bottoms for the predators. The possibility of gangrene prohibited human consumption. I wrote two early shooters, checked several "late morning" limits but no over bags and wrote one unplugged gun and one late shooter in the p.m.

Weis and I left the river to resume work on a deer investigation. I returned to work the close of the season on New Years day. Although some birds had returned to the river, it was nothing to compare with the opening day. The gunning was fairly constant and you might call hunter success – good. I wrote one more over bag case (only one over), one unplugged gun and three more late shooters, thus ending this late duck season. My violators forfeited over $2500.00 in appearance bonds. One late shooter chose to appear. He was found guilty and fined twice the amount of the appearance bond set by the Court.

Today, hunting seasons for certain abundant species such as Atlantic flyway "resident" canadian geese and migrant snow geese run well into January and February. The "late season" I write of in this story wouldn't be considered such.

I don't know how many of these late (in that day and time) seasons Ohio was granted as I left soon thereafter to enter the Federal Service. I do know I don't agree with the concept. This late season, targeting two not over abundant species, resulted in an abnormal slaughter, particularly of black ducks, a species then and now in trouble. The season wasn't a quality hunt for the Ohio duck hunter. It was an opening day massacre that served the blood lust of a greedy few. We made many quality cases. We slowed the slaughter a little. I hope the resource and folks of this day and age benefited in some measure from our efforts.

14
The Eber Road Incident

In October of 1967 I was assigned an after-the-fact investigation in Lucas County, Ohio. John Staab, the Lucas County Game protector, caused my involvement in the investigation by submitting an Investigation Request (Form W-45) to the District Two Acting Law Enforcement Supervisor, Gil Palmer, at the Wildlife District Two Headquarters in Findlay.

John requested the assistance of a Wildlife Enforcement Agent to investigate the closed season deer killing near Eber Road and the Toledo Airport in Lucas County. The facts were a thirteen year old boy discovered a fresh deer gut pile some distance behind his home. The boy's mother (I'll call her Mrs. Smart) called Officer Staab reporting the discovery. John completed the initial investigation by photographing and inspecting the site. He thoroughly examined the gut pile and couldn't find a bullet, slug or buck shot. There were tire tracks; however, they were muted and weathered.

Shortly after I was assigned the case, John and I re-visited the scene and re-interviewed the thirteen year old boy and his mother. On this occasion, the boy's father and an older teenage brother were present. Both were very quiet and displayed what I can best describe as an "uncooperative spirit." As a matter of fact, I had the distinct feeling one or both had something to do with or knew something about the illegal deer killing. Later, I expressed my feeling and suspicions to John. If either of them killed the deer, the mother and the thirteen year old would almost have to know about it and it was doubtful they would have reported the violation to John. I theorized even though they (the father and/or teenage brother) didn't actually kill the deer, they knew who did and for whatever reason didn't tell the mother or thirteen year old.

The fact an access lane connected the crime scene property and the Toledo Airport property caused John to have an entirely different theory. John felt the guilty person or persons had something to do with the airport. Perhaps an airport employee or weekend warrior with the Air National Guard Unit that was located there. In any event, all we had at this point were theories only. We had no leads or traceable evidence of any kind.

Lucas County was outside my assigned work area of Williams, Defiance, Fulton and Henry Counties. I worked in Lucas County only on special assignments. Consequently, I had very few informants there. However, I did have one who was very reliable. I had planned to contact this C.I. (confidential informant) concerning this case to see if he had or could develop any leads. Several weeks passed since John and I visited the crime scene. During this time, Defiance County Game Protector, Dick Wolfrom and I conducted and completed an investigation involving non-residents illegally procuring resident fishing licenses in Defiance County. The investigation was prompted by the fact Officer Wolfrom was encountering an unusually high number of fishermen with out-of-state driver's licenses and license plates on their vehicles, fishing with freshly procured resident fishing licenses. The residency requirement was six months. Most illegally procured resident licenses listed length of residency as one year. One year seemed to be the standard lie.

We went to the county license issuing agents and examined their copies of issued licenses and made a list of those claiming one year of residence. We ran residency checks on all of them. We determined such factors as when their public utilities i.e. phone, electric, etc. were turned on. When they began rent payment or purchased a home, etc. All were a matter of public record. Just before contact we examined the license plates on their vehicles. Upon contact each subject would, in most instances, still possess his out-of-state driver's license, fishing and/or hunting license, vehicle registration, etc. We cited each violator into court. All admitted to the violations when confronted. Most forfeited the court established $35.00 bond.

We processed forty-five individuals for this violation when we were ordered by the Columbus Office, through the District Two Office, to cease and desist. We were never told why. A hard to understand order, especially in view of the fact our investigation extrapolated state wide and to include hunting licenses, clearly showed the Ohio Division of Wildlife was being swindled out of thousands upon thousands of needed dollars due to this violation each year.

I later learned Chuck Kniffin (Ohio State Game Protector at the time – soon thereafter a U.S. Game Management Agent for the U.S. Fish and Wildlife Service) conducted a similar investigation in Sandusky County years earlier only to be thwarted and stopped by the Columbus Office.

Ah, the mysterious ways of politics!!

Before I could contact my Lucas County C.I. concerning the Lucas County closed season deer investigation, he contacted me by phone.

"There's a situation going on at the Toledo Airport that your Game

Warden in Maumee should know and do something about," stated the clear, crisp voice of my Lucas County Informant over the phone.

"Yeah, tell me about it (I'll call him) Tom," I responded.

"Not on the phone. I've said too much on the phone as it is. You'll have to come here, my friend – and be sure you come alone," my C.I. stated. We made arrangements to meet the following evening at a specified location in Maumee.

"I'm a member of the Air National Guard. I attend weekend drills at the Air National Guard Armory at the Toledo Airport. We've got a certain A.P. (Air Policeman) who makes it his business, while on perimeter patrols, to hunt deer. There's quite a few of them (deer) on the airport property. I'm certain he's killed one or two – shot them out of his Jeep with a Carbine. The word is – he sneaked them back to the base near the end of a drill, put them in his pickup truck, covered them with a tarp and took them home. He hasn't been able to keep his mouth shut. He bragged to a couple Guardsmen," my C.I. stated opening our meeting.

"You say 'a certain AP', what's his name?" I asked.

(I'll call him) "Eddie Pence", the C.I. replied.

"Do you know of any Guard members who have actually witnessed Eddie kill or possess a deer?" I asked.

"No, it's his running off the mouth," My C.I. replied.

"Describe his pickup truck," I stated.

"It's a beat up GMC – about a '58 or '59," the C.I. responded.

"Do you know the license plate number," I asked.

"No, but I'll get it and give it to you later," my C.I. replied.

"Do you happen to know where Pence lives," I asked.

"I know exactly where he lives?" my C.I. replied and gave me directions to the Eddie Pence residence.

Well Bailey, you sure didn't pick up the right vibes on this one, I thought while en route home after my meeting with my C.I. John Staab hit the nail square on the head with his Air National Guard weekend warrior theory. Later that evening my C.I. phoned and gave me the license number on Eddie Pence's red pickup truck.

The following morning I ran a license check on the pickup. It checked out to a 1958 GMC. That afternoon, I traveled to Swanton, Ohio where I soon located the Eddie Pence residence situated in the Swanton outskirts. The red '58 GMC pickup, along with a sedan vehicle were parked in his driveway. It was about 5 p.m. My knock on the front door resulted in Eddie himself opening the door.

"My name is Ron Bailey. I'm an Ohio State Game Protector and I'm looking for a Mr. Edward Pence," I stated.

"You're speaking to him," replied the five foot ten,brown haired Pence.

"Mr. Pence, I'm investigating the illegal killing and taking of one or more white tail deer, during the closed season at the Toledo Airport. Our

193

investigation thus far, tells us you are responsible for these illegal acts. The investigation has reached the point where I'm required to talk to you about your illegal deer hunting activity. I'm required at this time to advise you of your rights," I stated. I read Pence the Miranda Warning.

Pence nervously agreed to questioning. At my invitation, we went to my patrol car where I sat behind the wheel and Pence sat in the front passenger's seat. "I understand you're a member of the Air National Guard Unit located at the Toledo Airport – am I correct?" I asked.

"Yes, sir, that's true," Pence replied.

"Eddie, I'm going to come to the point. I'm giving you the opportunity to tell me all about your deer poaching activity at the airport. If we had no evidence against you, you and I wouldn't be talking now. There is no sense in this matter going beyond you, me and the court. In other words, there's no sense in me having to contact your Commanding Officer or the Airport Authorities. Let's keep this entire affair between you, me and the court. Now, I want you to tell me all about it. It's your call," I told Pence.

Pence hesitated for what seemed like forever. He acted nervous as all get out. I felt certain a confession was forthcoming.

"Do you have any questions?" I asked, breaking the silence.

Continued silence as Pence was obviously wrestling with his conscience and at the same time weighing the odds.

"What do you expect me to say?" Pence finally asked.

"I expect you to tell me the truth. As you tell me all about it, I'm going to write it down on a statement form that I'll ask you to read and sign," I replied.

Continued silence. Then suddenly, "I didn't kill no deer," Pence blurted.

"Wrong answer, Eddie! You're not adding things up right – you've got the wrong sum total. You don't see the hand writing on the wall – the direction I've got to go if you don't level with me. Do you want to stick with that answer?" I asked the now more nervous Pence.

"I didn't kill no deer," he again responded.

"Okay Eddie, I'm through playing games. We can settle the matter of your innocence or guilt quite simply. Do you know what a polygraph examination is?" I asked.

"Yeah, I know what it is," he answered.

"Fine, if you're innocent of these deer killing allegations, you won't mind taking a polygraph examination, will you? As a matter of fact, I've got a little form for you to sign agreeing to take the examination at the Patton Detective Agency located near here," I told Pence as I quickly retrieved one of my self initiated Polygraph Agreement forms from my brief case. I clipped it to a clipboard and thrust it in front of Pence along with a pen. To my surprise, Pence grasped the pen and signed the form. "Yeah, I'll take the polygraph test," he stated.

"Okay, fine Eddie. I'll notify you when and where to appear to take the examination. This hopefully will settle the matter. This concludes our business for the time being," I told Pence.

As Pence started to exit the vehicle, I asked, "Eddie – one more question. (I'll call them) Jim and Bob Smart, who live near the airport, tell me they know you, is that true?" (A fib, but I had to test my theory concerning a nexus between Pence and the Smarts.)

Pence hesitated before answering. It was obvious my question had him guessing as to what the Smarts (father and teenage son) may have told us. "Yeah, I know them," he quietly yet nervously answered.

"Fine, Eddie, I'll be in contact with you soon," I stated just before Pence's exit from my patrol car and my departure from his home.

At eight a.m. the following morning, I phoned Gil Palmer, Acting Law Enforcement Supervisor at the Wildlife District Two headquarters in Findlay. Gil approved payment for the Pence polygraph examination and stated, "You sure do like that machine don't you Mr. B – good luck!"

That afternoon, I phoned Dick (nicknamed Slick) Patton, Polygraph Examiner, Patton Detective Agency in Toledo. Arrangements were made for the Pence polygraph examination to take place two days hence on Friday.

On examination day, Officer Staab and I arrived at the Patton Detective Agency to find Pence's battered red GMC pickup in the parking lot and Eddie Pence waiting for us in the lobby. During the few minutes we had to wait before our appointment with Dick Patton, I wrote a list of questions for Patton to ask Pence during the examination. That chore completed, Officer Staab and I entered the Patton Detective Agency where we met and exchanged the usual amenities with Pence following my introduction of Officer Staab. Shortly, Examiner Patton entered the room and greeted us. All introductions completed, Examiner Patton, armed with my questions written on a yellow tablet, invited Pence to accompany him to the examination room.

I can only describe Pence's demeanor as "resigned". He wasn't unusually nervous nor was he unusually calm. He was definitely cooperative. I knew he would fail the test. For the next forty-five minutes, John and I discussed the case while the polygraph examination took place.

"Mr. Pence failed his polygraph test, gentlemen. He confessed to the closed season killing of a buck white tail deer that he shot and field dressed on the property of a Mr. and Mrs. Smart on or about mid October, 1967," Examiner Patton stated upon entering the room. Eddie Pence stared at the floor as I wrote a check and handed it to Dick Patton in payment for his services.

"Please mail the examination results and your written report concerning Mr. Pence's confession to Officer Staab," I told Patton. John handed Patton a business card and we departed the Patton Detective Agency Office.

"Eddie, you could have saved all concerned a lot of time and trouble had you leveled with me to begin with. Officer Staab will notify you as to where and when you are to appear in court. After court we can all consider this case closed," I told Pence as we parted company.

"John, I'll leave getting the Prosecutor's approval of the charges against Pence and the court proceedings up to you. It's your case. Don't bother with giving me an assist on your arrest report and call me if you need me as a witness," I told John just before I left for home. Eddie Pence ultimately forfeited an appearance bond in Maumee Municipal Court. Thus, ending the case. I wasn't being generous by telling John to take the case, thus naming him on the arrest report as the arresting officer. At this point, I was ninety-nine percent sure I would soon be entering the Federal Service as a Park Ranger for the U.S. Army Corps of Engineers. Credit for the case or another "notch" on my gun stock wouldn't mean much on my work record as my fourteen year career with the Ohio Division of Wildlife would soon end.

John's image standing beside his patrol car in his uniform reminded me of all the great Ohio State Wildlife Officers I had worked with all those years. I'll have to admit I choked up a little as I asked myself, "Bailey, are you doing the right thing?" I knew my new duties as a Park Ranger would be somewhat similar to my old Game Warden duties but certainly not the same. I wondered how well I would make the adjustment. I knew in my heart I would always be a Game Warden.

15
The Essayons

The Army Corps of Engineers, known as the Essayons in the early years, is one of our country's oldest military organizations. Its history dates back to a resolution of the Continental Congress on June 16, 1775 under which General George Washington appointed Colonel Richard Gridley as Chief Engineer of the Continental Army. The first Corps of Engineers was formally organized in 1779, and in 1802 the present Corps was constituted and charged with the responsibility of conducting a military academy at West Point, N.Y. For 64 years, until it was turned over to the Army-at-large in 1866, "West Point," the first – and for nearly a quarter of a century the only – engineering school in the nation, was a Corps installation managed by the Chief of Engineers. I'm blessed to have a Grandson who graduated from this great Institution.

The primary mission of the Corps has always been to provide combat support to our fighting Army. Engineer troops have written a distinguished battle record in every war and campaign in which the Army has been engaged, from Bunker Hill to the jungles of Vietnam and the desert sands of Iraq.

Engineer troops were first in action among American forces in World War I and suffered the first casualties. They were the first ashore in Normandy in World War II. In all the wars in which the United States has participated, the Corps has both fought in the front lines and constructed the field military installations, roads, bridges, and fortifications the Army has needed to do its job.

Immediately after the attack on Pearl Harbor in 1941, the Army Engineers were also assigned the responsibility for military construction in the United States previously accomplished by the Quartermaster Corps. It built more than 3,000 command installations, 500 camps, 765 airfields, 300 major industrial projects, 167 storage depots, and thousands of miscellaneous military facilities. It also constructed the Alaska (Alcan) Highway reaching 1,523 miles from "head of steel" at Dawson Creek, British Columbia to Fairbanks, Alaska.

During the Korean War, the Army Engineers built strategic air bases at remote locations throughout the world, including Greenland and North Africa. They also constructed a complete line of supply and communications facilities across France, and air raid warning systems in Labrador and Greenland.

In Vietnam, Engineer battalions constructed many military facilities supporting American, South Vietnamese, Australian, and Korean troops.

The military construction mission of the Army Engineers included construction for the Air Force in the United States, including long-range missile bases, and the design and construction of test and launch facilities for the National Aeronautics and Space Administration. Recently the Corps had a role in the Post Office facilities building program.

The first civil responsibilities were delegated to the Army Engineers immediately following the Revolutionary War. The new nation needed roads, railroads, lighthouses, bridges and many other engineering works to support economic advancement, and the Corps was called upon to build them.

Beginning in 1815, when Lieutenant Zebulon Pike explored the Missouri Valley, the Army Engineers were the principal agents of the Government in the exploration of the West to locate wagon and railroad routes. Lieutenant John C. Fremont surveyed the Oregon Trail and opened up California. Lieutenant A. J. Donelson surveyed the line of the Northern Pacific Railroad. Other Corps survey parties located the transcontinental routes of the Santa Fe, Union Pacific, and Southern Pacific. In 1871, Lieutenant George M. Wheeler commenced a survey of all the territory of the United States west of the 100th meridian, and completed it 13 years later. The Corps also surveyed and mapped the Great Lakes and marked all the boundaries of the United States and most State boundaries.

During this period of exploration, the Army Engineers systematically catalogued the wildlife and other natural resources in the areas of their expeditions. They fought for and carried out the first measures to preserve from private exploitation (mainly poaching) such national treasures as the areas which are now the Yellowstone, Yosemite, and Sequoia Parks. The Corps administered the Yellowstone area until the founding of the national park system and administered the Yosemite and Sequoia areas from 1864 until California accepted them as State Parks, and again from 1890 until 1916 when they became national parks. The Corps was, in fact, the first "Park Managers". Army soldiers were the first "Park Rangers".

Since 1824, the Corps has been the principal developer of the nation's water resources. In that year the Congress assigned it the task of clearing snags and sandbars from the Ohio and Mississippi Rivers to facilitate navigation – the small beginning of its civil works program. This program was limited to improvements for navigation until 1879, when the Mississippi River Commission was created with flood control in the alluvial valley of the Mississippi as a function incidental to the improvement of the river from the mouth of the Ohio to the Gulf of Mexico.

Later the Corps was given the responsibility for regulating hydraulic mining in California's Sacramento and San Joaquin Basins, and for the construction of debris basins and the institution of other measures to prevent the creation of hazards to navigation. In 1917, flood control on the Mississippi was authorized as a purpose in its own right, and the Corps was directed to undertake similar work on the Sacramento River. The Congress added coastal protection to its functions in 1930, and in 1936 its responsibilities were greatly enlarged to embrace flood control activities nationwide. Subsequently the construction of projects to provide multiple (use) benefits, including, in addition to flood control and navigation, the generation of hydroelectric power, water supply, recreation, and the conservation of fish and wildlife, was authorized.

During the last 148 years, the Corps has completed more than 4,000 civil works projects. It has built more than 19,000 miles of inland and intracoastal waterways now in commercial use, and 500 coastal, Great Lakes, and waterway harbors, including almost all those through which the United States carries on its vital domestic and foreign trade and 250 small boat harbors and harbors of refuge. It has constructed some 350 reservoirs, and local flood control projects incorporating more than 9,000 miles of levees and flood walls and 7,500 miles of improved channels. Flood control projects built by the Corps have so far prevented more than $19.3 billion in flood losses, more than three times the amount invested in flood protection. Corps hydropower plants in more than 50 projects have a total generating capacity of more than 12 million kilowatts. Hydroelectric power is the most environmentally clean form of electricity, since there is no air and water pollution as there is with the burning of fossil fuels, and no thermal pollution as with contemporary nuclear plants. The average annual recreation attendance at Corps reservoirs is 300 million. Two hundred and fifty fish and wildlife management areas have been established around these lakes, as well as 400 state, county, and municipal parks.

In time of flood or hurricane, the Corps provides assistance in damage control, rescue work, and rehabilitation both under its own authorities and as engineering agent of the Office of Emergency Preparedness. Since 1963 it has been involved in more than 150 disaster operations, including floods and hurricanes.

In May of 1968, another Ohio State Wildlife Officer, Dick Wolfrom, and I became infinitesimal parts of this great organization. We went to work for the Resource Management Section, Operations Division, Louisville, Kentucky District, Ohio River Division of the Army Corps of Engineers. Following physicals, we were hired and sworn in as Park Rangers.

After the issuance of uniforms and credentials, we underwent a one week orientation of all the Louisville District Office components with emphasis on Corps personnel regulations, Corps history, and the federal judicial system.

This was followed by two weeks travel that included inspections and briefings of all operational Corps flood control projects in Indiana and Kentucky – thirteen in all. (Seven projects were under acquisition and/or construction in Ohio and Kentucky that we didn't tour.) Emphasis briefings were given on all the parks and wildlife management out grants issued to the relative State Fish and Game, and/or Parks Agencies. "Riding herd", so to speak, on all Corps and "other party" leases, out grants and agreements would be a big part of our duties as Park Rangers. We both evaluated our three week orientation and briefings as darn good "down-to-earth," "nuts and bolts" typical Army training at its best. We were assigned our duty stations before we were actually hired. Dick returned to Ohio, assigned to a Ranger-at-large position in what was officially the Miami River Area. It consisted of four flood control reservoirs, three of which were under construction – an assignment I envied. I went to what was known in the District as the "nightmare" – Mansfield (now C.M. Harden) Lake in what was officially the Middle Wabash Area. The Middle Wabash consisted of Monroe Lake at Bloomington, Cagles Mill Lake at Poland, Patako Lake at DuBois and my "nightmare" at Rockville – all in Indiana. We reported to our duty stations in mid-June, 1968. (Two years later, Dick Wolfrom was promoted to Park Manager and transferred to Buckhorn Lake, Kentucky. He passed away of a heart attack on duty inspecting a wildlife management lease sometime later. He was a friend and true champion for wildlife.)

Mansfield Lake was authorized by the Federal Flood Control Act of 1938. Construction began in 1956 – the project became operational in 1960. The lake is a part of a comprehensive plan in the Ohio River Basin to effect reduction in flood stages down stream from the dam, primarily in the Big Raccoon Creek and lower Wabash watersheds. The lake provides water related recreation and was intended to enhance fish and wildlife shoreline habitat. The property comprises about fifty miles of Corps owned boundary line (often referred to as "fee" or the red line) that surrounds about 2,000 acres of property above the lakes summer pool of about 2,000 acres of water. Above the "red line" the Corps purchased flowage easements (or the right to flood) about 1,200 acres under private ownership. The flowage easements prohibited structures for human habitation and septic systems. The flowage boundary line was called the "yellow line". Illegal use of Corps owned property and flowage easement provisions were called encroachments. Upon my arrival at Mansfield there were approximately 185 documented fee (Corps owned property) and flowage easement encroachments.

The Ranger who preceded me was a professional land surveyor. He had meticulously documented all encroachments in written reports with photographs and plotted each encroachment on detailed maps. A separate file was maintained on each. They were all on file at the Project Headquarters – copies of all had been sent to the Resource Management and Real Estate Sections in the Louisville District Office. Of the 185 encroachments, 104 were on Corps owned land; the rest were on easement. All these land encroachments plus an excursion boat that operated out of Raccoon State Park and dumped human excrement (poop) into the lake is what prompted Glen Bayes, Resource Management Branch Assistant Chief in Louisville to call Mansfield "A nightmarish pile of poop." The excursion (or party) boat's poop shedding days ended very early in my tenure. One bright Saturday morning an Indiana State Game Warden's patrol boat merged into the wake behind the excursion boat. Afloat in the excursion boat's wake was observed a sizeable portion of human excrement (a turd).

"I do believe that's a turd," exclaimed Indiana Wildlife Officer, Bill Folmer, as he turned his patrol boat tightly to the left and circled the evidential turd. Confirming his earlier observation was in fact correct, Officer Folmer engaged in hot pursuit of the offending craft. Soon he boarded the craft and confronted the operator.

"Sir, we've observed what appears to be human excrement afloat in the wake of your boat. I'll have to inspect your toilet facility. As you know, your holding tank must be closed while your boat is in operation. You are to dump it at the facility provided at the State Park only – not in the lake," Officer Folmer informed the boat operator.

"What do you mean, human excrement?" The boat operator asked with some indignity.

"Poop", Officer Folmer answered, in a word, so to speak, as several lady passengers emitted sighs of mild shock. Officer Folmer inspected the "Mens" and "Womens" toilet facilities aboard ship. In each, he flushed an inked marked piece of tissue and ordered the boat operator to move the boat forward a few feet. Both pieces of ink marked tissue floated up behind the boat; thus, cinching Officer Folmer's case. The boat operator was cited into court.

Following a brief and debatable (whether or not needed as evidence) and unsuccessful search for the original evidential turd, the case was closed pending the court outcome. The boat operator paid a substantial fine. Ultimately the State of Indiana cancelled his concessionaire contract and the excursion boat days at Mansfield ended. "After all, a noticeable turd floating in a lake no larger than Mansfield, sorta stands out," Officer Folmer mused.

Shortly thereafter, while on patrol with Officer Folmer, we received a radio call from the Raccoon State Park Office.

"Officer Folmer, we've received a complaint that there's a couple 'cavorting' in Campground C, site 3 – would you please take care of this?" radioed the park secretary.

"You say they're 'cavorting' – do you mean they're fornicating?" Officer Folmer responded.

"Well, if they're not married, I suppose they're fornicating; but if they're married, it's cavorting, I guess," the secretary answered.

"When did you receive this complaint?" Folmer inquired.

"Just a few minutes ago," the secretary answered.

"Okay, it will take me a minute to check the Game Laws to see if it's a violation to cavort or fornicate in a State Park," Folmer advised the secretary, joking of course.

"You don't have to arrest them, do you? Can't you just stop them from cavorting or fornicating or whatever it is they're doing? They seem to be creating a disturbance in the campground with their behavior," the secretary replied.

"Are they doing whatever they're doing in public? Are other campers standing around watching them?" Folmer asked.

"Oh dear, I don't know. Two more have come into the office and are complaining," the secretary stated.

"If the last two complainants are still in your office, get them to tell you exactly what they saw and relay the information to me," Officer Folmer requested.   (Pause — then)

"Oh dear, Officer Folmer, I don't believe I can broadcast what these two people have told me. It will suffice to say, the couple in C-3 are either cavorting or fornicating, depending on their marital status," the now frustrated secretary broadcast.

"Okay, we have a speeder stopped at the entrance road. As soon as we get him cited into court, we'll proceed to the campground," Officer Folmer responded.

"Very well, please hurry," the now noticeably upset secretary answered.

We patrolled up and down the state park entrance road for about fifteen minutes – it was obvious Folmer was stalling. Finally, we proceeded to and arrived at Campground C, site 3. There seated in folding chairs, holding hands, and having a glass of iced tea was a young couple undoubtedly enjoying the afterglow of love making.

After a short and most cordial explaining exchange between Officer Folmer and the honeymooning couple during which the young man stated, "Well, we may have gotten a little noisy," we left the happy couple at campsite C-3

"You did a beautiful job of stalling in that one, Bill," I told Folmer.

"Right, we weren't about to ruin that young couple's pleasure, now were we?" Folmer replied. We both chuckled and considered the case closed.

Past policy in dealing with encroachments was the Corps Real Estate Section in the Louisville District Office, sent letters to the encroachers. The letters admonished the guilty party to cease and remove his or her encroachment from Corps (or public) owned property and restore the property involved to its original state.

Encroachments on Corps owned lands at Mansfield took many forms i.e. roads (paved and/or graveled), retaining walls, boat docks, electric power lines, concrete walkways, outhouses (or privies), water lines, boat ramps, tree and shrub clearing, incorporation into private lawns and gardens, structures of many kinds, fish cleaning facilities, septic systems, night lights, patios, fences (privacy and otherwise), etc. You name it, it was all at Mansfield. Most flowage easement encroachments amounted to structures for human habitation and septic systems. An issue of a locally published civic publication featured, "The beautiful lawns and gardens at Mansfield Lake" – all illegal encroachments on Corps owned property. Preservation of the natural shoreline and its wildlife habitat for the outdoor recreation enthusiast and enjoyment of the general public sure didn't take place at Mansfield. It was destroyed by encroaching adjacent landowners for what they deemed their own personal benefit. What's worse, the Corps and State of Indiana let them get away with it.

The encroachment files were filled with letter exchanges between the Corps and the encroacher. Not one encroachment had been resolved. Not one encroachment was in the process of effectively being removed or corrected.

I quickly decided this policy wasn't working. There wasn't a single instance in which the Corps Ranger met one on one with the encroacher and simply advised the encroacher (violator) to correct his encroachment and restore the Corps owned property to its original state or face charges in U.S. District Court. Nor was there a single instance in which the Corps simply removed the encroachment (which it certainly had every legal right to do), restore the property and bill the offender. All of the preceding became my policy. I went to Mansfield in June, 1968. When I left Mansfield in August, 1969, of the 104 encroachments on Corps owned property, 4 remained. I did a lot of "xo#x kicking." I freely admit my methods departed from the official Corps – Real Estate Section—policy, but quickly add that my superiors in the Resource Management Branch at the Louisville District Office, particularly Mr. Fred Huelson and Mr. Glen Bayes, supported me 100%.

My time at Mansfield – short as it was – certainly was an eye-opener. Mansfield was the worst encroachment reservoir in the Louisville District, perhaps the nation. It was the ultimate example of what shouldn't be allowed to happen on any public owned project, intended whole or in part, for public outdoor recreation use and enjoyment. It was a perfect example of yielding to a select few, even though such permissiveness was totally illegal. Because of Mansfield, the Corps land acquisition policy had already changed for new flood control projects. No more (or very little) easement acquisitions. Land was acquired up to the flood elevation. Written shoreline management policy and rules were adopted along with a tougher "enforcement" policy – the new changes worked!

203

16
Carr Fork Lake

My year and two months at Mansfield was "exhausting" to say the least. In August of 1969, I transferred to Carr Fork Lake, Kentucky (name later changed to Carr Creek Lake) as a Park Ranger but was soon promoted (as promised) to the Park Manager's position. The lake is located in the mountainous region of southeastern Kentucky about 16 miles from Hazard and 18 miles from Whitesburg. The dam is located 8.8 miles above the mouth of Carr Fork, a tributary of the North Fork of the Kentucky River. It provides flood protection for Hazard and smaller downstream communities. The entire project is within Knott County.

Carr Fork (or "the project" I'll call it) was an altogether different experience. The project was new – still in land acquisition/construction phase. It provided an opportunity to see and experience a Corps flood control project develop from the ground up.

The Corps maintained a Real Estate Office at Hindman, KY, north of the construction site. It was staffed with a surveyor, a negotiator (land buyer), an appraiser, a management and disposal specialist, administrative support persons, and a project manager. As was the Corps policy at that time, they placed the first of the operations personnel (those who would operate the project after completion) usually a Ranger, with the Real Estate folks before their work was completed. I maintained an office and worked out of the Hindman Real Estate Office. One of the real estate secretaries was assigned to me part time. During my time at Hindman, the Management and Disposal position was vacated. I was temporarily assigned those duties (largely selling and disposing of buildings acquired within estate tracts) in addition to my Ranger duties – an enlightening experience.

The Corps construction office and personnel were located at the project site. They consisted of a Project Engineer, three to four Construction Inspectors, and one Administrative Assistant. Road, power line, and cemetery relocations were in progress. Construction of the outlet works tower was complete. The dam and spillway were under construction. All the Corps contractor construction, plus the fact much of the project watershed was being auger-strip mined for coal, made Carr Fork a beehive of heavy equipment activity. When complete, the project would have approximately 43 miles of boundary line enclosing 3,161 acres above the summer pool of 710 acres. It would have 24 miles of shoreline, a state park, 7 recreation areas, 25 picnic sites, 70 camp sites, 8 playgrounds, 1 swimming area, 7 miles of hiking trails, 2 fishing docks, 3 boat ramps, 1 marina and 144 boat slips. Most of its 3,161 acres would provide upland and forest game hunting opportunities. The lake would provide an excellent sport fishery especially known for its walleye fishing. The tail water below the dam would provide very good trout fishing.

All the before mentioned would someday be, but then it was all seriously threatened by mine acid pollution and heavy silt loads being deposited in the empty lake basin with every significant rain – all coming from contour strip/auger coal mining operations within the watershed. Trace Branch, a tributary of Irishman Creek (Irishman is a tributary of Carr Fork) ran red as blood with acid drainage from the No. 9 coal seam high on the mountain above. It was mined many years earlier and never properly reclaimed. Pyrite (fools gold) that lay above coal seam No. 9, exposed to air and water, came down the mountain and into the Carr Fork Lake basin as sulfuric acid, commonly known as mine acid pollution. I began running PH tests on all the tributary streams of Carr Fork within the lake watershed. One other source of little significance was identified near what today is known as the Littcar site. Based on the PH data and the inflow contribution of Irishman Creek, the hydraulics and water quality professionals in Louisville were of the opinion that one or more additional mine acid contributors of the Irishman magnitude would have a serious detrimental effect on the water quality (and thus the fishery) at Carr Fork Lake. In addition to the coal mine acid drainage and siltation problems, arsonists were active in the Irishman Creek Area. Knott County, as most eastern Kentucky counties in that day and time, had no countywide waste management system. The entire Carr Fork Lake basin was being used as a dump site by many Knott County residents. My work was most certainly cut out for me. I set the priorities; mine acid pollution and lake basin siltation posed the most serious threat – it became priority No. 1. Arson was priority No. 2, and waste dumping was No. 3.

By written request, I proposed a meeting between the Corps and the Kentucky State Division of Strip Mine Reclamation (KDR). Kentucky state law required all coal strip mine operators obtain mining permits from the KDR. The permit application must include a land reclamation plan that conformed to state reclamation law. State Reclamation Inspectors "walked out" each area to be mined that was applied for in each permit application. Permit issuance depended largely on the "method of reclamation" proposed by the coal mine operator. State inspectors inspected mine operations at least weekly to insure that mining and reclamation methods complied with state law and the provisions stipulated in the mining permit. A little legal research revealed "third party input" with respect to mine permit approval was not only legal; it was in some cases, welcomed by the KDR. I saw this as an opportunity to insert Corps influence into the approval and issuance of mining permits as well as reclamation methods within the project watershed. At all costs another source of mine acid pollution had to be prevented. Of equal importance, the Corps needed to be aware of all watershed mine permitted areas past, present and future. The meeting between the Corp and the KDR took place during my second year at Carr Fork. The outcome was a "Memorandum of Understanding (MOU)" between the Corps and the KDR.

The MOU stipulated that within the Carr Fork Lake watershed (later amended to include all Corps project watersheds within the eastern Kentucky coal fields):

1. A Corps Ranger accompany each State Reclamation Inspector during the pre-mining, ground inspection phase of the permit application process.
2. Established the inherent right of the Corps to comment and recommend changes in the reclamation plan favorable to the environmental welfare of the Corps project involved.
3. All mining permits must be submitted to the Corps, Louisville, KY District for review before the mining operation could begin.

The time had come for me to go to work. I quickly discovered why all the State Reclamation Inspectors were in such good shape! Dodging copperheads and rattlers wasn't the least of it.!

Soon after my arrival at Carr Fork, Corps owned (and to a lesser extent, privately owned) property in the Irishman Creek area was periodically set on fire – the work of arsonists. One fire starter's method of operation was to drive the main road up Irishman as well as many adjacent abandoned strip mine roads and throw out ignited kerosene soaked rags. The fires continued well into September. I spent many non-productive patrol hours trying to catch the arsonist. I also spent considerable time questioning adjacent landowners, coal operators and construction workers, attempting to ascertain the arsonist's identity. I'd had no training in arson investigation, or for that matter, experience working arson cases. I assumed going after an arsonist wasn't much different than going after a poacher.

At the suggestion of Don Burchette, Surveyor at the Hindman Real Estate Office, I contacted the Kentucky State Forestry Division seeking help. According to Burchette, the State Forest Rangers were well trained in arson investigation (for obvious reasons) and they worked arson cases on any forest property, be it government or privately owned. Soon thereafter, State Forest

Ranger Cox, who specialized in arson investigations, contacted me at the Carr Fork Real Estate Office in Hindman. We went to and inspected the Irishman Creek area where past fires were set and extinguished by local volunteer fire departments, construction and mine workers, the citizenry, and the Kentucky Division of Forestry. I explained the arsonist's method of operation (previously described) to Officer Cox.

Following his inspection and my report of the kerosene soaked rags, Cox asked, "How do you know your arsonist was using kerosene soaked rags? Did you collect any evidence?"

"Yes, I have several partially burned rags, collected at the scene in labeled evidence bags at my office," I answered.

"Good", Cox responded. Immediately he opined, "Based on his method of setting fires that will ignite quickly, your arsonist wants a quick fix. I feel he is always close by observing his handiwork. He will not be a part of the fire fighting crew as some are. He'll not be one of the obvious observers. He'll be concealed and my guess is, he'll be deriving some sort of sexual excitement or gratification as he observes his fire. This may take the form of masturbation at the site or sexual arousal to be vented on his lover – be it male or female – when he returns home."

"In other words, we've got a real sick-o here," I stated.

"They're all sick-os," Cox responded.

Before departing, Ranger Cox gave me his card showing his office phone and how he could be reached by radio. He instructed me to call him the very minute another fire was detected.

We didn't have to wait long. Four days later a section of Irishman was ablaze. I notified Cox and he arrived at the Carr Fork construction office a half hour later. Up Irishman Creek we went in his patrol vehicle. Very soon we observed an old battered pickup truck parked in the lane of an abandoned home site (bought by the Corps). We both seemed to instinctively know the vehicle belonged to the arsonist.

"You take the right side of the branch, I'll take the left. He's somewhere on the ridge watching his fire. If you find him, be careful. Some of these people are very dangerous. One kept me pinned down with a 30/30 deer rifle for two hours. I radioed for help. Two of our guys managed to come in on him from the other side of the mountain and get the drop on him. He still tried to whip all three of us two times before we got him out of the hollow to our vehicle. I mean it when I say they can be dangerous. They've been caught doing one of the worst low-down acts a human being can do. They know this and one of their greatest fears is how they'll look to their family and community," Cox stated as we went our separate ways in search of the arsonist.

I soon realized the arsonist didn't go in the direction I was searching. There was absolutely no trail of any kind. I immediately began hiking in Cox's direction. In no time at all I observed Officer Cox coming toward me with the suspect arsonist handcuffed and scuttling down the mountain ahead of his capturer. The suspects fly was noticeably open.

"He was leaning up against a big rock, looking across the hollow at the fire saying aloud, 'I've started me a good-un! I've started me a good-un!' while he was whackin' away (masturbating)," Cox exclaimed breathlessly.

"I'm sorry I done it. I'm sorry I done it," the arsonist stated.

"Sorry you did what – started the fire or played with yourself?" Cox asked.

"Started the fire," the suspect responded.

"Alright, zip up your pants. You're going to jail in Hindman, pal," Cox advised his captive.

The arsonist appeared in court a few days later. He plead guilty to the arson charge. His sentence was a few more days in jail and a work detail. No fine, as he had no assets. A longer jail sentence would mean that much more burden on a very poor Knott County.

"This is about all they get in eastern Kentucky. Of course, what they need is professional help which they seldom get. That too costs the county," Cox explained after court.

After instructing me to call him again if I needed him, Officer Cox left. Interesting is the fact, this one arrest seemed to curb the arsonist set fires at Carr Fork. It never reared its ugly head to any extent again during my tenure there.

By late summer 1970, the Hindman real estate function was winding down. Some of the real estate specialists had transferred to other projects. The time had come to establish the Operations Division (Resource Management) office at the project site. A mobile home was leased and set next to the Construction Division trailer at the dam site.

Virginia Everage, who worked several years at the Hindman Real Estate Office and served as my part time secretary, came on board as the Operation's Division secretary and Administrative Assistant. Virginia, who by then, was quite familiar with all aspects of managing a project resource management office, "hit the ground running." She was the last word in efficiency and soon had the project operations office firmly established. She would work her entire thirty plus year award winning career at Carr Fork Lake. Her loyalty to the Corps and outstanding performance stands as a monument to the American work ethic. We name our great engineering and construction feats, many times, to sooth the egos and further the political gain of our politicians and others of fame and fortune. It's time – long overdue -- to name such projects in honor of those who "tilled the fields and tended the crop" rather than after those famous who did little more than "reap the harvest." To The Honorable Congressman representing the fifth District of Kentucky, let me suggest the second name change of Carr Creek Lake. In honor of a daughter of eastern Kentucky, a beautiful mountain girl who gave "the project" her all, I propose the name Carr Creek Lake be changed to Virginia L. Everage Lake. A lasting tribute to one great lady who mothered "the project" from infancy to fruition.

In 1971, Dan Barrett, following a District Office water quality assignment, came on board as the Carr Fork Park Ranger, filling my old position. Dan, an Eastern Kentucky University graduate with a BS in Aquatic Biology, was of the same mettle as Virginia. He too, "hit the ground running" and was quick to see what needed to be done. He required only assignments – no supervision. He would later earn his Master's Degree based on his comprehensive water quality studies of the Carr Fork Lake watershed in 1977. Ultimately, he retired as the Area Manager in charge of the Upper Kentucky River Area, consisting of Buckhorn Lake, Carr Creek Lake, Cave Run Lake, and Taylorsville Lake. His thirty plus years -- award winning career was exemplary.

An occasional "visiting" Ranger was a young Phil Bayes who worked as a Ranger-at-Large out of the Jackson Area Office. Phil was fresh out of college and squared away. He was a catch dog Ranger who helped immeasurably at Carr Fork with my No. 3 priority (trash dumping). He later served as Park Manager at Buckhorn Lake and ultimately retired as Park Manager at Barren River Lake. His award winning career was, as Dan Barrett's, exemplary.

With Virginia and Dan's arrivals, my workload lightened. It ushered in a time for planning and I completed several off-project assignments including authoring the Corps' first Wildlife Management Appendice to a Project Master Plan, a black walnut tree theft investigation and intermittent travel presenting lectures and slide presentations on strip mine abatement as it related to Corp projects.

Dan and I teamed up to close the case on the last of my three original priorities – trash and other waste dumping within the lake basin and future shoreline properties. We hit every dumping site, old and new. We diligently searched each for traceable evidence that would lead to the perpetrators. Once traceable leads were found, we would interview the suspect violators (following Miranda, of course). Most admitted guilt and subsequently plead guilty or forfeited collateral (a fixed penalty set by the court) in U.S. Magistrate Court in Pikeville. The Magistrate was a retired FBI Agent who dealt fairly with those who appeared in his court. Before I left Carr Fork Lake, it's safe to say the trash dumping problem was under control and mostly curtailed. Later, Dan Barrett would say, "I think our efforts at Carr Fork did a lot of good and heavily influenced the fact Knott County was the first eastern Kentucky County to implement a county waste collection, management and disposal system."

My time at the Carr Fork Project ended in July of 1973. I was selected to attend a lengthy in-service training "School for Administrative Leadership" at the University of Montana in Missoula. There I heard some of the Corps Districts in the west were "looking to the east" for Rangers and Managers – mainly due to the fact the Nashville, Tennessee and Louisville, Kentucky Districts were years ahead of the rest of the nation with the relatively new Resource Management Sections (and function) within the various District Operations Divisions. I applied for an Area Manager's position over the Mid-Willamette Area in the Portland, Oregon District. I was selected and left Carr Fork Lake with a sense of accomplishment. I'll always cherish the experience and the place.

Many years later, while on an assignment in Kentucky for U.S. Fish and Wildlife Service, I digressed for a time and went to Carr Fork Lake. I visited no one – it was a time for just me and "the project". As I viewed its beautiful shoreline, it's tidy well-kept public use facilities and dipped my fingers in its clear, clean, sparkling waters, I thought, my dear little Carr Fork Lake – the name you'll always be to me – how truly magnificent you are. A star in Kentucky's crown. You're more than worth all the battles fought and won for you so long ago.

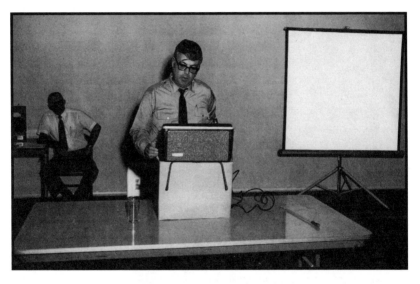

The author giving a lecture/slide presentation on the effects of contour auger strip mining and mine acid pollution on Corps Lakes. Louisville District Conference – Barren River Lake, Kentucky, 1971.

(Background) Fred Huelson, Assistant Chief, resource Mgt. Branch, Louisville District.

17
The Thieves
of Rough River

During my time at Carr Fork Lake, it was not uncommon to receive off-project assignments. This duty consisted of conference attendance (giving talks and slide presentations, usually on watershed strip mining), flood duty, special investigations and visitation surveys.

At this point, let me say a few words about the Corps' visitation surveys. Of the four government agencies I worked for, the Corps was by far the most sensitive to the needs and concerns of the public. Their method of determining these two public attitudes and other public use determinations was through its visitation surveys. The surveys are accomplished by direct contact (questioning) with the visiting public at various public use sites on Corps projects at strategic times of the year. Visitation survey results govern significantly the design, location, and services offered at Corps campgrounds and other public use sites. Considering camping alone, most Corps projects offer everything from primitive camping to full hook-up camp sites. Many Corps Lake projects offer luxurious overnight accommodations and gourmet dining. Their campgrounds and other public use facilities are unequalled. The Corps is most cognizant of the fact the lands and waters under its control are owned by the public and therefore, should be used by the public to the maximum. It's safe to say "something for everyone" is a Corps philosophy.

Now we'll go to Rough River Lake, Kentucky. Near the middle of my tenure at Carr Fork – on a rainy morning, my office phone rang. The caller was Fred Huelson, Assistant Chief of the Resource Management Section in the Louisville Office.

"Ron, a Corps surveying crew, working at Rough River discovered the theft of a significant number of mature black walnut trees, some on Corps property, some on private property. Black walnut logs from this part of the country are the highest quality and bring the highest prices. This matter warrants our own (Corps) investigation and the bad guys caught. Think you can handle it?" Fred stated and asked.

"I'd sure love to give it a try," I replied.

"Good enough, I've already cleared it with Russell Brown (my Area Manager). We'll cut your travel orders here – stop by the District Office on your way to Rough. I'll notify Ken Skaggs (the Area Manager over the Green River Area including Rough River) you've been assigned the investigation – he'll be expecting you. Incidentally, you can have anyone you feel you need to assist you with this investigation – got anyone in mind?" Fred stated and asked.

"Sure do – Kenny Skaggs if he's got the time and doesn't mind working with a subordinate in rank," I replied.

"Kenny will have the time. I'll tell him he's got the time. I think you just made a good choice. Kenny is mainly concerned with rank when he's got some butt-kickin' to do. He'll make you a good partner," Fred responded.

Skaggs was a tall, thin, raspy voiced, distinguished looking gentleman – white haired and wore glasses. He was an imposing figure, especially in uniform. I had visited with him briefly on two occasions at District meetings and pretty well ascertained his "law enforcement philosophy." It was simple, "Catch-em and don't take any gaff."

Glenn Bayes, Assistant Chief of the Resource Section, told me several war stories about Skaggs and his boys (Rangers) working closely with or without "local law" catching everything from hub cap thieves operating at public use sites to drug busts in Corps campgrounds. "Kenny keeps things clean down there," Bayes commented.

I knew Skaggs carried a Deputy Sheriff's Commission and didn't hesitate to "throw-um in jail." Skaggs came up through the Corps Lock and Dam Branch. He was iron-jawed and tough. He was the man for me. Little did I know at that time, he would also prove to be a good after-the-fact investigator and (a-hem!) interviewer.

The following day, I went to the Louisville Office. I spent the rest of that day and the following on the phone, running down timber buyers in the immediate area around Rough River Lake and the Louisville area. I came up with six. One would later prove "fruitful". The next day I went to Rough River Lake and met with Ken Skaggs. Ken pointed on a project map, the location where the black walnut trees were cut. We proceeded to the site. Five black walnut stumps gave mute witness of their theft. We surmised part of the stumps were on an adjacent landowner. (I'll call it the Taylor farm – a later survey showed four of the trees were on the Taylor farm and one on Corps property.) All appearances indicated the adjacent landowner cuttings and the Corps theft occurred at the same time. It was obvious the logs were rolled down to the lake, floated to a nearby boat ramp, loaded, and hauled away. We photographed the stumpage at the site and the skid and roll marks indicating the logs were rolled into the lake.

We decided our next step was to interview residents within any reasonable proximity to the scene, particularly those nearest the boat ramp. After ten contacts and interviews, a farm lady looking out her window who lived closest to the boat ramp in question stated, "I saw a big truck loaded down with logs stuck in that field," pointing to a field that lay between her house and the boat ramp. "A wrecker from the Ford garage in Leitchfield came and pulled them out," she further stated.

"When did you see all this?" Ken asked. She gave us a date and approximate time of day.

"How do you know the wrecker came from the Ford garage in Leitchfield?" I asked.

"Cause it was painted on the side of the wrecker," the lady answered.

"Would you be willing to testify in court as to what you've just told us?" I asked.

"Yes," she answered.

"Are you willing to give us a signed statement recording what you've told us?" I asked.

"Yes," she answered.

I prepared the statement and she signed it. Kenny and I witnessed her signature. We thanked her for her time, complimented her on her powers of observation, and left for the Ford garage in Leitchfield. What a break!

At the Ford garage, we interviewed the wrecker driver who "snaked the log truck out of the mud" as he put it. We obtained a copy of the bill for the towing service made out to (I'll call it) Ajax Timber Company, Hunters Trace, Kentucky (suburb of Louisville). The wrecker driver stated four male subjects were present when he arrived at the scene. One subject who signed the towing bill, obviously worked for Ajax Timber Company. The wrecker driver gave good descriptions of the other three lads at the scene.

The next day we went to the Ajax Timber Company at Hunters Trace. We asked for and made contact with the manager. We advised him of our investigation results thus far.

"We're reasonably sure you have knowingly or unknowingly received stolen government property, and probably stolen private property. At this time it's our responsibility to advise you, on behalf of your company, of your constitutional rights." With this statement, I read him the Miranda Warning. "Having been advised of your rights, are you willing to discuss this matter with us and let us examine any records you may have that relate to the incident we're investigating?" I asked.

"We bought those walnut logs in good faith and we'll stand on that. We had no knowledge the logs were stolen. We bought walnut logs from those three boys on one occasion. It took one trip to haul them all out. Yeah, we'll talk about it with you and show you our records," the Manager (I'll call him Tim) stated. Tim instructed his secretary to retrieve a copy of the invoice recording the purchase of "those black walnut logs the (I'll call them) Merriwether brothers sold us."

Shortly, Tim's secretary returned. She produced an invoice showing the date and recording the purchase of a quantity of black walnut logs from Les, Tom and Joe Merriwether.

"It's interesting the invoice is made out to all three," Ken observed.

"That's the way they wanted it made out. They came here to get paid. It was as though they didn't trust each other. They wanted their check made out to all three," the secretary stated.

"Then all three would have to endorse the check to get it cashed," Ken observed, almost under his breath.

"That's correct – they did just that," the secretary confirmed.

"Do you have the cancelled check?" I asked.

"Yes," she answered.

"We'd like copies of the purchase invoice plus the cancelled check," I stated.

"Certainly," Tim replied after his secretary looked at him for a response to my request. Shortly, the secretary supplied us with both.

"Does this check and invoice relate to the load of logs that was stuck in the mud?" I asked.

"Yes, it does," Tim answered.

Kenny and I asked for and received a statement from Tim, the Manager, recording all he'd told us. Tim signed the statement and we witnessed his signature. The statement included wording showing the Ajax Timber Company bought all the black walnut logs in good faith.

"We need a forester to measure the stumpage and estimate the board footage at the site so we can compare it with the board footage shown on the invoice. Let's hope they compare favorably and add to our case. I'm sure Ben Schoby (Area Manager, Upper Wabash, Indiana) is a graduate forester and can handle it. Do we have anyone closer?" I asked.

"Bob Barnett, the new Ranger at Barren River, is a graduate forester. We'll check with Huelson tomorrow – we should brief Fred on what's happened so far," Ken stated.

"Looks like you-all are perkin' down there. Yeah, Bob Barnett is a graduate forester – put him to work," Fred responded following our up-to-date briefing and inquiry about the new Ranger at Barren.

Kenny radioed Barren River Lake and requested Ranger Bob Barnett's presence at Rough River ASAP. The following morning, Bob arrived before noon. We went to lunch where Kenny and I briefed him on our black walnut theft investigation and the services we needed of him.

Bob visited the timber removal site that p.m., radioed Kenny and stated he would hand deliver his report with his estimates of the board footage removed.

The following day Bob came to Rough River with his report showing his findings. Bob's report compared almost to the board foot with the Ajax Timber Company's invoice showing the Merriwether sale.

Kenny ascertained John Taylor, owner of the farm adjacent to the Corps property, lived in Leitchfield. We called on Mr. Taylor who advised us Joe Merriwether was a tenant who resided on his farm. Mr. Taylor stated, "I, at no time, authorized Joe or anyone else to cut any walnut logs on my property. If anyone cut any logs on my farm, I'll have him arrested and sue him for damages." Mr. Taylor was not a happy camper. We asked him to hold off on confronting Joe until we'd had a chance to interview him. Taylor agreed.

Later that afternoon we made contact with Joe Merriwether at his residence on the Taylor farm. He fit one of the descriptions given by the tow truck driver. Following the Miranda Warning, he agreed to interview nervously claiming, "I've got nothing to hide." When we confronted him with our investigation results and the documentary evidence (sales invoice and cancelled check) he stated, "Yeah, we sold Ajax those logs but they came from my brother Tom's farm – we can prove it – you can't prove a xo#x thing."

"How?" I asked as I noticed Kenny Skaggs' jaw muscles tighten. I could sense Skaggs wasn't happy with Joe Merriwether's attitude or answers.

"Yeah, how can you prove the logs came from your brother's farm? You'd better make it good because I think you're a xo#x liar," Skaggs asked and proclaimed through clinched teeth.

"I can show you, I can show you," the now intimidated and even more nervous Joe Merriwether stated.

"Good, get in the car! We're going to your brother's farm!" Skaggs declared as he opened the front passenger's side door on our patrol car. Merriwether immediately seated himself. We proceeded to the Tom Merriwether farm about three miles distant as Joe gave directions. No one was at home.

"Show us the stumps of the black walnut trees you claim you sold to Ajax," Skaggs stated. As we walked through the barnyard into an adjacent empty pasture field, Merriwether immediately began pointing out black walnut stumps – all located in fence rows. As we inspected the stumps, Kenny and I noticed tractor tire and skid marks going from the stumps to a deep ravine in the middle of the field. We followed the tracks and discovered a sizeable quantity of black walnut logs (much smaller than those stolen on the Taylor and Corps property) deposited, along with other trash, in the bottom of the ravine.

Why would anyone place the logs in a ravine mixed with trash as though throwing them away? I wondered in thought. The expression on Kenny's face made me think he was wondering the same thing.

"Why did you or someone place your logs here? You've lied about selling them – it's as though they're alibi logs or something," I asked and opined.

"Tell us all about it, Joe and don't lie," Skaggs ordered as he stared Joe square in the eye.

"They're fence row logs," Merriwether blurted.

"So?" Skaggs asked.

"So, we tried to sell them to a buyer over by Leitchfield. He wouldn't buy them because they have fence wire, staples, nails and bullets in them. He told us they were worthless. We were going to doze them over but didn't get to it in time. Yeah, we thought we could show the stumps to anyone who questioned our sale to Ajax," Joe Merriwether confessed.

"You might call them alibi logs," I suggested.

"Yeah, you could call them that," Merriwether responded.

I immediately went to the patrol car and prepared a statement recording all Joe Merriwether told us and confessed to. Soon after Kenny escorted Merriwether to our patrol car, I read the statement to him. "If this statement is true, I'll ask you to sign it," I stated.

"It's true," Merriwether stated.

"Sign it!" Kenny stated handing Merriwether a pen.

The statement no sooner signed, Tom Merriwether arrived home from work. "What's going on?" he demanded. We introduced ourselves and read Tom the Miranda Warning.

"They've caught us Tommy!" Joe told his brother.

"What the xox you talkin' about – caught us doin' what?" Tom said in response to his brother's proclamation.

"For cuttin' and sellin' those walnut logs to Ajax," Joe responded.

"We cut those trees right here," Tom stated.

"It's no use, Tommy, they found the logs in the ditch. I told them the truth. It's no use – they've got us. I gave them a statement," Joe stated.

"You dumb xo#x," Tom stated and fell silent.

"Tom, I'm going to read Joe's statement to you and advise you of our investigation so far. If you agree with your brother's signed and witnessed statement, I'll ask you to sign a short statement simply acknowledging your brother's statement is true," I told Tom

"Both of you get off my farm – I ain't signin' nothin'," the now "chesty again" Tom shouted.

I could see Ken Skaggs had had it with this gentleman. "How'd you like to take a trip to the county jail – now!" Skaggs told Tom.

"I've heard about you Skaggs – you'd take me to jail over this, wouldn't you?" Tom asked.

"You gotta live with me, boy – even when this mess is over. Now are you gonna shape up and act your age or are you goin' to jail" Skaggs admonished Tom.

I thought, xo#x, Kenny may lock the Merriwethers up and decide to prosecute them in State Court. I for sure, want them in the U.S. Magistrate's Court in Louisville.

"I'll settle down – write the statement -- I'll sign it," the now humbled Tom stated.

I prepared the brief statement previously noted. Tom Merriwether signed it. Kenny and I witnessed his signature.

"Alright, we're gonna take a few photographs, then we're leaving. Have your brother, Lester, in my office at the Dam by 9:00 a.m. tomorrow. I've spent enough time with this case. Have Lester in my office – hear?" Kenny told the Merriwethers.

We returned to the ravine where the "alibi" logs were dumped, photographed them and left. The following morning the Merriwethers were waiting for Kenny and me when we arrived at the Corps Office at 8:00 a.m. After Miranda, Lester cooperated 100%. He signed a short statement acknowledging the statements signed by his brothers were true and correct. We advised the Merriwethers we would notify them when and where to appear in court with the issuance (to each) of a Violation Notice later. We suggested they settle their issue with John Taylor before their appearance in Federal Court. I returned to Carr Fork.

On a Monday morning, I wrote a complete investigation report in much the same format I used while I worked with the State of Ohio.

I phoned Fred Huelson and gave him an overview of the case. Fred advised that Kenny and I should meet the next day with Fred Rager, Attorney in the Legal Section of the Louisville District Office. I phoned Rager and made the arrangements.

At 11:00 a.m. on Tuesday, Kenny and I met with Rager. He reviewed the investigation report and documentary evidence. He complimented us on our work and advised us we had very good cases against the Merriwethers. He stated he would submit the case to the U.S. Attorney for prosecution approval in U.S. Magistrate Court, Western District, Louisville, Kentucky and we would be notified when and where to appear in Court. I returned to Carr Fork.

The following week, Kenny Skaggs, Ranger Bob Barnett and I, with Corps Council Rager, and an Assistant U.S. Attorney, appeared in U.S. Magistrate Court in Louisville. Present were the three Merriwether defendants with their council as a result of being served with Violation Notices by Kenny Skaggs. Charged with theft of U.S. government property, in violation of Title 36 of the Federal Code, the U.S. Attorney also asked for full restitution and replacement of the stolen black walnut tree. The three Merriwether's entered pleas of no contest on advice of their council. Following a brief prosecutorial statement advising the court of Corps investigative results, the U.S. Magistrate found the defendants guilty and imposed a fine of $500.00 on each of the defendants for violating Title 36. The defendants were ordered to pay full restitution to the Corps in the amount they were paid for the stolen black walnut tree (in excess of $1000.00 – do not recall the exact amount). Their attorney advised the Court the Merriwethers had "settled" with adjacent landowner Taylor.

Timber theft in the U.S. is as much a problem today and it was then. I was never privileged to work another timber theft case. When I remember this case, my thoughts automatically focus on three individuals. Kenny

Skaggs has passed on – he was a great Resource Manager and darn good cop. Ranger Bob Barnett, a bright young graduate Forester who cinched our case. Fred Huelson, (the quintessential gentleman from Clarksville, Indiana) -- my "big boss" in Louisville who always supported his troops 100% when they did their jobs. All have my utmost respect then and now.

The wintering elk herd at Green Peter Lake, Mid-Williamette Area, Oregon. Five members of the herd are not pictured.

18
The Mid-Williamette

My time as an Area Park Manager over the Corps' Portland, Oregon District's Mid-Williamette Area was very short (July, 1973 – June, 1974). Although short, it was rewarding and eventful. I was fortunate to be the first Park Manager hired. My first priority was to establish the Operation's Division – Mid-Williamette Resource Management Section. I selected and hired a Chief of Maintenance, three Park Rangers, one of which may have been the Corps first female Park Ranger. My office and the new Resource Management Headquarters were located at the Foster Lake Dam Office complex, Sweet Home, Oregon.

Detroit and Big Cliff (on the North Santiam River), Green Peter (on the Middle Santiam River) and Foster (on the South Santiam River) Dams and Lakes constituted the Mid-Williamette Area. Located at Foster Dam is the South Santiam Salmon Hatchery constructed by the Corps. It is operated by the Oregon State Fish and Game Department. The hatchery raises spring chinook and summer steelhead. Upstream, migrant adults are captured from March to October. Spawning occurs in September for chinook -- December to January for steelhead. Juvenile fish are raised year around. There is a 1200 gallon aquarium for viewing fish.

Within the four projects are about 8,500 acres of water when full. About the same land acreage above pool and about 100 miles of shoreline. The four power dams have a total kilowatt capacity of 218,000 kw. There are fourteen public use sites, including campgrounds, boat ramps and day use areas. The Corps, U.S. Forest Service, Oregon State Parks, and Linn County operate the various public use sites. The primary purpose of the four projects is power production. They were managed by a Project Engineer who I answered to. A full military Captain was assigned to my section for training. Larger (at that time) than the Resource Management Section was the long established Power Dam Operators and Maintenance Crew who, through a supervisor, also answered to the Project Engineer. The Power House Labor Crew was shared between the Power House Section and the Resource Management Section – a situation that could prove "difficult" but didn't. I selected my new Chief of Maintenance from within the Power House Crew. I knew he had the respect of the entire crew as well as their superiors. His name was Gordon Wright. He proved to be a master at maintaining good relations with our sister section. He also became my one of my best friends. He has since passed on. He's another I'll "look up" someday.

In that day and time, the operation of Corps power production and/or flood control projects were governed by a "Master Plan." These "how to" instruments directed the accomplishment of virtually every project's purpose and function. About midway through my time in the Louisville District, Corps Headquarters in Washington issued a directive requiring Master Plan updating. The updating included the preparation of forestry, soil, water, fish and wildlife Appendices to each project Master Plan. I was selected by Fred Huelson to do the first (in the Louisville District) Fish and Wildlife Management Appendices to the Master Plan for Rough River Lake, Kentucky.

In December, after my arrival at the Mid-Willamette, I was summoned to the Project Engineer's Office to attend a meeting with the contractor (a private Environmental Consulting Firm) who won the bid to do the fish and wildlife management Appendices to each Project Master Plan in the Mid-Willamette Area. In attendance were three contractor representatives, Bud Ossie, Chief of the Resource Management Section in Portland, Paul Peters, Project Engineer, and yours truly.

I wondered, surely, the Portland District hasn't contracted the work on their Master Plan Appendices. That's got to be expensive. There must be enough talent on board to accomplish the mission.

I'd met two new Rangers from other Portland District Projects. One with a degree in forestry, another, a soil scientist who had worked for the Soil Conservation Service As the meeting began, the contractor handed out a "sample" Fish and Wildlife Management Appendices they had received from the Corps Headquarters in Washington, DC. Its cover page read, "Appendices D & E to the Master Plan, Rough River Lake, Kentucky, Louisville District, Corps of Engineers. Prepared by Ron Bailey, Park Manager."

There it lay in front of me – the Fish and Wildlife Management Appendices for Rough River that I had completed almost two years earlier. I decided to sit mute. As the meeting progressed, Bud Ossie asked, "Ron, didn't you come here from the Louisville District?"

"Yes," I answered.

"Is this you?" he asked as he held up the Rough River Appendices and pointed to my name.

"Yes," I answered.

"Then, why are we contracting the work on these Wildlife Appendices in the Mid-Willamette? For that matter, the Portland District?" Ossie asked.

"That was our call at the time, Bud. If you'll remember we didn't have the talent on board to do these Appendices when the directive came down from OCE in Washington," Paul Peters, the Project Engineer, stated.

Before Ossie could respond to Peter's statement, a member of the contractor contingent jumped to his feet, "Gentlemen, this contract has been signed – our company will hold the Corps' feet to the fire if this becomes an issue," he stated in a somewhat loud and indignant tone.

Well, I guess that takes care of that, I thought, then stated, "Folks, I suggest we move on, past is past."

"Agreed," stated another member of the contractor's party.

The contractor handed out an "outline" of the Appendices proposed for the Foster and Green Peter Projects. As we reviewed this document, I quickly noticed the general theme was "wildlife habitat maintenance" not "wildlife habitat maintenance and improvement." No mention was made of a thirty animal elk herd that wintered on the exposed flats due to discharge to winter pool at Green Peter Lake. Luxuriant grass growth occurred on the flats between draw down to winter pool and cold weather. We had already top dressed (and planned to continue annually) these flats with an all-purpose fertilizer that greatly improved growth. My plan was to establish shoreline – above pool selected grasses, saltlicks, and encourage natural succession of herbaceous plant and shrub growth. Thus, giving the herd much improved wintering conditions. There was no mention of artificial nesting structures for waterfowl and other migratory birds and no mention of the fishery other than salmon. Why the contractor addressed salmon I'll never understand as the salmon management strategy was historic – already covered in the original Master Plans of the power dam projects in the Pacific Northwest.

Green Peter and Foster Dams are equipped with fish ladders and elevators that aid spring and summer steelhead migrations upstream. When the fish reach the top of the fish ladder, they are collected and moved over the dam by an elevator system.

At the time of my departure from the Mid-Willamette, meetings with the contractors awarded the work on the forestry, soil and water Appendices had not taken place. The fish and wildlife management Appendices had not been received. Paul Peters, the Project Engineer (a super guy) told me to "go ahead and do what you know how to do – that's why we hired you. We'll worry about the Appendices mandates later."

Like Carr Fork, a trash dumping problem along with an off-road vehicle problem existed, especially at the Foster and Green Peter Projects. I felt the more "public participation" I could encourage, the better. I was able to enlist the services of the Santiam Four-Wheel Drive Association, the Senior Citizens of Sweet Home Association, the Assembly of God Church of Sweet Home, and the Boy Scouts. We implemented a "Johnny Horizon Operation Clean Sweep" day. The Senior Citizens prepared and served a mid-day cafeteria style dinner

223

for the Four Wheelers, Boy Scouts & participating private citizens, who all devoted one day to the clean up of the two Projects. Over 400 were served. Over 3 tons of trash including automobile bodies and discarded household appliances were collected and hauled away in Corps trucks. With this effort and an all out Ranger law enforcement effort (citing dumping violators into U.S. Magistrate Court), we cleaned up Foster and Green Peter. Our efforts won congressional recognition mainly because of the public's participation.

Ranger, Jerry Paige, whom I hired fresh out of Humbolt State College with a degree in Resource Management, designed, implemented, and supervised the Interpretive Program for the Mid-Willamette Projects. He did a super job. His prepared presentations gave dramatic illustration of all aspects of natural resource management and power production. At Foster, Jerry established an arboretum where experimental plantings (grasses, trees and shrubs) were established for use in the wildlife management program as well as ornamentals for public use sites.

Rangers Lee Ellison and Debbie Smith (who had a degree in police science) were outstanding all-round Rangers who carried out all aspects of their duties with a great degree of professionalism.

Captain Tim Reynolds, a full military trainee and graduate engineer, proved to be one of my greatest assets. He was a master at solving engineering and other problems. Particularly adept, along with Gordon Wright, at lake snagging and clearing. This involved crowding and booming (by heavy steel hulled tugs) huge Douglas fir logs that clogged Foster as a result of high water runoff from watershed logging operations. The logs were branded by the timber companies who would remove them at lake boat ramps after they were herded and boomed by the Corps.

It will suffice to say, the Mid-Willamette Resource Management Section was established in short order – my short time there was most successful. I hired the right people to get the job done.

While attending a joint Interior Department/Corps meeting in Portland, I met Mr. Al Missledine, Special Agent in Charge, District 2, with the U.S. Fish and Wildlife Service's Law Enforcement Division. His office was in Portland. Al was a former State Wildlife Officer. We traded a couple "war stories" and I found myself longing to return to fulltime wildlife law enforcement work. Within the federal service, satisfying this "longing" meant only one target – the U.S. Fish and Wildlife Service, so I thought. I inquired of Al, "What was happening" with respect to Special Agent hiring in the USFWS.

"Ron, there's been a freeze on hiring Agents for sometime. Forget the Fish and Wildlife Service for now. Sometime ago, the Bureau of Commercial Fisheries was removed from the Service and placed under the National Oceanic and Atmospheric Administration. The new National Marine Fisheries Service under NOAA now does the work of the old Bureau of Commercial Fisheries. They're hiring law enforcement agents. I have some of their vacancy announcements at the office. If you can get on with them and find yourself dissatisfied – wait your chance and shoot for an interagency transfer to the

Service. Hiring will loosen up with the Service, but Lord only knows when," Al advised me.

"Would you mind giving me copies of those vacancy announcements?"

"Not at all – we'll go to my office after the meeting and take care of it," Al responded.

The National Marine Fisheries Service (NMFS) vacancy announcements listed Special Agent vacancies in Alaska and two Regions stateside. I applied for positions in Alaska and the Boston Region. Dan Russ, Special Agent in Charge, soon notified me I had the Special Agent's job at Cape Cod, Massachusetts and told me when to report to him at the Regional Law Enforcement Office in Glouster, Massachusetts. My seven year career with the Army Corps of Engineers ended in June, 1974. Just after giving my departure notice, late one night my home phone rang. The call was from a person "very high in rank" (is all I can say. By policy, this person was not supposed to involve himself in civilian personnel matters) in the Portland District. He was attending a meeting at Coos Bay.

"Ron, I've just been advised you're leaving your position at the Mid-Willamette," the caller stated.

"Yes sir, that's true," I answered.

"Your career is certainly yours to manage. Your efforts and timely results in the Mid-Willamette have not gone unnoticed. I feel your abilities far exceed the Mid-Willamette position. Be aware the Chief of the District Resource Management Section in the Portland Office will soon open. I certainly can't promise you the job, but if you're inclined to reconsider, I'm safe in saying your chances of being named to the position are better than average," the caller advised.

"Sir, I am humbled and honored but now I'm committed to the National Marine Fisheries Service. Thank you so much for this call and your confidence in me. My time with the Corps has been more than a privilege," I responded.

"So be it. I wish you and your wife the best of everything," the caller stated leaving me very much "moved" by his call.

Soon thereafter, I received the most commending and congratulatory letter I've ever received from Colonel Clarence D. Gilkey, District Engineer over the Corps Portland District. I also received a similar one from my boss, Mr. Paul Peters, Project Engineer over the Mid-Willamette.

On the eve of our departure, my entire Mid-Willamette crew, the Project Engineer, and the personnel at the South Santiam Fish Hatchery honored Shirley and I with a goodbye party featuring a grilled salmon feast. A few tears were shed. Our last night in Oregon was spent on the banks of the Calapooia River in the home of Gordon Wright, my Chief of Maintenance and one of our lasting best friends. The next morning as we were leaving for Massachusetts (driving a Dodge and towing a Volkswagen), Gordon hugged and kissed both of us – then broke down and cried like a child – so did we.

19
NMFS

When Shirley and I left Kentucky and traveled west to Oregon in 1973, an event stands out in our memories. Near Twin Falls, Idaho, we stopped at a roadside produce stand and bought a quart of fresh Bing cherries. As we continued our journey west, we relished the plump, crisp, cherries - - - for about an hour. Then the worst case of the green-apple-quick-step besieged both of us. We hit every roadside restroom all the way to and beyond the Oregon State Line.

When we left Oregon and traveled east to Massachusetts in 1974, two events stand out in our memories. Both involved State Troopers – one in Oregon and one in New York. Both are sickening examples of almost everything a law enforcement officer shouldn't be. The two incidents are stories within themselves. I won't take the time or effort to elaborate.

I reported to the National Marine Fisheries Service Law Enforcement (LE), Special Agent in Charge (SAC) Office on July 8, 1974. As previously instructed on the phone by SAC, Dan Russ, I met with a very amiable Special Agent (SA), Alan Mager. I was replacing Alan (who transferred to the SAC Office as the Agent in Charge of Marine Mammal enforcement) at the Provincetown duty station on Cape Cod.

Two days orientation at the Regional Office followed, that included all processing through personnel and the issuance of credentials. I was also issued an ICNAF Identification Card. My duties mainly included the enforcement of:

The International Convention for the Northwest Atlantic Fisheries (a treaty).

227

The Endangered Species Act of 1973.

The Marine Mammal Act of 1972.

The Lacey Act of 1900 as amended in 1969.

The International Convention for the Northwest Atlantic Fisheries became effective in 1950 with ratification by Canada, Iceland, the United Kingdom, and the United States. Ultimately, participation increased to include 18 member nations. Its purpose was the investigation, protection and conservation of the Northwest Atlantic Fisheries, to include mollusks, finny fish, harp and hooded seals. The main concern of the United States and Canada was the depleted stocks of cod, haddock and yellow tail flounder. It established five management areas within the Convention area in the Northwest Atlantic Ocean. It established the International Commission (made up of members from each nation) for the Northwest Atlantic Fisheries (ICNAF). Known as "The Commission", it was the responsible body for managing the fishery in the Northwest Atlantic. It had regional advisory panels, advisory committees, scientific committees and sub-committees composed of members from the contracting nations. It enacted open and closed seasons, annual and seasonal catch quotas (in metric tons) for each contracting nation, by species, in each of the five management areas.

Enforcement of these regulations, along with fishing gear regulations and the "Creature of the Continental Shelf" (lobsters) law was accomplished through U.S. Coast Guard surveillance flights and sea patrols. NMFS Special Agents participated in both. Sea patrols ran from 7 to 21 days. Detected violations of ICNAF regulations were reported to the Commission and State Department who issued complaints to the violating member nations' Management Authority. The Management Authority (in theory, at least) saw to it the offending vessel or fish company was penalized in some manner when the fishing vessel involved returned to its home port. There were no provisions for verifying these "penalty" actions. They were apparently "assumed" and it was questioned they actually took place, especially in the "Iron Curtain" countries where the fishing vessels and/or companies were rigidly controlled and owned by the government.

ICNAF failed. It was unable to prevent the decline in fish stocks in the Northwest Atlantic. The fact that it failed caused the enactment of The Magnuson Fishery Conservation and Management Act of 1976 (MFCMA), renamed the Magnuson-Stevens Fishery Conservation and Management Act when amended on October 11, 1996. It established a U.S. exclusive economic zone which ranges up to 200 miles offshore, and created eight regional fishery councils and management areas to manage the living marine resources within each area. The Act was passed principally to address heavy foreign fishing, promote the development of a domestic fleet and link the fishing community more directly to the management process. Pursuant to the original MFCMA of 1976, the ICNAF Convention was replaced with the Convention on Future Multilateral Cooperation in the Northwest Atlantic Fisheries (CFMCNAF) in 1978. The Act provides very stiff civil and criminal penalties for violations of its fishery regulations. Violators are processed through the U.S. Court System. However, fish stocks continue to decline in the Northwest Atlantic as they are in all the traditional commercial fishing salt waters of the world.

During my short tenure with NMFS (July, 1974 to November, 1975), I participated in 8 sea patrols aboard 7 Coast Guard Cutters, spending 63 days at sea. I participated in 22 surveillance flights, spending 84 hours in the air. I detected and reported significant ICNAF violations on 6 of the 8 sea patrols. Not once was I notified of a penalty or sanction of any kind being levied against the violating vessel or violating ICNAF member nation. Not once was I ever summoned to a hearing of any kind. On several of my surveillance flights I observed violations that involved fishing vessels of various nations engaged in closed area fishing violations – mainly yellow tailed flounder, In these instances, sometimes I was able (by radio) to get Coast Guard Cutters, on patrol with a NMFS Agent aboard, to the scene.

I resolved one "gear conflict case" while on sea patrol. This took place off the northern coast of Massachusetts. Two Soviet trawlers fished through a field of U.S. lobster traps, destroying them all. After considerable efforts with Coast Guard help, I managed to make radio contact with a Soviet inspection vessel that had five Soviet ICNAF inspectors on board. A Coast Guard Officer (the XO) and I boarded the Russian Inspection Vessel. Through an ICNAF interpretation guide, we were able to inform the Chief Russian Inspector of the "gear conflict" violation. He was a very jovial, red faced, gentleman who kept repeating, "No probl-e-e-m, no probl-e-e-m". At this point we thought he was conveying the message, "We're not going to do anything about your destroyed lobster traps." The opposite proved to be true. After lengthy radio conversations (in Russian, of course) with the Captains of the violating Soviet trawlers, the two Captains came (by small boat) to the Inspection Vessel. I had a list of the American lobster vessels violated. The list included dollar values of all the traps destroyed, plus estimates of the wholesale value of the lobster catch had each U.S. vessel returned to port and sold his catch. The Russian Inspectors collected a quantity of cash in U.S. dollars from each Russian Captain and paid the entire bill in cash. Rather than accept the cash, we radioed each U.S. lobsterman who suffered damages. One by one they came to the Russian Inspection vessel and accepted payment. The Americans thanked the Russians and the Russians thanked the Americans. The Soviet Inspectors ordered the Russian trawlers "off the grounds". By daylight the following day, all were gone. It took 20 day and night hours to get all this accomplished. I wasn't certain this was the proper way to handle a gear conflict case. The Coast Guard cutter skipper assured me, "This is the way we're going to handle it," case closed.

During June of 1974, two very rare leatherback sea turtles (Dermochelys coriacea) made their appearance in Cape Cod Bay. This species is protected by the Endangered Species Act of 1973. Leatherbacks are the largest turtles on earth, weighing up to 1500 pounds. Some marine biologists claim up to a ton. Front flipper spans have been measured at 8 feet. They feed almost exclusively on jelly fish. Their meat is unpalatable. They have no hard shell and no commercial value.

It reached the point where the turtles were seen often by commercial and non-commercial fishermen, tourists and others. They were, more or less, adopted as pets or mascots by the folks on Cape Cod. Their value to the tourist trade and consequently the economy of Cape Cod was considerable. The turtles and their welfare were frequently mentioned by the news media. Due to the past commercial value of the green sea turtle and to some extent, the loggerhead, I felt it was only a matter of time until someone "harvested" and attempted to sell one or both turtles, believing the meat edible and therefore, saleable.

Sure enough it happened. In mid-August, I was summoned to the Provincetown Fishermen's Cooperative, managed by Frankie Reis. One of the turtles was found floating, headless, in the bay. A few days earlier during a tuna tournament, it was towed to the Co-op where Frankie stored it in a cooler. It had four bullet holes in the carapace. The next day Marine Biologists from the New England Aquarium in Boston identified the turtle as a female leatherback. She was weighed at the Co-op at 1200 lbs. Frankie towed the turtle (due to the stench) to a small island off Provincetown where she awaited my inspection.

I summoned the Coast Guard for help. A Coast Guard patrol boat, complete with crew, picked me up at the Provincetown dock and transported me (in wet suit) to the turtle's location. They anchored about 50 yards off the Island. I jumped overboard equipped with my issued Navy survival knife, swam a short distance, and then waded ashore.

I was amazed, almost intimidated by the size of the creature. My first thought was, How truly magnificent and beautiful you are, but then aren't all God's creatures? My next thought was, You unique, rare and wonderful creature, all the years you roamed the seas only to have your life snuffed out in an instant by a greedy and uncaring outlaw. I choked and teared as I approached her lifeless form, knife in hand, and proceeded to do what I had to do.

I cut squares around each bullet hole in the top of her soft, pliable carapace. As I did this, gas caused by the internal decomposition taking place within her body cavity began escaping through the cuts. An orange fizz rose from each cut. It was caught by the wind and carried toward the Coast Guard patrol boat. I was upwind of all this. Although I noticed a bad odor, I wasn't experiencing the full blast of the stench as those aboard the patrol boat. I removed the first square plug and thrust my hand and arm, to the armpit, through her oozing, goopy, slimey, decomposing innards to the plastron. Immediately my fingertips felt a bullet. I grasp it and brought it to the surface of the carapace. It was a perfect specimen. I guessed it was a .45 caliber. I removed the remaining three plugs and executed the same procedure as the first. I groped through the three holes as long as I could stand it. I recovered no more bullets. By now the gaseous fizz exiting the openings I had made in the carapace changed in color to a greenish-orange. As the fizz rose into the fresh Cape Cod air, only to be captured by the wind and blown towards the Coast Guard vessel, it appeared beautiful. However, the stench, even at my upwind location, was by now more than I could bear. I've performed my amateur evidence seeking autopsies attempting to remove bullets, arrow points, etc. on many forms of wildlife. None, in the deceased state, smell as bad as the marine mammals and reptiles. (I performed or helped perform autopsies, usually with Dr. James Mead of the Smithsonian, on a minke whale, a finn whale and a right whale along with several seals and dolphins. My wife had to "cook" my wet suite and under garments outside on a grill to remove the odor. She could smell me at the front door where she made me undress on the porch.) Meanwhile, three of my downwind helpers were bent over the rail of the patrol boat barfing into the clear blue waters of Cape Cod. At the same time they were "urging" me, in no uncertain terms, to hurry. Why they didn't move their boat upwind, I'll never know. I managed to loop a hawser around the turtle and return with its opposite end to the boat. We towed her out past the Cape where she was unceremoniously buried at sea.

My investigation of her demise began and continued as information and evidence developed over the next eight months. It included contact with and/or the assistance of the New England Aquarium Marine Biologists, an Audubon Society Biologist, the Massachusetts Fish and Game Department, the Provincetown Fishermen's Coop, fishermen, a bar room waitress and two customers, U.S. Coast Guard, Orleans Police Dept., ATF, Braintree Police Dept., Massachusetts Division of Recreational and Marine Vehicles, two sporting good stores, suspect associates, New England Divers Co., New Bedford Police Dept (Ballistics), NMFS Agents – Southeast Region, a Florida Bangstick Manufacturer and Dealers, Massachusetts State Police, Florida Marine Patrol, and the Palm Beach Shores Police Dept. All the aforementioned investigative contacts resulted in the following:

1. Exact identification of turtle species.
2. Identification of the weapon used to kill the turtle – a bangstick – a single shaft with a firing device on one end that fires a 12 gauge smooth bore slug of the .44 caliber. Used on sea going vessels mainly to kill sharks.
3. Identification of two suspects as a result of bar room admissions.
4. Proof that one of the two suspects owned a bangstick manufactured by Bay Front Industries of Florida (the only manufacturer in the U.S.)
5. Identification of the boat suspects used when they killed the turtle.
6. Location of both suspect's residence and workplace in Florida by Florida Marine Patrol undercover officers.
7. My travel to Florida where I met with three NMFS Agents who earlier assisted with the investigation.

One Agent was assigned to assist me and witness the interview of the two suspects (I'll call) Peter Conkle and Joe LaPointe. LaPointe's residence was a mobile home in a swampy, mosquito infested, park on the outskirts of Ft. Lauderdale. According to the Marine Patrol undercover officer who located his residence, the location was one of the worst drug and other crime infested locations in the Ft. Lauderdale vicinity. We located the LaPointe trailer – he wasn't home. I made the decision (at about 4 p.m.) to maintain surveillance of his home until he returned – all night if necessary. Suddenly, my assisting NMFS Agent became very nervous, exclaiming, "Bailey, you got guts." He "remembered" he had an "urgent" investigation to work on in Tampa and promised his wife he would be home the following day. It was more than obvious he wasn't comfortable with my "all night surveillance" decision. He departed with my encouragement. I contacted the Florida Marine Patrol and requested assistance. I was advised Officer Ken Clark would meet me in Ft. Lauderdale the following morning at 7:00 a.m. I maintained surveillance of the LaPointe residence until 1:00 a.m. when LaPointe and a male associate I had interviewed in Boston, arrived – both drunk. It wasn't the time to interview LaPointe. At 7:00 a.m. Officer Clark, Florida Marine Patrol, met me in Ft. Lauderdale. "We thought you had a backup Agent with you – what happened?" he inquired.

"He apparently had more important priorities elsewhere," I replied.

"Ask me why I'm not surprised?" Clark (who knew the NMFS Agent) responded.

"No comment," I stated.

We went to the LaPointe trailer – he was not at home. Inquiry of a neighbor revealed he was at a Ft. Lauderdale Marina having a tuna tower installed on a boat he had just purchased. At the Marina we were told he was on a nearby waterway trying out a boat. Clark radioed an "all points." Within minutes Marine Patrol undercover Officer Akey had the boat located. Akey summoned a nearby Marine Patrol boat who had LaPointe and companion "docked" in short order. They further advised they had LaPointe aboard their patrol boat. Clark and I went to the location and contacted LaPointe. I read Joe the Miranda warning. After agreeing to questioning, LaPointe looked at me and stated, "You've been working on this one a long while, haven't you?"

"Yeah, sure have Joe – you want to tell me all about it?" I asked.

"Sure do, it's been on my mind long enough – you gonna arrest me and take me back to Massachusetts?" LaPointe asked.

"That depends on your cooperation and what you tell me," I replied.

"Okay, all I'll say is we didn't know the turtle was an endangered species and was protected. We're watermen, we try to abide by the law. We thought we could sell the turtle. Beyond that, all I'll say is I cut its head off to have it mounted. I threw it away when we read the newspapers. You'll have to get Pete to tell you the rest," LaPointe admitted.

"I'm going to prepare a statement recording all you've told me. Are you willing to sign it? Officer Clark and I will witness your signature," I advised LaPointe.

"Yeah, I'll sign it – am I going back to Massachusetts?" LaPointe stated and asked.

"No, I'll notify you by mail when and where you are to appear in court. You may be able to handle this by mail. I don't know at this time," I told him. On that note, I prepared LaPointe's statement. He signed it and we witnessed his signature.

"You'll be hearing from me after I get back to the Cape," I told him as Officer Clark and I departed.

At Ft. Lauderdale, I thanked Officer Ken Clark for his help. He asked if I needed help with Pete Conkle who lived at Palm Beach Shores.

"No, I'm going to the Police Department there to get help in locating him. I believe he operates a charter boat there. If I need help I'm sure the Palm Beach Shore Police will help me," I told Ken.

At Palm Beach Shores PD, I contacted a Patrolman, Dick Myers, who knew Pete Conkle well. After I gave Myers an investigation briefing, he stated, "I know Pete – he had a little drug problem some time ago. Nothing serious – don't worry, he'll cooperate," Officer Myers answered. Shortly, we arrived at the dock where Conkle's charter boat was moored. He and a very pretty blonde were aboard. Myers knew both. "How's it goin' Patty?" he spoke to the blonde.

"Pretty good Dick, how about you?" she replied.

"Pete, hop in the patrol car – we need to go downtown for a little while. We'll have him back soon, Patty," Myers announced. Conkle complied with Myers request without a word. At the Police Station, I introduced myself and presented my credentials.

"Yeah Bailey, we knew you would be here sooner or later. We already knew your name. Friends on the Cape told us you'd been everywhere up there checking on us," Conkle blurted. I read Pete the Miranda Warning.

"Yeah, I'll talk about it. Let's get it over with," he responded.

"I'm going to read you a statement signed by Joe LaPointe. If it's true, tell me," I told Conkle.

After reading him the LaPointe statement, he stated, "Yeah, it's true."

"Were you the trigger man? Did you kill the turtle with a bangstick?" I asked.

"Yes," Conkle responded.

"Did you know the turtle was protected by law?" I asked.

"No, we thought it was legal to catch and sell it. We didn't know it was illegal until we read it in the newspapers," Conkle stated.

I wrote a statement acknowledging the LaPointe statement was true and added wording that incriminated Conkle as the one who shot the turtle and recorded his lack of knowledge of the fact the turtle was protected. Conkle read it and signed it. Officer Myers and I witnessed his signature. I advised Conkle I would contact him by phone or mail and advise him of the next step in the litigation process. We returned Conkle to his charter boat and with the usual amenities, we departed.

I thanked Patrolman Myers for his cooperation and help and departed for Tampa. The following day I returned to Provincetown. Because Conkle and LaPointe, in committing the unlawful act of killing (and aiding) the leatherback sea turtle, did not meet the Acts' culpability standard for criminal prosecution, I had to file civil charges against the two after consulting with an Assistant U.S. Attorney in Boston. Conkle was charged with unlawful taking (killing) the turtle and subsequently fined $500.00. LaPointe was charged with aiding and abetting Conkle in the unlawful taking of the turtle and fined $250.00 by an Administrative Law Judge. The citizens of Cape Cod were highly critical of the fines. They thought it should be much more. Their opinions were vividly reported in several subsequent news articles. They voiced no criticisms of the investigation. To the contrary, I received many compliments for tracking down the violators.

In February 1975, through a tip I received from a CI (confidential informant) on Cape Cod, I interviewed, took statements and seized 175 pounds of sperm whale teeth, illegally possessed -- to be sold in the whale-ivory, scrimshaw trade -- from two Portuguese Nationals residing in Rhode Island. I also obtained an airline bill of lading labeled "fish bones". The two subjects admitted they misrepresented the shipment of sperm whale teeth as fish bones and imported them into the U.S. – all in violation of the Endangered Species Act, Marine Mammal Protection Act and the Lacey Act. I prepared a case report charging them with the violations that was filed with the U.S. Attorney for approval and prosecution. A copy of the report, of course, went to the SAC Office. Later that same CI stated he received reliable information indicating the same two individuals had much earlier (before the 175 lbs.) smuggled 400 lbs. of sperm whale teeth from Portugal into the U.S. They reportedly sold them all to scrimshaw engravers (known as scrimshanders) up and down the east coast. If my CI's information proved true, this would certainly develop into a major and most significant case. I re-interviewed the two subjects who denied guilt but agreed to a polygraph examination that I scheduled with the Rhode Island State Police. When the SAC learned of this, he called me at my home on Sunday – a day off – and told me to cancel the polygraph examination. He refused to discuss the matter, stating "I told you to cancel it." I cancelled the examination. The case was pursued no further. When I left NMFS, the following December, the existing case against the two violators had not been litigated. I never heard any more about it.

In late March of 1975, I was summoned to the Cape along with Dr. James Mead of the Smithsonian and the Coast Guard. A 40 foot Sei Whale had stranded itself in the mouth of the Herring River (headed upstream) inside the Cape off Cape Cod Bay. I arrived about the same time as Dr. Mead and the Coast Guard. The local Cape Coders had formed a bucket/boat brigade and was doing an excellent job of keeping the whales' exposed skin (above water line) wet. Cape Cod natives are used to taking care of stranded whales and other marine mammals. They know what to do and usually do it well. The whale was blowing (breathing) and appeared to be in good flesh and good health. Mead examined the whale as best he could and opined her problem may be an inner ear parasite. (I always refer to the great whales as "her" or "she". It's because, like the ladies – they're beautiful.) We attached a 100 foot hawser (with slip knot) around her tail ahead of the fluke. The Coast Guard vessel began pulling her west towards the Bay. Gradually she became unwedged and quietly towed behind the Coast Guard vessel. We towed her around the point of the Cape to about 12 miles out to sea. Then she began to sound (dive, then surface and blow (breath) through the blow hole). Now, she was towing the Coast Guard vessel, almost pulling the vessel under like a fishing bobber. Two Coast Guardsmen in wet suits went overboard to try and remove the hawser from her tail. Her fluke tossed them in the air like ping-pong balls. Finally, the hawser was cut, releasing the whale. In view of the fact the hawser was affixed with a slip knot, it was hoped she would eventually shed it. When last seen, she was still headed out to sea and freedom.

During April of 1975, I was assisting another NMFS Agent who was investigating a reported over-limit of haddock landing by a New Bedford based fishing vessel. I called on (I'll call it) the Shagnasty Sea Food Company located on the New Bedford docks where the haddock were sold. When I requested the most recent weigh-out slips recording the suspect vessel's landings (fish sold and species); I was ordered off the property. When I advised the Shagnasty Seafood's owner he was making a big mistake, due to the fact I would file interfering charges (with a federal agent in performing his duties) against him in Federal Court, he ordered three thugs who worked for him to "throw his ass off the premises." I immediately went to the New Bedford Office and prepared a case report against the Seafood Company owner for approval and prosecution by the U.S. Attorney's Office in Boston. Shortly after I advised my immediate supervisor, the Senior Resident Agent in New Bedford and the SAC Office in Glouster that I was on my way to the U.S. Attorney's Office to present the case, I was phoned by the SAC and told not to file the case. "Forget it – you should expect to have a few problems with the Industry." I was enraged! I decided to file the case anyway. Later, after thinking it over and considering the earlier sperm whale teeth case, I decided on a different course of action – get out of the National Marine Fisheries Service – ASAP! -- Get back with an Agency that will stand behind me. I recalled Al Misseldine's advice, "If you find yourself dissatisfied, shoot for an interagency transfer."

In October 1975, I contacted ASAC Jeff Blackmore, U.S. Fish and Wildlife Service, Law Enforcement District 13 in Boston. I told Jeff point blank, "I need a Special Agent's position with the Fish and Wildlife Service." I told him of my problems with NMFS, ending my statement with, "Jeff, I've got to get back into serious, job satisfying, wildlife law enforcement work with an agency that will back me up, some how, some way. If this sounds like I'm desperate, I am."

Jeff smiled, "I understand, what's your background before NMFS?" he asked. I answered his question in a hurry. "Well, you've got a full sea bag that's for certain. An Agent's position in Philadelphia will soon open. Pennsylvania is within District 10, headquartered in Baltimore. I'm on the AD-HOC Committee that will make the selection. I'm certainly not promising you anything. There will be several within the Service who'll go after the position. I'll assure you the Committee will make a fair evaluation of each applicant. In any event, you need to get a 171 (application) to Bill Kensinger, the SAC in Baltimore. Bill is one fine fellow – he and I worked as Florida State Game Wardens together," Blakemore stated. During that interview with Jeff, two words he spoke stood out in my memory, "I understand."

By 10:00 a.m. the next morning I had a 171 completed and in the mail to Bill Kensinger. I notified my boss, NMFS SRA George Schneider, of my application with the USFWS. Schneider, to his everlasting credit, wrote a letter, "To Whom It May Concern" giving me the highest of recommendations. 'I hate to see you go, Ron, but I know you're not satisfied here and you never will be," George told me.

On November 11, 1975, I was phoned by SAC Dan Russ. "I've heard about this fin and feather business (Fish and Wildlife Service). I'm prepared to offer you the supervisory (Senior Resident Agent) SRA's position in Maine if you want it. I can fill the job in the next three months. Now, as for this fin and feather thing is concerned – you xo#x or get off the pot."

"I'll let you know, Dan. There's a lot of competition for the job I've applied for with the Fish and Wildlife Service. I probably won't get it," I responded.

"I need an answer on the Maine job within three weeks," Russ stated.

"You'll get one," I replied.

On November 24, 1975, the day after my birthday, I received notification by mail from Bill Kensinger, SAC, USFWS, Baltimore, that I had the Philadelphia position. In it was a note to call Bill.

"I just got the job notification, Bill. Thanks!" I told Kensinger.

"You have a full sea bag, Hoss. You received the highest rating of all the applicants. All your past supervisors gave you very high recommendations. I might add you're the only applicant without a college degree. The Committee checked you out thoroughly. Heck, they know who you played in the sand box with back in Ohio," Kensinger stated.

I told Bill I was having a few problems with my SAC at NMFS.

"Don't let ol Dan get to you. We all know him well – he used to be with us, you know. Before that, he was a Pennsylvania Game Warden. A good one, I might add. Dan's just trying to keep his shop together. He likes you or he wouldn't have offered you the job in Maine. When this is all over, he can be a good friend. When does your pay period end up there?" Kensinger advised and asked.

"My pay period ends December 6th. How did you know Russ talked to me about the job in Maine?" I asked.

"Report to me in Baltimore on the 8th. About the Maine offer – we have ways of finding out about things, stud. Heh – heh," Kensinger chuckled.

That iced it! As of December 8, 1975 I became a Special Agent with the U.S. Fish and Wildlife Service stationed at Philadelphia. My new boss was SRA Leo Badger, Harrisburg. Leo was a former Pennsylvania State Game Warden. He would prove to be one of my best friends; the best boss I ever had; and one of the best Game Wardens I ever worked with. When the good Lord smiled on me in November of 1975, he really smiled. I sure didn't realize then how truly rewarding and adventurous the rest of my career would be.

Headless 1200 lb. leatherback sea turtle – Endangered Species – shot in Cape Cod Bay, being towed to sea for burial following autopsy – August, 1974. Violators apprehended eight months later.

The Author at beginning of aerial seal count – Cape Cod. Monomoy Island Wilderness Area and Martha's Vineyard, April, 1975.

Autopsy of a 40 ft. beached Right Whale, Monomoy Island National Wilderness Area. Dr. James Mead, Smithsonian (foreground), Lt. Proulx, USCG (left), Dr. W.E. Schevill, Harvard University (right) Photo by Author – May, 1975.

Head of Right Whale (above photo). dr. James Mead (foreground), Lt. Proulx (left), Dr. W.E. Schevill (center). Photo by Author.

Beginning
surveillance
flights to locate
the foreign fishing
fleet. ICNAF
Sea Patrol
– U.S. Coast
Guard Cutter
DECISIVE.
December, 1974

ICNAF Sea Patrol. U.S. Coast Guard Cutter ACTIVE approaches
Polish fishing trawler FINWAL for fisheries inspection. June, 1975

20
The Feather Merchant

A significant mail-order hunting and fishing equipment supplier, headquartered in the Midwest, was in full swing business during the 1950's. They published an inch thick catalogue offering for sale a very comprehensive line of hunting, fishing, and camping items. They specialized, to an extent, in fly tying, spinning and bait casting lure components. A customer could purchase all the components necessary to tie his own flies, manufacture his own spinners or bait casting lures (plugs) at significant savings. They listed and sold all manner of fly tying components including game and non-game bird plumages, game and fur bearing animal hair for fly tying purposes, as well as hooks, wire, etc. and unpainted plug bodies for the bait casting lure maker. Their business was nationwide, their prices reasonable. As a game biologist I worked with said, "They'll nickel and dime you to death." Their customers included fly fishing and fly tying celebrities who gave testimonials attesting to the quality of their products. To this day, somewhere in the maze I call my hunting and fishing shed, I have spinner components I purchased in the 1950's from this company.

Unfortunately, certain plumages and furs they were buying and selling in interstate commerce, mainly to those who tied flies, came from wild migratory non-game girds, native game birds, and mammals protected by State and Federal laws. Laws that prohibited the sale of these species or "parts thereof", laws at the federal level known as The Migratory Bird Treaty Act and The Lacey Act. Back then, young in my career before entering wildlife law enforcement, I'd heard selling certain migratory bird parts was illegal. I wondered how this company could openly engage in this illegal activity for such a long time. Then it finally happened. They were raided by wildlife authorities and their illegal "parts thereof" dealings in protected wildlife in interstate commerce was brought to a halt.

Little did I know that a business, exactly as the one described, was operating in eastern Pennsylvania (my new duty station) right under my nose.

In February of 1975, U.S. Fish and Wildlife Service Special Agent (SA) Jay D. Miles, who was stationed in California, visited a fly fishing (including fly tying) supply business at McKinleyville, California. There, he obtained a 1974 and a 1975 catalogue put out by the (I'll call it) Roland G. Downey Company addressed to a town in eastern Pennsylvania. Listed for sale in the 1975 catalogue were plumages and parts of migratory non-game and game birds, marine mammal fur and wolf fur. Also listed to buy and sell were parts of native (to Pennsylvania and other states) game animals and game birds. Entries in the 1974 and 1975 catalogues solicited the purchase of "well handled furs". In the 1975 catalogue was a solicitation to "buy or trade" certain migratory non-game bird parts. All this indicated possible violations of the federal Lacey Act, the Migratory Bird Treaty Act, the Marine Mammal Protection Act and the Endangered Species Act. Also, the California Penal Code, the Pennsylvania Game Laws, and the laws of the various states from where the company suppliers shipped. Of interest, was the fact that only the 1975 catalogue contained listings that indicated violations of the federal laws other than the Lacey Act. This indicated the Downey Companies' dealings in parts of species protected by federal law were of recent vintage. During his visit, Agent Miles also secured a copy of an invoice recording, among other things, the purchase of kingfisher skins by the California Fly-Tying Supply business from the Downey Company.

In May of 1975, SA Miles made an undercover mail order purchase, by personal check, from the company. The buy included migratory bird plumages, a quantity of fur advertised as wolf fur and a quantity of fur advertised as seal fur. Subsequently, the migratory bird plumages were identified by expert, Roxie Laybourne, Zoologist of the Smithsonian Institute, Washington, DC. The plumages were from species as advertised for sale in the Downey catalogue and protected by the Migratory Bird Treaty Act that prohibited their sale. The wolf and seal fur was examined by Michael A. Bogan, Wildlife Biologist, Mammal Section, National Fish and Wildlife Laboratory, Museum of History, Washington DC. A positive I.D. of the advertised wolf fur could not be made; thus a violation of the Endangered Species Act could not be proven. A positive I.D. of the advertised seal fur could not be made, thus a violation of the Marine Mammal Protection Act could not be proven.

On October 29, 1975, SA Owen Seelye, assigned to Western Pennsylvania, visited the premises of the Downey Company in an undercover capacity. He obtained a 1975 catalogue. In December of 1975, SA Seelye, using a Downy catalogue order blank, ordered plumage from three species of protected migratory non-game birds, making payment by personal check. In Mid-December, Seelye received his order. Again, Roxie Laybourne identified the plumage as the species advertised for sale and protected by the provisions of the Migratory Bird Treaty Act that prohibits their sale.

In February of 1976, I made a covert visit to the Downey business establishment posing as an avid fly fisherman and fly tier. I made contact with a male Downey employee.

"I need to acquire some real flicker, kingfisher, grouse, and crow skins or feathers – whatever you have," I told the young clerk.

"We have whole kingfisher skins, crow wings, and the feathers most fly tiers use from flickers or yellow hammers we call them, and grouse," he replied. He disappeared into an adjacent room and shortly returned with four separate trays, each containing the plumages – merchandise he previously described. I selected a kingfisher skin, two crow wings and several separate flicker and grouse feathers.

"Sure is good to find a place where I can buy the real thing. I've been using artificial dyed stuff up until now. I've been told and always thought selling real wild bird plumage was against the law," I commented to the clerk as he made out an invoice recording my over-the-counter cash purchase.

"Aw, they don't pay any attention to selling a few feathers and fur," he responded.

"Who are they?" I asked.

"You know, the Game Wardens," he replied.

I bid the young man good day and left the premises. All the plumage I purchased was subsequently identified by expert, Roxie Laybourne as the species represented at the time of the sale.

On March 17, 1976, I obtained a Federal Search Warrant through an Assistant U.S. Attorney and U.S. Magistrate for the Eastern Federal Court District of Pennsylvania. Probable cause for the warrant of course, was the covert purchases from the Downey Company by Agents Miles, Seelye and yours truly. The positive identifications of Roxie Laybourne firmly established violations of the Migratory Bird Treaty Act. Advised of the results of this investigation, Pennsylvania State Fish and Game Officers obtained a State Search Warrant to be executed simultaneously with our Federal Warrant.

On March 18th at 9:00 a.m., State and Federal Search Warrants, authorizing seizure of illegally possessed, "for the purpose of sale," wildlife and/or parts thereof along with all pertinent business records were executed at the Downey business establishment. Participating officers were W.J. Lockett, H.T. Nolf, B.J. Schmader of the Pennsylvania Game Commission and Agents Leo Badger, Darcy (take no prisoners) Davenport and myself of the U.S. Fish and Wildlife Service. I served Mr. Downey with a copy of the Federal Search Warrant. Immediately thereafter, he was served with the State Search Warrant by State Officer H.T. Nolf. Mr. Downey was physically shaken – as though exiting a dream world, as I read the Miranda Warning to him. He responded by humbly stating, "We'll cooperate to the fullest."

The searches effected seizure of a considerable volume of illegally possessed wildlife skins, furs and plumages. Also seized was a considerable volume of documentary evidence recording the illegal purchase and sale of wildlife parts advertised in the Downey catalogues. Mr. Downey settled with the Pennsylvania Game Commission, on the spot, in the amount of $1,161.00 under the Pennsylvania Game Commission's "Field Acknowledgment of Guilt" system. Following positive identification of migratory non-game bird parts seized during the search, Downey was charged with the illegal possession, sale and shipment of parts of migratory birds in violation of the Migratory Bird Treaty Act. Appearing with counsel, Downey pled guilty in Federal Court for the Eastern District of Pennsylvania. He was fined $1,500.00. A Lacey Act charge was litigated by the Fish and Wildlife Service through the civil provisions of the Act. It resulted in a negotiated civil penalty paid by Downey in the amount of $1,500.00. Of greater significance was the fact that many thousands of dollars worth of illegal wildlife inventory was forfeited to the State of Pennsylvania and the U.S. Fish and Wildlife Service. The wholesale value totaled $57,000.00. The retail value was estimated at well over $100,000.00.

Following the Downey raid, the seizures (wildlife parts and records) were logged and stored at the Harrisburg Office. State and Federal Officers made a cursory examination of the Downey records, lasting well into the night of March 18th.

Two Eastern Pennsylvania business establishments, very quickly "stood out" as having engaged in significant illegal wildlife transactions with the Downey Company. State search warrants were obtained and executed on March 19th and 20th at both businesses. State Officers Gosnell, Fox, Nolf, Locket, and Federal Agents Badger and yours truly participated. More illegal wildlife parts and records regarding illegal transactions were seized. Both businesses settled, paying significant penalties under the Pennsylvania Field Acknowledgment of Guilt system. Their illegal wildlife inventories were forfeited to the Pennsylvania Game Commission. Examination of their business records led to still more convictions under state law.

The Downey business records were so voluminous, a special records examination team was sent to Harrisburg from the Fish and Wildlife Service's Washington Office. Their examination resulted in "undeveloped leads" sent to Federal Agents in twenty-six states for further investigation of possible state and federal wildlife law violations committed by the Downey Company suppliers. These investigations ultimately led to many state and federal convictions in most of the various states.

This case was my first exposure to major illegal wildlife commercialization as an investigator. The case was reminiscent of the many accounts I had read about in my library of wildlife management books -- accounts of wildlife commercialization that took place in the 1800's and at the turn of the century -- wildlife exploitation and commercialization that lead to our regulating wildlife management practices and laws of today. I recall thinking at one point, Heck, this is no different than it was back then. At least we nipped this one in the bud. I hope I never have another investigation like this. Dream on – new Agent – dream on!

An Ilegal
Wildlife
Dealer's
Stockrooms

Above left, foreground: Newly arrived shipments of wildlife pelts, hair, wings and plumage awaits inventory, processing and sale. Background: Packaged and labeled wild bird plumage.

Above right: Borax tanning racks containing wild skins and bird wings.

Lower left, foreground: Hanging clumps of freshly tanned wildlife pelts await packaging and shipment. Background: Small labeled plastic bags containing wild bird plumage waiting sale and shipment.

21
The Bird Man
of Hazleton

Ten letters spelled his last name ending in s-k-i. Too many Pennsylvanians, those last three letters nicknamed him a "Ski" (I'll call him Joe). His lineage was proud and hard working Polish-American. He was a big, no fat, hulk of a man, a decorated ex-marine and Korean Vet, who worked hard with his hands. He drank a little too much on occasion when he'd square-off and fist fight any challenger including a cop now and then; jailing him for drunk and disorderly conduct. His drinking usually followed a Korean War battle nightmare, reliving one of too many battles he fought.

He married his high school sweetheart – the only girl he ever dated or loved – truly the love of his life (I'll call her Ann). She was as small as Joe was big. Their marriage was childless – a fact that burdened both. Joe and Ann were born, raised, married and lived in Hazleton, Pennsylvania.

In June of 1976, I was contacted by Pennsylvania Wildlife Officer, H.T. Nolf. He forwarded information he received from the Hazelton Police Department reporting they received numerous complaints from residents of a city neighborhood alleging their neighbor (Joe) was live-trapping song birds. Many in the neighborhood maintained bird feeders and were avid bird watchers. They resented Joe's bird trapping activity and wanted it stopped. If the complaints against Joe proved true, he was violating the Federal Migratory Bird Treaty Act as well as the Pennsylvania Game Law. Nolf asked me to assist with the investigation.

Shortly thereafter, I met Officer Nolf at the Hazleton Police Department and we began our investigation. Our first contact was one of Joe's next door neighbors (and police complainant).

"We don't have a single cardinal left in the neighborhood – he's caught them all," (I'll call her Mrs. Adams) stated.

"How is he catching them?" Nolf asked.

"With traps he's made – his backyard was full of them. He baits them with bird seed, the same as you put in feeders," Mrs. Adams replied.

"Have you observed him taking birds from his traps?" I asked.

"No, but I've seen birds in his traps – the traps weren't hard to see – all you had to do was go down the alley in back of his home and you could see them in his back yard. His traps looked like they're homemade out of little wood slats. One type he uses is made like a box. He props one side of it up using a stick with a string tied to it. The string runs to a little shed. He hides in the shed and pulls the string when the birds go under the box to feed. His neighbor on the opposite side of his house told us he sits in the shed for hours catching birds. He's got another type of trap that is funnel shaped and the birds follow the bait through the funnel into the trap. He hasn't had his traps set for the past week – he's put them away," she responded.

We thanked Mrs. Adams for her information and concern for the birds. As we departed, she said, "Oh, there's something else I feel I should tell you."

"Please do," Officer Nolf responded.

"Joe can be very mean. He's bad to drink and gets into fights. The Police have thrown him in jail for fighting and being drunk. I've heard he's fought with the Police too. It's a shame, because he's married to a very fine lady – her name is Ann," Mrs. Adams advised.

"Thanks for the additional information, we received the same information from the Police before we contacted you," I told Mrs. Adams as we departed.

Next, we contacted a neighbor who lived on the opposite side of Joe. (I'll call him Mr. Jones). Following introducing ourselves and stating the purpose of our visit, Mr. Jones (a Police complainant) gave substantially the same report as Mrs. Adams, adding, "I spoke to Joe about his bird trapping and told him it was illegal. He told me to go home and mind my own business."

"Do you know what Joe is doing with the birds he traps?" I asked.

"He puts them in his garage. I watched him take them out of his traps and go into his garage with them. Some in the neighborhood say he's eating them; some say he's selling them, but I don't think so. I think he's got every bird he's trapped right there in his garage. If you walk down the alley behind his garage you can hear them chirping," Mr. Jones replied. We thanked him for his information and concern for the birds. We assured him we would put a stop to Joe's illegal activity.

There were many neighborhood complainants we could have interviewed for both information and eye witness purposes; however, we felt the Adams' and Jones' interviews were sufficient. The time had come to interview Joe.

"In view of the reports we've received regarding Joe's temperament, I suggest we contact Ann while Joe's at work. I have the feeling she'll cooperate with us and perhaps alleviate any problems we might have with Joe," I told Nolf.

"I was going to suggest the same," Nolf responded.

We contacted Ann mid-morning at her home. Following introductory amenities and display of our credentials, Ann immediately stated, "I knew you'd be here sooner or later regarding Joe and his birds. I know Joe's bird capturing activities are illegal – Joe does too because I've cautioned him. But before this goes any further, I want to tell you a little about my Joe. We're childhood and high school sweethearts. I never dated or wanted to date any boy but Joe. Joe's not the smartest guy in the world but he's honest, caring, and has never known anything but hard work. The handsome young Marine I hugged and kissed goodbye wasn't the same Joe we all new and loved when he came home from Korea. He'd seen and experienced too much in that hell-hole over there. He had, and still has nightmares – always the same one where he's trying to rescue a buddy who's pinned down and being shot to pieces. When Joe finally gets to him, he dies in Joe's arms. The helplessness Joe felt then still haunts him today and causes him to dream. Before he came home, Joe started drinking and fighting. He fights only when he's drinking. He stopped going to church. He claimed, "No God in heaven would allow wars." He's had several encounters with the law – always when he was drunk and in a fight. All of our neighbors feed and watch the birds – they all talk about it. Someone, I don't know who, but one of the neighbors got Joe interested in the birds. Joe bought two bird feeders and put them in the backyard – didn't say "boo" to me about it. I looked out the kitchen window one morning and there were the feeders with birds all over them. Those wild birds absolutely fascinated Joe – he'd watch them for hours and looked them up in a bird identification book I bought him. Soon he could identify every kind of bird that came to his feeders. The cardinals totally captivated him. Over a period of time, Joe's drinking and fighting slowed down and finally stopped. I even got him back in church. I don't know why or how the wild birds in our backyard had such a calming and peaceful effect on Joe, but believe me, they did. Joe would get in endless bird discussions with the neighbors. Joe decided he wanted to see if he could capture – and turn loose, of course – some of the birds he loved to watch, so he constructed some traps. He made them out of a soft wood because he reasoned wire would hurt them when they fluttered in the trap. His traps worked – he was good at catching them. Joe would examine the birds all over before he released them. When Joe was handling those birds, I believe he was the happiest man alive. The effect the birds had on Joe was almost unreal. He decided he wanted to try to raise the cardinals – his favorite bird. He made some cages out of that same soft wood. He put little feed and water pans in each cage and hung the cages in the garage. At this point, I cautioned Joe – I told him that catching and keeping the birds might be against the law. I don't believe he ever heard me – he began keeping the cardinals he caught in his traps. He placed a male and a female cardinal in each of his cages in the garage. They're still out there. He tends to them every day before he goes to work and after he gets home. He spends hours out there," Ann related.

"May we see the birds in the garage?" I asked.

"Of course, let me get a sweater and I'll take you out there," Ann replied. At this point I filled out a "Consent to Search" form that Ann willingly signed. In the garage we found ten beautifully constructed wooden cages, each containing a male and female cardinal. We also found three additional cages, one containing a pair of towhees, one containing a pair of blue jays and one containing a single female cardinal. The conditions were spotless and orderly. We thanked Ann for her information, her permission to observe the captive birds and her cooperation. We told Ann we would return later to interview Joe. We asked that she persuade Joe to cooperate with us when we returned. She assured us she would see to it that Joe cooperated when we returned about 4 p.m.

At lunch in downtown Hazleton, I told Nolf, "Harry, if what Ann tells us is true -- I'm sure it is, and Joe cooperates one hundred percent, I'm not the least bit interested in prosecuting him in Federal Court. To the contrary, I think Joe would make an excellent Licensed Bird Bander for the U.S. Fish and Wildlife Service. What's your thought?" I asked.

"Bailey, I'm glad you said that; I agree. They didn't pin these badges on us to make this kind of a case. If Joe cooperates and goes along with releasing the birds back to the wild, the State of Pennsylvania is satisfied. Furthermore, I'll support the issuance of any state permit he may need," Officer Nolf replied.

At 4:15 p.m. we returned to Joe and Ann's home. Ann introduced us to Joe. He was a big man with black and gray hair, broad shouldered and narrow hipped. I felt the firm grip of his calloused hand as we shook hands. Nolf noticed the same.

"Joe, I'm sure Ann has told you why we're here. Before we go any further, it's my duty to read you the following," I stated, then read the Miranda Warning to Joe."We're going to seize the birds you have in the garage, Joe. They must be released back to the wild," Officer Nolf told him.

"Yeah, I guess that's the way it's got to be, but I love those boids," Joe grunted in a raspy voice. As we started to go to his garage, I noticed a quiver in Joe's lower lip and a quickly brushed away tear in one eye.

"Wait a minute, let's sit down here at the table and discuss this whole matter a little more. Ann is that a fresh pot of coffee over there on the stove?" I asked.

"It sure is – all of you sit down and I'll get the cups," Ann quickly responded as though she sensed something good was about to happen.

All seated, I asked, "Joe would you be interested in becoming a volunteer Bird Bander for the U.S. Fish and Wildlife Service and the State of Pennsylvania?"

"What do you mean?" Joe asked following a quick sip of his freshly poured cup of coffee.

"I mean that if you cooperate with us in the release of the birds you have in captivity; Number one -- you won't be prosecuted in State or Federal Court for the unlawful taking and possession of the wild song birds you have in your garage. Number two – Officer Nolf and I will do all we can to see that you're issued the necessary permits to legally live trap, band, and release migratory birds during their spring and fall migrations." I told Joe.

"Are you telling me I can trap and turn loose birds after I've put a band on their leg and it won't be against the law?" Joe asked as he looked up from his cup of coffee. Ann's face was aglow as she exclaimed, "Oh yes, officers – he can! he would! he will!"

"That's right Joe; you'd be performing volunteer work for the U.S. Fish and Wildlife Service and the Pennsylvania Game Commission. There's a certain amount of paper work you'd have to do such as submitting reports that show the band numbers, species of birds you band, the date, and so on. Think you could handle that?" I stated and asked.

A big grin broke across Joe's concerned face as he replied, "You bet I can, that would suit me just fine – get me those permits."

On that note, an elated Joe, a happy and relieved Ann, Officer Nolf and I went to his garage. Joe gently unhooked each bird cage from the garage rafters and brought them to the alley behind his home where Ann, Officer Nolf and I released them. Two cardinals had been in captivity too long and were unable to fly. They fluttered to the ground where Joe gently picked them up. "What do I do with these?" he asked.

"Release them in your garage so they can learn to fly again at will. When they regain their flight ability, release them. Would you do that, Joe?" Nolf stated and asked.

"I sure will," Joe replied.

Joe went on to become one of Pennsylvania's top Bird Banders. His neighbors, many of whom had reported him initially, became his cooperators – permitting Joe to set his mist nets in their yards. A bad thing became a good thing. Had we prosecuted and convicted Joe, his Banding Licenses would not have been issued.

With mention of the accolades Joe later received from the Audubon Society and news media as being one of Pennsylvania's top bird banders, I'll end my story "The Bird Man of Hazleton" – a story about a big man, a gentle man and an All American. A man I call "Joe".

22
Hell Hath No Fury...
like a woman's scorn

This is a story of the eternal triangle . . . and big game poaching at its worst. It's a story about greed, wealth and "what money can buy." It's a story about a loss to you and me; the loss being a part of our big game wildlife resource. It's a story about a hunter, lover, and multi-millionaire who owned one of the nation's most important transport firms and homes hither and yon. It's about (I'll call him) Big Ben King.

"An Officer with the Federal Protective Service wants to meet with us in Harrisburg. He's received information from a woman who has laid the dime on her estranged husband concerning his illegal out-of-state big game hunting habits. She's asked the FPS Officer to put her in touch with the authorities who handle hunting law violations. She and hubby are in the middle of a messy divorce. We're to meet him at our office tomorrow morning at 9:00. I'll see you in Harrisburg in the morning," my boss, Senior Resident Agent (SRA) Leo Badger, notified me by phone during the evening of 8/17/76.

On 8/18/76 at 9:00 a.m. FPS Officer (I'll call him Bob Fussell) met with Fish and Wildlife Service Agents Leo Badger and yours truly at the Senior Resident Agent's Office in Harrisburg. Fussell reported according to (I'll call her) Mrs. Cary King, the estranged wife of Ben King, Ben took illegal big-game species in Florida, Colorado, Wyoming, and Montana. He transported or caused to be transported the same wildlife to Pennsylvania. Fussell could arrange for a FWS Agent to interview Mrs. King on 10/28/76.

On the 28th, FPS Officer Fussell introduced me to Mrs. King at her home. Following an introduction, she informed us of the following:

During 1973 while vacationing in Florida, King paid an unknown person who lived in Winter Haven, to capture two juvenile alligators for him. The alligators were taken from the Kissimmee River. King knew this was a violation of Florida state law. I photographed the alligators in an aquarium in the King home with the consent of Mrs. King after executing a consent to search form.

King, during a ten day hunt in Colorado in 1973, with guide and hounds, killed a legal black bear and an illegal bear cub. King claimed the hounds killed the cub. She named the guide (who I'll call Bill Smith) and gave his address and phone number. King transported both bears back to Pennsylvania. She gave the name, address and phone number of the PA Taxidermist (I'll call him) Loyd Tyner, who mounted both specimens. The bears were not in the King home.

King didn't get a non-resident Wyoming elk license in 1973 or 1974. He hunted elk anyway using his guide (I'll call him) Tom Thompson's license both years.

During 1975 King was licensed to hunt deer and mountain goat in Wyoming. He killed a legal mountain goat in September. He returned to Wyoming in November and killed a six point bull elk on Thompson's license. King was caught for this offense by a Wyoming Game Warden. He paid a substantial fine and lost the elk. While on the 1975 hunt, King killed an illegal antelope, using the license of a Wyoming resident, (I'll call) Ted Capone. King paid Capone $50.00 for the use of his license. King transported the antelope from Wyoming to Pennsylvania. I photographed the antelope's antlers in the King home.

During 1975, King was licensed to hunt big horn sheep and (either sex) elk in Montana. King was unsuccessful in bagging a sheep or elk during the legal open seasons. Following the close of the sheep season, King offered to pay his guide (I'll call him) Carl Rich, $1000.00 for a shot at a big horn sheep that proved to be blind in one eye. King shot the sheep on its blind side and killed it. The guide, Carl Rich, hired two unknown subjects to retrieve the sheep and skin it. King transported the sheep from Montana to Pennsylvania. It was mounted life size by PA Taxidermist, Loyd Tyner. The sheep was not in her home but I was provided with a photo (life sized mount) by Mrs. King. She opined the sheep, along with the bears, were at one of King's other properties or in the home of his "concubine." Mrs. King provided documentary evidence of her allegations against Ben King in the form of used hunting licenses, big game tags, letters to and from guides, cancelled checks and photos. Using the information received from Mrs. King, plus the documentary evidence she provided, I prepared investigation reports that included "undeveloped leads" to be investigated for violations of the respective state laws as well as the Lacey Act (illegal interstate movement of illegal wildlife or parts thereof). These investigative requests were sent to: Special Agent Charles Kniffin, Florida; SA Dick Hart, Colorado; SA Tom Sechrist, Wyoming; and SA Bob Freeman, Montana. Naturally, I took care of the undeveloped leads in Pennsylvania. The results of these undeveloped leads investigated in all states substantiated and proved state Fish and Game Law violations in all the states as well as King's Lacey Act violations. This was another example of the outstanding investigative skills of the Agents of the Fish and Wildlife Service as well as the State Fish and Game Officers who assisted them.

Subsequently, all those involved with King, who assisted him and/or committed state law violations were convicted -- a total of five individuals paid a total of $1700.00 in fines. King, who was prosecuted under the Lacey Act, paid a $2500.00 penalty plus the substantial fine he paid for his illegal elk in Wyoming in 1975. The two alligators he bought illegally in Florida were returned to the Kissimmee River at his expense and released to the wild. King "enriched" the Florida state coffers by $500.00 for his alligator episode. All of King's mounted "trophies" taken in violation of the various state laws and the Lacey Act were forfeited to the U.S. Fish and Wildlife Service. In all, those involved paid well over $4700.00 in fines and penalties. In addition, certain individuals suffered the loss of hunting privileges and/or license revocations.

Big Ben King's divorce settlement with Cary, his wife of many years, amounted to well over two million. Soon thereafter, he suffered and died of cancer. I'm told, he again became aware of the "true values" in life before passing. I'd be willing to bet he was also cognizant of a great truth in the old saying, "Hell hath no fury like a woman's scorn."

A Montana Big Horn Sheep – blind in one eye.
Subject of investigation paid guide $1000 for one shot at sheep during closed season. His shot "blindsided" and killed the sheep. Sheep was transported interstate in violation of the Federal Lacey Act.

23
Death From Above

Part 1

During the month of December, 1976 I was privileged to be assigned two after-the-fact Airborne Hunting Act investigations by my boss, Senior Resident Agent, Leo Badger. One alleged violation of the Act took place in Cambria County near Fallentimber, PA; the other in Rayne Township, Indiana County, PA. The Pennsylvania Game Commission asked U.S. Fish and Wildlife Service for assistance with both investigations.

The Airborne Hunting Act of 1971 prohibited the use of aircraft to shoot, attempt to shoot or harass wildlife. The Act further prohibited piloting (or assisting) any aircraft used to shoot wildlife and prohibited any person on the ground from taking or attempting to take wildlife by means, aid or use of an aircraft. Although the Law of the Land, the Act was generally thought of as a "western law." It was enacted mainly to curtail the use of aircraft in the taking of big game in the western states and Alaska where the practice was common. Many western aircraft became the property of the U.S. Fish and Wildlife Service under the forfeiture provisions of the Act.

I grew up on the Ohio prairie. A neighboring farmer shot one hundred and twenty foxes from his airplane during one winter. He collected a county funded bounty on each and sold their pelts. The practice of hunting fox and other wild game by aircraft was not uncommon throughout Ohio and the mid-west. Although Ohio law prohibited taking game from a "motor driven conveyance," few airborne hunters were apprehended. I venture to say the practice of taking game from an in flight aircraft was far more common in the mid-west and the east than it was in the western states. In any event, I remember how excited I was to start work on my two Airborne Hunting Act

257

investigations.

On 12/03/76, the Ligonier Office, Pennsylvania Game Commission received a complaint from Bill Wertz, an ex-Deputy Game Protector from Cambria County, PA. Wertz told of hearing radio traffic indicating deer hunting was taking place by use of a helicopter.

On 1/07/77, I interviewed Bill Wertz, Altoona, PA. Wertz reported that

it was common knowledge in Northeastern Cambria County (I'll call him) Merle Jones and his son Gary of the Mills Coal Company, Bollentown, PA hunted deer from and by the aid of a helicopter during the past deer season. They engaged in this activity in years past and hunted other species such as bear and turkey in the same manner.

Wertz's work-vehicles were radio equipped with frequency 42.96 (FM). At certain high elevation locations where the Wertzs' hunted in Northeastern Cambria County, the frequency used by Merle Jones "blead in" to Wertz's frequency. Consequently Wertz could overhear Jones' radio traffic.

During the latter part of the first week of buck season, Wertz, his wife Jean, Bill Wertz, Jr. and Gary Owens hunted together in Northeast Cambria County on a farm owned by Wertz.

They heard a "Merle" in a helicopter talking to some hunters in a truck on the ground. Wertz and his party determined the helicopter and its party on the ground were near the Jr. Traux farm and near a school about ten air miles north of them. From the helicopter they heard: "The deer are coming towards you! Go up (certain road – not audible): Stop right there! Stop right there! Get out of the truck! Don't slam the door! One to the right, one to the left, the others stand back!" Then a party on the ground said, "There are five of us." The helicopter pilot responded, "Alright, two to the right and two to the left! Don't go in the woods! Don't go in the woods! They're right in front of you! Coming right at you!" From the ground: "Are you going to shoot from the helicopter?" From the helicopter: "No, I'll let you fellows shoot."

During the second day of the season, Wertz heard the following in the same general area. The helicopter was trying to locate deer. From the helicopter he heard, "I have ten in the brush – they're in the middle of the field! I have six in the brush here in the middle of the field! These are going to be a little hard to get out to you!" Then from someone on the ground, "Do you think we could drop (name not audible) close enough to get a shot?" From the helicopter: "I don't think so – I got a little fellow in here that's getting a little sick. I'll have to go in and let him off." From the ground: "It's dinner time anyway and I have a deer in the truck I'll have to take in."

Wertz heard basically the same thing on another occasion during the doe season but this time Gary Jones was piloting the helicopter. Jean Wertz, Bill Wertz, Jr. and Gary Owens confirmed Bill Wertz's report.

I spent parts of six days interviewing FAA officials (Pittsburgh), Airport officials (Altoona) and Ag-Rotors Helicopter Sales Co. (Gettysburg). I ascertained Jones owned a red, white and blue Enstrom F-28C helicopter, the helicopter number and that Jones crashed his helicopter near the close of deer season. He walked away from the crash alive and sold his wrecked helicopter.

I conducted extensive interviews of persons residing in northeast Cambria County. I interviewed hunters from Lamar, PA, Chambersburg, PA and Johnstown, PA who hunted in northeast Cambria County. Although many saw a red, white and blue helicopter flying low (tree top level) and irregular, no one reported the helicopter number or witnessed an actual "shooting" or "taking" violation of the Airborne Hunting Act.

On 3/3/77 I contacted Merle Jones, Fallentimber, PA by phone to schedule an interview. He stated he was glad I called, he was trying to reach me; he agreed to an interview and would come to the Holiday Inn, in Altoona where I was staying. He added, "You've been everywhere asking too many questions. I need to get this whole thing quieted down and settled."

Jones arrived at the Holiday Inn at 6:30 p.m. I read him the Miranda Warning. He signed a waiver agreeing to interview without counsel present. However, he stipulated he would be completely candid concerning the matter, provided he and no one else took the blame for any violations. Advising Jones, "I can't guarantee that, but I'll see what I can do." Jones, nevertheless gave and signed an Affidavit.

I advised Jones I would need some member of his hunting party to verify his account of what happened. Jones phoned (I'll call him) Bud Smith who claimed to hunt with him on the dates in question. Smith arrived about one hour later. He gave and signed an Affidavit verifying the contents of the Affidavit signed by Merle Jones. Jones named (I'll call him) Jack Waddel of Export, PA as a witness.

Two days later, I interviewed a surly and indignant Gary Jones at his home. I attempted to question him concerning the deer hunting activity that took place while he piloted his father's helicopter during the past doe season. Following introduction, credentials display and the Miranda Warning, Gary Jones stated, "You took care of all this with my Dad. He assured everyone you wouldn't come around asking anyone else any more questions – he would handle everything. No, I won't agree to questioning. I have nothing to say to you." I thanked the young snot for his time and left. This was one of the few times in my career a suspect declined questioning following the Miranda Warning.

On 5/13/77 Jack E. Waddel, Export, PA, who hunted with Jones and Smith, was interviewed by SA Owen Seelye. He gave a statement that neither denied nor confirmed the Jones and Smith statements concerning violations of the Act.

The Merle Jones, Smith, and Waddel statements did not confirm shots were fired from the airborne helicopter. They did confirm deer were "spotted" for hunters on the ground by Jones in his helicopter; and deer came close to hunters; thus, providing an opportunity for hunters to "take" them.

I felt the evidence showed a clear cut case of "harass" "aiding" and/or "attempting to take" under the Act. I prepared a case report showing violations of the Act for the U.S. Attorney in the Western District of PA. After carefully going over my case report, Joel Straus, the young Assistant U.S. Attorney assigned to the case, declared, "I want a smoking gun fired from an aircraft and a dead deer." He declined prosecution. I left his office – not a happy camper. I thought, I'll give him his smoking gun and dead deer before these cases are over. I'm going to get a pound of flesh out of this one – one way or other.

I radioed Dan Jenkins, the State Game Protector assigned to Cambria County and met with him at the Ligonier Office. We went over the Jones, Smith and Waddel statements. "You got anything here under the PA State Game Laws?" I asked Jenkins.

"I believe I have under Section 704," Jenkins replied.

"Good! We're going to re-interview Merle Jones. I'll set it up," I told Officer Jenkins.

Subsequently Merle Jones was re-interviewed by PA District Game Protector Dan Jenkins and yours truly. "Merle, I'm going to give you a break. I'm also going to honor your request to take sole responsibility for any violations. You've been candid with me. As you know, the Airborne Hunting Act carries a very stiff penalty. If you care to settle this matter under the provisions of the State Law, I'll pursue this matter from the federal standpoint no further," I advised Jones.

"Yes, I'm more than willing to settle all this under the State Law. Thanks Agent Bailey. I appreciate your consideration," Jones stated.

PA Officer Dan Jenkins took the floor. He explained to Jones the Pennsylvania "Field Acknowledgment of Guilt" system. The law violated (illegal use of a motor drive conveyance to assist others in taking game) and the penalty ($200.00) payable on the spot.

Officer Jenkins receipted Jones for his check made out to the Pennsylvania Game Commission for $200.00. Case closed!

24
Death From Above

Part 2

The staccato—chatter of a helicopter cracked the snowy stillness of the afternoon on December 3, 1976. The airborne machine flew an irregular pattern at tree top level over the (I'll call it) Harold Young farm in Indiana County, Pennsylvania. The monster of death from above spit gunfire as it pursued a four point buck white tail deer in violation of the Federal Airborne Hunting Act. A young deer hunter (I'll call) Albert Santini with his father and deer hunting companion (I'll call) Gildo Santini watched it all. Its downdraft fell dead timbers, as the copter came close to both hunters while it pursued the deer. At times, it was no more than seventy-five yards away. Three shots from the copter rang out as it and the deer disappeared over a ridge. Soon both copter and deer re-appeared as another shot fired at the deer, marked the helicopter's landing one hundred yards away from the Santinis. The deer was down. As the enraged Santinis charged the scene, two men exited the helicopter – one carrying a rifle. They ran toward the deer, stopped, the rifle bearer fired another round as both men ran into a nearby wooded area where the buck lay dead. As all this was happening, the pilot seeing the charging Santinis, lifted the helicopter and landed in a nearby field. Then he raised the helicopter again and returned to his original landing site. By then, the Santinis arrived as the man without a gun emerged from the wooded area. Following a few "heated" words with the pilot and the gunless airborne hunter, the Santinis charged the wooded area. There they encountered the gunner with his rifle slung over his shoulder in the process of dragging the gutted buck towards the helicopter. Another "heated" word exchange ensued during which the gunner threatened, "I'll burry you right here." Ignoring the gunner's threat, the Santinis seized the deer and told the gunner, "Your gun better never move from where it is now." The Santinis escorted the gunner the remaining distance to the helicopter. There the Santinis demanded the three airborne hunters produce identification. The three refused. Albert Santini recorded the blue and white helicopter's number as well as accurate descriptions of the trio. As the airborne hunters departed, the Santinis assured them, "We'll see you in court." (Lord, if all hunters could be like the Santinis.) The Santinis carred the deer to landowner, Harold Young's house. They telephoned PA Game Protector Charles Hertz, notifying him of the violation.

A subsequent, and I add "darn good", investigation by PA State Game Protectors Charles Hertz and James Deniker followed. It established and proved beyond doubt the identities of the three airborne hunters including the separate identity of the gunner who shot and finished killing the wounded deer after landing. (I'll call them) Don Radclif, pilot; James Honaker, hunter (copter leasee); and Tony Bondini, gunner. Officer Hertz ran the helicopter's number recorded by Albert Santini through the Federal Aviation Administration. He ascertained the copter was owned by a leasing company and leased to James Honaker. The aircraft was based at Jimmy Stewart Airport, Indiana, PA. Officers Hertz and Deniker interviewed Honaker following the Miranda Warning. Honaker stated on 12/3/76 the helicopter was piloted by Don Ratclif and occupied by Honaker and Tony Bondini. He denied any shots were fired from the aircraft. He claimed there was only one gun in the aircraft which belonged to Tony Bondini and they were en route to his hunting camp when they saw the deer from the air, followed it a short distance and landed. Tony exited the aircraft, then shot the deer on the ground. He continued with his version of the encounter with the Santinis. No written statement was taken. Officer Hertz delivered the deer to Pathologist Alan Woolfe, PhD, Rachelwood Wildlife Preserve, Florence, PA for examination.

In late December of 1976, my boss SRA Leo Badger received a request from the Pennsylvania Game Commission Law Enforcement Chief, Earl Geeseman, asking the U.S. Fish and Wildlife Service investigate the preceding for violations of the Airborne Hunting Act.

Soon to retire, SA Owen Seelye and yours truly received the assignment. On 1/04/77 Agent Seelye and I took sworn statements relating to their investigation from State Game Protectors Charles Hertz and James Deniker. Later, the same day, Agents met with Pathologist Alan Woolfe. His examination of the deer clearly showed three shots (two fatal) penetrated and exited the deer, two shots came "from above and behind." A third shot penetrated and exited the neck just below the head – the final and killing shot. His written report and briefing clearly showed he would be an excellent witness. His examination "shattered" suspect James Honaker's version of what happened.

On 1/12/77 Agent Seelye and I interviewed both Santinis. Their sworn statements recorded in detail the events that took place on the third of December, 1976 on the Harold Young farm and told at the beginning of this story.

Following the Santini statements, Agent Seelye had to reluctantly "bow out" and go home. Owen was in poor health and became very ill. I phoned Leo Badger and advised him of Owens's departure and illness. "I'll call and check on him right away," Leo stated.

"Leo, our investigation is going well," I continued with an in-depth account of the investigation results so far. "However, ..." Leo cut me off.

"I've just been told by Bill Kensinger (SAC) this is the first Airborne Hunting Act case in the Eastern United States since the Act's enactment. Bill said to tell you to 'cinch this one' and he'll buy you a steak dinner with all the trimmings. Let me add – I'll buy you and Owen one too," Leo stated.

"I'm glad you told me this, Leo. I was going to ask to stay a little longer in Indiana County. We've got three bad guys and we've got three good guys – our witnesses the Santinis and the Pathologist. That's even-up going into battle. I want to uneven the scales. I feel I can go door-to-door around the scene and come up with more witnesses. I also feel, provided I get more witnesses, I can get confessions out of the bad guys. You know – I'd like to put a little frosting on the cake," I told Leo.

"From what I've seen of you to date, I'd say you'll get all that accomplished – go ahead with my blessing!" Leo responded, chuckling.

Over the next two days I knocked on every door near the Harold Young farm. I came up with thirteen eye witnesses who saw a blue and white helicopter flying irregular and abnormally low, not only on 12/3/76, but on other dates near and before 12/3/76 (none after). Seven of these witnesses actually saw and heard gunfire come from the helicopter. Two saw the helicopter in pursuit of a deer while shooting. Four recorded the helicopter's number (the same number recorded by Albert Santini). I took written and signed statements from all of them. The good old door-to-door routine I'd used so many times as an Ohio Wildlife Officer paid off.

My next step was to interview pilot Don Radclif, who I figured was the weakest link and had the most to lose (his pilot's license). I made contact with Radclif at the Jimmy Stewart Airport. Following introduction and showing Radclif my badge and credentials, I told a very nervous Don Radclif to accompany me to my patrol car. There, I advised Radclif of the nature of my business including the provisions of the Airborne Hunting Act. I read the Miranda Warning to him. He agreed to questioning. "Don, I'll tell you up front what I'm prepared to do providing you tell me the truth. I'll do all I can with the U.S. Attorney to see that you don't lose your pilot's license. Whatever it takes, I'll do it – you have my word. Now, are you willing to answer my questions concerning the Airborne Hunting Act violations you were involved in on 12/3/76?" I asked Mr. Radclif.

"Yes, I'll answer your questions. I'll tell you the truth. I know Honaker lied to the State Game Warden. I won't lie to you – I'll be xo#x if I'm going to lose my livelihood over this mess!" Ratclif declared.

"That's fine Don, let me make this as easy as possible. I'm going to read two sworn statements given to Agents of the U.S. Fish and Wildlife Service by Albert and Gildo Santini, the two eye witness hunters you encountered when you landed Mr. Honaker's leased helicopter on the Harold Young farm on 12/3/76. If you agree, I'll ask you to sign a simple statement acknowledging the Santini's statements are true. To this I'll add a plea to retain your pilot's license and any other statements you care to make – okay?" I asked.

"Okay," Ratclif replied. As I read the Santini's statements to him, he intermittently nodded his head indicating he agreed with what was being read. At the conclusion of the readings, Ratclif asked, "May I read the statements?"

"By all means," I responded and handed him the statements. Concluding his reading, Ratclif stated, "It's the truth, that's how it happened." I prepared a statement acknowledging the Santini statements were true. I added (in his words) a plea for the preservation of his pilot's license. At conclusion, I asked, "Is there anything you wish to add?"

"Yes, I wish to add this . . . although it didn't seem right to me to hunt deer this way, I didn't know we were violating any hunting law. The Santini's reaction scared xo#x out of me . . . I don't want to ever tangle with them again."

I added his additional words to his statement, handed the statement to him and asked him to read it. As he finished reading his statement, I gave him my pen. He signed the statement and I witnessed his signature.

Next stop – Mr. James Honaker. I asked Radclif to notify Honaker (but not Bondini) that I was coming and what he had admitted. Not my usual procedure but for some reason in this case, I sensed this ploy would serve the investigation well.

A day later I met with J. Honaker at his place of business in the privacy of his office. Prior to this meeting, I assembled copies of all my witnesses' statements, sixteen in all. I folded them and with a light weight rubber band around the bundle, placed them in my inner coat pocket. Following introduction, I showed Honaker my credentials and read him the Miranda Warning even though earlier he was advised of same by PA Wildlife Officers Hertz and Deniker. He agreed to questioning after I advised him of the provisions of the Airborne Hunting Act.

"I talked to Radclif yesterday. Just what do you think you've got on us, Bailey?" an arrogant James Honaker asked before I could ask my first question. I retrieved the bundle of witness statements from my coat pocket, leaned slightly across Honaker's desk toward the seated poacher and "swished" the bundle close to his nose.

"How's a dead deer, a pathologist's report and sixteen sworn statements from eye witnesses for openers?" I asked the startled James Honaker.

Setting a shaking cup of coffee on his desk pad, Honaker stated, "Okay, let's talk."

"You shouldn't have lied to the state officers, Jim. All you got for your lie was a much more intensified investigation. At this point, I don't need to talk to you or Bondini at all. I'm certain I've got enough evidence to win indictments against the three of you. However, I thought it only fair to offer you the privilege of telling me your side of the story. I'm going to make your interview very easy. I'm going to read the statements given by Albert and Gildo Santini along with Don Radclif's. If you agree, tell me so and I'll prepare a statement for your signature acknowledging they are true. With that I read the Santini and Radclif statements to Honaker. Are these statements true?" I asked.

"Yes, they're true but I'm not going to sign any statements," Honaker responded.

"Very well, suit yourself. You certainly don't have to sign a statement. You've admitted to me the Santini and Radclif statements are true – do you swear the Santini and Radclif statements are true?" I asked.

"Yeah, I swear they're true. We've discussed it all by phone. Neither Tony nor I want to see Don's pilot's license in jeopardy. I know you're going to question Tony when you leave here. I believe Tony will tell you the truth," Honaker stated.

Later the same day, following contact by phone, I met with Tony Bondini at his home. His interview took place in my patrol car parked in the driveway of his residence. Following introduction, I showed Bondini my credentials and badge. The Miranda Warning followed along with an explanation of the provisions of the Airborne Hunting Act. Bondini agreed to be interviewed. I opened the conversation by stating, "Tony, it's my hope to make this short and sweet. You know why I'm here. I know you've discussed this matter with Jim Honaker since the U.S. Fish and Wildlife Service became involved. I assume you've also had similar discussions with Pilot Radclif. I'm going to read you the statement of two of the sixteen witnesses to the events that took place over and on the Harold Young farm on December third. They are the statements of Gildo and Alfred Santini. I'll also show you the results of a pathologist's examination that supports the Santini statements. Jim Honaker and Don Radclif have acknowledged the Santini statements are the truth," I stated. I read Bondini the Santini statements and pathologist report.

At conclusion, Tony stated, "Their statements are the truth; that's what happened."

"What caliber rifle were you using?" I asked.

"My thirty-o-six," he replied. Without asking, I prepared a short statement on an affidavit form that acknowledged the Honaker admissions, the Santini statements and the Radclif statement were true. Bondini signed the statement and I witnessed his signature.

"I probably should seize the rifle you used Tony, but you were straight with me so I'll forget the rifle," I told Bondini. With few parting words, I headed for Harrisburg.

The Airborne Hunting Act cases against Radclif, Honaker, and Bondini were approved and prosecuted by Assistant U.S. Attorney, Joel Straus, Western District of Pennsylvania. The three plead guilty in June of 1977 before Judge D.J. Snyder, Western District Court. Jim Honaker and Tony Bondini were fined $750.00 each. Don Radclif was sentenced to one year deferred prosecution, meaning the charge would be dropped in one year if Radclif did not commit any federal, state, or local law violations. He did not and the FAA took no action concerning his pilot's license.

Of all those involved in this case, two stand out in my memory – Gildo and Albert Santini. Those two All-American sportsmen had the guts and courage to do the right thing. It was a privilege to meet and know them.

Airborne Hunting Act Violation scene.
PA State Game Protectors, Deniker (left) and
Hertz conducting metal detector search for spent
30/06 shell.

Airborne Hunters Bag $750 Fine
Pittsburg Press

Washington (UPI) – The director of the U.S. Fish and Wildlife Service hopes the "swiftness and severity" of a conviction of two Pennsylvania men will deter airborne hunters in the East.

Lynn Greenwalt said yesterday that _____ 47, and _____45, both of Indiana, PA., were convicted of using a helicopter last December to kill a buck deer and fined $750 June 20.

"We hope that the swiftness and severity of this conviction will serve as a deterrent to others who would engage in such a practice," said Greenwalt, calling the case the first of its kind in the East.

He said the fine was the largest ever imposed for a violation of the Airborne Hunting Act of 1971.

Greenwalt said "even though the deer are not a federally protected species, "they are protected in this case by law which prohibits the airborne hunting or harassing of any animal except under federal or state permit for the protection of wildlife, livestock and human health and safety.

Wound # 1 (fatal)

Wound # 2

Wound # 3 (fatal)

25
Blue Mountain
Hawk Killers

On November 3, 1977 I received the following report from Lowell E. Bittner, Law Enforcement Supervisor, Pennsylvania Game Commission, Southeast Division, Reading, PA.

On September 16, 1966, Bittner (then a District Game Protector) apprehended (I'll call them) Jesse Simon and Donald Shuster hunting raptors from a blind beside the Appalachian Trail on Blue Mountain near Pine Grove, PA. Both subjects claimed to be hunting crows; however, Simon had a hawk call hanging from his neck and the rigging at the blind was typical of that used in hawk hunting. Shuster admitted they were hawk hunting and vividly described the thrill of gunning raptors. Both Simon and Shuster paid fines for hunting with unplugged shotguns. Hawk hunting was not illegal in Pennsylvania at that time.

Subsequent to these arrests, Bittner got reports Simon bragged about shooting eagles. In 1968 Deputy Game Protector F. Mason Spancake found a dead golden eagle in his front yard one morning. It had been shot. Several days later he was approached by Simon who asked Spancake if he "had received his present?" Simon then laughed and walked away.

Simon has since become a member of the Hawk Mountain Sanctuary (a raptor preservation organization). Since becoming a member he has made off-hand remarks to Director, Alex Nagy and other members about shooting hawks and eagles. Simon owns his own company and is independently wealthy.

On October 28, 1977, Bittner, flying in a State Police helicopter, noticed the blinds known as the "north blind" and the "south blind" at the same location he apprehended Simon and Shuster in 1966 appeared active. A blue and white four wheel drive Jeep vehicle was parked near the north blind.

On November 2, 1977 (long after raptors were placed under federal protection in 1972), Bittner and District Game Protector, Rod Dilling, made a ground inspection of the blind sites. At the north blind they found a red tailed hawk that had been shot and hidden under some brush. They found evidence (plumage) an undetermined number of raptors had been killed. Recently constructed hawk hunting rigging was found (dismantled) behind the blind. There was a clay bird trap at this site the officers felt was a cover for illegal hawk shooting.

At the south blind site, they found recently constructed hawk hunting rigging that was dismantled and more plumage evidence of raptors that had been killed.

Bittner believed Simon and Shuster were involved. The land where both blinds were located was owned or leased by the Brookside Gun Club, Pine Grove, PA.

Bittner stated this matter has top priority as far as the PA Game Commission was concerned. He asked for Federal assistance and prosecution in Federal court. According to Alex Nagy, Director of Hawk Mountain Sanctuary, the best time to shoot raptors was from 9:00 a.m. to 3:00 p.m. – he would notify Bittner and/or Federal Agents on days of heavy flights for stakeout purposes. Bittner stated week days offer the best stakeout periods as weekends have too much activity with hunters and hikers on the Appalachian Trail.

"The thermals are right. The birds are moving. Tomorrow morning is a good time for you to be on the mountain. I feel your chances of catching your hawk gunners are very good," Alex Nagy reported by phone during the late evening of November 13, 1977.

"Thanks for the information, Alex. I'll be there," I replied, even though I knew I was coming down with the flu and feeling worse by the minute. I guess I could turn this over to Leo and stay home on sick leave and nurse this flu, I thought. ("Leo" being Senior Resident Agent, Leo Badger, my boss and one of the best Game Wardens the good Lord ever made) Yeah, but I believe Leo is in travel status somewhere, besides Bailey, you've got a lot of surveillance time invested in this one and you may never get the chance again to make a case quite like this one. It's a rare collector's item. Better be there, I thought as I took two aspirin and went to bed hoping sleep would relieve some of my misery.

My quest the following day would be the apprehension of two hawk killers "from out of the past" you might say. Prior to placing raptors (birds of prey) under the protection of the Migratory Bird Treaty Act in 1972, "hawk hunting" was a traditional and annual event within Pennsylvania's Blue Mountain range and elsewhere. Especially during the fall migrations when the birds rode the mountain thermals (updrafts) from north to south for miles on end. The birds were shot from blinds made of on-site rocks and brush.

Many of these blinds were still in place and being utilized by legally licensed bird banders to capture and band raptors during their migration. The bird banders used some of the same techniques the hawk gunners of the past used to lure the birds to their mist nets and talon snare traps. The mist net is a very fine gauge monofilament or nylon string net (barely visible) stretched loosely over a large hoop frame that is suspended several feet above the ground. Under the net is tethered a lure, usually a white or light colored pigeon. The talon snare trap is a wire mesh cage (cylindrical or square) with a pigeon inside. Secured to the top of the cage are many monofilament loops tied in slip knots. Both devices ensnare the hawk stooping (diving at a high rate of speed) on the lure. Upon capture, the banders rush from their blind, unsnare and band the bird, record certain data and release the bird unharmed. Most banders in Pennsylvania were associated with Hawk Mountain Sanctuary. I considered it a privilege to watch their banding operations. They are certainly committed to their cause.

I thought about the hawk banders I watched during two previous day long surveillances trying to catch my hawk killers, as I awoke at five a.m. on November 14th, now sick with the full blown flu. "Coffeing up" and eating as much breakfast as my Shirley June could get in me and over her concerned protest, I shouldered my .357 Smith and Wesson. By 6:00 a.m. I was behind the wheel of my patrol car leaving my home at New Providence, PA en route to a location on the Appalachian Trail near Pine Grove, PA, where hopefully I would find my culprits at play.

After several roadside stops where I "lost" all my breakfast, I parked in a PA Game Commission parking lot adjacent to State Route 501 near the Appalachian Trail and due east of my "target" area. The following is the actual record of my observations, made in part through binoculars and prepared from my field notes on 11/14/77. Between several of these entries I was plagued with instances of the green-apple quick-step. My flu malady didn't get any better. Perhaps I'll give the flu-who-who to the hawk killers – heaven forbid! I thought. From the 11:17 a.m. entry on, I detected the tantalizing aroma of steak cooking on an open grill. Later, "take down" confirmed my two Blue Mountain Raptor killers enjoyed a T-bone steak dinner including a tin foil encased baked potato, fresh hot coffee and the comforts of a fine blended whiskey. Overhearing parts of their conversation reminiscing hawk hunts of the past, along with their present chuckles and laughter, I ascertained they were not only enjoying the hunt – they were having a ball! I must admit – flu and all – I found myself "caught up in the hunt." Once again, my unnatural love of my adversary kicked in. I thought, you rascals, you've privileged me with a glimpse into a hunting custom of the past that in all probability will never be legal again. What an era of carnage it must have been when the ridge of this Blue Mountain range was lined with blinds, decoys and hawk hunters just like you! I spoke to my Creator, "Lord, help me – how I love it all."

MY FIELD NOTES: "9:07 a.m. Arrived PA Game Commission parking lot -- Rt. 501. Brisk north -- northwest wind – can't hear from here. Moved to position half way (west) to blinds on Appalachian Trail.

271

<u>10:50 a.m.</u> Two shots (shotgun) fired; rapid succession -- north blind. Crawled to position -- next described. Observations made from 40 yards south; elevation 4 ft. above north blind. Observed blue and white Jeep, canvas top parked 30 yards behind and west of blind. Observed two live white and buff colored pigeons harnessed; hooked to strings dangling from elevated poles; either side of blind. Two men in and milling around site. One, noticeably black hair; the other a black fur hat. Both in hunting garb; hunting licenses on backs.

<u>11:05 a.m.</u> Both subjects in north blind. Strings attached to pigeons jerk. Both pigeons flutter, attempt to fly. A raptor -- hawk family (silhouette against sky) decoys, comes over me from the south/southeast.

<u>11:06 a.m.</u> Three shots fired at hawk from guns used by both. Hawk flares, goes back over me to right (east).

<u>11:17 a.m.</u> Man in black hat walks to Jeep -- returns. Black haired man picks up spent shotgun shells.

<u>12:24 p.m.</u> Both subjects in north blind. Strings attached to pigeons jerk – both pigeons flutter, attempt to fly. Raptor -- hawk family (ID'd bird silhouette -- sky) decoys fast, straight at pigeons from same direction-- first bird.

<u>12:25 p.m.</u> Two shots fired; both guns. North gun hits bird hard while bird is decoying – high. Second shot – south gun hits bird lower – before it hits the ground. Man with black hair leaves blind; picks up dead goshawk – takes it behind blind; hides it under piece of tar paper. Goes back where hawk fell; picks up plumage.

<u>12:39 p.m.</u> Both subjects in north blind. Pigeons jerked and flutter; attempt to fly. Buteo family raptor (ID'd by silhouette) decoys, comes in over my head to right. Four shots fired; both guns. Bird passes over my head to south – appears crippled; plumage falls to ground in front of me. Plumage collected – placed in my shirt pocket.

<u>12:43 p.m.</u> Man with black hat walks to Jeep. Man with black hair retrieves goshawk; cuts it apart with a knife. Puts parts of bird under tar paper. Takes the rest of bird, disappears behind thicket to north. Returns from thicket, begins taking strings -- harness off pigeons. Man in black hat backs Jeep to blind, begins loading gear.

<u>12:51 p.m.</u> Subjects leaving – moved in -- apprehension.

Upon my arrival behind the subjects in the blind, I was unnoticed for a few seconds. Both men turned and looked at me. One subject stated, "You're the man, aren't you?"

The other stated, "Yeah, he's the man and he's a Fed – no uniform."

"Yeah, gentlemen, I'm the man and don't try to tell me you're crow hunting. I've enjoyed your hunt right along with you and I've seen it all," I stated as I "rolled the gold."

"We're up here shooting a few clay birds," the "noticeably-dyed" black haired hawk killer stated.

"Don't start that! I've told you, I've been here and seen it all!" I responded.

I obtained their I.D.'s and filled out pink slips (forms that record date, names, violation, etc.). Subjects were identified as J.L. Simon and R. P. Shuster of Pine Grove, PA.

On November 15, 1977 the north blind site (where Simon and Shuster were apprehended) and south blind site as described in Officer Bittner's original complaint were searched by PA Game Commission Officers Lowell E. Bittner and Rod Dilling, SRA Leo Badger, Special Agent (SA) John Meehan and yours truly of the U.S. Fish and Wildlife Service. The remains of raptors were found at the north blind site in the thicket described. Raptor remains were also found near the south blind site. Photographs were taken of both sites and the raptor remains found, by SRA Leo J. Badger.

"Ron, you're sick as a dog. You get home and I don't want to hear from you for at least a week," my ever caring boss, Leo Badger ordered at the end of our search.

November 30, 1977 – The raptor remains found at the north and south blind sites on 11/14/77 and 11/15/77 were identified by Roxie C. Laybourne, Zoologist, Smithsonian Institute, Washington, DC. By letter dated December 9, 1977, Laybourne identified the remains as those of seventeen Red-tailed Hawks (Buteo jamaicensis), one Crow (Corvus brachyrhychos). One Goshawk (Accipiter atricapillies) observed shot by me on 11/14/77 and four feathers as those of a Red-tailed Hawk (Buteo jamaicensis) which was collected by me after it was shot and crippled on 11/14/77.

My two hawk killers were found guilty and fined $2000.00 for violating the Migratory Bird Treaty Act in Federal Court at Philadelphia. Their convictions marked the end of a historical hunting custom that annually took place within Pennsylvania's Blue Mountain Range. A custom, ill conceived and oh, so wrong, that was a part of our national culture. A custom of days gone by that caused the needless and wasteful slaughter of raptors by the thousands. A custom that failed to realize the valuable and vital role our precious birds of prey play in our exploited and ever deteriorating environment.

The author and evidence collected at crime scene on
11/15/77.

The remains of seventeen raptors (background).
Dismembered goshawk and plumage from crippled
red-tail hawk (foreground) – the later representing "take"
violations observed by the author on 11/14/77.

Blind, control string and clay bird release box. Used as a "cover" by violators.

(Below) Crime scene search. Agent Leo Badger walks the control string from dismantled pigeon pole to blind. PA State Game Warden,Rod Dilling (background). Note second string to the right.

26
You're Going to Raleigh

Leo Badger, the Senior Resident Agent in Pennsylvania, was the best boss I ever had. It could be said, "He stood head and shoulders above them all" (six foot-five, about two hundred eighty). He was easy-going and among many, nick named "Gentle Ben." "With my size and all, I learned as a kid I could hurt someone if I got mad – I guess that's one reason I don't have much of a temper," he told me. By the same token, an Agent assigned to the Chesapeake, once commented, "You don't want to see the big man mad. He cleaned a whole diner out in Delaware. Half a dozen head who were sacked that morning for over-bagging and hunting over bait, couldn't keep their mouths shut. They kept harassing the Agents who were trying to have dinner. Leo politely told them to "cool it" twice – they didn't; so Leo cleaned house."

Leo had an unequalled ability to command the respect of those he knew, worked with and supervised. He was brutally honest and truthful. He could professionally plan, supervise, and successfully execute an operation like no lawman I had experience with before, largely due to the admiration and respect those involved held for him. He was a devoted family man and one of my very few "true friends." He has gone on to his reward above. He is another I look forward to seeing again soon.

A year after my arrival in Pennsylvania, Leo summoned me to the Harrisburg Office. "Ron, soon after you came to Pennsylvania, I realized all I had to do was see to it you had a good set of wheels under you and the money to travel. You needed virtually no supervision – only assignments. Your waterfowl and other field work in the Chesapeake and Eastern Pennsylvania proves you're a catch-dog Game Warden. You're one of the best

277

after-the-fact investigators I've ever seen. Your past supervisory experience and training, especially with the Army Corps of Engineers indicates you're a capable administrator and supervisor. We, and I speak for the SAC, feel it's time to discuss your career plans with you. There's certainly nothing wrong with working the rest of your career as a journeyman grade, field agent. Many darn good agents are content with this. We feel and hope you're interested in going beyond the field agent level. I've been asked to apply for the SAC position in Denver. I've been briefed on the Denver position and it seems there are some acute problems in that District. A big "if" I'm selected, I'd like to know if you'd be interested in coming to Denver as my Assistant Agent-in-Charge (ASAC). I'll need a loyal "right hand" out there if this all comes about."

"Leo, I won't be able to report for duty in Denver before 8:00 a.m. the day following your notification I've got the job," I answered. (Shortly thereafter, while small mouth bass fishing with Leo on the Susquehanna River and catching fish right and left, Leo looked up and down the river and commented on the beauty of it. Suddenly he stated, "Ron, I'm going to withdraw my Denver application. I've told Marilyn (his wife) to "think Denver" but she really doesn't want to go west. She's supported me in four duty station moves – this time it's her call. We're born Pennsylvanians and I guess we'll die here. Leo submitted one of his famous one-liners withdrawing his Denver application the following day. I happened to be in the Harrisburg Office a few days later when Leo's withdrawal letter reached the desks of the powers that be. Leo's phone rang all morning; calls from Baltimore, Washington, DC and Denver asking him to reconsider. He remained firm.)

"If, for some reason you don't go to Denver, I've heard there will be a Senior Resident Agent's position opening in Raleigh, North Carolina under Willie J. Parker, the SAC in Nashville. If I can't work under you as an ASAC or SRA, I think I'd like to work for this Parker I've heard so much about," I told Leo.

(While working waterfowl enforcement details on Chesapeake Bay and environs, I heard many stories about the "Parker Era"; stories about Willie J. Parker and his crew cleaning up the Chesapeake – the worst geographical area in the nation for waterfowl hunting law violations. Stories, of course from the agents involved, but more impressive were the stories told by the hunting guides and duck club operators. One son of the Chesapeake and seasoned guide summed it up, saying, "Now listen to me, cause I'm gonna tell ya. We never worried much about the state or federal wardens till that Parker and his bunch got here. They'd flat put-a-catchin' on ya. They put the fear of God in all of us. If you was violatin' – bait, whatever – they'd get ya; just a matter of time. They had us all thinkin' there was one of them behind ever bush in the marsh. There weren't nothin' like 'em before and I doubt there will ever be again." During the eight Parker years, his "bunch" consisted of Agents Leo Badger, Bud Davenport, Larry Thurman, Bill Richardson, Jeff Blakemore and Bill Kensinger. I thought many times I'd sure like to have been a part of the Parker team but alas, that time had passed, the Parker team disbanded.

Parker was now the SAC in Nashville, Tennessee, District 10. Bill Kensinger, my SAC in Baltimore, District 11. Leo Badger, my SRA in Pennsylvania. Bud Davenport, the SRA in Virginia. Jeff Blakemore, the ASAC in Boston. Bill Richardson, the SRA in South Carolina. Larry Thurman, the SRA in Maryland with its infamous Chesapeake Bay, was now manned by SRA Thurman and a very capable Agent, Bob Germany. Agent Bill Richardson left his SRA position in South Carolina and returned to the Chesapeake. Where there had been seven agents, there were now three.)

I was privileged to work temporary assignments in the Maryland goose fields, the famed Susquehanna Flats and Chesapeake Bay three consecutive waterfowl hunting seasons. These assignments certainly introduced me to duck hunting – east coast style. As an Ohio state warden, I'd had little exposure to serious waterfowl baiting. Maryland changed all that. My limited exposure there most certainly served as a most valuable precursor for the Carolina years to come.

In January of 1978 the SRA positions at Louisville, Kentucky and Raleigh, North Carolina were both open to applicants. I applied for the Raleigh position. On February 4th, I was contacted by SAC Parker and asked if I would consider the Louisville position as well. I told him I would accept Louisville but preferred Raleigh. Shortly thereafter Leo stated, "Don't be concerned about Louisville; you're going to Raleigh." I recall expressing serious doubts about actually landing the Raleigh position. Rumors abounded that the applicants for Raleigh were many. Again, I was re-assured by Leo, "You're going to Raleigh." On February 22, 1978 I received a radio message to call Willie J. Parker in Nashville ASAP. "We don't pre-select, but you've got the job in Raleigh; I'll be in touch," Parker advised me by phone. On April 26, 1978 I was officially notified by Mr. Parker and Leo Badger that as of May 5th, I was the new SRA in North Carolina. It was agreed that I would report for work in Raleigh as soon as I finished several near complete Pennsylvania and Maryland investigations along with the resulting court work. I reported for work at the Raleigh Office on May 23rd following a day-long court trial in Baltimore on the 22nd during which five members of Maryland's famous Bishop's Head Club were convicted of waterfowl hunting violations.

Leo informed me, "Ron, you're going to a great state. It has a tremendous wildlife resource base. It has everything from ski slopes, the Smoky Mountains and black bear in the west to great fresh water fishing and hunting in the Piedmont to duck hunting and salt water fishing on the Coast – it has it all. You're lucky because you'll have one of the best professional state wildlife agencies in the country to work with – the North Carolina Wildlife Resources Commission. It's no wonder they're the professional organization they are (smiling) – their Director is Bob Hazel, a native Pennsylvanian and he's the first man you need to meet. He's top of the list all the way. The second man you need to meet is Warren Lupton. Warren is an ex-North Carolina Wildlife Officer and retired Fish and Wildlife Service Agent-in-Charge of North Carolina. His brother, Floyd Lupton, is also an ex-North Carolina Wildlife Officer.

Floyd is now the Chief Administrative Aid to North Carolina Congressman, Walter Jones, who chairs the committee that controls our purse strings. Warren is the present Chief of Law Enforcement for the North Carolina Marine Fisheries Division. Warren knows North Carolina politics inside and out. I've never known or heard of Warren using his political connections in the wrong way. To the contrary, he's always used his connections for the good of the resource. He's remained fiercely loyal to the Fish and Wildlife Service. He can be one of your greatest assets in North Carolina so don't forget what I'm telling you. I'll call Warren and pave the way for your meeting with him." I thanked Leo for his information and advice – it proved right on the money in the years to come.

Mr. Parker, during a scheduled phone call, continued with a briefing on my new duty station. "I want you to understand you're going to one of the most desirable duty stations in the country. You're got three young and new agents in North Carolina -- I hand-picked all three. They've preceded you by a duck season during which they cut a swath. They understand one word – catch! They've stirred every duck hunting politician in the state, most of whom have called me. Frankly at one point, they had me scared to death! All three arrived in North Carolina last year with the duck season opening close at hand – right on top of them you might say. They put together their own waterfowl enforcement program with no supervision, and went to work. Bennett took on Currituck County – the hottest county on the coast. Sommers and Curtis split the rest of the coast and of course, handled all the aerial surveillance. Their equipment was in deplorable condition. You might say, the aircraft was down and the boats were up, for repairs, that is. Their patrol cars weren't much better – well used, to say the least. They didn't know the coastal geography – they learned it the way you should, they worked it! Bob Hazel, State Fish and Game Director, was made aware of your agents need for help. To his everlasting credit, he ordered his Coastal Captains to put the new federal agents in their boats and 'get them where they need to be.' I'll always feel indebted to Bob for that. Speaking of the North Carolina Resources Commission – they're the best. They've perfected the finest aircraft enforcement program in the country with aircraft stationed all over the state. They keep their planes up and looking day and night. They are well funded and financially solvent. To watch those North Carolina officers take down an illegally baited dove field with their airplane overhead is no less than poetry in motion. Like most southern states, they bait in North Carolina – waterfowl and doves. It's an old southern tradition. In addition to the cases you and your agents make, you're going to be processing literally thousands of Migratory Bird Treaty Act cases your state officers make. The state takes ninety percent of their duck and dove cases through the federal court system. There is a need for some good undercover work in western North Carolina. It concerns the Great Smoky Mountain National Park, the eastern black bear, and Lacy Act violations. We'll discuss all this later. Soon after you get to Raleigh, I'll come there and we'll meet with all your U.S. Attorneys, U.S. Magistrates, District

Court Judges, and Bob Hazel. Julia Hamilton will put our schedule together in short order. Welcome aboard, Hoss – I'll talk to you later."

My SAC, Bill Kensinger, threw a farewell party for me at Glenburnie, Maryland. I was presented with a framed waterfowl print by a famous wildlife artist. With a short and choked farewell speech, I left District 11, my Agent's position in Pennsylvania and my great boss, Leo Badger.

My first phone call to Raleigh was answered by a lady with the sweetest southern accent I ever heard. "Good morning. U.S. Fish and Wildlife Service, this is Julia Hamilton speaking," thus beginning a long and wonderful working relationship with my new Administrative Assistant who soon became my right hand. The three Special Agents who preceded me in North Carolina were Agents, Jerry Sommers (an ex-IRS Agent) and Ted Curtis (an ex-Kentucky State Wildlife Officer), both pilots. Jerry with an assigned helicopter and Ted with an assigned fixed wing were stationed with their aircraft at Little Washington, North Carolina on the coast. Agent Tom Bennett (an ex-California State Wildlife Officer and NMFS Agent) was assigned to the Raleigh Office. One by one each Agent phoned me prior to my official arrival and welcomed me to North Carolina. I reported for duty in Raleigh and was off and running with a team who, in my biased opinion, would prove to be the best in the nation.

27
Operation Rawhide

    Utilizing the skins of animals, wild and domestic, for shelter, clothing, and much more dates to the beginning of mankind. Trapping wild animals classified by law and the fur trade as "fur bearers" dates to the beginning of our great nation. Trappers were the first to "open" the west. Companies evolved such as the famous Hudson Bay, American Fur and Northwest Fur Companies, along with many others. They bought and processed for manufacture, the trappers furs. The fur industry past was vibrant and employed many. New and innovative clothing materials, the "anti" movements, and other factors caused the gradual decline in the demand for furs and prices slumped. The 20th century experienced low fur prices with occasional "highs" due to the foreign market, mainly Russia and Japan.

    One of these "highs" occurred in the late 1970's and early 1980's. Once again fur prices soared – so did the illegal activity associated with taking and marketing the pelts of wild fur bearing animals. The laws of all the various states require licenses to take, sell and buy the pelts of wild fur bearers. All states require licensed fur buyers to keep and submit records of purchases and sales. Limits by species are set by many states. States such as North and South Carolina require the tagging of pelts. South Carolina law also required a law-compliance inspection and permit issuance (by a S.C. Wildlife Officer) take place before any fur shipment could be exported from South Carolina. These regulations are designed to measure harvest and thus aid State Fish and Game Agencies manage their native fur bearer resource. The harvest and export of bobcat and otter, two fur bearing species native to the Carolinas, is regulated in the U.S. by the Convention on International Trade in Endangered Species

(CITES). CITES is an international agreement between governments. Its aim is to ensure that international trade in certain wild animals and plants does not threaten their survival. Consequently only limited numbers of bobcat and otter pelts could be trapped in each state and bought, sold and exported. This regulation was implemented by a tagging (each pelt) requirement. Dealing in untagged bobcat or otter pelts was, therefore, illegal.

Prior to and during the 1979-80 fur trapping seasons, North and South Carolina State Fish and Game undercover officers attended trapper-fur dealer conventions in both states. Intelligence was gained there as well as thorough confidential informants (CI's) and other covert infiltrations. This intelligence clearly showed blatant violations of all the before mentioned state fur harvest regulations was taking place. In addition, the illegal trafficking in pelt tags – both within and interstate was occurring. All these illegal black market furs were transported, shipped, bought and sold in interstate and foreign commerce in violation of the Federal Lacey Act.

In late November, 1980, Vernon Bevill, Director of the N.C. Wildlife Resources Commission, through his Chief of Law Enforcement, Gene Abernathy, formally requested the assistance of the Special Agents of the U.S. Fish and Wildlife Service. The request proposed a joint state-federal covert investigative probe into the illegal fur industry in North Carolina. The request won U.S. Fish and Wildlife Service approval and the investigation dubbed "Operation Rawhide" officially began.

However, N.C. State Wildlife Officer Sgt. Tommy Williams and US FWS Agent Tom Bennett were already ahead of the game. During October, 1980, Officer Williams contacted Agent Bennett. Williams reported a Virginia buyer not licensed to buy fur in N.C., was soliciting the purchase of illegal N.C. furs (protected species) during the open trapping season within Officer Williams' patrol area. Williams' information came from a CI much involved in the fur industry who Williams and Bennett recruited as a possible undercover operative. In subsequent official reports, Bennett proposed an undercover investigation and projected investigation costs including POI&E (purchase of information and evidence) funds.

Following investigation approval at all levels, I designated Agent Bennett as the case-agent-in-charge of Operation Rawhide. Let me say at the outset; in the Preface, I hailed Tom as a "swath cutting" agent before and after this investigation, Tom more than lived up to my claim. His management and supervision of Operation Rawhide was brilliant. Little did we know then how wide scoped, comprehensive, all inclusive and dangerous this investigation would be. There were over 200 covert contacts made. Many would make a good short story.

Excluding a few "buy and bust" covert investigations, Operation Rawhide was our first major undercover case. In light of the soon to be discovered multi-million dollar illegal black market fur industry, it became overwhelming. Rawhide took place before many "guidelines" governing covert operations were formulated and handed down by the Law Enforcement Office of the USFWS (and others) in Washington, DC. Most of these later guidelines served the mission and the resource well. Others, conveyed the message to me at least, "slow down boys, you're movin' too fast and we're runnin' skeered." In other words, it might be said, during this, our first significant covert operation we were "flying by the seat of our pants." In spite of it all, Case Agent Tom Bennett kept us free, clear and out of administrative and legal trouble.

Illegal untagged furs were supplied by two covert-store front suppliers and furs seized in state overt investigations. State and federal – N.C. based undercover operatives, posing as trappers and/or fur dealers with illegal furs and/or fur tags to sell, investigated 44 North Carolina, 6 Tennessee, 3 South Carolina, 5 Virginia, 5 West Virginia, 3 Kentucky, and 2 New York illegal fur dealers. All were identified by pre-investigation reliable intelligence and intelligence gained as the investigation progressed. All were convicted; most under the criminal, some under the civil provisions of the federal Lacey Act and other federal laws. Many were also convicted of State Law violations. Unfortunately, I don't have at hand the total amounts of fines levied or values of property (furs and 30 gallons of white liquor) forfeited. I do recall the penalties levied were very stiff and the value of property forfeited ran into many thousands. Post investigation intelligence clearly indicated the sentences more than caught the attention of the fur industry.

The investigation began in Greenville, N.C. October, 1980. Before it ended (in North Carolina only) with the last N.C. defendant convicted in April, 1982, it encompassed the entire Tar Heel State. In addition to the states mentioned, the investigation's tentacles reached Ohio, Pennsylvania, New Jersey, Indiana, Missouri, Texas, Washington, DC, and Canada. These "tentacles' or undeveloped leads, as they're officially known, were the result of raid-day searches, seizures and examination of illegal fur dealer records. These leads generated ongoing investigations leading to many, many arrests for state and federal violations in all the mentioned states; much too monumental to tell about in this story. Example – 57 unlicensed fur dealers were detected and prosecuted in Kentucky alone. Probably of little interest to the reader, I'm listing the Wildlife Officers and others who participated in this investigation. Why? Because they proved they're among the best law enforcement officers in the nation. I was privileged to work among them with my main partner, N.C. Officer Lamar Worley. To this day, I am gratefully proud of them all. They deserve, at the very least, name recognition.

For the N.C. Wildlife Resources Commission; Officers, Tommy Williams (who started it all), Jim Twiford, Billy D. Hedrick, Don Hudler, David Grubb, Dwight Davis, Alan McCleod, Carlton Meeks, William A. Thompson, H.B. McKenzie, Mike Shirley, Fred Weisbecker, Kelvin Elliot, Doug Flake, Joe Story, J. Ferguson, Dwight Higgins, Foster Harrell, Steve Harris (Biologist), Mike Lambert, Leon Lineberry, Harold Ragland, Steve Morrison, Ben Wade, Dennis Holloway, Bruce Byrd and Sterling Baker.

For the South Carolina Wildlife and Marine Resources Department; Officers, Larry McClain and Bobby Joe Smith.

For the Tennessee Wildlife Resources Agency; Officers, A.J. Gulley, James Vaughn and Tom Stanfill.

For the West Virginia DNR Wildlife Resources Section; Officers, Rolli Eye and Keith Taylor.

For the Virginia Department of Game and Inland Fisheries; Officer, J. Calhoun.

For the U.S. Fish and Wildlife Service; Agents, Tom Bennett, Jerry Sommers, Ted Curtis, George Hines, Garland Swain, Dan Pooler, John Collins, Bud Davenport, Richard Marks, K.C. Frederick, Joe Wright, Joe Goulet, Kelvin Smith, John Webb (Attorney, Dept. of Justice), Julia Hamilton (Administrative Asst, Raleigh) and me.

Confidential Informants and Covert Operatives; There were two.

By March, 1982, Operation Rawhide had wound down. The undercover aspect of the investigation ended. Litigation of the accused was well underway with many already convicted. By written request submitted by Case Agent Tom Bennett and yours truly, the investigation's emphasis shifted to South Carolina. It was welcomed by S.C. assigned Agent George Hines and S.C. State Fish and Game Chief of Law Enforcement Bill Chastain. South Carolina Fish and Game had a relatively new undercover unit consisting of Officers J.C. Sims, Larry McClain, Tommy Norris, and a later addition, Dudley Britt. Their track record hence would clearly prove they were among the best, if not the best, State Fish and Game undercover team in the nation. The investigative "shift of emphasis" gained partial intelligence that would ultimately lead to "Operation Wild" – a state wide state and federal undercover investigation and crack down in South Carolina that would begin in 1985 with George Hines assigned as the Case Agent.

Rawhide was perhaps our greatest undercover/sting investigation. Looking back – remembering -- given the times and certain problems created within my own agency that I won't further mention – I wonder, amazed that we accomplished our mission. It was accomplished because the "grunts" in the trenches who took the risks and did the work were too professional to fail. I love them all.

Cash money received as payment for illegal NC furs from an illegal Tennessee fur dealer. Labeled and held as evidence.

(Top) Illegal-untagged bobcat and otter furs bought from illegal NC fur dealer. Here they are readied for shipment and sale to an illegal NY dealer.

(Bottom) Illegal-untagged grey fox pelts bought from illegal NC dealer and readied for shipment to an illegal NY dealer. (A double sting).

28
Operation Rock

"The boys from Palmer's Point have a load of fish to sell. They want to know how much you're paying?" an unknown female voice informed me over my undercover phone that tape recorded all calls during the late afternoon of February 20, 1984.

"You have a very pleasant voice, one I don't recognize. "Who is calling?" I asked.

"Never mind who I am – think of me as the 'Lady in Red'. How much are you paying for rock fish?" she asked.

"How about I just call you 'Red'?" I requested.

"Okay," she chuckled.

"We're paying one fifty to two fifty a pound in the round. The bigger the fish, the better the price," I informed her.

"Okay, if you don't get another call from me in the next fifteen minutes, it means the boys will do business with you. Come to the truck stop at the Norlina Exit (North Carolina) be there by nine tonight," Red informed me.

"Huh-uh Red, we don't do business this way. You have Hank or Ed call me right away – I'll stand by the phone. For all I know, this is some sort of set-up," I told her.

"I'll pass your message on," she responded and hung up.

State law prohibited selling rock fish caught in the inland waters of North Carolina and Virginia. Transporting the fish across a state line to sell them was a violation of the Federal Lacey Act. I was certain "the boys from Palmer's Point" were (I'll call them) Hank Wills and Ed Burns. Burns operated a country store near Palmer's Point on Kerr Lake. Wills farmed nearby and worked as a part-time fishing guide. Both lived and worked on the Virginia side of Kerr Lake. The lake is a large Corps of Engineers Reservoir divided by the North Carolina/Virginia state line with most of its waters in Virginia. Wills and Burns (based on intelligence from reliable informants) were actively engaged in the unlawful practice of selling rock fish (striped bass) taken from Kerr Lake, and to some extent, downstream Gaston Lake – another large reservoir separated by the state line. During previous months, covert contacts were made with Wills and Burns by me in the separate company of Agents Jerry Sommers and Tom Bennett. Using bogus identities, we posed as coastal seafood dealers on holiday enjoying the large mouth bass fishing at Kerr Lake. Our work paid off. If accomplished, this would be the first buy of rock fish taken from Kerr Lake. Our intelligence sources indicated Wills and Burns had liaison with virtually all the buyers and sellers engaged in the striped bass (rock fish) black market trade at Kerr and Gaston Lakes. Burns operated country stores at both lakes. His stores were often visited by most of the investigation's targets. Wills and Burns were "key contacts". Gaining their confidence could (and did) get Operation Rock started.

I waited for Wills or Burns to call. At 6:15 p.m. my undercover phone rang. It was Hank Wills.

"We'll sell you our fish," he stated.

"What's all the cloak and dagger stuff with the Lady in Red?" I asked.

"We didn't want our names or voices used over the phone. Don't know if we can trust you. We thought you might tape record our call," Wills Stated.

"I like that Hank, I do, shows you're no dummy. I think we can do business, but I'm not driving up there – it will be too late. You meet me at the Holiday Inn in Henderson. We'll do business in the back parking lot. You know the location, don't you?" I asked.

"I know where it is. Come alone, don't bring anyone, be there by 9:30. We'll have the place scouted before you get there," Wills stated.

"Scouted out, for what?" I asked.

"For cops. We're still not sure we can trust you," Wills continued.

"Look Hank, I've got the same suspicions about you. We've reached the point where we both have to take the step of faith. Either we do business or we don't. I'll see you at nine," I stated. From this point, I was able to get Wills to admit on tape, where in Kerr Lake the fish were caught – all in Virginia waters. Wills ended the conversation saying, "We'll be there, bye."

I phoned Case Agent (in charge of supervising the investigation) Ted Curtis, then Agents Jerry Sommers and Tom Bennett. I informed all three what was happening.

"Get that buy made, Bailey. I don't have to tell you how important it is. Keep me informed. I'll be considering a target for you to sell to," Curtis admonished. Agent Bennett called North Carolina Officer Dennis Thompson and made arrangements for State Officers Thompson and Julian Alman to serve as my back-up. Both officers, concealed in the red tip shrubbery sur-rounding the Holiday Inn parking lot, witnessed the buy. Warned of Wills "scouting" statement, the Officers weren't detected. They were there if I got into trouble. I'll never forget how comforted I was knowing they were nearby. Wills past behavior during our covert contacts troubled me. The fact he was a committed cocaine user had much to do with my apprehension.

At 9:00 p.m. I arrived at the rear parking lot of the Holiday Inn at Hen-derson, driving my "fish truck", a 1983 Dodge pickup with a camper shell. I no sooner parked when Wills parked his black GMC pickup beside me. He exited his truck, lowered the tailgate and pulled two large coolers of iced-down rock fish onto the tailgate.

"Where's Ed?" I asked as we met.

"He's around – got scales, coolers and ice?" Wills asked.

"Sure do – got a lot of fish?" I asked.

"Only nine, they're big ones," Wills answered.

"Let's do business," I stated. I lowered my truck's tailgate, pulled two sea-going coolers on to it, and hung a set of scales from the camper shell roof. We weighed one to two fish at a time, repacked them in ice, and put them in my coolers. I recorded the weights and price per pound on an invoice with our bogus Fish Company name printed at the top. They weighed eighty-six pounds – most over ten pounds each. I paid Wills in cash at the agreed price and offered him a copy of the invoice. He refused it. While the transaction took place, I got Wills to reiterate he and Burns caught the fish by line and hook baited with live shad from the Virginia waters of Kerr Lake. The fish were caught the preceding night.

"How about the net Joe got for you. Have you used it?" I asked. (Agent Tom Bennett, alias Joe Black, previously acquired a gill net for Wills and Burns from a coastal supplier at Wills and Burn's request.)

"Naw, not much luck with the net. This time of year we catch them best from the bank off the rocky points. They're still working the shoreline in singles. When the water warms, they school and we use boats and finders in open water," he replied. Wills when asked, described the manner they sold fish to a buyer (I'll call) Dale Burke.

"We dig pits a good ways behind where we're fishing. The pits are filled with ice. Then we put the fish on the ice and cover them with a camou-flaged tarp. Burke comes around before daylight, gathers our fish and heads for the coast. He sends us a check by mail. We never contact each other. No unloading and loading like we're doing. Nothing for Game Wardens to watch. You should operate the same. By the way, Burke heard about you guys – he's not happy with ya'all."

"We're not about to run around Kerr Lake early in the morning dig-ging fish out of pits and sending checks through the mail. What you and I did is illegal enough; using the mail is a federal offense," I responded.

"Thought I'd let you know . . . ," Wills continued.

"Why're you selling your fish to us, not Burke?" I asked.

"You're paying a little more," he answered.

"We pay market price – no higher. As far as Mr. Burke being unhappy with us buying a few fish, all I can say is TS … TS. Tell Mr. Burke he should consider doing business with us," I suggested.

"I'll pass it on. Burke says there's ways of 'taking care of you guys,'" Wills responded.

"Tell Burke he'd be better off to sell us his fish. That way we'd 'take care' of him. We need to take care of each other. We don't get mad at our competition on the coast – neither should he; it's stupid and bad for business," I told Wills.

"I'll tell him," Wills stated.

"We've done business. I'm comfortable with our transaction. Looks like we can trust each other. When you've got more fish, let us know. Oh, tell Ed I spotted him parked over there hunkered down behind his steering wheel. Tell him I suggest we do future business in the back room of his store and the next time wear a different colored cap – that one sort of stands out (iridescent orange)," I told Wills as we parted company.

'Will do," Wills chuckled.

Elated with the transaction success, I drove my "first buy" (load) of rock fish to Agent Tom Bennett's home. We photographed the fish and agreed to meet the next day at 5:00 a.m. We transported the fish to the coast and sold them to a seafood dealer. Our identities changed from seafood buyers to sport fishermen who fished for rock fish in the inland waters of Kerr and Gaston Lakes. Fishermen interested in illegally selling their catch to a seafood dealer who would knowingly, illegally buy the fish. A dealer located on North Carolina's Albermarle Sound who, during earlier covert contacts, indicated to both agents he knowingly illegally bought inland caught stripers in the past and would do it again. A targeted seafood dealer, Case Agent Ted Curtis, considered a priority.

Departing Raleigh at 5:00 a.m. with our load of rock fish, we met Case Agent Curtis at a mid-point location where we exchanged trucks. Proceeding on, in a truck with Virginia plates, we arrived and made covert contact with (I'll call him Fred of Luckey's Seafoods) on Albemarle Sound, NC. Agent Bennett, wearing a body wire, identified and introduced both agents as fishermen (bogus names) from South Hill, VA with a load of rock fish to sell.

"I remember you two, you fish Kerr and Gaston," Fred stated.

"I got a net from you for some friends," Bennett stated.

"Right, how'd the net work out?" Fred asked.

"Okay, I guess. Don't know for sure, haven't seen them in a while," Bennett responded.

As our fish were unloaded and weighed, Bennett commented, "Long trip over here. Had us kind of worried – you know selling and buying rock fish being illegal and all. Even crossing a state line with them is against some kind of federal law. You heard anything like that?" Bennett asked.

"Look, when they get here, they don't know but what they're caught in the sound out there," Fred stated nodding out the window towards Albemarle Sound (legal waters for saleable rock fish).

"We're going to do a lot more fishing now that the fishing's getting good. May have more stripers a little later on," I stated as we concluded the transaction and started to depart after Fred gave Bennett a copy of the invoice (preserved as evidence) recording the sale.

"Bring um on," Fred replied.

We sold our "first buy" (load) of rock fish for a profit. As Case Agent Ted Curtis would later say, "Operation Rock was off and running".

Days later, the evening of February 27th, my undercover phone rang. "Got more fish to sell," Wills stated.

"How many pounds, Hank?" I need to be sure and bring enough cash, unless you'll take a check?" I inquired.

"Near three hundred pounds – no checks – how much a pound you paying?" Wills asked.

"Price is market, same as before. Where and when?" I asked.

"Palmer's Point, in the morning at nine," Wills stated.

"We'll be there. Joe will be with me. He wants to take a look at a boat for sale," I told Wills.

"No problem," Wills stated.

At 9:00 a.m. on February 28th, Agent Bennett and I drove to Palmer's Point at Kerr Lake, Virginia. Wills, his truck and load of rock fish were waiting. Again, Burns wasn't present. "He's minding the store," Wills stated. Wills' fish weighed two hundred and ninety two pounds. I paid him in cash and once again attempted to give him a copy of the invoice recording the sale; he refused it. The same conversation was invoked regarding where Wills and Burns caught the fish (Virginia waters – Kerr Lake). Buy and sell transaction concluded, Wills, somewhat surly acting, stated, "I've got something here I need to show you." His right hand went behind the driver's seat of his truck. It returned holding an older model .38 caliber revolver. He "brandished" the weapon. This is what's going to happen to you two if we ever find out you're undercover Game Wardens," Wills stated with a crazed look in his eyes. He's snorted some of his "nose juice" before he met us this morning, I thought as Bennett stated in a meaningful way. "Put the pea-shooter away, Hank – now! You don't want to play that game with us or we'll show you how to play it. We've been on the wrong side of the law a long time in this business. You're nothing but a pansy compared to some we've dealt with." My, Tommy could be nasty when he had to – he even scared me. Hank meekly placed his "pea-shooter" under the driver's seat of his truck. We exchanged strained amenities and departed.

"Whew, where'd that come from?" I asked Tom as we turned onto the main road leaving Palmer's Point.

"I don't know – he made me mad. Besides that, he scared me," Tom replied. Two hours later we met Case Agent Ted Curtis, exchanged trucks and proceeded to the North Carolina Coast. We sold our load of contraband to another "knowing and willing" seafood dealer (I'll call) Short Stop Seafoods, as instructed by Case Agent Curtis.

After the Wills gun encounter, I carried a loaded and concealed, shoulder holstered weapon; a four inch barrel Ruger Model GP 100, 357 Magnum. It was fitted with a custom made oversized, somewhat grotesque looking, burled walnut grip that fit my right hand perfectly. Its holster pouches contained twelve extra rounds. It appeared big, mean and wicked nestled next to my left rib cage. Range Officer, Agent Don Patterson at Richmond graciously qualified me to use and carry the weapon in accordance with agency regulations. I made several buys from Wills and Burns involving hundreds of pounds of rock fish during the ensuing weeks, accompanied by Agents Sommers or Bennett. Agent Sommers bought a large load of rock fish from Wills and Burns and talked both into accepting payment from me at a later date. "Charge them to our account," Agent Sommers told Burns and Wills as he departed with the load of fish following a line of BS one can only imagine. (Jerry was the only undercover operative to "charge" a load of fish.)

Time and events progressed rapidly. Soon Agents Bennett and Sommers were much committed to other targets and avenues of the investigation. I needed a new partner. Enter, retired Ohio State Wildlife Officer, Charles Cooper (Coop for short).

"Guess who's retired and living in Sanford, North Carolina?" stated Assistant Agent in Charge(ASAC – Atlanta), Tom Wharton (ex-Ohio Officer).

"Who?" I asked.

"Charlie Cooper," Wharton answered.

"I remember Coop – thanks for telling me. I'll look Coop up. Have you talked with him?" I asked.

"Sure did, by phone yesterday. He retired as Law Enforcement Supervisor in District 4 at Athens. He's sharp as ever, says he's in perfect shape and enjoying retirement," Wharton stated.

"Suppose he's interested in going back to work as a U.S. Deputy Game Warden? I could use a new partner in Rock," I asked.

"You can ask him. If he's willing, I'll see that he's re-issued his Deputy Commission," Wharton responded.

I contacted Coop at his home in Sanford. Although I didn't work with Coop when we were both Ohio State Wildlife Officers, I attended many meetings with him and got to know him quite well. It's safe to say, "We were on the same – catch the violator – wave length." At our first meeting, he was the same Coop – a big man with large powerful vice grip hands who loved to tease, torment and eat fried chicken. He hadn't changed. He was in great physical shape, lean and mean. He possessed the same old guttural chuckle he exhibited when he found something amusing. Usually the embarrassing or uncomfortable moment of others (most invoked by himself). He always emitted a low (heh-heh-heh) chuckle on these occasions. He agreed to accept the re-issue of his Federal U.S. Deputy Game Warden's Commission and be my new partner.

"You know when Coop goes up home, he sometimes patrols with the guys (Ohio Wardens). His radio call signal is O F 1, meaning Old xo#x No. 1," Wharton stated.

"You're kidding," I stated.

"No, it's the truth, they call him O F 1," Wharton re-assured.

"My, how appropriate," I responded.

I summoned Coop to the Raleigh Office the day after his credentials arrived from Atlanta and presented them to him – he was back in harness again. During the two days following, Coop and I went to Kerr and Gaston Lakes; I introduced him simply as "Coop", my new business partner.

Shortly thereafter, on March 24th, I was summoned via my undercover phone to Ed Burns' store. Wills and Burns claimed they had another load of rock fish to sell. Coop and I arrived at Burns' store mid-afternoon. Unusual for Saturday afternoon, we noticed the customer parking lot was empty except one vehicle belonging to another well known violator. One who sold us his fish through Wills and Burns – a slippery character who wouldn't do business directly with us. As we approached, he hurriedly exited the store and sped away in his truck. We noticed Wills' vehicle (that usually transported the fish) was not parked at the back door. "Something's not right here, Coop," I stated.

"Stay on your toes," Coop responded. I don't know how we sensed it – the "signs" at the scene -- old Game Warden instincts, I suppose. Burns greeting was decidedly cool.

Coop asked, "Where's the restroom?" Burns nodded to the back of the store. I knew instinctively Coop was using his need to use the restroom as an excuse to scout as much of the store as possible.

"Where's Hank?" I asked.

"He'll be along soon," Burns said smugly. As Burns and I engaged in strained conversation concerning his and Wills fishing success, Coop returned from the restroom, winked at me and told Burns, "Tell Hank to come out from behind the stack of dog food and keep his gun pointed toward the floor." With that statement, I unbuttoned my jacket rendering my 357 quickly available. Coop (also "carrying") was already unbuttoned and ready.

"Come on out Hank, do as they say," Burns announced. Wills appeared approaching us with gun pointed down. Close to me, he waved the weapon in front of my nose. He was "high" on something. With the gun gesture, Coop, standing at Wills right side, grasped Wills gun hand. Wills grimaced as Coop bore down with his vice-like grip. Wills' weapon dropped to the floor. Coop picked it up, unloaded it and placed it in his pocket – the cartridges in another. The weapon was the same chrome plated break-down action antique .38.

"Be thankful you got disarmed, Hank. I have one here that's much bigger than yours," I stated as I pulled my jacket open displaying the .357. It'll take a diesel engine out of a truck or the biggest outboard off the back of a boat. Think what a nice new and extra xo#0-hole it would give you," I told Wills.

"How'd you like a new xo#o-hole, heh, heh, heh," Coop chuckled in his low guttural, in this instance, "chilling"chuckle.

"Joe Black warned you about playing this game, Hank. Is it safe to say, you've got the message?" I asked Wills."It's safe to say that," Burns stated as Wills messaged his mangled gun hand.

"You broke my hand," Wills told Coop.

"Smarts, don't it," Coop chuckled.

"Okay, knot-heads, what's this all about?" I asked both.

"We went to the address on your business card – it's nothing but an empty building. You guys are undercover agents and we know it!" Burns exclaimed.

"What age do you think they retire cops," I asked.

"About 55 for State Troopers," Wills answered.

"Tell them how old you are, Coop," I ordered.

"Born in 1914 – let them figure it out," Coop replied.

"He's too old to be a Game Warden," Wills concluded.

"Yes, the address on the card is fake. Now that you've been smart enough to check that out, tell me why we'd be using a phony address?" I asked both.

"Because you're undercover Game Wardens," Burns stated.

"You know good and well we're not Game Wardens. If we are, then why aren't you already arrested? Let's assume we're not – what other reason could we have for using a phony address. Think! Tell me and I'll conclude you're almost smart enough to continue to do business with us," I proclaimed.

"I don't know," Burns declared.

"The IRS, stupid! The paper trail – where does it lead? To the false address knot-head, to the false address!" I yelled.

"Never thought of that," Burns responded.

"Aw xo#x" Wills stated. (Case Agent Ted Curtis confirmed, following a meeting with a legitimate coastal seafood dealer on March 21st, the dealer was successfully recruited. He would serve the investigation as the business front we badly needed.) Thank goodness Teddy, you got that business front just in time, I thought as I asked Wills and Burns, "Have you got a load of fish for us today?"

"No, we got you up here to confront you about being undercover agents," Burns acknowledged.

"How soon will you have a load?" I asked, to see if we had regained their confidence. I was sure of our success as both acted much more relaxed.

"Soon," Wills replied.

"I'm going to arrange for you to deliver your next load of fish directly to our store on the coast. This is something we never do, but I want the two of you to be sure you can trust us and no more of this gun play, okay?" I asked.

"Okay," both answered. On departure, Coop and I shook hands with both, Wills offered his "good" hand. Coop placed Wills' gun on the store counter and kept the cartridges.

"Now, is all well -- do we understand each other?" I asked as we parted company.

"All's well," Burns answered, smiling.

"Whew! That was a close one. How did you come up with that line of B.S.? They bought it hook, line and sinker," Coop asked as we began our return trip to Raleigh.

"I don't know, Coop. It remains to be seen if they bought it," I answered.

On March 27th, Wills and Ed Burns phoned telling they had another load of fish to sell. "This time gentlemen, you're going to haul your fish directly to our place of business on the coast where you can sell them in person to the man who runs our plant," I informed both. The following day Wills and Burns met Agent Bennett and me mid-way between Kerr Lake and our new business front near the Coast. They followed us to the dealer where both agents witnessed the sale. I went to the store office, posed as the big shot who owned the place, while Agent Bennett, and deck hands Agents Curtis and Sommers helped unload the fish. The store owner paid Wills and Burns by check (they would never before accept) and played his part to the hilt. Content they were on "safe ground", our violators departed on their return trip home to Virginia.

Covert buys continued resulting in over 2600 pounds of rock fish were purchased from Wills and Burns. They proved to be very good suppliers. All their fish were sold, usually by two-man undercover teams consisting of State and Federal Wildlife Officers to "knowing and willing coastal seafood dealers. At least one other officer, N.C. State Wildlife Officer James Ward received life threats while working as an undercover operative. On January 7, 1985, Officer Ward and yours truly bought a load of illegal, inland caught, rock fish in North Carolina. We transported and sold the fish to a "knowing and willing" seafood buyer in Montross, Virginia, thus concluding the last covert transaction of Operation Rock. "Raid" day soon followed on January 16th.

The scenarios I've described were some (not all) of mine and my various partners experiences. They convey the "method of operation" used to accomplish the mission. Similar scenarios, excluding the "gun play" but just as dangerous, took place many times by other undercover teams.

The following edited paper was presented by Case Agent Ted Curtis at the Southeastern Association of Fish and Wildlife Agency Conference in November, 1985. The overview it records of Operation Rock is far better than I can write. It follows:

"The objectives of the covert operation, known as "Operation Rock", were to identify, apprehend and prosecute those individuals involved in the taking, selling, transporting and purchasing rock fish taken from certain inland waters of North Carolina. This was accomplished by infiltrating the black market trade, using undercover teams made up of Agents of the Fish and Wildlife Service and Officers of the North Carolina Wildlife Commission, posing as fishermen, black market dealers and seafood dealers.

In June of 1979, North Carolina Wildlife Officers asked an Agent of the U.S. Fish and Wildlife Service in North Carolina if there was anything that could be done to help combat the large scale poaching and illegal commercialization of rock fish taken from the spawning grounds of the Roanoke River. In March 1980, a case was opened and the investigation was initiated.

The problem was identified and found to be more complex than it appeared:

1. Rock fish (Striped Bass) are protected by North Carolina Law as a game fish when found in inland waters.

2. Rock fish are further protected by North Carolina Law; "it is unlawful to buy or sell, to offer to buy or sell, or to possess or transport for the purpose of sale any species of inland game fish." Striped Bass, when taken from inland waters are classified as a game fish.

3. Rock fish taken by commercial fishing activities in coastal and Atlantic Ocean waters may be sold on the open commercial market.

4. Rock fish, under growing commercial pressure in the early 1970's, reached an all time annual commercial harvest of over 12 million pounds in North Carolina. However, due to over harvesting and other biological problems, the rock fish harvest began to decline and dropped to about 330,000 lbs. in 1983.

5. To add pressure on the spawning grounds, a North Carolina statute enacted to provide a source of food to the local population, allowed for the selling of rock fish taken from the spawning grounds in two counties adjacent to the Roanoke River. This was allowed in the months of April, May and June, the primary spawning period, opening the door for illegal commercialization of rock fish taken from inland waters.

In 1979, local Wildlife Officers believed illegal commercial poaching had also spread into Roanoke Rapids Lake, just upstream in the Roanoke River from the spawning grounds.

During 1979-1981, there were virtually no funds available for fisheries investigations by the Fish and Wildlife Service and a very limited investigation was possible. But the surface was scratched and a few local arrests were made. Records seized from one coastal seafood dealer for years 1979 and 1980 showed that over $240,000 worth of illegal rock fish had been moved in the commercial market. More information gathered from informants showed this was not only a problem in the Roanoke River and Roanoke Rapids Lake, but there was large scale poaching and commercialization of rock fish taken from Lake Gaston and Kerr Lake further upstream in the Roanoke River system.

The initial investigation revealed in the Roanoke Rapids area, there were primarily two black market dealers. These dealers had a group of suppliers—local fishermen, who for the most part, complied with the state creel and size limits on rock fish. The fishermen fished with rod and reel in the swift waters of the Roanoke River and Roanoke Rapids Lake. In the Roanoke River, the creel limit was eight fish per day with a minimum size limit of sixteen inches. Rock fish taken from the river averaged six to twelve pounds, but a twenty pound fish was not uncommon. In Roanoke Rapids Lake, the creel limit was four fish per day with a minimum size limit of twenty inches. Fish taken from Roanoke Rapids Lake averaged twelve to twenty pounds. A twenty-five pound fish was not uncommon. In the evenings, the local fishermen would drop off their daily catch at the home or business of one of the black market fish dealers. The dealers were paying from $1.00 to $1.50 a pound and would keep the fish on ice until they had enough to take a load to the coast. Usually in 2-5 days the black market dealer would have enough for a load. He loaded a pick-up truck with the fish iced down in coolers and traveled the 150 mile drive to sell the fish. He sold the fish to a commercial fish dealer where he would receive $1.75 to $2.50 a pound. It was later learned that during the peak of the spawning season, the black market dealers would make trips daily and sell as much as 2,000 pounds of rock fish each trip.

As the investigation continued, we learned that in the Kerr and Gaston Lake areas, there were three large scale fish buying operations as well as two part-time buyers. These black market dealers had a large network of local fishermen to buy from. The black market dealers and the fishermen did business at night. The dealers would weigh the fish and pay the fishermen $1.00 to $1.50 a pound for the fish.

Because of the depleting populations of rock fish along the Eastern Seaboard States, the U.S. Fish and Wildlife Service identified rock fish as a priority species and fisheries funds were allotted. The new Lacey Act Amendments put teeth into the Federal Wildlife Laws and applicable state laws. In 1982, the North Carolina Wildlife Commissioner representing the Kerr and Gaston Lake Regions forwarded public complaints he received concerning the illegal rock fish activities taking place at both lakes to Vernon Bevel, the Director of the North Carolina Wildlife Commission, and demanded Director Bevel do something about it. In addition, relatives, who lived in the Kerr Lake area, of James Pulliam, Regional Director for the U.S. Fish and Wildlife in Atlanta, made similar complaints and requests to Mr. Pulliam. A meeting between Directors Bevel and Pulliam along with Special Agent in Charge of Law Enforcement (Atlanta Region) Dan Searcy, ensued. The investigation was put into a covert, intelligence gathering phase. Information was collected concerning the legal commercial market in North Carolina and the overall rock fish market in Baltimore and New York. It was also ascertained many illegal rock fish were bought and utilized aboard several sea-going luxury liners operating in the Atlantic. Contacts were made in the illegal black market and numerous informants were located and developed.

In the spring of 1983, Fish and Wildlife Fisheries funds became available and an agreement in the form of a written Memorandum of Understanding between the North Carolina Wildlife Commission and the U.S. Fish and Wildlife Service was signed. "Operation Rock" was born, with a new investigation identifying number, as a joint Federal/State covert investigation.

A three point plan was devised to achieve the operational objectives. First, two groups of undercover operatives, composed of State and Federal Agents, would attempt to enter the network as fishermen, make contact with local fishermen and ultimately sell rock fish to the local black market dealers. A second group of operatives would attempt to enter the network posing as seafood dealers. The operatives would purchase rock fish from local fishermen as well as the black market dealers. Third, another group of operatives would pose as fishermen and black market dealers. They would sell their fish to established seafood dealers on the coasts of North Carolina and Virginia previously identified as those dealers who were knowingly purchasing illegal rock fish.

The first portion of the plan was the least successful. Several good contacts were made with local fishermen and a lot of valuable information was obtained concerning black market dealers. Unfortunately, only one sale was made to one black market dealer. They were very cautious of undercover agents and would not do business with any new associates.

The second part of the plan was the most difficult to administer. The agents posing as seafood dealers had only a business card and a telephone number to show as a front. Special funds were allotted by the Fish and Wildlife Service and the North Carolina Wildlife Commission, but these were insufficient to operate a full scale covert store front seafood business. However, greed was on our side, there were some very good contacts and a few purchases were made. Finally, a seafood dealer surfaced that cooperated fully and became the business front so badly needed. During summer and fall of 1983, three federal agents infiltrated a group of three inland poachers, two of which in February 1984, sold the first load of illegal rock fish to a Federal Agent while two State Wildlife Officers serving as back-up, witnessed and documented the transaction. Shortly thereafter, we were able to get this same group of fishermen, who were very suspicious of our business, to make a delivery of rock fish to the cooperating store front dealer. "Operation Rock" was off and running. We were able to purchase over 4,000 pounds of rock fish from the Kerr and Gaston Lakes area and in turn used those fish in the third portion of the operation.The third part of the plan, posing as fishermen or black market dealers, proved to be very successful. We would first make a telephone call to one of the identified seafood dealers and tell him that we had caught a large amount of rock fish and ask what price he was paying. We would then inform the dealer that we had caught the fish at Kerr, Gaston or Roanoke Rapids Lake, that it was illegal for us to sell fish and we were worried about getting caught. The most common responses we received were: "Once you get your fish down here they can't tell where they came from", and "When you get here, don't say where you caught them—just bring your fish down". The last such transaction occurred January 7, 1985 when a State Wildlife Officer and Federal Agent sold a load of North Carolina inland rock fish to targeted Virginia coastal dealer – nine days before takedown.

During those covert activities, contact was made with numerous subjects along the coast and in the Kerr Lake area. Several of the subjects expressed concern about the depleting rock fish populations. We followed with a covert contact and found that several were very willing to work as confidential informants. These new informants were able to supply so much good information that in October, 1984, the operation turned, almost entirely, to a covert surveillance operation.

Three surveillance teams were set up, one each in Henderson and Roanoke Rapids, to observe the black market dealers as they loaded and transported their illicit fish to the coastal dealers. The third team worked at the coastal seafood dealers to observe the unloading and selling of the rock fish.

The surveillance teams in Henderson and Roanoke Rapids, consisting of four to eight North Carolina Officers and Fish and Wildlife Service Agents, established surveillance on five black market dealers. When information was received that one of the dealers was planning to haul a load of rock fish to a coastal seafood dealer, the surveillance would begin. The subject's residence would come under constant observation to document the loading of the fish, which usually took place between 10 PM and 2 AM. Two unmarked vehicles would be placed, as well as one of the state's aircraft readied, to keep the subject under continuous surveillance from his residence along the 200 mile route to the coastal seafood dealers.

The coastal surveillance team was responsible for surveillance of the black market dealer upon his arrival at the fish house where the fish would be unloaded, weighed and sold.

These covert surveillance operations were set up with the objectives of documenting the illegal activities of five black market dealers and to gain enough evidence to obtain Grand Jury Indictments. The surveillances were 100 percent successful.

All five of the black market dealers were observed loading coolers filled with fish into pick-up trucks and on two occasions, a large U-Haul truck was used for transporting. Surveillance was maintained along the entire route of travel and at the fish houses at the coast. By introducing a female undercover agent at the fish houses, the unloading, weighing and selling of all five subjects were observed. Four of the illegal transactions were photographed and on two occasions, the female agent was able to engage the subjects in incriminating conversation concerning their illegal activities.

In January 1985, 42 Wildlife Officers of the North Carolina Wildlife Commission, 3 South Carolina Wildlife Officers, 8 Wildlife Officers of the Virginia Game Commission, 7 National Wildlife Refuge Officers and 24 Special Agents of the Fish and Wildlife Service executed arrest and/or search warrants on 25 subjects in Virginia and North Carolina. These individuals repre-

301

sented commercial fish dealers, fish house owners, operators, fish buyers from the coasts of Virginia and North Carolina, as well as black market dealers, poachers, and fishermen from the area surrounding the inland lakes. These 25 subjects accounted for a total of 20 misdemeanors and 75 felony counts for violations of the Federal Lacey Act. In conjunction with these arrests, search warrants and subpoenas were executed. These resulted in the seizure of vehicles, fishing boats, freezers, coolers, ice makers, scales, gill nets, and approximately 700 pounds of rock fish.

In conjunction with the 25 arrests on January 16, 1985, business records from 13 coastal seafood dealers and one inland seafood dealer, and the New York Fish Market were seized for business years 1983 and 1984. This amounted to approximately two pick-up truck loads of purchase and sales invoices, as well as cancelled checks, check book stubs and cash payment receipts.

After six weeks of reviewing all the records, the entire scope of the illegal rock fish black market was revealed. The total surpassed all estimates. Eleven commercial seafood dealers along the coasts of North Carolina and southern Virginia were illegally buying rock fish taken in the inland waters of North Carolina and Virginia from Kerr, Gaston and Roanoke Rapids Lakes and the Roanoke River. The records showed that the fish were purchased from 15 black market dealers and fish poachers. There were five black market dealers who accounted for 86 percent of the total illegal sales for 1983 and 1984. Their total documented illegal rock fish sales was 223,934 lbs. which netted $518,805.87 to the black market dealers.

The follow-up investigation of the business records as well as the statements given by seafood dealers established sufficient evidence to obtain Grand Jury Indictments for eight subjects in July of 1985. These eight defendants accounted for 30 additional felony charges under the Lacey Act.

Throughout the course of the investigation, the United States Attorney's Office continually reminded the undercover officers of the elements of a Lacey Act violation to insure that all elements were present before a subject could be indicted. Only one defendant plead not guilty and went to trial in United States District Court. At the conclusion of the trial, Judge W. Earl Britt, Chief Judge for the Eastern District of North Carolina, impressed on the jury that all elements of the offense must be proved by the government. The Judge highlighted those elements in his instructions to the jury. The following is an excerpt from the Judge's instructions:

"...... Count One charges that .... defendant herein, did knowingly and unlawfully sell and purchase in interstate commerce fish, that is, Rock Fish (Striped Bass), with a market value less than $350.00, which were taken, possessed, transported, and sold in violation of the laws and regulations of the State. Title 16, USC, 3372 (a)(2) (A) provides that: It is unlawful for any person .... to sell or purchase in interstate or foreign commerce .... any fish or wildlife taken in violation of any law or regulation of any State. 16USC3373 (d) provides that: Any person who knowingly engages in such conduct . . .

and in the exercise of due care should know that the fish or wildlife taken, possessed, transported, or sold in violation of, or in a manner unlawful under, any underlying law . . . or regulation shall be guilty of a criminal offense . . .".

The Judge continued: ". . . In order to find the defendant guilty . . . you must find:

First: That the defendant sold or purchased fish in interstate commerce;

Second: That the fish were taken, possessed, transported or sold in violation of State laws or regulations;

Third: That the defendant knowingly engaged in such conduct;

Fourth: That the defendant knew or, in the exercise of due care, should have known that the fish were taken, possessed, transported or sold in violation of State Law."

In regards to Count Two of the Indictment which differed from Count One in that the value of the fish were in excess of $350.00, a felony, the Judge instructed the Jury that: ". . . you must find beyond a reasonable doubt.

First: That the defendant sold or purchased fish in interstate commerce;

Second: That the defendant knowingly engaged in such conduct;

Third: That the fish were taken, possessed, transported or sold in violation of State Laws and Regulations;

Fourth: That the defendant knew that the fish were taken, possessed, transported or sold in violation of State Law; and

Fifth: That the fish involved had a market value in excess of $350.00."

During the trial the defendant asserted that he was a victim of entrapment. Judge Britt instructed the jury that:

"Where a person has no previous intent or purpose to violate the law, but is induced or persuaded by law enforcement officers or their agents to commit a crime, he is a victim of entrapment, and the law as a matter of policy forbids his conviction in such a case.

On the other hand, where a person already has the readiness and willingness to break the law, the mere fact that government agents provide what appears to be a favorable opportunity is not entrapment. For example, it is not entrapment for a government agent to pretend to be someone else and to offer, either directly or through an informer or other decoy, the opportunity to engage in an unlawful transaction."

Throughout the trial the defendant also asserted that the government undercover agents had tricked him and set him up to violate the law. Judge Britt informed the jury:

"The government has presented testimony of undercover agents involved in its investigation of this case. Indeed, much of the evidence that has been introduced was derived directly or indirectly from the use of these agents.

Such undercover activity is a recognized and permissible means of investigation necessary to gather evidence of illegal conduct. An agent does not violate any federal statute or rule by such undercover activity. The undercover activity may take many forms including persuasion and fraudulent representations. A solicitation, request or activity, standing alone, is not an inducement. Law enforcement officials are not precluded from utilizing artifice, stealth and stratagem such as the use of decoys and undercover agents in order to apprehend persons engaged in criminal activity provided that they merely afford opportunities or facilities for the commission of the offense by one predisposed or ready to commit it. They may properly make use of undercover operations, in which they use false names and false appearances. They may properly assume the roles of criminals."

Of the 32 people indicted, five defendant's charges were dismissed due to their limited involvement and overall good cooperation; two were transferred for civil litigation; and one young defendant was placed under pretrial diversion under the supervision of the Federal Probation Officer. Twenty-six defendants were found guilty in the United States District Court. Of those 26 convicted defendants, eight received felony convictions. Penalties handed down by the Chief District Judge, W. Earl Britt, reached total monetary fines of $112,549.05. Of this, $81,040.05 was ordered paid to the North Carolina Wildlife Commission as restitution for the wildlife taken. In addition, active jail time was given to four defendants totaling four years, ten months. A total of 33 years, nine months jail time was suspended and the defendants placed on a total of 93 years probation. Nine vehicles, two fishing boats and motors, thirty-seven coolers, six freezers, one ice maker, and four gill nets were forfeited to the U.S. Fish and Wildlife Service and the North Carolina Wildlife Resources Commission. As part of the terms of probation, most subjects were prohibited from engaging in any hunting or fishing activities for the length of their probations.

In addition, two defendants were arrested and convicted in Virginia State Court. They paid a total of $520.00 in fines on misdemeanor charges."

In March, 1986 the conviction of the one defendant, who appealed his conviction in District Court in North Carolina, was upheld by the 4th Circuit Court of Appeals in Richmond. Operation Rock ended. This eye-opening covert investigation was one of our best. It curtailed the wholesale slaughter of rock fish in the inland waters of North Carolina and to a great extent, Virginia.

(Right) Federal Agent/Pilot Jerry Sommers, who, with Agent Tom Bennett and the author, infiltrated the first outlaw fishermen on Kerr and Gaston Lakes who sold illegal rock fish to covert operatives. Here he "suffers" on a surveillance detail. Rough duty – huh Jer?

(Below) Bad guys at work rock fishing at Kerr Lake. They had 200 lbs. on board. (Background) NC state Officer Sgt. Dennis Thompson in fisherman's garb has them under surveillance.

First covert buy of rock fish made 2/20/84 by the author at Henderson, NC. Fish taken from the Virginia waters of Kerr Lake.

NC Wildlife Officer James Ward, who with the Author, made the last covert sale of rock fish on 1/7/85 – nine days before "take–down", Operation Rock. The shipment of rock fish was bought from an illegal NC dealer and sold to an illegal VA dealer.

Gold Rock, NC, 1/15/1985. Much in command Case Agent-in-Charge, Ted Curtis (left-standing) addresses participating officers in the Operation Rock "take-down" on 1/16/85. His briefing was all-comprehensive. His overall management of the investigation was nothing short of genius. U.S. Fish & Wildlife Service Region 4 Director, Jim Pulliam is seated below. (Extreme right-back to camera) Dan Searcy, Special Agent in charge Region 4. Both, as always, supported us 100%.

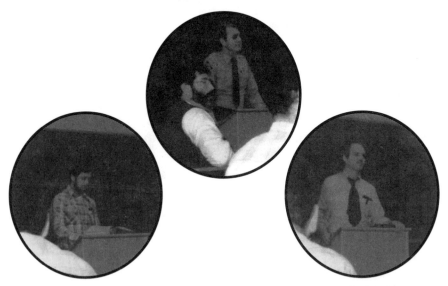

(Top) Col. Gene Abernathy, NC Wildlife Commission. (Left) Agent George Hines. (Right) Agent Tom Bennett – U.S. Fish & Wildlife Service, give instructions to raid team leaders, Day 1 of Operation Rock raid breifing.

U.S. Deputy Game Warden Charles Cooper inventories seized property (vehicles, boats, coolers, freezers, nets) following raid team deliveries to a NC Wildlife Commission compound.

NC Eastern District U.S. Attorney Sam Currin conducting a press conference the morning after "take-down".
Press conferences following all undercover raid days, telling the public what we did and why we did it, paid off. We always received public praise and support.

29
Operation Wild

Bill Delahoyd was a young, heck of a good Assistant United States Attorney for the Federal Eastern District of North Carolina. He won every Lacey Act--Operation Rock case he prosecuted in the Eastern District Court.

He deserved a reward. "Bill, how would you like to go on a guided fishing trip for hybrid stripers at Lake Hartwell in South Carolina – all expenses, including your fishing license paid?" I asked him by phone one afternoon in mid-June, 1985.

"Does a bear do-do in the woods? Of course I'd like to go – when?" he asked.

"July first, second, and third. We'll go down there on the first, fish on the second, and return to Raleigh on the third," I replied.

"Sounds good. When and where do I meet you on the first?" he asked.

"I'll pick you up at your home at 8:00 a.m. but I must let you in on something - - - ," I informed my new fishing buddy.

"What?" Bill asked.

"You'll be working with me on an undercover assignment for the Service and South Carolina Fish and Game. Still want to go?" I inquired.

"Is this something I'm going to have to prosecute?" Bill asked.

"No, this one will to go a state or a federal court in South Carolina," I answered.

"Let's do it," he responded.

"Oh, Bill - - - there's another little hitch," I stated.

"Okay, let's hear it," he responded.

"We're going to do another little undercover job on the way down," I told Bill.

"For who?" he asked.

"For North Carolina Fish and Game and South Carolina Fish and Game and, when it's all said and done, probably the Fish and Wildlife Service," I answered.

"A Lacey Act thing?" Bill asked.

"Maybe, don't know yet – will have to see how everything falls out," I answered.

"Okay, if it goes federal, it's in the Western District – right?" he asked.

"Right," I answered.

"Okay, Ron, let's go fishing," Bill replied.

I received a request from S.C. Wildlife Officer, J.C. Sims, (head of the S.C. undercover team) to check a seafood dealer in Charlotte, NC I'll call Westside Seafoods, ascertain if the dealer was illegally selling game fish (white bass or hybrid stripers taken in S.C.); make a buy and try to ascertain who was supplying the fish. (S.C. intelligence indicated the supplier was the same guide Delahoyd and I were booked to fish with at Lake Hartwell on July 2nd – I'll call him Reggie McFarland.)

On July 1st I picked Bill up at his home and we headed for our first covert stop in Charlotte at Westside Seafoods. There, we observed white bass, gutted and scaled, but otherwise in the round for sale. I purchased two pounds. "I've never seen such nice fresh white bass for sale – where in the world do you get them?" I asked the clerk.

"I don't know – some guy from South Carolina brings them in," she replied.

"He's got to catch them somewhere – we're headed down there fishin' – sure would like to get up with him; maybe we could get him to tell us and our guide where to fish. What's his name?" I asked.

"Hey Les – what's the guy's name in South Carolina who brings us fish?" the clerk yelled to Les in another room.

Les came to the sales room and jokingly asked, "You guys buying fish when you're going fishing – is that so if you don't catch any, cause your up to something else, you can show the little lady some fish in the cooler when you get home, heh, heh, heh?"

"No, we're going to Hartwell – we've got a camper there. We won't fish until morning with our guide. We want some fish to cook and eat in camp tonight," I replied.

"Who's your guide?" Les asked.

"Reggie McFarland – they say he's the best," I answered.

"Reggie, he's the one who brings us fish! I've heard he's the best guide on Hartwell," Les responded.

"Did he bring you the white bass we just bought for camp chow?" I asked Les.

"Sure did!" Les affirmed.

"Well, I guess we're in luck. I sure didn't know you could buy white bass over the counter. I thought it was against the law," I commented.

"Aw, we don't worry about that – we just call them perch," Les responded.

We left Westside Seafoods and iced our "perch" down in a cooler. They would be frozen, tagged and held as evidence. We departed for Lake Hartwell -- a huge body of water separated by the South Carolina and Georgia state lines; an Army Corps of Engineers Project. Its fishery is jointly managed by the South Carolina and Georgia Fish and Game Agencies. Two of Hartwell's game fish offerings are striped bass and hybrid striped bass. As in North Carolina, both species were classified as "game fish" when caught in South Carolina's inland lakes. Buying and selling them was illegal. The same was true in Georgia.

At Hartwell, we acquired Bill's fishing license. We hooked to a Service owned camper stored at a South Carolina Fish and Game facility and moved it to a lakeside KOA campground. The following morning we met our guide, Reggie and his son, at the boat ramp he designated during a previous phone conversation when I engaged him as our guide. Reggie's boat, a sixteen footer, equipped with sun canopy, fishing station seats aft and fish finders, was launched and ready. As we began unloading our tackle, Reggie stated, "I should have told you – no need to bring your tackle, I've got everything you need on board." Reggie and son were dressed in uniforms consisting of blue silken jackets and caps advertising Reggie's Guide Service.

This garb was typical of the guides on Hartwell. Undercover, I previously fished with two of them in the company of Agent Charles Bazemore and S.C. Officer Dudley Britt (using aliases of course). I'll call these two guides Bo Black and Bubba Stout. During both trips we caught over limits at the suggestion of and with our guides help. The catches were turned over to S.C. undercover officers who photographed and sold the fish to "knowing" buyers or froze the fish to hold as evidence.

At 8:00 a.m. sharp, we left the dock – our guided fishing trip began.

Due to intelligence received over a considerable length of time, I was told by S.C. Officer J.C. Sims, "McFarland is the number one target of Operation Wild. He's dealing in all kinds of protected wildlife – deer, fish, ducks, doves, furs – you name it, he'll buy and sell it." I was "privileged" to be the operative selected to work McFarland.

During our day of fishing, we caught fifteen hybrid stripers, two large mouth bass and several nice sized bream (bluegills, up North). Near the end of our trip ending at 5:00 p.m., Delahoyd and I engaged in a pre-arranged discussion after letting it be known I was a Raleigh based seafood wholesaler. Bill posed as a Raleigh seafood retailer.

"What's going on, John (my alias) – why can't you get us any stripers?" Bill asked.

"Ask me that! You know the state and feds just finished a big undercover case on stripers in North Carolina. I was scared they'd get you and me but they didn't. I'm having to rely on coastal caught, legal stripers; they're expensive and hard to come by," I replied.

"How about these hybrids like we're catching here. Can you get me some?" Bill asked.

"Same deal – just as hard to get, but I'll see you get your share when and if I get any," I answered. That was our total "staged" conversation.

McFarland heard it all with no response. "Gentlemen, I'll filet your fish," Reggie stated as he readied a 12 volt electric filleting knife.

"Filet the bass and bream – just gut and scale the hybrids if you will Reggie," I requested.

"You got it," he replied. McFarland iced our cleaned fish down, packing them in a styrofoam cooler he taped shut. We paid him his guide fee, gave him the customary tip, and exchanged amenities stating we enjoyed our trip and would engage his service again. That evening we enjoyed a bass, bream, french fries and beer dinner in camp.

On the morning of the 3rd we broke camp, returned the camper to the storage facility and headed for Westside Seafoods in Charlotte after photographing our hybrid catch. There, we entered the store and asked for Les. He soon appeared. "Less, our fishing trip at Hartwell with Reggie McFarland was great. You're right, he's probably the best guide on Hartwell. We've got more hybrids than we need. Thought we'd check and see if you could use them," I told Les.

"Bring them in – are they dressed?" he asked.

"Reggie gutted and scaled them yesterday evening. They've been on ice since," I answered. We fetched our cooler of hybrids; Les inspected them and stated, "I'll give you a buck and a quarter a pound,"

"You just bought them. We're a little uncomfortable with this. We're sure it's illegal. We've been reading about an undercover case the state and federal wildlife people just finished," I told les.

"Don't worry about it. They didn't get to Charlotte with their undercover case – like I told you before, they're perch," Les stated. He paid us by check (later copied as evidence) for the hybrids and we left. Shame on you Lester!

En route home to Raleigh, Bill commented, "It's hard to believe McFarland is up to his neck in illegal wildlife dealing; he's sure a nice guy." "That he is Bill, time will tell how good a nice guy he is," I responded.

On July 11th at 9:30 p.m. my undercover phone rang – it was Reggie McFarland. The conversation was taped. "John, I-I-I know where I can put you onto some fish," he stated.

(Playing dumb) "Oh good, have you found a new place on the lake where they're biting? If so, book us and we'll be down," I responded.

"These ain't the catchin' kind, John – these are the buyin' kind – heard you and your partner talking on the boat about needin' some stripers or hybrids maybe – didn't want to say nuthin' then on account of the boy (his son)

– are you interested?" he asked.

"Of course I'm interested, I'm in the business -- it ain't been too good as far as stripers or hybrids are concerned. Do you sell them?" I asked.

"About all you'd want," he answered.

"Okay Hoss, it's time to get serious. Dealing in these game fish is illegal as xo#x. I'm a little leery after what's happened up here in North Carolina," I told Reggie.

"You mean that undercover thing the feds pulled off?" he asked.

"Right, they got a lot of my competitors. Since then we don't know who to deal with, if you know what I mean," I stated.

"Look John, I've been a guide on Hartwell a good while. I've been dealin' a lot longer, ain't never been caught, ain't gonna get caught," McFarland bragged.

"Dealin', what do you mean – dealin'?" I asked.

"Man, I can get you anything you want – deer, ducks, doves, rabbits, alligator meat, coons, possums, squirrels, ground hogs, you name it, I can get it for you," he replied.

"You buyin' and sellin' all this stuff?" I asked.

"Right," he answered.

"Ducks, you mean wild ducks?" I asked.

"Yeah, wood ducks and mallards mostly. These swamps around here are loaded with them. These boys down here shellac the xo#x out of them. I buy what they don't want. No trouble sellin' any of this stuff. There's a lot of folks that like game and fish to eat," he answered.

"Whew! Guess you are in the business," I responded.

"Have been for a long time, John. I've got to do somethin' to pay for these boats, gas and all," he stated.

"Okay Reggie, I'll buy your fish. When will you have some?" I asked.

"In a couple of days – what are you payin'?" he asked.

"Market price – right now about a buck and a half to two bucks a pound. We'll take them in the round. They've got to be fresh and iced; we'll scale and gut here," I answered Reggie.

"Okay, we'll do business! I'll call you in a couple days. A small load – you pick up here at my home. A big load I can afford to meet you somewhere not too far away," he stated.

"Okay, good enough. Let me hear from you," I told him.

"Good enough John," he stated.

"Oh, by the way, are you interested in buyin' some deer meat?" I asked.

"Always – I can always sell venison," he answered.

"What are you payin' for venison?" I asked.

"Always pay a dollar a pound, processed or not," he replied.

"Okay, got a friend here in North Carolina who kills quite a few in season or out. He's a meat cutter -- processes them himself – does a nice job.

He's always tryin' to sell the meat," I told Reggie.

"I'll buy his venison if he'll take my price," he stated.

"I'll tell him I've got a buyer and how much you'll pay. We'll see what works out," I stated.

"Good nuf John, I'll be in touch," Reggie stated concluding our taped conversation.

The following day I met with Assistant U.S. Attorney, Bill Delahoyd, concerning an Eastern District case. I played the McFarland tape for him.

"Well, I guess our nice guy turned out to be a bad boy – a really bad boy. Looks like South Carolina's intelligence turned out to be right. You guys know your targets, don't you?" Delahoyd commented.

"We don't go after them if they're clean – just the dirty ones," I replied.

Two days later, at 7:00 a.m., my undercover phone rang – it was McFarland. "I've got twenty-one nice stripers; when can you pick them up?" McFarland asked.

"So happens I was just headed out the door for Charlotte. I'll be driving a tan 1983 Chevrolet pickup. I'll have scales, ice and cooler on board. I won't use our regular refrigerated truck – it's got advertising on the side. We don't need to do any advertising now, do we?" I asked.

"We sure don't," Reggie replied.

"Give me directions to your house," I inquired.

Following McFarland's instructions, I arrived at his home in a community near Lake Hartwell. My arrival found Reggie in a spry and cheerful mood. He brought me a cup of coffee and proceeded to tell me a lewd joke. With faked laughter I joined Reggie laughing over his disgusting joke. Amusement concluded, he stated, "The fish are in the garage, follow me." I inspected twenty-one nice, big and plump, hybrid stripers. They were iced down in a large sea-going cooler. "Those are real nice, Reggie. Market price today is a buck fifty a pound, okay?" I asked.

"Can't do any better?" Reggie asked.

"Not and haul them all the way to Raleigh," I answered.

"Okay, you've got a deal," Reggie responded. We weighed the fish, I paid him wholesale market price and repacked the hybrids in my coolers. As I departed, McFarland stated, "I'll call you soon with some more fish and don't forget about that deer deal – I can always use good venison."

En route to Raleigh, I met South Carolina Undercover Officers, J.C. Sims and Larry McClain. There the McFarland fish buy was photographed and turned over to the state officers. They in turn sold the fish to a "knowing" buyer; another Operation Wild target.

This same scenario would be repeated many times hence with McFarland bought fish. On two of these occasions, I sold McFarland's fish to two other targets of the investigation. Both transactions were sound recorded on video tape (I wore a body wire) by South Carolina Undercover Officers Sims, McClain, and/or Tommy Norris. Ultimately, I introduced Agent Charles Bazemore (alias "Chuckie", my ex-con nephew) into the scene. Uncle employed "Chuckie" drove my fish truck. He bought, transported, and sold illegal fish and other wildlife to Operation Wild targets. Bazemore was one of the best after-the-fact overt investigators I've ever worked with or encountered. His reports were exemplary. He once informed me he didn't like to do undercover work. For an agent who didn't like to do undercover work, he was a superb covert operative. Truth be known, I think "Chuckie" actually enjoyed it.

The Columbia Office of South Carolina Fish and Game authorized the purchase of a professionally made surveillance van from a company in Maryland. The van's purpose was for undercover work. It would be utilized primarily by their undercover team, who was authorized to go to Maryland and make the purchase direct from the manufacturer.

After Sims and McClain went to Maryland, toured the plant and observed the manufacturing process resulting in a state of the art surveillance vehicle, they left the plant without making the authorized purchase. "We can make one at one-third the cost," J.C. Sims advised his Chief, Bill Chastain, and they did!

Beginning with a new van, they installed a 360 degree rotating video camera. It was equipped with sound tract recording capability that picked up body wire conversations. Its lens peered through a typical, slightly opened, camper vent centered in the van's roof. It was undetectable – it captured all the action. Its lens had the zoom capability; hence, it would zoom in on many money exchanges during undercover buys and sales. Utilizing power trim assemblies from surplused (replaced) patrol boats, they stabilized the van's suspension. As J.C. put it, "You can trim that baby up and square dance inside – she won't move or wobble." A 12 volt air conditioning system was devised utilizing aluminum tubing, dry ice and a 12 volt fan. The camera operator sat in rotating, comfortably padded camper sized chair that was secured to the van floor. A second operative could be comfortably seated. Last but not least, it was quipped with a toilet. During years hence many state and federal operatives, along with the bad guys, would star in many J.C. Sims film productions.

Shortly thereafter, I delivered and sold three hundred and ninety five pounds of processed venison covertly purchased from a North Carolina violator by Agent Tom Bennett. The packaged venison had the words "Deer – unlawful to buy or sell" stamped in red ink on each package. The shipment was, of course, photographed before delivery. At the conclusion of this transaction, wearing a concealed body wire, I engaged Reggie in conversation concerning his illegal wildlife trafficking. Suddenly, Reggie stated, "I want to show you something, John. It will give you some idea of what I have to put up with." He went inside his house and returned shortly carrying a ledger. Opening the ledger, he showed me pages of handwritten entries recording dates, names, species of wildlife, weights and cash amounts. "These are dudes who owe me money," he stated.

"What are you doing, selling wild game and fish on credit?" I asked.

"What's a feller to do – I know these dudes and I give them credit out of the goodness of my heart. Then, with some of them – like these – I have a xo#x of a time collecting what they owe me. Sad, ain't it?" he complained.

"Sometimes it just don't pay to be a good guy, does it Reggie?" I commented. "Do you keep records on those who do pay you?" I asked.

"Sure do John, they're in the house," Reggie replied. With that earful, I exchanged amenities with Reggie and left. Later, I met with South Carolina Officer J.C. Sims and briefed him on the contact.

Later, in May of 1986 on "raid day", at the time of Reggie's arrest, a search warrant for records was also executed. Reggie's business records showing cash purchases and sales, and the ledger he showed me, was seized. These records led to many arrests.

Ultimately, covert purchases and sales of all the wildlife species, South Carolina intelligence indicated Reggie McFarland was trafficking in, took place. The media would later hail him as the "focal point" in upstate South Carolina of Operation Wild. He would pay $10,000 in fines for three of ten plea bargained counts of the federal Lacey Act plus a one year suspended prison term and five years probation. It would cost him $30,000 in additional state and federal fines, plus attorney fees. He forfeited his truck and boat and as part of a plea bargain agreement. He turned state's witness on many other violators with whom he had conducted illegal wildlife transactions. He lost his hunting and fishing rights for five years. What a price to pay!

Before, during, and after my small part in Operation Wild, South Carolina Undercover Officers J.C. Sims, Larry McClain, Tommy Norris, Dudley Britt, Tommy Haile, Ivan Holden, Billy Holmes along with Federal Agents George Hines, Pat McIntosh, and Charles Bazemore were "cutting a swath" from the coast to Santee-Cooper to the Piedmont and mountains of South Carolina. They covertly worked and nailed seventy violators illegally commercializing in South Carolina wildlife. All accomplished in one year and two months!

On May 14th and 15th, 1986, a pre-raid day briefing was held at the South Carolina Wildlife and Marine Resources Department's (SCWMRD) Styx Compound near Columbia. South Carolina Undercover Team Chief, J.C. Sims, and other team members, along with USFWS Case Agent, George Hines, briefed each of the many raid teams. Each team consisted of state and federal officers. The teams were briefed on the subject or subjects they were to arrest for violations of the Lacey Act, the Migratory Bird Treaty Act, the Endangered Species Act and many state wildlife laws. They were given a "raid team packet" containing directions to and photos of their subject's homes, subject descriptions as well as arrest and search warrants to be executed. Instruction was given regarding "a call in following arrest" plan to be implemented on raid day, the 16th. The raid teams departed after the briefing to their various state wide destinations.

During the pre-dawn hours of May 16th, "Raid day – Operation Wild" began. That afternoon a press conference was held. It was attended by NBC,

CBS, ABC, state and local news media.

Following are the words of Bill Chastain, Director of Law Enforcement and Boating, SCWMRD, as he addressed the media:

"State warrants and federal indictments, which involve 300 counts of violations of state and federal wildlife conversation laws, are being served, beginning this morning, on 70 individuals all across South Carolina. Several teams of state wildlife officers, federal agents and other law enforcement officers will make most of the arrests today and will report confirmation.

This investigation into the illegal commercialization of South Carolina's wildlife is continuing and we believe many more arrests will be made as a result of these initial apprehensions. Arrests are being made in each of the state's nine wildlife law enforcement districts.

In March 1985 the state wildlife department entered into an agreement with the Law Enforcement Division of the U.S. Fish and Wildlife Service to investigate the illegal commercialization of South Carolina's wildlife. Through information gathered by our conservation officers and tips to the Operation Game Thief Hotline, we concluded unlawful commercial harvest, sale and resale of game and fish were on the increase.

About two years ago we placed a priority on setting up an undercover investigative unit to deal with the more serious conservation law violators, who were difficult to approach through usual methods.

The steps being taken today should drastically curtail the illegal commercialization of wildlife in South Carolina. Our recent covert investigation yielded 14,000 pounds of deer meat, more than 700 migratory game birds, 13,000 pounds of game fish and 600 furs, purchased from illegal poachers and dealers.

We have no estimate on what these dealers have sold to others willing to buy black market wildlife and wildlife products. But we know there is a market for wildlife in this state and others. The illegal wildlife we bought or confiscated during our investigation includes a long list of species: white-tailed deer; furbearers, such as fox, raccoon, bobcat, otter, muskrat, mink, beaver and opossum; migratory birds, including doves and ducks; wild rabbits; grass carp, game fish, including striped bass, hybrid bass, largemouth bass, bream and crappie; and endangered species, such as alligators and others.

Through special investigators working undercover we were able to trace illegal South Carolina wildlife goods to nine other states and three foreign countries. It would be difficult to put a dollar value on the unlawful wildlife sales in the state, but it certainly could run into the millions. Our investigators found that deer carcasses were being sold for $25 to $75 and that most game fish were bringing from $1 to $2.50 a pound.

Obviously the illegal taking and marketing of game animals and fish is year-round and does not conform to the seasons set by law. In addition to illegal sales and purchases of wildlife, we found a lot of the wildlife involved was harvested either out of season or by unlawful means. Illegal trapping of game fish or night hunting for deer is nothing unusual for such wildlife law violators.

We appreciate the excellent working relationship the wildlife department has maintained with the Law Enforcement Division of the U.S. Fish and Wildlife Service and the emphasis its agents have given to this investigation. The two agencies complement each other. This investigation had to be a joint effort to be as successful as it was.

The assistance of many South Carolina law enforcement agencies was necessary to bring our investigation to a head and proceed with the resulting arrests. The wildlife department owes a debt of thanks to the South Carolina Law Enforcement Division, the South Carolina Department of Highways and Public Transportation, the South Carolina Alcoholic Beverage Control Commission, the U.S. Marshall's Office, the U.S. Attorney's Office, state solicitors, local magistrates, county sheriff's departments and other agencies.

A great deal of the information used in the investigation was provided by people who called the Operation Game Thief Hotline. We hope the public will continue to call the hotline 1-800-922-5431.

The penalties for commercialization of wildlife should not be taken lightly. The federal Lacey Act, which involves interstate and foreign transportation and commerce of illegal wildlife, carries a maximum penalty of $20,000 and five years imprisonment on each count. It also provides for confiscation of all equipment used. The Migratory Bird Treat Act has a penalty of $500 and 6 months imprisonment.

State laws for buying and selling deer and game fish have penalties which begin at $100 and 30 days and escalate to $1000 and 60 days for repeat offenses. The penalties for buying or selling illegal furs range from $300 to $1000."

Dan Searcy, Special Agent in Charge for the U.S. Fish and Wildlife Service's Regional Law Enforcement Office in Atlanta, Georgia, said, "Only through a cooperative effort of this type can we get to the root of a very serious problem: the illegal commercialization of wildlife. This joint federal-state investigation points out the magnitude of the problem – one that will not be tolerated. Hopefully, this is just the start of an effort whereby we assist the state of South Carolina to identify and investigate commercial operations that impact upon our irreplaceable wildlife resources."

Note: Undeveloped leads developed from raid day record seizures and bad guy interviews led to ninety-five additional arrests and convictions in both state and federal courts.

As the press conference continued, I glanced around the assembly. One by one, I observed the attentive face of each covert operative who participated in Operation Wild. I thought of them as 'The Silent Row'. Each encountered situations where they laid their very life on the line as they brought South Carolina's worst wildlife law violators to justice.

I thought, 'You magnificent soldiers. How proud and privileged I am to work, know, and be a part of you!'

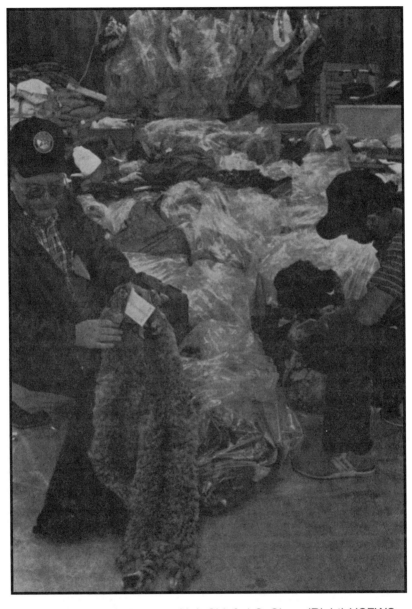

(Left) SCWRD Undercover Unit Chief, J.C. Sims. (Right) USFWS Agent, George Hines tag and inventory illegal wildlife goods, primarily furs, deer and game fish which were covertly bought or confiscated during Operation Wild.

Assistat U.S. Attorney, Bill Delahoyd on covert duty at Lake Hartwell, SC enjoying a camp meal – Operation Wild.

The author "pigging out" at Lake Hartwell fishing camp while on Operation Wild undercover duty.

Three of my favorite people (L to R) SC Undercover Officers,
Larry McClain (Ol Hoss)), Tommy Norris (Little Hoss), and
J.C. Sims (The Grand Foopah).
Background: 78 Lincoln undercover vehicle (drug seizure)

Federal Undercover Agent Charles (Chuckle, the ex-con) Bazemore
fishing with the bad guys at Lake Hartwell, South Carolina Operation
Wild.

30
Operation Smoky

    Two decades of gathering intelligence, one aborted and two failed undercover investigations haunted and preceded this investigation dubbed Operation Smoky. Smoky was yet another covert investigative probe into the illegal hunting and killing of eastern black bears within the 800 square mile Great Smoky Mountain National Park (GSMNP) in North Carolina, Tennessee and surrounding environs. Operation Smoky addressed new and emerging law violations; the illegal commercialization of black bear parts, mainly gall bladders eagerly sought by the Asian black market. Korean buyers, both foreign and domestic, were paying hunters high prices for bear gall bladders; the same being worth thousands more in Korea and other Asian markets. A brisk and historic black market trade, both foreign and domestic, also existed in other bear parts such as teeth, claws, paws, penises, hides and skulls. The estimated value of an eastern black bear on the international market was over $3,000.00; a grizzly, more; a polar bear much more -- $5,000.00. Black market, Smoky Mountain, bear parts, mainly gall bladders, were bought, sold, transported and/or shipped in interstate and foreign commerce in violation of the federal Lacy Act.

    An Asian medicinal text, appropriated and examined during Operation Smoky, listed many wild animal parts, plants and insects that after processing (some ingested raw) were claimed to be cures for certain human ailments. Example: sun dried bear ball bladders were ground into powder, capsuled, and taken internally for heart disease, sexual enhancement, and a host of other maladies. The listings went on and on. These Asian cure beliefs evolved over thousands of years and are deeply held in Asian cultures. This is bad news for North American (and other) wildlife – the market will probably always exist.

During the most recent covert investigative attempt preceding Smoky, a federal operative's cover was blown. He had successfully infiltrated a small close-knit group of southeast Tennessee suspect hunters that included an ex-state game warden. The group was bivouacked in a hunting camp and engaged in a hunt. The ex-game warden arrived on the scene and informed the group the covert operative was an undercover federal agent. Then he confronted the agent. "My brother is an IRS Agent in Louisville, Kentucky. I had him run the VIN number on your vehicle – we both know who it checked out to – you're a federal agent." The agent vehemently denied his accuser's claim. Nevertheless, he grabbed his 30/30 rifle and jacked a cartridge into the chamber. As he backed toward his vehicle, one of the hunters stated, "Dan, I like you and we've had some good times, but we know who you are. If you value your life, the best thing you can do is get." Keeping his gun on the group, the agent got to his vehicle and left the scene.

Its little wonder this attempt failed. Not only had the U.S. Fish & Wildlife Service (USFWS) failed to provide the agent with a "check proof" vehicle – an earlier attempt to set up a cover for an operative in a nearby town also failed. The cover, supposedly set up by a federal agency (other than the USFWS), involved a plan whereby the operative was to go to work at a local business establishment frequented by the bad buys and thus gain contact with and exposure to them. Before the operative ever arrived to go to work, one of the bad guys entered the business establishment and asked, "When's the federal agent coming to work?" How's that for security? Two federal agencies were involved in establishing the operatives cover. None of the planners had ever worked as a covert operative or set up an operative's cover. Too many people knew what was going on. It didn't take long for the whole plan to leak in the small mountain community – stupid!

The (GSMNP), Tennessee Wildlife Resources Agency (TWRA), North Carolina Wildlife Resources Commission (NCWRC), and the U.S. Fish and Wildlife Services' Raleigh and Nashville Offices law enforcement files reeked with documented complaints concerning the violations mentioned. Complaints received from reliable and confidential informants, made to uniformed law enforcement (LE) officers of each agency, from the general public and agency "hotlines". The problem reached acute and serious status. Something had to be done. Each agency knew the answer – a major cooperative undercover investigation; this time done right!

A "meeting of the minds" and planning session was held at a GSMNP facility, Gatlinburg, Tennessee on September 23, 1985. In attendance were Gene Abernathy (Chief of undercover investigations NCWRC); Bob Harmon (LE Chief TWRA); John Cook (Supt. GSMNP); J. D. Moore, Mike Zetts, Captain Ben Wade (NCWRC); Dan Searcy (Special Agent in Charge, Atlanta Region 4); Agents Tom Bennett, Dave Cartwright, Tom Wharton, and yours truly (USFWS). There, bad guy intelligence and identities were shared and targeted.

Loose-knit groups who hunted together along with their geographical areas of operation were recognized. An agent was assigned to each. It was each agent's responsibility to establish his own foolproof undetectable cover. A cover, appropriate to and for his assigned "theater of operations" (TOO).

Park Service Ranger/Biologist Bill Cook was assigned to head the investigation's Repository located at the GSMNP's headquarters. Bill was recognized as one of the nation's foremost authorities on the eastern black bear. All covert bear part buys made by the operatives were brought to Ranger Cook. His responsibilities included:

1. Preservation of all evidence (bear parts) purchased to include cold storage and/or freezing.

2. Positively (and legally) identify and photograph each evidence item purchased and provide the operative with an official identification report.

3. Supply professionally identified bear parts destined for sale by operatives to investigation targets.

4. Maintain the chain-of-custody (a legality that requires recording each occasion, and why, an evidentiary item changes hands).

During the post-raid litigation phase of Smoky, he would qualify as an "expert witness" many times.

N.C. Wildlife Officer Mike Zetts was designated as the official Operation Smoky bookkeeper. He computerized the bookkeeping system. He documented POI&E (purchase of information and evidence) funds, both incoming and outgoing on monthly statements. By written agreement, POI&E funding was shared equally by the participating agencies. His records passed even the most exacting examinations. His bookkeeping system followed the guidelines set by the USFWS. Mike was an electronic whiz. He wired the main vehicle used in the "GSMNP and environs theater of operations" – a 4x4 GMC pickup truck (Operation Rock forfeiture). Thanks to Mike's handiwork, the operative totally undetected, could activate a tape recorder concealed within the truck.

All the federal agents in attendance were seasoned and experienced covert operatives. They appreciated the importance of and knew how to set up foolproof undetectable covers. Thus, each "theater of operation" (TOO) agent established his own cover. His cover was unknown even to those in attendance at the Gatlinburg Conference. His cover was revealed only to other seasoned and trained operatives he may have to incorporate as his investigation progressed. Agent Cartwright had already established a cover. Agents Bennett and Wharton had covers in the mill. Basically,Agent Bennett handled the Fontana TOO. Agent Cartwright – the GSMNP and environs TOO, incorporating yours truly – Me, the Southern TOO. Not one operative's cover was blown during Smoky, although it came dangerously close to happening.

Given the cultural nature of our targeted outlaws (mountain folk), Operation Smoky would prove to be our most time consuming, many faceted, complicated and dangerous undercover investigation.

GSMNP and Environs Theater of Operations

At the first of the second week in January, 1986, I left my office in

Raleigh and went to Newland, North Carolina. Newland is a quaint mountain village in Avery County near the Tennessee border, at the edge of the Pisgah National Forest and northeast of the GSMNP. It's situated in the heart of some of North Carolina's best ski and bear hunting country.

I took lodging at a graciously hosted bed and breakfast. My mission was to make covert contact with a chap I'll call Herb. Herb was identified at the Gatlinburg Conference as a target of Operation Smoky. NCWRC intelligence indicated Herb was a bear, bobcat, and coon hunter (in and out of season). A houndsman with an excellent pack of hounds and a bear gall bladder (and other bear parts) buyer and seller.

I arose early after an excellent night's rest. From downstairs I could whiff the odor of fresh brewed coffee. I enjoyed an early morning cup of coffee with my lady host, but declined breakfast. I had other plans for breakfast! I donned my coon hunting garb, stepped outside and inhaled some of Avery County's fresh sweet Smoky Mountain air; warmed up my '83 Chevrolet pickup coon hunting rig (complete with dog crate in the bed) and headed downtown. I drove into a restaurant parking lot where several pickup trucks, some recognizable as coon and bear hunting rigs, were parked. Rigs, some of which had indoor/outdoor carpet glued to the top of the engine hood with big screw eyes bolted in the center for tethering a hound; otherwise known as a "rig or strike" dog. This particular restaurant was identified as "one of the best places in the county to make contact with bear hunters," by Doren Robbins, the State Wildlife officer assigned to Avery County. My target, Herb, lived near Newland.

I had a description of Herb's rig and license plate number. I didn't see it in the parking lot; a good thing as I didn't want to make contact with Herb yet. I wanted one or more individuals he knew to send me to him. Past experience taught me to never make contact with a target "out of the blue". A complete stranger appearing suddenly in his life usually arouses suspicion, especially among mountain folk. I needed to be able to use the names of hunting friends or acquaintances to truthfully claim he/she "suggested I contact you."

Entering the restaurant, I purposely took a seat at a table with three additional empty chairs around it. Soon a little green eyed waitress asked, "What're you havin' this mornin' podner?" "A short stack, a side of sausage, coffee and water, sweetie," I ordered.

"You got it"! she replied and shortly returned with my coffee and water. I waited a few seconds, looking around sizing up the crowd. I stood up and tapped on my water glass with my spoon. "Any bear or coon hunters in here?" I yelled above the early morning hub-bub.

"Yea," "You bet," "Bout everyone in here," "You're in coon dog country, Hoss," I heard in response from four separate hunters.

"They call me Buck. I lost or someone stole my coon dog while I was huntin'," I hollered. I continued, "Boys, bring your plates and come join me. I need your help – your breakfast is on me," I announced. As the four arose to come to my table the little waitress stated, "I'll get your plates, ya'all get over there and help that man out." Three seated themselves, one sat at a nearby counter.

"Let's hear what you've got to say," one stated. "When did he come up missin'?" another asked. "Where's you huntin'?" a third asked. "Have a trackin' collar on your dog?" the fourth asked as I distributed a black and white photocopy of "ol Nap" the best coon dog I ever owned. He had passed away twenty-five years earlier. In the upper left hand corner of Nap's photo it read, Call: Uncle "Buck" at (covert phone number) or nephew, Dave at (covert phone number). At the bottom of the photo it read, $1000.00 reward – no questions asked.

"My nephew and I was huntin' up on (a location near Herb's home) ridge night before last. Ol Nap had locked down -- treed solid, every breath, and we headed to him. We were pickin' him up on the trackin' collar. I'd say he was on the other side of the ridge (near the road Herb lives on). Then he stopped treein', the trackin' signal went dead – been huntin' the dog ever since," I told the four.

"Where's your nephew?" one asked as all four studied Nap's photo.

"Tennessee – had to go to work," I replied.

"What breed is that dog?" another asked.

"His daddy was a registered English – mama was a quarter bull. He's a grade dog – a potlicker," I answered.

"Got a calico ear, ain't he?" one commented.

"Yeah," I responded.

"What color is he?" one asked.

"Tan and white," I answered.

"Any tics?" one asked.

"None," I answered.

"Sure got a nice big ol chuckle tree head, ain't he?" one commented.

"Yeah, got a good clear eye too," another responded.

"Anything kind of unusual about the dog that a feller might be on the lookout for – did ya tattoo him in the ears by any chance?" my first inquisitor asked.

I was getting the third degree and I knew it. They were talking houndsman language and I knew they wanted to see my reaction. "Yeah, matter of fact there is. Ya'all ever seen and ol hound with a close-quartered hind end – you know, one that looks like his hind legs never quite caught up with his front end – growin' that is?" I asked.

"Yeah, you're talkin' bout that ol houny look when he's walkin' or runnin' in front of you," one stated.

"Yeah, yeah – they'll kinda run a little side ways," I responded.

"Yeah, my uncle used to have the old timey saddle backed black and tans. When they'd get bout four or five, they'd get that ol houny look in their rear ends," another commented.

"He ain't got no tattoos – sure wish he did," I stated. "Speakin of those ol saddle back black and tans – my grandpa up in Ohio had 'em years ago. Darn good hounds. Folks used to call them combination hounds. You could hunt rabbits and birds with them in the day time and fur at night. To begin with, pap got his beginin' brood stock saddle backs down near Greenup, Kentucky," (an old coon hunter myth, the old time saddle backs always came from Greenup) I told the group.

"By golly you know your hounds, Buck. Most folks now-a-days never heard of the ol saddle backs. Greenup – that's where the blood my uncle had came from," the saddle back tale teller stated.

"Yeah, they seemed to have died out – ain't seen one in years – darn shame, they's good ones," another stated.

"You from Ohio, Buck?" one asked.

"Sure am – raised there – been gone awhile," I answered.

"Ever go to the Grand National?" one asked.

"You mean the Grand National Leafy Oak at Kenton, Ohio? The biggest coon hound day trial, bench show, water race, and night trial event in the U.S. over Labor Day. I try to go every year. The Pfieffer family who started the Leafy Oak back in 1929 are some of my distant kin. When I was a kid, I remember the Leafy Oak got pretty bad – whores, gamblin' and such – dirty. I remember going to the big cement block outhouse they had when I was about thirteen – you peed in a trough. A drunk was settin' on a stool with his head layin' in the pee trough down near where it drained. Everyone was peein' up-trough from the drunk with the pee a filterin' through his hair and under his right cheek. I took pity on the poor feller and peed on the floor. I went outside and tried to get someone to help the poor ol drunk but no one would pay any attention to me. I'll never forget that," I told my listeners who didn't seem to want to finish their breakfast.

"That's pretty bad, Buck," one commented.

I continued, "A little later on, Mr. Eddie Ross, who owned the old time Mountain Music magazine in Columbus, bought the rights to and owned the property at the Grand National Leafy Oak. He cleaned the Leafy Oak up – no more whores, drinkin', gamblin' or peein' on drunks. He fenced the whole property and put up two big fancy entrance gates near Trader's Row. On the opening day of the big Labor Day event, the crowd would gather at the gates all excited, waitin' for the Leafy Oak to begin. The purdiest country music you ever heard would come over a PA system. A deep voiced announcer would say, "Ladies and Gentlemen, welcome to the twentieth (or whatever anniversary year it was) Grand National Leafy Oak!" Then the gates would slowly open. There came Eddie Ross down the midway. He'd be dressed in a light blue tailored western cut suit, wearing a big white ten gallon cowboy hat and high top white leather cowboy boots. Two of the purdiest big English-Bluetick hounds you ever saw would be on gold leashes in front of him. Those hounds wore diamond studded collars! The crowd went through those big fancy gates, whoopin and hollerin. All that didn't happen but a few years – Mr. Ross sold the rights to the Leafy Oak. Those were the best days of the

Grand National Leafy Oak. I was just a dirt poor kid then, dreamin' of some day ownin' my own coon dog. A good one like ol Nap. Yeah, those were the days . . . . . (my voice trailed off as though lost in the past).

"Gentlemen! (snapping to) I appreciate your time. Help me out if you can. Are there any known dog thieves around that you can tell me about?" I asked.

"Buck, I don't know of anyone in Avery County who would steal or shoot another man's huntin' dog. Anyone around these parts who would do such a thing wouldn't stay alive very long and everyone in Avery County, includin' the law, knows it," one of my breakfast guests stated. The other three agreed. "You know Buck, the way you describe your hunt, your dog all of a sudden stops treein' and loosin' that trackin' signal, it sure looks like someone took him. Someone may have come near him with a female in heat or sumpthin," one stated and asked, "Was he bad to go to strangers?"

"Never, that's the only way he'd leave a tree – if a stranger came near him, he'd come to me," I answered.

Following a rather lengthy discussion of the various hound breeds, I asked, "Do you know of any houndsmen who live out near where ol Nap, me and my nephew was huntin?"

"Well, there's Herbie Thompson – he lives out that way. I guess Herb is about the only one. You might want to see Herb; he'll help you if he can. Come to think of it, I'd sure recommend you see ol Herb," one stated as the other three agreed. They gave me directions to Herb's home – BINGO!

"Boys, I'll sure enough get in touch with Herb. Let me have your names – I'll tell Herb you'all recommended I contact him," I told the four. With that request, they gave me their names as I jotted them down on a restaurant napkin. That evening I knocked on Herb Thompson's door, a young lady opened the door. "Hello ma'm, I'm looking for Mr. Herb Thompson. I've got a coon hound missing and several hunters I met in Newland this morning suggested I contact Mr. Thompson for a little help," I told her.

"He's out back feeding his dogs. Just go back of the house and look up on the hill; you'll see him," she stated.

I soon introduced myself to a very amiable Herb Thompson. As the hounds quieted while eating, I told Herb the same story I told the hunters at the restaurant in Newland. I named the hunters and told Herb, "They all said you'd help me out if you could."

"I sure will if I can, Buck," Herb responded as he studied the same photocopy of Nap I gave to each of the group in Newland.

"Haven't seen or heard anything about your hound. Have you got many of these pictures?" he asked.

"Sure have," I answered.

"Leave me a few – I'll post them here and there on telephone poles – whatever – suggest you do the same. Put some in the shops in Newland," Herb advised.

"I'll do that," I responded.

329

"Where'd you say ya'lls huntin'?" Herb asked.

"If you've got a few minutes we'll take a ride and I'll show you. It's daylight now but I think I can show you about where ol Nap was treed," I stated. Herb said he had the time.

As we rode, I invoked conversation concerning coon, bobcat and bear, hounds and hunting all three species. After considerable discussion, I stated, "I hear the Koreans are going through this country buying bear gall bladders from the bear hunters."

"Yeah Buck, they do come around the bear huntin' camps and such wantin' to buy galls," Herb stated.

"They pay pretty good?" I asked.

"Yeah, but we can do better by takin' them to a Korean Doctor down in Sylva," he answered.

"Yeah, I've heard there was a Doctor down there buyin' galls. He's a little competition for us, or I should say my nephew – the boy that was huntin' with me when ol Nap came up missin'. We've got a little import-export business in Nashville. My nephew runs it. He just started buyin' a few galls for a Korean business client of ours – sort of a favor thing," I stated.

"Your nephew buyin' bear galls for a Korean?" Herb asked.

"Yeah, the Korean told him to be careful because it's illegal. You ever hear about it being illegal?" I asked.

"Yeah, it's sure-nuf illegal. You can't sell any part of a bear. The Koreans tell us the same thing. Be careful, they harp about that a lot," Herb stated.

"My nephew has been able to buy a few now and then when he's been over here in North Carolina huntin' with me. You'all might want to keep Dave in mind – he'll meet you somewhere near where you live and buy your galls – could save you a trip to Sylva. I'm sure he can meet the Doctor's price," I told Herb.

"Can you have him give me a call?" Herb asked.

"Well, yeah, I can have him call you – do you have some galls on hand now?" I asked.

"Yeah, a few, some are from bears I've killed and some are ones I've bought from a few bear hunters around here," he answered.

"You'all kill all those bear around here? – didn't suppose there were many," I asked.

"Oh, we got bear – we also kill a few up north," Herb stated.

"Okay, I'm sure Dave will give you a call – what's the Korean Doctor's name? I've heard it but can't recall – just curious to see if we're talkin' about the same guy," I asked.

"Dr. Han," Herb replied.

"Yeah, that's it. Dr. Han," (making a mental note) I responded. We returned to Herb's residence, exchange amenities and I departed. Mission accomplished.

Recorded phone conversations ensued between Herb and Dave Sloan

330

(Agent Dave Cartwright) and Herb and Uncle Buck (me). During these conversations it was firmly established Herb knew it was illegal to buy and sell bear parts. He spoke of selling bear gall bladders to "a man from Singapore" many times in the past. He indicated he would sell galls in the future. On January 16, 1986, Agents Cartwright, Maureen Mathews (posing as Sloan's wife) and yours truly met with Herb at Pineola, North Carolina. Agents Cartwright and Matthews purchased six dried bear gall bladders for the sum of $450.00. The entire transaction was video-sound recorded from their surveillance van by South Carolina Wildlife Officers Brian Wilson and J.C. Sims. During this transaction, Herb again told of the "man from Singapore" who visited the local bear hunters in April each year and bought their bear galls. Herb indicated an interest in knowingly illegally selling bear claws and hides stating he usually got $100.00 for a hide with head attached. He identified a relatively nearby fur and hide dealer who bought bear galls but didn't pay nearly as well as the "man from Singapore". He stated he would phone Agent Cartwright when he had more bear galls to sell, indicating he would sell his and those he bought from other hunters.

Subsequent investigation showed "the man from Singapore" and "Dr. Han" to be one and the same, a practicing Gynecologist in Sylva. In July, 1986 Agent Charles (alias "Chuck") Bazemore and yours truly, wearing a body wire, sold the Doctor four bear galls for the sum of $200.00. The entire transaction was video-sound recorded by NCWRC Officer, J.D. Moore from our now, newly constructed surveillance vehicle – a bed camper equipped (with surveillance equipment therein) Ford pickup truck.

During this and two subsequent transactions, along with pre-transaction taped phone conversations, the Doctor's predisposition to knowingly violate state laws and the Lacey Act was firmly established.

During the final transaction, TWRA undercover Officer Lee Luening and I sold Dr. Han six bear galls. From there, Leuning and I traveled to a flea market just outside the Cherokee Indian Reservation where we sold a quantity of bear claws to a many times reported and targeted vendor in bear parts. This was a scheduled transaction preceded by several taped conversations between the vendor and "Buck" during which the vendor's predisposition to knowing and willfully violate both N.C. Wildlife law and the Lacey Act was firmly established. The episodes were filmed from our surveillance vehicle by Mark Swartz Productions of California. This and other Operation Smoky transactions appeared in the television documentary "Greed, Guns, and Wildlife" narrated by film actor Richard Chamberlain. The film's production was contracted by the Turner Network in conjunction with the National Audubon Society. It is a graphic portrayal of the systemic destruction of our national and international wildlife resource through exploiting -- illegal commercialization. The film has aired on national television several times.

"Ya know Buck, some of the boys in the Del Rio Club are thinkin' your nephew – that Sloan feller who's been buyin' galls and whatever, might be an undercover Game Warden or Drug Agent," Lee McGill (I'll call him) abruptly told me as we drove to a nearby Radio Shack to get parts for McGill's hound telemetry collar-tracking system. Parts he hoped would enable his tracking system receive the frequency used by TN State University and GSMNP Biologists on telemetry collared bears within the GSMNP. Collars that aided the Biologists in their biological studies of the animal.

Danny Russo, the investigations number one target, bragged (tape recorded) about accidentally discovering the multi-channeled dog tracking telemetry system he used, could pick up the bear collar frequencies. To quote Russo, "We picked up the frequencies on four bears them Park Rangers collared. We tracked and killed all four." Russo uttered his gruesome claim as we (Dave Sloan and Uncle Buck, body wired) attended a live bear fight at Cowpens, South Carolina with Russo and many Operation Smoky targets. During these events, hunters pay to let their hounds fight a live adult bear that is tethered to a heavy rope The hounds are "packed" to fight the bear in groups of four to eight. Some are competition events judged as "the best fightin' dog" with trophies and/or prize money awarded. I video-taped the footage used in the TV documentary, "Greed, Guns & Wildlife" at the Cowpens event.

What xo#xo did you just say?" I asked McGill in a very loud tone of voice. His proclamation was sheer dynamite – I knew it was time for the mad act. McGill repeated his accusation. Getting louder, "Do you mind telling me where this leaves me – his uncle – how in the xo#xo could my nephew be an undercover cop and me not know it? What's he doing, workin' me, his own uncle? Maybe I'm one too—ever think of that." I asked, now yelling at McGill.

"Take it easy Buck -- take it easy! I shore didn't mean to make you so mad! The boys don't think you're a undercover agent – they think you're too old," McGill responded.

"There's one (cuss words) thing about it. There's no way Dave could be an undercover cop and me not be one too. If this is true, then with all the outlawing ya'all and us has been up to, why ain't ya'all been arrested? You and the Del Rio boys, ever think of that?" I asked my now apologetic target. I continued, "Where and when did all this get started?"

"A Game Warden ran his mouth at a truck stop up on I-40. A couple of the Del Rio boys heard him," McGill answered and continued. "He made some statements sayin' these bear poachin' hunters around here are gonna be in for a surprise of their lives – they're all gonna be arrested in a little while. As far as the Del Rio boys are concerned, this meant an undercover case was goin' on."

"What do you think?" I asked.

"I personally trust ya'all, Buck. Shoot Buck, I've got to trust ya'all. I've been caught (He had forty-seven prior wildlife arrests by Park Rangers, TN & NC State Wildlife Officers) so many times, my heart just couldn't take gettin' caught agin."

"Well, there's this much about it, Lee, if Dave or both of us are undercover cops, you and your compatriots had better get to the foot of the cross

– there's enough on all of you to put ya'all away for a long time," I told my outlaw.

"Ain't it the truth Buck!" McGill responded.

"Well, this does it for us. I'm gonna call Dave and tell him to pick up our hounds from Russo. We're out'a here. It's sure a shame – we came over here, got acquainted with ya'all, bought two of the best bear hounds in the country that we board with Russo – dogs ya'all are free to use even when we're not here. We enjoyed huntin' with ya'all, you might say it was a little R & R for us – bein' able to come to these beautiful mountains and hunt with ya'all – ya know what I mean? Gettin' away from our business cares and worries – lettin' our hair down a little. Sure nothin' wrong with that. I guess I met your brother first, tryin' to find my ol coon dog, Nap, remember that? But it's time to channel our huntin' activities elsewhere. We're sure not gonna associate with folks who don't trust us. Huh-uh, we're not gonna put up with that," I told McGill.

"Now Buck, don't be that way. I'll tell you what I'm gonna do. I'm gonna tell them Del Rio boys that I trust ya'all. I'm gonna tell them I put you through the test and you passed it. I'm gonna tell them I don't believe for one minute Dave is an undercover Game Warden or Drug Agent. Ya know Buck, a lot of the Del Rio boys do (do drugs). They can be dangerous when they're doin' while they's on a hunt. One asked Dave why he didn't do. Dave grabbed him by the back of his neck and shoved his face into the door mirror on his truck. He said Dave told him, 'Here, look at yourself – that's why I don't do. My Uncle Buck would have me killed if I did drugs. I may supply now and then but I don't do.' He sure hurt that boy's neck – he must have a strong grip," McGill informed me and continued. "No need in you and Dave pullin' stakes. If I think I haven't convinced the Del Rio boys, you'll hear from me. I'll let you know in a minute if I think Dave or you are in danger," McGill assured.

"Okay Lee, sorry I blew up. I guess we can keep on huntin' with you and your brothers anyway, for the time being that is. Dave's right, if I caught him doing drugs – ya know, I can't beat the tar out of him; he's too strong and I'm too old. But I've got a few boys who work for me that could sure take care of it. I'd have them beat him to within a inch of death. We drink a little; hunt a little; and might party a little but no drugs in this family. I personally see to that," I told McGill.

McGill and I finished our telemetry parts mission. Returning to McGill's home, I made a "confidence buy" of a walker hound pup before departing.

Naturally, I informed Cartwright of the McGill scenario immediately. Dave, just one day prior, had heard the same thing. He stated he'd used a "tactic" to counter it. He felt the situation was somewhat dangerous but he could handle it -- typical Cartwright. We kept going. Later we ascertained there was no Game Warden running his mouth at a truck stop on I-40. The McGill scenario was all staged. The best several of our outlaw targets could come up with as an "undercover agent test."

From January of 1986 to June of 1987, over twenty covert contacts were made with the McGill brothers (I'll call them Harry, Lee and Bob) and three other associated targets of Operation Smoky. Initially, I used my search for my missing coon dog Nap, as the ploy. It ingratiated me with Harry, the oldest of the McGill brothers, who introduced me to the other five. During the time frame mentioned, I introduced my gall buying nephew, Dave Sloan, who introduced TN undercover Officer Ray Swift (hunting buddy) into the scene. With these Transylvania County, N.C. targets, we participated in illegal bear hunts both on and off the GSMNP. We bought bear gall bladders and other bear parts from all five and one live bear cub. The purchase was arranged by Lee McGill. The Cub was taken to a state game farm where it was raised to maturity. It was released into the wild after what's known as a "hacking in" period. Meaning a slow and gradual introduction into the wild environment. It was saved a tortured life as "bait" for the hounds in the inhumane bear fighting contests.

The Opryland Sting

Agent Dave Cartwright, duty station Nashville, Tennessee, was the best covert operative I've ever known. He could cry (tears and all), embarrass (red face and all), show violent anger or the saintly countenance of a priest, at will. He knew country music star, Mel Tillis. He and his parents were on a first name basis with many Grand Ole Opry country music stars. Dave knew his way around Opryland in Nashville, Tennessee. Cartwright's father once told me, "My son, David, could have been a great actor. He has all the inherent qualities of one. He is also a con-artist par ex-cel-lence." He wrote country music songs. He had worked as a professional hunting dog trainer (retrievers). He was a knowledgeable houndsman, having at one time, an association with one of the greatest black and tan houndsmen of all time – Mr. Joe Bloodworth of Tennessee.

Danny Russo (I'll call him) was identified at the Gatlinburg Conference as the number one target of Operation Smoky. The intelligence concerning Russo reported to the conference by NCWRC Officer J.D. Moore, assigned to Haywood County where Russo lived, was overwhelming. Russo outlawed with a group of bear hunters from Cocke County, Tennessee and from three state-line counties in North Carolina. Many were members of a Tennessee based bear hunting club known as the Del Rio or Brushy Mountain Club. They hunted illegally on the GSMNP, a nearby bear sanctuary on the Tennessee-North Carolina state line, named Harmon's Den, another bear sanctuary named Sherwood, various bear sanctuaries in Tennessee and other surrounding environs. Russo was into other illegal fields of endeavor, i.e. arson, drugs, stolen vehicles and other forms of thievery. Agent Dave Cartwright successfully infiltrated this group in record time. He incorporated me as his "Uncle Buck from Raleigh" who was the money source behind his Nashville, Tennessee based cover. Before the investigation's end, he incorporated TN state undercover officers Tom White, Ray Swift, Lee Luening, Bill Holiday, Jim

Kennedy and N.C. Officer Dennis Holloway. I was the assigned case agent in charge of Smoky at the insistence of my SAC, Dan Searcy in Atlanta. I was a better operative than case agent.

Soon after Cartwright infiltrated the "Russo et al gang", he phoned me in Raleigh. "Ron, if we're going to get anywhere with this bunch of outlaws, I'm going to have to have a rig (meaning a 4 x 4 pickup truck with rig dog carpet and tether on the hood) and a couple of good bear hounds. One of these hounds should be a good trained rig dog. If you've got a good rig dog you're in like Flynn."

"Okay, the truck is no problem; we've got a good GMC 4 x 4 pickup here in Raleigh that was forfeited during Operation Rock. You can rig the hood. I'll get Mike Zetts (NCWRC officer) to wire it with a hidden tape recorder – he's good at that sort of thing. How does that sound?" I informed Cartwright.

"Great," Cartwright responded.

"Those hounds you need are going to cost some big bucks. I'll call the SAC," I told Dave. Immediately, I phoned SAC Dan Searcy.

"What will the dogs cost?" he asked.

"Probably around $5,000.00," I responded.

"Whew! Think you can sell them before take down and recover some of the price?" Dan asked.

"We'll try," I replied.

"Do it!" Searcy stated in his usual supportive voice.

Utilizing Danny Russo's guidance, Cartwright purchased one of the best rig dogs in the Smoky Mountains. He was a big raw boned UKC (United Kennel Club) registered English Redtick nicknamed "Knot Head". Perched on his lofty throne on the carpeted hood of a bear hunting rig, he could "wind" a bear a mile away. He could trail a bear track twelve hours old – he was one great rig dog. He'd bawl with his deep-course voice the second he smelled a bear. Released, he would trail and "jump" the bear. After he'd warmed up the track and one or more additional hounds were released or "packed" to him joining the chase, he'd return to the truck. He knew his "rig dog" job was done. He wouldn't join the pack again until it was time to kill the bear.

The second hound bought was a male UKC registered plott hound. He was a beautiful brindle colored hound of about fifty pounds. He'd been neutered by his former owner because "he was bad to fight other hounds". His name was "Trooper". He was a supurb long lasting track and tree dog. During a hunt near Fontana Lake on the southern border of the GSMNP, eight hounds were packed to a bear that swam Fontana Lake twice and stayed on the ground while the hounds trailed it for three days. One by one all but two hounds gave up the chase – give out – couldn't trail any more. The bear finally treed on the GSMNP. The outlaw hunters, including Cartwright, left their guns at their rigs before going to the two hounds barking treed. They knew after hearing the hounds trailing the bear for three days, the Park Rangers would be there hidden and waiting – and they were! It takes Dave to tell it;

"When we finally got to the tree, there was a nice sized bear in the tree's very top. Only two hounds were at the tree. An old redbone female had made a bed near the base of the tree. She was completely give out. Nevertheless she would occasionally raise her tired head and bark treed; and there was Trooper. He was skin and bones. You could count every rib in him. He was up on the tree with his front claws inbedded in the tree's bark. He was bawlin' and choppin' every breath with his head thrown back lookin' at the bear. Man, was I proud of that plott hound. The only dog out of a pack of eight – on the tree where he'd been for hours, still treein' his heart out. He raised goose bumps all over me! I rushed to him – scooped him up in my arms and kissed him! The Rangers confronted us but let us leash Trooper and the old redbone and leave because we had no guns and the dog training season off the Park was in. Every hunter in the group tried to buy ol Trooper – he wasn't for sale – not yet anyway!"

Near the end of Operation Smoky, before takedown, we sold Trooper and two "confidence buy" hound pups at a profit. Knot Head, our super rig dog sadly died of a heartworm infection.

On February 5, 1986, following my fourth covert contact with target, Lee McGill during which he accused "Dave Sloan" of being an undercover agent, Cartwright phoned me in Raleigh. "Russo called and invited himself and his girlfriend to Nashville. He wants to come the weekend of the twenty-second. He wants to see our shop (cover) and meet my wife and family. He smells a rat – he's checking us out," he informed me.

"It's in your ballpark Dave. The cover won't be a problem (an existing cooperating Nashville business), but what about the house you live in? No way is he coming to your actual home. You've got to come up with at least a five hundred thousand dollar home complete with cat poop in its litter box and your dirty clothes in the hamper, unless you can think of something else," I advised my pretend nephew.

"I'll come up with something and call you later," Cartwright responded.

Russo made a mistake – he gave Cartwright too long to think. Four days later my office phone rang. It was Agent Cartwright. "I've got it all set up. I've rented the suite next to the Presidential Suite at Opryland, USA. I got if for next to nothing, thanks to Opryland Security. The Chief of Opryland Security is "in the know" – it's okay, he can be trusted. They've cooperated with law enforcement in the past. I've got Agent Maureen Mathews flying in from Miami. She'll pose as my wife. I've contacted Russo and invited him and his girlfriend to Nashville for the weekend of the twenty-second. I told him the company (cover) would put all of us up at Opryland. The suite has three bedrooms, three baths and a grand piano. On Sunday, the 23rd, we'll all have a steak dinner at my home before Russo and friend depart for home which won't happen because on Saturday night we're going to stage a bitter marital breakup between Matthews and me. I've arranged for a big white Lincoln limo to pick us up at the hotel and deliver us to the Opryland Theater.

There Matthews and I will start bickering as we all watch the show. After the show, the bickering will come to a head in the Hotel's Jack Daniels Lounge. My "mistress", a cute little red haired TBI (Tennessee Bureau of Investigation) Agent will appear on the scene. TBI has a keen interest in Russo – he's been stealing vehicles in Tennessee. They will be video taping everything from a balcony above. I'll be wearing one of their body wires. My mistress will spot us, particularly me, and come cheerfully to our table. Quite embarrassed and scared, I'll feebly introduce her around the table to Russo, his girlfriend, your "mistress from Richmond" you and Matthews. As Matthews is introduced, she'll jump up from her seat and state, 'yeah, slut, I'm his wife!' My mistress will react by rising from her seat and looking at me, state, 'you rat, you didn't tell me you were married!' Both mistress and wife will leave with wife yelling, 'I'm leaving this little party and you for good. Don't worry about bringing your guests to our home tomorrow because the kids and I won't let you in the house and there won't be any steak dinner!' Matthews and TBI Agent will leave with me following them pleading with my wife to reconsider. Exit Matthews and TBI Agent – performance finished.

After I return from running after my wife, I'll ask you to pay the tab, tip the waiter and go find Matthews to help plead my case. This will be you and your mistress's cue to leave the scene – performance finished. I'll put my guests to bed in the Opryland suite, then come to an apartment my folks own where you'all will spend the night. All performances finished. This should get us off the hook.

Completing his description of the plan, Cartwright asked, "How's all that sound, Uncle Buck – think it will work?"

"I think so, you got all this arranged with Opryland, right?" I asked.

"Everything is all set with management and security at Opryland," Cartwright replied.

"Who am I going to get to act as my "mistress from Richmond"? I pondered out loud.

"Try Agents Mary Monahan or Marsha Cronan in the Washington Office," Cartwright suggested.

"How about my real life sweetheart – Shirley June Bailey?" I countered.

"Great! Will she do it?" Cartwright asked.

"Hoss, Shirley June's the best actress in the world! I'll have her all dressed up with jewelry all over her – she'll look like Joan Crawford," I replied.

"We're all set then. We'll all meet at the Opryland suite on the morning of the twenty-first. We'll do a one day rehearsal before our guest's arrival!" Cartwright stated.

And so it was; with rehearsal completed the previous day, at ten a.m. on the twenty-second, our guests from North Carolina arrived. After escourting Russo and friend to the suite and getting them settled in, we all had lunch at a very plush Opryland restaurant on the main floor. Then we all toured

Opryland, USA. Returning to our suite to "dress" for the evening show, we found an ornate bucket containing an iced bottle of Champaign resting on top of the grand piano. Attached was a note that read, "Dave, you and your guests have a great stay at Opryland. Doris has sure enjoyed the diamond necklace you imported for her from Europe, thanks! Your friend, Mel." Cartwright popped the cork and we all enjoyed a glass of Champaign as Cartwright muttered, "Got to remember to thank Tillis for the Champaign."

The rehearsed chain of events continued pretty much as planned except for a little added "flavor". During the show at the Opryland Theater featuring Roseanne Cash, Porter Wagner, Emmy Lou Harris and others, Matthews and Cartwright began their bickering – getting louder by the moment. An usher quietly invited Matthews and Cartwright to adjourn to the vestibule to settle their differences. Both left the stage performance and went to the theater lobby accompanied by Uncle Buck and Russo. There the married couple went at it hot, loud, and heavy with Uncle Buck trying to counsel both stating, "The two of you should be ashamed. You've got to think of your kids." Russo, amused by the happening, whispered in Cartwright's ear, "You need to get rid of that old bag." Finally Uncle Buck got the fighting couple to quiet down and all returned to the theater.

Later at dinner, during the Jack Daniel's Lounge scene, Cartwright's TBI supplied body wire went dead, not to mention the fact it heated up while it was still functioning. The wire, a state of the art machine, installed by TBI was taped to Cartwright's center chest cavity beneath his undershirt. No longer able to record the sound with the video taping from their balcony above, TBI dispatched a plainclothes agent to the scene. The agent, who happened to be Cartwright's son, passed by our table scratching his ear. Thus giving us the standard signal that says, "your body wire is not working." Making the restroom excuse, Cartwright and I left, got the body wire functioning again and padded Cartwright's chest with toilet tissue, between skin and wire. Then we returned to the lounge.

Later, during the "eternal triangle scene", as dear wife (Matthews) rose to her feet, addressed Cartwright's mistress (TBI Agent) and delivered her lines, she added a coup-de-grace by throwing her drink directly into Cartwright's crotch, stating, "Here, lover boy, take this, maybe it'll cool you off for a while." While this "eternal triangle" confrontation was taking place, a beautiful performing female harpist, dressed in flowing white robe and perched on a nearby golden pedestal, surmised it was time for her performance to end. With all the grace in the world, she stopped playing, gently shoved her harp forward to the resting position and lowered her beautiful body from her perch. On the floor, she raised the hem of her flowing white gown to the knee level, then she put it in high gear, taking off on a dead run and exited the Jack Daniels Lounge like a bat outa Hades!

As the evening continued (ahem!); during the "tearful and pleading pursuit of wife and mistress scene," Cartwright, wet crotch and all, streaked through the hotel lobby in pursuit of his escaping women. "Please sweetheart, let's talk this over – please don't leave me, as Buck says, think of the kids." (Next breath, addressing mistress) "Becky, I'm so sorry – I should have leveled with you – can't we talk about this?" Cartwright yelled as both women ran out of the Opryland Hotel disappearing into the darkness. As all this was taking place, other Opryland guests in the hotel lobby were "hugging the walls" as Opryland hosts tried to assure them everything was "okay, just a lover's misunderstanding." "To say the least!" one guest was heard to mutter while several elderly ladies gasp.

Cartwright returned to our dinner table. There he stood – wet crotch (looked exactly like he'd peed himself), crying with a white handkerchief in hand. "Go after her Uncle Buck. She's poppin' speed. Go find her please. She's probably gone to her mother's, where the kids are," he requested.

I couldn't resist, "But what about your mistress?" I asked as Russo broke up laughing while his girlfriend sobbed.

"Heck with her – go find my wife!" Cartwright ordered. With that command we all rose to leave the Jack Daniel's Lounge. I placed a generous tip on the table as Cartwright and I met the maitre'd and paid the tab. The maitre'd was holding his own trying desperately not to laugh. Then he burst out, addressing Cartwright, "This just ain't your night, is it fella," he blurted; then broke all the way down, laughing as Cartwright glared at him.

"Not funny, buddy," Cartwright mumbled. "I'll see our North Carolina guests to our suite and join you'all later at our house. Hurry Buck, see if you can find her," Cartwright pleaded. This was my dear Shirley June's and my cue to exit – stage left. Exit we did to our parked undercover Lincoln (a Custom's drug seizure) with Agent Matthews inside waiting. Then across town to the Cartwright apartment.

Cartwright arrived at the apartment at 2:30 a.m. He was spent; he had undoubtedly just finished the greatest performance of his undercover career. He related the events that took place at the Opryland Hotel after our departure. "I escorted Russo and his ladyfriend (Brenda) to our rented suite. Others on the elevator noticed and snickered at my wet crotch. In the suite, Russo started talking about all those Cadillacs and Mercedes parked in the Hotel parking lot. He actually proposed stealing one to take back to North Carolina. I blew up! I told him I'd just lost my family and all he could think about was stealing another vehicle. Then I sat down on the sofa and started crying my eyes out. 'I've lost my wife – my kids – even my girlfriend, I sobbed. Brenda sat down beside me. She draped her arm over my shoulders and leaned close to my face. She stated, 'Now honey, you've got to get hold of yourself and go on. You've got to support your children. These things happen even in the best of families – now settle down and stop crying.' Then coming even closer, she whispered in my ear, 'You're a first class butt. If you want a shoulder to cry on, give me a call – maybe we can go do dinner.' I didn't acknowledge her proposal – just continued crying."

"Do you think we've got the job done?" I asked.

"Yeah, I think we have, Uncle Buck," Cartwright replied. Then a very tired (as were all were) Special Agent Dave Cartwright, alias Dave Sloan, left for home and some well earned sleep in the arms of his dear wife, Mary. So ended the "Opryland Sting."

I note that during the evening of the twenty-first (dress rehearsal day) we all decided we deserved an after dinner drink in the Jack Daniels Lounge. Our two actresses decided it would be nice to adorn themselves in the "costumes" they would be performing in on the evening of the twenty-second. Cartwright and I went to the Lounge sometime before our "leading ladies", leaving both to dress and join us later. Enjoying our second drink at the dimly lit – sparkle illuminated bar, I noticed a breathtakingly beautiful woman enter the Lounge. She wore a light blue, two piece outfit with slightly lengthened skirt. The open jacket she wore was heavily shoulder padded and covered a "revealing" low cut white blouse! The infrequent sparkle lights of the bar picked up the highlights of her beautiful auburn hair. She wore oversized horn rimmed glasses that nevertheless revealed her mascared eyes that had a Cleopatra look. Her complexion was peach pale. Her lipstick – maroon, yet conservatively applied. She glided past us seemingly blinded by the bars darkness and took a seat at a nearby table. I nudged Cartwright in the ribs, "Get a load of the gal that just walked in. The words -- good lookin' – just don't get it. If I was single, would I make a move on her," I whispered in Cartwright's ear. Turning around on his barstool, Cartwright eyed the object of my admiration. With drink in hand, he slid off his seat and headed for the beautiful lady's table. "Come on Uncle Buck, she's Shirley, your wife!" he informed me with certainty. Through squinted, perhaps somewhat alcohol influenced eyes, I peered at the lady more closely. Sure enough, she was my Shirley June! At that moment, as many times before and after, I fell in love with her all over again.

Soon a "tantalizing" Agent Matthews arrived on the scene. We all enjoyed a much deserved after dinner drink before our much needed rest preparing us for the following day's performance. During the entire Opryland's evening performance on the twenty-second, Shirley June's facial expressions went from a pleasant smile to scorn and disapproval to wiping away a pretext tear. All this acting and she didn't say one word! As a matter of fact, Shirley's performance was stellar.

Brushy Mountain Homecoming

The fact our Opryland sting restored the confidence in us with Russo and the Del Rio or Brushy Mountain Bear Hunters Club was soon thereafter evidenced by three events. First, we were invited to attend the "Brushy Mountain Bear Hunter's Club Homecoming". This event was an annual affair during which an award was presented to the hunter who entered the best bear mount. The event featured a feast of bear meat, cooked and/or prepared many ways – fried, roasted, barbequed, bear burgers, broiled and dried (bear jerky). Served with the bear meat were fresh cooked vegetables, gravy, salads and homemade deserts. I must say, everything was delicious. Mountain women certainly know how to cook bear meat and I was able to acquire a couple recipes.

Mid-day a Southern Baptist Preacher and wife arrived. He gave a blessing before anyone partook of the feast, then led us in singing Amazing Grace, ate and left. Just before the good Reverend's arrival, all the marijuana, cocaine and alcoholic beverages disappeared. After his departure, all the "goodies" reappeared.

Cartwright donated several items of costume jewelry as door prizes. We entered the scene with a life sized, very well mounted, bear that Cartwright acquired as an undercover buy; part of a separate undercover investigation. Tom Bennett was the Case Agent. The delivery and buy took place at the Knoxville Zoo. Before arrival, we affixed the specimen to the roof of Cartwright's sinister looking undercover vehicle – a hold over from his undercover days in Louisiana. It was a late model custom painted all black Chevrolet pickup with blackened windows and black upholstery. All chrome was removed except for the bumpers and sparkling chrome wheel covers. The "Grim Reaper" was professionally painted in very muted pink tones on both sides of the bed. On the lower right hand corner of the tailgate was an ever so small professionally painted Hornet. Cartwright, romantic that he was, felt these paintings symbolized him. He was in fact, the "Grim Reaper" who "stung". He loved to walk the very dangerous "deception-discovery" line. I once asked him if a bad guy had ever figured out the symbolism painted on his truck. "Not a single one," Cartwright chuckled.

We entered our mounted bear in the competition and won first prize. Several of the women present began sitting on our bear and posing for photographs, including Brenda, Russo's very attractive girlfriend the same who proposed "dinner" during Cartwright's tearful breakdown at the Opryland Suite. A little middle aged and very attractive lady took a liking to "Uncle Buck". Every time I turned around she was there. She prepared my dinner plate and we dined together. After awhile she slowly asked, "I s-h-o-r-e do l-i-k-e y-o-u B-u-c-k, do y-o-u l-i-k-e m-e?" I told her I liked her and appreciated her fixing my dinner plate. Cartwright, picking up on this brief exchange, took me aside. "The drunk sitting over there on the bleachers is her husband, be careful," he warned. The husband appeared stoned out of his skull on alcohol or drugs totally unconcerned about his wife's antics. Nevertheless, I knew it was time to shake my sweet little accommodating brunette. Before I could accomplish this she asked very slowly, "B-u-c-k, c-a-n I s-i-t on y-o-u-r b-a-r, w-h-i-l-e y-o-u t-a-k-e my p-i-t-c-h-e-r?" Before thinking, I answered, "Honey, you can sit on anything ol Uncle Buck's got." Cartwright heard this, laughing, yet grimacing, he whispered, "Take that broad's picture and drop her like a bad habit." I took Cartwright's advice, telling my new found sweet thing, "Honey, you're a married woman. I happen to know the gentleman (nodding toward her stoned husband) seated over there is your husband. I think we'd better cool our togetherness before there's trouble."

"I-t's a-l-r-i-g-h-t B-u-c-k, h-e's d-r-u-n-k. I-f'n he w-a-s s-o-b-e-r he

341

w-o-u-l-d-n't c-a-r-e no w-a-y. He d-o-n't c-a-r-e n-u-t-h-i-n b-o-u-t me," she drawled in her sweet and tempting mountain accent. After hearing this, Cartwright grabbed my arm and whisked me away into the crowd, telling my "mountain sweetie", "My Uncle Buck's married to my Aunt June. It's time for us to hit the road."

As we joined several who were already leaving the Homecoming, my pretty little mountain sweetie waved goodbye. After we loaded our mounted bear, we said goodbye to a few including Russo and Brenda. Traveling down the long lane to the nearest county road, Cartwright stated, "You're crazy to be foolin' with one of those mountain women. They're all some mountain boy's girlfriend or wife and that makes them all dangerous." "I wasn't foolin' with her, I couldn't shake her," I responded.

"Couldn't shake her? You were enjoying that little gal like a barnyard cat drinkin' fresh cows milk!" Cartwright declared, so ending my brief romance and our Brushy Mountain Bear Hunter's Homecoming adventure.

The next event took place within the Harmon's Den bear sanctuary where bear hunting was illegal. The bear season off the sanctuary was closed. At Russo's invitation, we participated in a closed season bear hunt with him and hounds including old Knot Head and Trooper. We met Russo at his parent's home and proceeded to Harmon's Den. Knot Head, tethered on the hood of Russo's hunting rig, soon opened on a fresh bear track. Russo released him. After a short while, we packed Trooper and another hound to him. No sooner after Knot Head made his customary return to the truck, we heard Trooper and Russo's hound barking treed. Russo, grabbing a rifle and hand held radio from behind the seat told Cartwright, "They've got one up – c'mon," he and Cartwright left and headed to the hounds. Before departing, Russo threw me the keys to his truck and a second hand held radio, stating, "Here Buck, patrol the roads and be on the lookout for Rangers or Game Wardens! If you see any, tip us off on the radio."

I began patrolling the roads in Harmon's Den as ordered. Soon I heard the crack of Russo's rifle. Russo's voice came over my radio, "Where you at, Buck?" he asked. I radioed my location.

"Keep comin' south. About a half mile you'll see Dave's hat layin' near the right side of the road. We're hid in a little holler behind his hat. Hurry, we've just drug out a real nice bar. When you get to the hat, jump out of the truck and open the tailgate. We need to load this bar in a hurry and get," Russo ordered.

"Gotcha, be right there," I replied. I soon arrived at the "hat" location, leaped out of Russo's truck, ran to the rear and hurriedly lowered the tailgate that came off the truck in my hands. Russo and Cartwright quickly arrived roadside dragging a 200 pound bear. As I stood in the road holding the get-away truck's tailgate, Russo yelled, "What happened to the tailgate?" While Cartwright, sweating, gasping for breath, tongue hanging to his waist, proclaimed, "I'll never smoke another cigarette!" We didn't just drag this bear down this mountain, we ran with it!" Russo wasn't so much as out of breath

– this outlaw was in shape!

Hurriedly, the three of us heaved the still warm, limp, bear in the truck bed behind Russo's dog crate. "Don't just stand there – ya'all help me get this tailgate fixed!" Russo ordered.

"Fix the tailgate! There's Game Wardens about four miles behind us on this very same road," I announced (a lie). I was getting a kick out of the situation, especially Russo's frustration. Cartwright, pretty sure I had just told a lie, giving me that Bailey, get serious look, yelled, "Throw the cotton-pickin' tailgate on top of the bear and put that cement block behind the bear and let's get out of here."

"We gotta round up and ketch them hounds," Russo stated.

"Are you nuts?" I asked Russo as I hurriedly took off my hunting coat, removing its pocket contents and shoving them in my pants pockets. "Get your coat off – we'll lay both coats in the brush in the mouth of the hollow – the dogs will be laying on them when we get back. Right now we've got to get this bear stashed in a hurry!" I told Russo in a serious tone. We finally got underway and soon reached I-40. At a roadside park, we re-affixed the truck's tailgate and traveled to Russo's parent's home up a remote Haywood County hollow. We unloaded the bear and hung it, head up, in a shed near the main barn. We returned to Harmon's Den where our hounds were laying on our hunting coats, as I predicted.

"I didn't know hounds would do that, " Russo stated.

"Do what?" I asked.

"Come in and lay on your huntin' coat like that," Russo answered.

"How long have you been huntin' with hounds, boy?" I asked.

"Ever since I can remember," Russo answered.

"Well, now you've learned something new. When a hound checks in and you're not there, if there's something there that smells like you, he'll lay on it or be near it till you come and get him. Especially if you leave a little something for him to eat." I continued, "If he's not there, you can pretty well assume something's happened to him.

"I know they'll usually come to the place you turned them loose but I didn't know they'd come to your coat," Russo stated.

"About every time," I responded.

We returned to our stashed bear. I photographed the critter before Russo quickly skinned it, gutted it and carved out the tenderloins. He tied off the gall bladder, severed it, plastic bagged it and handed it to me. Then he rolled the hide with the head and claws attached into a very neat bundle and bound it with rope. "This goes with ya'all", he stated.

"I'll pay you half of what the gall, hide and claws are worth and we'll keep the other half," Cartwright told Russo, counting out and handing Russo the cash. Cartwright continued, "Here, another ten to top off your gas tank, as he handed him the extra ten.

"Fine with me," Russo stated, pocketing the money.

Near the end of the preceding, I noticed a very old gentleman with a

343

cane coming towards us down a mountain path from a cabin. Upon arrival, the old man entered the shed and examined the remainder of the hanging bear carcass. Russo introduced us, "This is my Grandpap – he's a retired preacher man."

"What denomination?" I asked the old gentleman.

"Baptist, if'n it's any of yore business, which it ain't," the old man angrily replied. Then, pointing a shaking cane at the three of us, he lit in. "Ya'all don't know what these bars meant to us in these mountains in the old days, do ya? What ya'all's doing here is wrong. I'm tellin' ya'all, hits wrong! Ya'all don't kill bars this time-o-year, they's young-uns (meaning bear cubs) in the woods!" he shouted. Then he took a step towards Russo, raising his shaking cane as though he was going to strike his grandson, shouting, "I'd orta take this cane to ya boy! I'd orta whail the stuffin' clean outa ya. If'n I's ten years younger and had the strength, I'd whup you like yore pappy ort to a done a long time ago," he shouted at Russo.

"Now you calm down, Pap – you calm down and go on back up to the house," Russo told his grandfather.

"I'm a goin' Sonny boy, I'm a goin! But when I get thar, I'm a gonna get on my knees and I'm a gonna pray for the wrath o God to come down on ya'all! Ya'all hear me – the wrath o God!" the old preacher shouted as he left the shed. Halfway up the path to his cabin, as dry thunder cracked in the distance, the old preacher, his snow white hair blowing in the wind, turned and faced us again, "Ya'all hear me – the wrath o God! The wrath o God!" he shouted once more pointing at us with his shaking cane.

I glanced at Russo. He stood motionless and quite sobered. He quickly brushed away a tear on his right cheek. The old man had got to him – to all of us for that matter. Cartwright was still as a mouse. "Ol Grandpap's tetched – he's a little tetched," Russo quietly commented. I thought, No Danny, you're wrong, your old Grandpa is right, as we departed, leaving Russo with his head bowed, walking slowly toward his parent's home. His posture showed he felt his Grandfather's scorn. He would be the most penalized of all the Smokey Targets. He would go to prison and lose what little he owned. Perhaps he sensed the "wrath" yet to come.

Later, by invitation, Uncle Buck and Dave Sloan with bear hounds, Knot Head and Trooper, accompanied Russo and five Cocke County Tennessee hunters on another illegal bear hunt within the Harmon's Den Sanctuary. The December season off the Sanctuary was open. Although bear, coon, bobcat and opossum hunting was prohibited in the Sanctuary, camping and trout fishing was legal. This group of outlaw bear hunters annually established their hunting camp within the sanctuary at a developed U.S. Forest Service campground. If checked by Rangers or Game Wardens, they claimed they only camped there and did their hunting off the sanctuary. Of course, the opposite was true. They actually hunted the far-flung fringes of the sanctuary and killed bears, in season and out, within the sanctuary.

This hunt proved most interesting. After establishing camp, Russo and I departed on a trip to a nearby town to buy camp provisions. I drove our 4x4 "wired" GMC pickup truck. Naturally, I engaged the truck's concealed tape recorder as soon as we got underway. Two days earlier, we staged an aircraft "big money delivery from Miami" (combination locked briefcase and all) at the Knoxville Airport, with Russo present. Although at no time did we actually lay claim to it, Russo was convinced we were part of a drug and/or organized crime cartel. For the second time, he hit me up for a job.

"Buck, I know ya'all got sumthin' more goin' for ya besides that business in Nashville," he began.

"Oh," I stated.

"Back at the bearfights, you said you might have a hole for me," he stated and continued. "I can take a man out for ya for ten thousand, Buck."

"That's cheap enough Danny – cheap enough. What other talents do you have?" I asked.

"I do fires, Buck – fool proof fires," he claimed.

"You mean insurance fires, right?" I asked."

"Yeah, that's it – insurance fires," he affirmed.

"What do you mean, fool proof fires?" I asked.

"They can't tell they've ever been set," he answered.

"Most of you guys take claim percentages; how about you?" I asked.

"What ya mean?" he asked.

"Do you get a percentage of the insurance settlement or do you charge a fixed amount?" I asked.

"Whatever works out," he replied.

"That's no answer Danny! What percent of the insurance settlement do you charge or what do you charge for doing the job?" I asked, acting somewhat irritated.

"Well, thirty percent or whatever me and whoever works out," he replied.

"Thirty percent's too high. Doesn't make any difference anyway, we're not into fires," I stated and continued, "How about vehicles – you wanted to lift a car at Opryland according to Dave?" I asked.

"How'd you like a new four wheel drive Toyota for $2500.00? Now that's our price to you only, Buck. We usually get more," he answered.

"Thanks but no thanks – too much trouble with the paper work; dummyin' up titles, licenses, and all," I stated.

"Oh, I can take care of that. Gotta do it in Kentucky though," he stated.

"I see, are you movin' many trucks?" I asked.

"Some, not too often though – just now and agin. Got a deal goin' with a dealer," he replied.

"Another insurance thing, right?" (Collect insurance on the stolen truck and sell it also).

"You got it," he replied.

"How's the Kentucky thing work?" I asked.

"Sellin' trucks to the strip miners in east Kentucky. Trucks never leave the job – never get on a public road. But if they do the strip miners got the connections to get them titled and licensed in Kentucky," he claimed.

"Really, what about VIN numbers, serial numbers and whatever?" I asked.

"Change um," he answered.

"Interesting, Danny, interesting. Just what all do you do for a living.? We've never really known. You always seem to have plenty of money," I asked.

"Pot and tomaters too," he replied.

"Marijuana, fires, tomatoes and vehicles – that's it?" I asked.

"A few pigs," he replied.

"How about cocaine – seems to be plenty of that around?" I asked.

"You've never seen me use it. Know where to get it but not enough to peddle unless I can get some from ya'all, heh, heh, heh," he stated.

I decided to play games. I wanted to see just how sharp Russo was.

"You'll not get any cocaine from us, Danny. Forget it," I stated and continued. "Okay, I'll admit it, we operate a little in the gray zone, very little. Have to sometimes when regular profits are down but we're careful – the feds. There's one bunch of feds we don't ever fool with – we keep them happy," I told Russo.

"Who," he asked.

"The IRS chum, don't ever mess with them. They'll nail you, but good," I proclaimed.

"The tax guys?" he asked.

"Yeah, the tax guys. How about the tomatoes and pigs – sounds legit." I asked.

"I lease a lot of ground in the French Broad River bottoms where I raise tomatoes and sell to the canneries. Got a halfers deal goin' with some kin on pigs. We sell um mostly to the barbeque pits – more money in them there," he replied.

"How about the pot?" I asked.

"Raised some right in with the tomaters, heh-heh-heh, but raise the most way back in. Pot's good money," he answered.

"Well, it's up to you just how you do it, but you'd better be reporting all, and I mean all, your income to the IRS and paying the tax due on it. Are you doing that?" I asked.

"How in tarnation am I gonna pay taxes on what I get outa pot, setting fires, stealin' trucks and the like?" he asked.

"The bottom line Danny, is total income and total taxes. The way you dummy up how you made the money is up to you. Your real concern is the bottom line. Don't ask me how they do it but they can trace every dime you spend if they pick you out to check. You pay your back taxes if you owe any and be sure and pay them for this year. Take a tip from ol Uncle Buck," I admonished Russo.

"Thank you for tippin' me off, Buck. I can't exactly remember what I made last year or the years before that but I'll sure nuf figure it up this year," Russo stated.

"Now, as far as you coming to work for us. First, Dave does the hiring, not me. Second, we have some expansion plans soon. Maybe you can fill a hole then. Third, if we do offer you anything it will be within our legitimate business. Frankly Danny, you wouldn't last two weeks working in the gray zone I mentioned. You've sat here and told me things you shouldn't have – you don't know me that well, you talk too much. If we could use you in our gray zone, we'd ascertain these things anyway. Rather than think I've offended you, I'm going to believe I've taught you something. Something that some day may help you qualify for work in the gray zone," I advised Russo. What a line of crap. Time to knock it off Bailey," I thought.

"Buck, I understand what you're sayin'. Guess you're right, I do talk too much but if you get something you think I can handle, I'd sure appreciate commin' to work for ya'll," Russo stated.

"We'll see what works out. I'll make Dave aware of our little talk," I informed Russo.

After returning to camp and stowing the provisions, Cartwright caught my attention. He nodded for me to go to our camper. Making the "gonna take a nap excuse", I went to the camper. Five minutes later Cartwright

joined me. "We've got two undercover drug agents who arrived in camp and they're screwing up big time," Cartwright told me. Looking out the camper window, Cartwright didn't have to point them out; they were obvious. They were dressed in brand new hunting garb; Eddie Bauer quality. Their camping gear was new; a new tent, among all the other banged up bear hunter campers. New Coleman camp stove, new gas lantern, new 4x4 Ford Bronco – showroom clean with no dog rigging on the hood and no dog transport crate in back (amidst all the banged up, strike dog rigged, dog crates in he beds, dirty, muddy bear hunters pickups), and last but not least, two pin headed walker hounds of obvious fox hound ancestry (as Cartwright mumbled, "Straight out of the Nashville dog pound"). Comparing either of the dudes with any bear hunter in camp would be like comparing an under-the-bridge unwashed troll with a member of the British Royal family.

"State or Feds?" I asked as I continued observing through the camper window.

"I'd say DEA," Cartwright answered.

"Got their stool (stool pigeon) spotted," I asked.

"Yeah, it's ol Gabby, he gave them several obvious high signs including one when you an Russo drove in.

We went up on the northeast boundary after you and Russo left. Ol Knot struck wide open soon after I got him rigged and turned loose. We packed Trooper to him, then two more hounds. Ol Hump went back the line to the DEA turkeys and told them it was time to pack one of their hounds to the bear. The DEA guys didn't know what ol Hump was talking about. They just sat there in their nice new Bronco, grinning. Ol Hump grabbed one of their walker hounds out of the back end of their Bronco and tried to pack him to the bear. The poor thing hid under their Bronco, pissin' and scared to death. Ol Hump grabbed their other hound and tried to put it on the bear. It bit ol Hump, then joined its buddy under their truck. Those two hounds never ran any kind of game in their lives. The hounds running the bear, treed it smack in the middle of the sanctuary. Our good buddies stashed their guns – too much chance of getting caught. We caught the hounds, left the bear in the tree and took off out of there."

"Did that second DEA hound piss too?" I asked Cartwright, chuckling over his account of the morning's hunt. Cartwright didn't bother to answer.

"Every bear hunter here's got um pegged as undercover drug agents. They claim they've had ol Gabby pegged as a DEA stool for a long time," Cartwright informed.

"Ol Gabby's an alcoholic," I stated.

"Yeah, and you can bet he buys all that booze with the bucks DEA gives him," Cartwright stated and continued. "The drug guys have been runnin' their mouths all morning about throwing a party tonight at the Holliday Inn in Newport – booze, whores, the whole nine yards. That's a typical drug gig. None of the bear hunters are going except Gabby – he says he's going."

"They're working us, aren't they David?" I asked.

"You bet they are," Cartwright affirmed. "We probably shouldn't have staged the money delivery at the Airport. Russo ran his mouth to someone. Gabby's heard about it and put the DEA guys on us. DEA's got backup somewhere – they always do. Think you could scout around and find them?" Cartwright requested.

"I'll handle it. We've got to get rid of them. We can't have them around messing up what we've got left to do. Gosh, you don't think these bear hunters would knock off the two DEA's, do you? We sure can't let that happen, even if it means blowin' our cover," I told Cartwright.

"Nah, they'd be more apt to pop-a-cap on us if they knew who we were. They're not paying much attention to the DEA's. They know who they are. We gotta be ready though just in case," Cartwright stated. "We need a heavy hitter to intercede with their SAC in Nashville and get them gone. At this late date, it's probably okay to let their SAC know we're going to give them all the drug stuff we've come across anyway. Got a heavy hitter in mind?" Cartwright asked.

"Searcy (our SAC) or Pulliam (our Regional Director) or both," I threw out. "I know Searcy would – would Pulliam?" Cartwright asked.

"With all the diplomacy in the world, I'm sure. The kind of diplomacy it's gonna take that we're a little shy of," I answered.

"Or - -", Cartwright was thinking. "Or maybe we should get a Tennessee State heavy hitter like Bob Harmon (LE Chief, TWRA) or Gary Meyers (Director, TWRA). It stands to reason, if DEA is as concerned about state-federal relations as we (USFWS) are, they might be more prone to react favorably.

There's Tennessee State operatives up to their necks in this thing the same as us.

It worked! Following this hunt, Cartwright solicited the services of TWRA's LE Chief, Bob Harmon. Bob "put the hammer" on the DEA SAC in Nashville. We never saw another DEA undercover agent during the remainder of Operation Smoky.

A beautiful little brook trout stream wound its way through the entire campground. I thought, what a good way to scout the campground and look for the backup DEA Agents. With waders on and fly rod in hand, I entered the little stream's ice cold water and began "nymphing". I didn't have to fish upstream very far; the DEA backups were camped at the very next camp site to the north. Their camp site wasn't visible from ours due to a large and protruding (upward) limestone rock outcropping between the two camp sites. I fished around a curve in the stream and there they were – a male and a female agent. The entire campground was completely void of campers except ours and the DEA backups. This wasn't "normal". A regular camper would choose a location some distance away to insure some degree of privacy – that's the way campers are. I'd had plenty of experience with them during my Ranger days. The male half of the duo, spotting me midstream, scurried to the ground from an elevated position atop one of the mentioned limestone rocks; his binoculars still hanging from his neck. All their camping equipment, including vehicle, appeared new like their fellow agents camped with us. I couldn't believe it; hanging from a clothesline pole was a shoulder holstered stainless steel .357 (I surmised) not unlike the one issued to me. They hadn't so much as hidden part of their cop weaponry. Then the male threw the female, fully clothed in new winter hunting garb, on a two-thirds unrolled sleeping bag and began "making out". I could actually see the space between their lips during a faked kiss. Following this passionate act, they acted as though they "just discovered" me because I'd just hooked a ten inch brookie that was cutting its shenanigans above and below the surface of the pool next to their camp. The little brookie timed his act perfectly. Normal campers or outdoorsman would have been excited to watch me land my fish. Not these two clowns; they rose to their feet, did some pretense throat clearing and disappeared into their half-pitched tent.

I thought, and to think, they took the same law enforcement training I did at the Federal Law Enforcement Training Center at Glynco, Georgia.

They, like their fellow agents camped with us, were probably good agents when functioning in their own environment. In the wildlife environment, they sucked! Regardless of the environment, they needed to do their homework. They didn't. The truly bad situation was the fact the two DEA Agents camped with us were known by the bad guys. We were not only troubled by the fact they were messing us up, we also had to worry about the bad guys killing them. We knew our bad guys were capable of doing it. The following day, after their party at the Holliday Inn in Newport, the night before fizzled, all four DEA's, their no account hounds and new camping equipment

349

disappeared, while the rest of us, excluding Gabby who disappeared with the DEA's, participated in a morning hunt.

Our Hamon's Den hunt ended with a single bear killed. Perhaps the unwanted DEA presence jinxed the hunt; a good thing for the bears.

The Southern Theater of Operations

Beverly Moser ably replaced our beloved Julia Hamilton as our Administrative Assistant in the Raleigh Office in November, 1985 when Julia retired. Julia served the U.S. Fish and Wildlife Service for over thirty years. She was my "right arm". She gave me seven of those years. We all loved her as she did us. In September of 1986, at age 73, she came out of retirement to do one last covert assignment with me. Her true identity changed -- she became my "Aunt Mary Ellen Du Pont from Linville Falls."

Our mission was to accomplish initial infiltration into a group of southeast Tennessee outlaw hunters; the same group written about earlier, who, before the beginning of Operation Smoky, "burned" an undercover operative through the investigative efforts of an ex-Tennessee State Game Warden. I'll call him Hank. I chose to start by working Hank because I knew if I could win his confidence the rest would be down hill. I knew from past experience that Julia's casual presence during my first contact with Hank would lend great credibility.

Hank and a close friend and hunting associate (I'll call him Bill) who resided in Chattanooga, Tennessee, co-authored a book about bear and wild boar hunting in the Appalachian Mountains. I acquired a copy and read it from cover to cover. It was well written and I knew it could be an "in" with Hank. I made phone contact with and consequently called on Hank's co-author friend in Chattanooga, a very accommodating individual whom I visited with for a good while. I praised the book and asked the gentleman to autograph my copy. Afterwards by phone, at my request, he sent me to Hank telling Hank, "This gentleman read our book. He came a considerable distance to my home to get me to autograph his copy. He'd like very much for you to autograph it also. I'm sending him to you. Please honor his request – he's a fine gentleman." Hank agreed to autograph my book.

Shortly thereafter I made a tape recorded phone call to Hank. I told him who I was (alias, of course), reminded him of Bill's phone call and my autograph request. I continued with small talk about how much I enjoyed his book. I informed him that on a date in September, I would be driving my Aunt Mary Ellen Du Pont from her summer home in Linville Falls, N.C. to her winter home in Atlanta. I told him it would be convenient for us to make a slight detour and come by his home to get my book autographed. Hank agreed to our visit wholeheartedly and gave directions to his home. I told him we would arrive around 4:00 p.m.

The day before our appointment with Hank, "Aunt Mary Ellen Du Pont" and "Uncle (I should say nephew) Buck" traveled to Knoxville, Tennessee. There, we spent the night. The next morning adorned in appropriate attire – Julia, in a conservatively rich, light red suit. Me, in a navy pinstriped suit, after arranging for storage of our government sedan, leased a shiny new Lincoln. I was equipped with a set of license plates that would, if ran, check out to our business cover. In our Lincoln, we drove to a somewhat remote corner of a shopping mall parking lot. Julia put on a beautiful cashmere overcoat, grasp each corner of the hem and fanned the coat out; providing me with a screen behind which I switched plates on the Lincoln. Placing the vehicle's regular plates in a combination locked brief case and securing it in the trunk, we proceeded southward to our target's home near a small southeast Tennessee village.

Early in our travel, Julia grew quiet. I glanced at her, noticing she had positioned the index fingers of each hand on her temples – her eyes were closed. "Got a headache, Julia?" I asked.

"No, mentally I'm getting into my Mary Ellen Du Pont role," she informed me. I thought, What a gal, my Miss Julia! Soon she was wide eyed and alert.

"You ready now?" I asked.

"I'm ready. Let's take 'em down," she declared as we continued on our journey.

We arrived at our destination on schedule. Our hosts (Hank and his wife) were most cordial – they invited us in. Julia and Hank's wife hit it off immediately. Talking a mile a minute, the ladies adjourned to the living room while Hank and I visited over a cup of coffee at the kitchen table. Soon Hank's wife appeared, fixed a tray with coffee and cake for her and Julia. She quickly informed Hank, "There's some cookies in the cupboard if you want any," and hurried to rejoin Julia.

Hank autographed my book. We engaged in conversation during which he spoke of his seventeen years as a Game Warden. As we talked about hunting and the great outdoors, his book, etc., I found I was beginning to like the guy. I touched lightly on my missing dog, Nap, my nephew and hunting buddy, Dave Sloan, and our business in Nashville. Hank invited me outside to look at his hounds – all plotts. There, he invited Dave and I on a wild boar hunt with him, his son and his hunting buddies. Some would prove to be Operation Smoky targets. I was "in" and I didn't relish being "in". By then, the thoughts of working another Game Warden, who I was beginning to doubt (the vibes were conflicting) was the outlaw portrayed and targeted by the TWRA, didn't appeal to me. I'd heard TWRA's side of the story concerning why Hank left TWRA at the Gatlinburg Conference. As time progressed, I heard Hank's side. Both were convincing and I was forced to recall my dear ol Pappy's saying, "There's not two; there's three sides to every story – yours, mine, and the truth".

Our time soon came to depart. As we were leaving, Hank's wife and Julia hugged each other goodbye. Hank's wife came to the drivers side of the Lincoln where I was seated behind the wheel and stated, "I just love your Aunt Mary Ellen, please bring her back to me for a longer visit."

"I'll try to do that ma'am," I responded. As we drove down their long driveway to leave, we both glanced back to see Hank and his wife waving goodbye to us until we were out of sight. We were both quiet a good while; each with our thoughts and impressions after meeting the couple.

"From what little I was able to gather Uncle Buck, I'd say you're in – am I right?" Julia asked.

"Yes, Julia, I'm in, but I can't say I feel all that good about it. Ol Hank burned one undercover Agent – perhaps he'll burn me before it's all said and done – we'll see," I replied.

"I doubt that, Ron?" Julia responded and then grew quiet again. Finally, she stated, "Ron, those two are good people."

"I know Julia, I know," I said.

"You won't be too hard on Hank when you take him down, will you?" she asked.

"Honey, I guess that's what makes you who you are – you come straight from your heart and that's why all your agents love you so much. We'll try not to be too hard on ol Hank," I told the sweetest, most caring undercover agent I ever worked with – my Miss Julia as she completed her last assignment.

From the initial contact with Hank, through September of 1987, Agents Dave Cartwright (Dave Sloan), Tom Wharton (bear hide seller), Tom Bennett (Joe Black, real estate developer), TN undercover Officer Ray Swift and N.C. undercover Officer Dennis Holloway (Harold Cobb) -- Sloan's hunting companions and yours truly thoroughly infiltrated the Southern Theater of Operations. Its targets included one Georgia and five Tennessee residents. The operatives set up buys and/or bought bear galls, other bear parts and engaged in bear, boar and wild turkey hunts. Cases were made against all the targets identified at the Gatlinburg Conference.

Two additional targets (man and wife) who emerged, not identified at the Conference, were rather unique and dangerous. Their part-time occupation was robbing the graves of the dead. They showed operatives Cartwright and Holloway much of the bounty they'd collected as the result of their gruesome pastime – gold rings and other jewelry, ancient coins, etc. They described in detail their method of operation that left the grave site appear totally undisturbed after their unholy invasion. The man in this devilish duo ultimately sold a quantity of bear claws to the operatives.

Near the end of the operative's exposure to this couple, I had lunch with Hank at a village restaurant at his urgent invitation.

"I hear your nephew and his buddy have been keeping company with ___ and ___," (the grave robbing duo) Hank abruptly told me seeming very concerned.

"I didn't know that (a lie) – why, is there a problem?" I asked.

"There sure is, Buck! Those two people are crazy and dangerous," Hank proclaimed.

"How so, Hank?" I asked.

"___ (the guy) gets his jollies by getting men to make a play for his wife and she goes along with it; then gets her jollies too. While she seduces the guy, he hides and watches – he likes to watch and she likes to have him watch. After it's all done, they beat the tar out of the guy. The beatin's the climax to the whole thing. It's rumored they've killed at least two boys who've been missin' from these parts a good while. Now you listen to me, Buck, you get your nephew and that other boy outa there!" Hank advised.

"That's scary, Hank – real scary. I can't imagine Dave and his buddy pickin' up with somebody like that; I'll get them out of there. Thanks for the tip!" I responded. That evening I phoned Cartwright and advised him of Hank's dire warning. Cartwright laughed, "Don't worry Uncle Buck, we've made a buy and we've dropped them. Hank's right, they are weird, we sure didn't know how weird. I can't imagine they do a lot of business along the sexual lines – that woman is uglier than snot. Thanks for the info – it's sure good to know I've got ol Uncle Buck and ol Hank looking after our best interests!" Cartwright informed me.

So ended the "adventure" with the grave robbers, for the time being at least. After the Operation Smoky take down, the devilish duo was reported to the Tennessee State Police. Their grave robbing habit was dealt with harshly.

On raid day, Hank and the other southeast Tennessee targets were arrested by teams of uniformed Tennessee State Wildlife Officers. The Georgia target was arrested by federal agents. I watched a TV news clip showing Hank being escorted into the Federal Court House for arraignment. The escorting officer had not handcuffed him. Hank had his arm hooked through the arm of the young officer who walked beside him. Hank, like all of us at one time or another in our lives, had been his own worst enemy. With sadness, I thought, Why Hank, why? He carried the badge proudly for seventeen years, then turned and traveled the opposite path. I prayed I'd never have to work a fellow Game Warden again.

Our Miss Julia

"Just an old southern girl is all you get,"
She said to me, when first we met.
In her rich old south accent that haunts me yet;
Her first words to me, I'll never forget.
She served Agents past - George, Al, Warren and John;
And of more recent vintage - Jack, Jerry, Ted and Tom.
And many others who came and went;
She served them all – at times totally spent.
And me, who came to know and love her so;
As did all the others, who want her to know.
"This is Julia Hamilton speaking," for many years her famous
telephone greeting;
It caused many to visit her office seeking;
With her only a personal meeting.
Clerks, Judges, Senators, Congressmen and such;
All wanting to meet the lady whose voice they loved so much.
She served covertly in both country and town;
Admonishing after each assignment, "Don't be too hard on
those folks when you take them down."
She'd find us even during unscheduled travel;
How? A puzzle we never unraveled.
"You're to call Julia Hamilton," on arrival we'd hear;
Then, her loving voice ever so clear;
Delivering our messages year after year.
She loved, mothered, and nurtured us all;
Winter, summer, spring and fall.
Now she rests at the Master's feet;
In Heaven's Garden, on a gold paved street.
One by one, we'll all hug and kiss her again;
Only the Master knows how soon and when.

We love you, Julia
Ron
and
All your Carolina Agents

The Author with "Miss Julia" who received an Outstanding Achievement Award

Two northeast Tennessee Smoky targets were identified at the Gatlinburg Conference as bear gall traffickers as well as dangerous drug dealers. N.C. undercover Officer Lt. Joe Story and I made a run on them with limited success. We couldn't set up a buy. My ploy (missing coon hound) didn't gain the exposure time needed. They weren't houndsmen or bear hunters. They were worse – dealers and traffickers only. This meant a buy transaction with them would be expensive. We would have to meet or exceed the prices paid by their Asian handlers. However, before they dismissed us from their thoughts, we implanted an awareness in their devious minds:

1. My nephew, Dave Sloan, was in the import-export business in Nashville; a business that included me as a silent partner.
2. Dave bought bear gall bladders for a Korean client.

I informed Cartwright of our limited success with the two.

"We'll see what Matthews and I can do," Cartwright advised.

"It won't be easy David. At no time did they admit to us they bought or sold bear galls. They'll remember that fact," I told Dave.

How Cartwright and Matthews did it, I don't know to this day. The next thing I knew our roles were reversed. Tennessee undercover Officer, Lee Luening and I were set up to make a buy of twenty three bear gall bladders from the trafficking duo. Somehow Cartwright and Matthews had used a ploy that utilized "role reversal" to get the job done. Tennesse undercover Officers Halliday and Kennedy were all set to serve as backup and sound-video tape the event. It all went down in a motel room located in a northeast Tennessee city. Lee wore a body wire. The entire transaction was filmed through a motel window with opened curtains. After heavy price negotiations and conversation that clearly established our trafficking duo knew they were violating the law, we bought twenty three dried and/or frozen bear gall bladders for the sum of $1600.00. The film footage recording the transaction later appeared in the TV documentary "Greed, Guns and Wildlife." This was the largest single buy of Operation Smoky.

Next on the northeast Tennessee agenda were two houndsmen and bear hunters identified at Gatlinburg as bear parts sellers. They were hunting partners. One (I'll call Oakley) owned and operated a restaurant. The other (I'll call the General) was a well to do business man who would pass for the famous World War II British Field Commander Sir Bernard Law Montgomery. I managed to "get in" with Oakley by using my missing dog ploy. I introduced Matthews, Cartwright and their cover to Oakley one afternoon while having dinner at his restaurant. Subsequently, Oakley invited us to participate in a legal, in season, coastal North Carolina bear hunt that took place near Kilkenney and Mattamuskeet, North Carolina on lands leased for bear hunting by the General. We (Cartwright and I) accepted Oakley's invitation. It was "understood" Dave would buy the galls from any bears killed and any other parts that may be for sale. We obtained Oakley's permission to bring along one of our bear hunting buddies, Harold Cobb (N.C. Officer Dennis Holloway). Holloway's purpose was to witness (and later prosecute) state law violations we knew would occur. Holloway was a superb undercover operative. He really got into his role. He grew a beard and dressed the part of a dirty, scroungy, bear hunter. His appearance was so appalling you'd swear he also stunk. He wore a crumpled wide brimmed hat that covered his eyes. He could portray the most sinister, untrustworthy, rotten, lowdown individual imagined.

On a cold day before the opening day of the November, 1986 coastal N.C. bear season, we all assembled with camper trailers and set up camp at the General's Kilkenny N.C. lease. Later that afternoon, two uninvited guests arrived who knew Oakley. (I'll call them) Little Stevie and Big Ralph. They towed a banged up camper and set up camp. They were from one of the deepest hollows in northeast Tennessee. They had no hounds or non-resident N.C. hunting licenses. They had many guns and an ample supply of cocaine. That night after eating, we all sat around a camp fire and got acquainted. All, that is, except the General who remained in his large and luxurious camper, after tending to his hounds. Little Stevie and Big Ralph told Oakley, "We knowed whar ya'll be huntin' – we came over cause we's wantin' to kill a bar."

The following morning after an early breakfast and before the hunt, Harold Cobb visited with Little Stevie for a short time while having an extra cup of coffee. "I shore wish I'd had a Pappy like ol Buck, Dave's Pappy, who set him up in business and whatnot. My Pappy was a drunk, beat on my Ma and went to prison for killin' a feller," Little Stevie told Mr. Cobb (Holloway).

"Buck is Dave's Uncle not his Pappy. Dave's Pappy died when he was a youngin'. Buck raised Dave – took care of him. Buck ain't got no kids of his own – he's gay," Cobb told Stevie.

"He's what?" Stevie asked.

"Ol Uncle Buck's gay," Cobb answered.

"What ya mean?" Stevie asked.

"He's gay – you know," Cobb answered.

"Ya mean he's quar – he's a wantin' to trifle with men folk – not no woman?" Stevie inquired.

"Yeah, you got it – ol Uncle Buck's gay," Cobb told Little Stevie.

"Does he try to trifle with ya'll – you and Dave?" Stevie asked.

"Oh no, he respects the fact we're straight. Ol Buck's got a friend in Raleigh," Cobb replied.

"We run them kind of fellers off where I come from," Stevie commented.

"I'm not surprised," Cobb responded.

I didn't learn of this conversation until long after the hunt. I wondered why Little Stevie, so friendly when we all got acquainted around the campfire the first night, took great effort to avoid me during the rest of the hunt.

The first day's hunt began soon after breakfast. In a short while Oakley's rig dog "bawled loud" on a hot bear track. Oakley released him from his truck hood tether – he was off and running, bawling every breath on the hot bear track. Shortly, Oakley released another hound who quickly joined his rig dog opening "full cry" on the track. About this time, Little Stevie and Big Ralph arrived late on the scene. They were much too scantily dressed for hunting. Their dripping, red, cocaine noses explained their tardiness. They were well armed with holstered hand guns and hunting knives. Twenty minutes into the chase, Oakley addressed the General, who was formally attired in British tweeds, a waist belted coat, leather leggings, and a little tweed touring cap.

"Do you feel it's time to pack "Lillian" to the chase?" Oakley asked the General.

"I dare say it is," the General replied and nodded towards his pickup truck with its custom made aluminum dog transport crate in the bed. Oakley obediently retrieved a leashed, very slight built and bawling, little redbone female hound from her compartment. She listened to the two hounds squalling on the truck, then strained for release. The General nodded and Oakley released sweet little Lillian. She went to the trailing hounds pronto. Soon, she opened on the track. As soon as she opened on the track of the now hotly pursued bear, the General raised his right hand skyward. Oakley, Big Ralph and Little Stevie immediately stood still with heads slightly bowed. Not understanding what was taking place, Cartwright, Holloway and I followed suit. The General, head bowed, crossed his arms on his chest. After a few seconds, all returned to normal. "What was that all about?" I asked Oakley in a whisper.

"It's an old European custom. When ____ (the General) crosses his arms on his chest, he's paying tribute to the bear. At the same time this symbol means 'dead bear'. He only does this when Lillian opens on a track. When she opens, ____ (the General) knows the pack is running a bear – no off game. Lillian is a straight bear hound; she won't open on anything else. Lillian is so fast, she'll push a bear so hard it will soon tree or bay on the ground. Then, it's a dead bear," Oakley explained. This ritual would take place five times, with the killing of four more bears during the next three days of the hunt.

Two more hounds were "packed" to the chase as a Mercedes arrived. From it exited a Doctor from Raleigh clad in hunting clothes. He paid the

General $500.00 for the privilege of shooting and claiming a bear. Within the hour, thanks mainly to Lillian, a bear of about 300 pounds was bayed on the ground in very thick cover. After some effort with machetes, all arrived at the scene. The hounds, except Lillian, were caught, leashed and tied to saplings. The Doctor took careful aim and dispatched the bear with one shot. Immediately Oakley, Little Stevie and Big Ralph pounced on the carcass. They did an expert job of skinning the bear leaving the head attached to the hide. Afterward, Oakley deftly opened the bear's body cavity. With a short pre-cut string he tied off the gall bladder before severing it, thus sealing the bile juices therein. He quickly put the gall in a plastic bag and quietly, almost unnoticeably, handed it to Cartwright who hurriedly brown paper bagged it. All helped packing the bear hide and skinned carcass (tied to a pole) to the nearest road, the Doctor departed with the hide and attached head. No effort was made to tag the bear before transport as required by state law. Stevie and Ralph transported the carcass (as ordered by the General) to a meat processing facility for later retrieval by the Doctor.

That afternoon bear number two was brought to bay in the thickest Pocosin Swamp imaginable, with little Lillian leading the pack. Following the General's European ritual, the group (excluding the General) formed a line. The lead man macheted the thick brush in front of him for twenty minutes, then the second man in line would move to the front position and so on. The progress was slow hard work. Suddenly little Stevie yelled, "Give me one of those two-way radios," as he burst his way ahead of the line. Armed with a holstered .44 Magnum, he began backing and elbowing his way into the thick thorns and brush. The brush was tearing his shirt clad back to pieces. Soon, the swamp enveloped him and he was out of sight. All you could hear was groaning and cursing as the brush tore at his flesh. After forty-five minutes, we heard the loud echoing report of Stevie's .44 Magnum. Then Little Stevie's voice over the radio, "Boys come and get Mr. Bar – I just blew his brains out." It took another hour and fifteen minutes to hack a trail to Little Stevie, a dead 500 pound bear and the hounds. The hounds, now quiet, were laying here and there licking their wounds; some inflicted by the thick thorny brush and some inflicted by the bear. There stood Little Stevie with his long stringy, bloody hair, holstered .44 Magnum and dripping, reddened cocaine nose. The back of his shirt was blood soaked and torn to shreds. Big Ralph lifted Stevie's shirt-tail; his back looked like ground hamburger. Little Stevie had already began skinning the bear. Oakley and Ralph followed suit. Soon they reached the bear's hind end where they cut into huge puss bag. The bear was obviously wounded with buckshot in the past. The stench was unbearable with no wind or breeze in the thick swamp, everyone got sick. The three skinners threw up but nevertheless finished skinning the bear, keeping the paws and claws intact. They scraped the puss off the hide and actually packed the stinking, heavy, hide out of the swamp. The carcass minus gall bladder of course was left to continue to rot. That evening at camp, Oakley and Big Ralph smeared Little Stevie's back with a salve used on the hounds to toughen their paws.

They bandaged his back with a big white (but dirty) towel. I'll never forget Little Stevie and his bear killing incident. I've often thought – Could he or would he have done it without cocaine – I doubt it very much.

The second day two more bears, one in the morning and one in the afternoon, were killed at the Kilkenney site. One bear was brought to bay on the ground, the other treed. Little Lillian was getting tired and couldn't catch this one on the ground. The third days hunt took place at the Mattamuskeet lease site. The hunt was without unusual incident, other than an encounter with trespass bear hunters hunting without permission on the General's lease. One bear was brought to bay on the ground and killed.

The gall retrieval procedure for bear number one was repeated four times during the three day hunt with the killing of five bears. Before breaking camp the third day, Cartwright negotiated price and bought five gall bladders plus the claws taken from four bears. Payment was made to Oakley who later admitted and testified half the money went to the General. Oakley, the General, and Little Stevie each laid claim to a bear. Big Ralph claimed the puss laden hide from bear No. 2. None were tagged before transported as required by state law. Stevie and Ralph hunted without the required N.C. non-resident licenses and bear permits. The four bears were transported to Tennessee. Bear parts were knowingly sold in violation of state law and in interstate commerce in violation of the federal Lacey Act. Following their arrests on raid day, August 23, 1988, the four were prosecuted in state and federal courts. They paid dearly for the errors of their ways.

The Fontana Theater of Operations

Basically, two families, I'll call the "Wills" and the "Burke" clans, claimed eight family members identified as Operation Smoky targets at the Gatlinburg Conference.

One of the most difficult challenges of covert investigative work is "initial infiltration". This single task usually requires all the talents the operative can muster. North Carolina Wildlife Officer Lt. Tony Lewis was a "natural" undercover operative. He could "walk the walk and talk the talk". He could portray the "aw shucks" kid himself, complete with both "country boy" dialect and mannerisms. Tony met with NCWRC Captain Bed Wade who supervised the geographical region where both clans lived and hunted. Ben supplied Tony with "buy money – just in case". Later, he met with local Officer Travis Whitson who supplied Tony with additional detailed intelligence and a map showing where the targets lived and hunted. Tony was off and running. In exactly one day; (1) he infiltrated the entire Wills clan; (2) made the first bear hide buy (fresh, with head attached) of Operation Smoky (and some wild boar tenderloins to boot); (3) arranged an invitation to participate in a scheduled closed season bear hunt (at night) on the GSMNP.

Later, due to a misguided, uninformed, outdated, yet sincerely felt philosophy regarding undercover work by a superior in the NCWRC Raleigh Office, sadly, Tony was removed from the investigation. I must add this superior's philosophy was temporary – it didn't prevail, thank goodness!

As a parting gesture by phone, telling the bad guys he couldn't go due to a death in the family. Tony arranged for "a close friend that could be trusted" to participate in the scheduled closed season bear hunt. That close friend was USFWS Agent Tom Bennett. Tom, using his established cover, entered the scene. As usual, Tom took the ball and ran with it! Before Smokey's end, Tom would incorporate undercover operatives, Agents Ted Curtis, Tom Wharton and South Carolina Officer Larry McClain.

Through body wires, taped phone conversations, witnessed conversations, and prior arrest records, they established all eight members of the Wills and Burke clans, plus two associated poachers and two Koreans, knowingly and willingly violated North Carolina law, GSMNP's law and consequently, the Lacey Act. They nailed a third Korean for an illegal ginseng violation. They established each target violated these laws in the past, was willing to violate the laws at present and intended to continue violating in the future.

On one occasion Agent Curtis talked the bad guys into allowing him to video tape an illegal hunt. Ted filmed all he could during the daylight hours. After dark, letting the camera remain hanging from his shoulder and left running, he recorded the conversations taking place as the hunt continued.

In addition to witnessing and documenting closed season hunts on and off the GSMNP, the operatives made (and in some cases) filmed undercover buys of the parts of illegally taken bears i.e. gall bladders, claws, hides and heads. They bought illegally sold protected migratory birds, a gallon of moonshine and witnessed a well attended showing of a porno movie.

All would successfully be incorporated and participate in the two other Operation Smoky "Theaters of Operation".

In mid-July, 1986, I was contacted by a superb mid-western assigned Agent, Doug Goessman. Doug was working his own mid-west based covert investigation involving the Asian bear parts black market. A part of Doug's investigation led to a Korean target in Atlanta. Subsequently, following covert-taped phone contact, Agent Goessman and the author sold the Korean importer four bear gall bladders. The Korean's case was successfully litigated under the Lacey Act with a significant penalty. A second lead developed by Agent Goessman led to another Atlanta Korean importer's apprehension, arrest and conviction.

The undercover part of Operation Smoky began in the fall of 1985. It ended on raid day, August 23, 1988. I've written for the most part, about my adventures during Smoky. All the while the other State and Federal Operatives involved in Smoky experienced adventures of their own while they nailed the bad guys. I can't write about their adventures, only they can, they were there. Forty three subjects were arrested on raid day. Seven subjects were arrested later as the result of investigative leads obtained on raid day and through post raid day interviews. Several subjects (Fontana Theater of Operations) voluntarily turned themselves in to Special Agent Tom Bennett, fearing Tom would soon come knocking on their door.

Within the federal court jurisdiction for eastern Tennessee we experienced very poor cooperation with the U.S. Attorney's Office. Identical criminal Lacey Act charges, approved for prosecution and successfully prosecuted by the U.S. Attorney's Office for the Western District of North Carolina, were declined for prosecution by the U.S. Attorney's Office in east Tennessee. Few were approved and prosecuted. Those few were won with significant penalties levied. Consequently, many east Tennessee cases were adjudicated in state courts (where all were convicted) or litigated under the civil provisions of the Lacey Act. All litigated civilly ultimately paid penalties. The litigations lasted well into 1990.

The total penalty results amounted to well over $200,000.00 in fines with three subjects sentenced to prison terms. 266 bear gall bladders, 285 bear claws, 77 bear paws, 9 bear hides, 1 live bear cub, 3 protected migratory birds and a gallon of illegal moonshine were purchased. Three stolen vehicles were recovered with the thief prosecuted; 70 pounds of ginseng were seized with the Korean possessor prosecuted. An unlawful human burial during a bear hunt and resulting gravesite, over which a federal undercover agent "said a few words" (Cartwright, of course—another story) along with two grave robbers were reported to appropriate authorities having jurisdiction. All were investigated and litigated. Many drug violations were detected and litigated by DEA.

I stated in the Preface, "I was blessed with good agents." I add to that, "We (the feds) were blessed with darn good State Fish and Game Undercover Officers." Together, after two previous attempts failed, we pulled it off!!

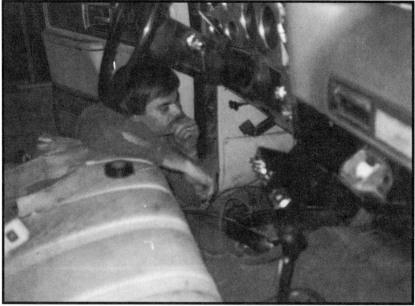

(Above) The Gatlinburg Conference. (L-R) Gene Abernathy, J.D Moore, Mike Zetts, Ben Wade, NCWRC; John Cook, GSMNP; Tom Wharton, Dan Searcy, Dave Cartwright, USFWS; Bob Harmon, TWRA; Tom Bennett, USFWS.
(Below) Stumped! NC Wildlife Officer, Mike Zetts, thinks it over while installing a concealed tape recorder in an undercover bear hunting vehicle.

(L-R) SC undercover officers Brian Wilson & J.C. Sims (surveillance van officers) CI, USFWS Agents Maureen Matthews & Dave Cartwright. Second bear gall bladder buy. Operation Smokey.

(Left) NC undercover Officer Joe story, planning strategy in North East Tennessee, doing preliminary work on largest single gall buy – Operation Smokey.

GSMNP Ranger/ Biologist Bill Cook (left) and TWRA undercover Officer Tom White with a load of bear hides and other bear parts bought by State & Federal undercover operatives – Operation Smokey.

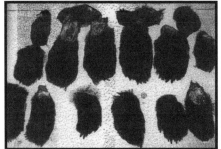

(Above and right center) 16 black bear gall bladders.
(Left Center) Black bear paws – destined fro "Bear Paw Soup" on the Asian market.
(Bottom) Black bear claws, teeth, penises and skulls. All bear parts bought by state and federal undercover operatives – Operation Smokey. Photos, Bill Cook GSMNP.

Agents, Maureen Matthews and Dave Cartwright relax in our Opryland Suit. "Rehersal Day", the day before the "Opryland Sting".

(Left) Black bear killed by a poacher following the "sting", during a "confidence" closed season hunt on a bear sanctuary where bear hunting was illegal. Undercover agents witnessed the killing and later bought the bear gall bladder, hide and claws.
(Center) a very tired undercover Agent cartwright takes a nap when we went back to pick up the hounds after "stashing" the bear to the left. One of the bad guy's hounds looks on.

Call "Uncle Buck" Farley at _____ or "Nephew", Dave Sloan at _____

$1000 Reward
No Questions
Asked

The Hounds of Operation Smokey "NAP" the best coon dog the Author ever owned or hunted. "He helped me catch poachers in the 1960's. Then again after death in the 1980's.

(Lower left, foreground) "Trooper" working as a Federal Agent. A Plott hound – a great track and tree dog.
(Lower right) "Knot" an English hound on duty as a Federal Agent. One of the best "rig" and "strike" hounds in the Smokey Mountains. Here posing with the Author.

Our Miss Julia Hamilton on duty – her last assignment.

Throughout my entire tenure in the Carolinas, sandwiched between overt and covert investigations, alone and beside North and South Carolina Wildlife Officers, we worked many migratory game bird (waterfowl and doves) hunting seasons. We apprehended, prosecuted and convicted thousands for violating our nation's migratory game bird hunting laws through the various Carolina U.S. Attorney's and Federal Court systems. The story of our migratory game and non-game bird law enforcement efforts in the Carolinas can only be properly told in another book. Carolina Agents completed and successfully litigated many overt, after-the-fact investigations and several lesser covert investigations.

Two overt investigations completed by Case Agent Tom Bennett, during Operation Smokey's tenure, stand out in my memory. One involved the destruction of red cockaded woodpecker habitat on and off a major military installation in N.C. in violation of the Endangered Species Act. The investigation was long and complicated. Tom saw it through to successful litigation.

The second case involved the wayward Director/Curator of the N.C. Museum of National History. Illegally misusing the provisions of a scientific Endangered Species Permit, he appointed various big game hunters throughout the nation as "associate curators". Using their museum affiliation, they enjoyed hunting and taking traditional and exotic big game species listed as endangered and banned from import into the U.S. by the Endangered Species Act. Utilizing the services of a well known big game trophy appraiser and co-conspirator, the "associate curators" claimed inflated tax deductions for their museum donations. Tom was assisted by the N.C. State Bureau of Investigation, the Internal Revenue Service and U.S. Customs Service. The Director/Curator was prosecuted in U.S. District Court by the U.S. Attorney's Office for the Eastern Judicial District of N.C. He plead guilty and was appropriately penalized. Ostracized by his peers, he retired.

This volume tells only part of the Carolina story. Perhaps some day, I'll pen "The rest of the story".

Operation Smoky was my last undercover assignment, for that matter, my last significant case. Near the end of Smoky, I participated in a night-closed season bear hunt set up by a confidential informant who participated in the hunt. The hunt took place near Blowing Rock, N.C. After a lengthy chase, the hounds treed. Locating their general location by their tracking collars, we soon arrived at their treed location. They were barking up a huge hemlock covered with leafy vines. The entire hunting group began shining the tree, attempting to locate our quarry. The treed critter proved to be a huge raccoon – not the expected bear. I was wearing a typical night hunters hard hat with affixed light. Walking backwards and looking up at the tree, I stupidly managed to step off a roadside cliff and fell thirty feet into the empty darkness. I was knocked unconscious. I recall seeing streaks of light (like meteors) on impact. When I came too, my head was lodged against a sapling and crushed into my chest. The rest of my torso was pointed upward. The light on my hard hat was still lit. My hard hat was lying on my left shoulder. I remember thinking, my neck is broken – I don't dare move. At the same time, I could hear shale-rock falling to my right and left. My torso began sliding to my right down the mountain. Without more thought of a broken neck, I dislodged my head and hooked my right arm around the sapling as my torso continued sliding. At the same time I realized my neck wasn't broken. Thank God, I thought. The light on my hard hat, now lodged against a rock below me, was still shining and illuminated a logging road about forty feet below me. I released my hold on the sapling and slid down the mountain to the logging road. En route I slapped at my hard hat. It dislodged and followed me. When my feet hit the solid surface of the logging road, I thought the top of my head was coming off – the pain was bad. Standing, I felt the back of my head – it was all blood. I dropped to my knees, fell back on my haunches and rested for a few moments. My head was throbbing. I could feel blood oozing down my neck and back. I remember thinking, be thankful you can feel that blood, Bailey—you're neck's not broken. After resting a few more moments, I walked a short distance discovering a rhododendron-laurel laden ravine that led to the logging road I fell from. Although the ravine was a thicket, I knew the growth therein would provide me with the hand-holds necessary to reach the road above. Climbing, fighting the thicket hand over hand, I could hear the hunting party above calling my undercover name (Buck). Their lights cast beams in every direction. I tried answering their calls but for some reason couldn't. It was a frustrating—near claustrophobic feeling. Reaching my destination, my CI grasp my bloody right hand and hauled me to safety. Needless to say the hunt ended.

My CI drove me to an all-night clinic in Boone, N.C. where they cleaned my wound and put nine stitches in the back of my scalp. I spent the rest of the short night at the home of my CI in a bed graciously prepared by his wife. I couldn't sleep, I was in too much pain. I arose just before daylight while my care giving hosts slept and drove my hunting rig to Raleigh – a big mistake as I was later informed by my Doctor. My Doctor in Raleigh referred me to a Neurologist who ordered a full body MRI and diagnosed a spinal condition I can't spell, pronounce and won't bother to consult my old medical records to write. My continuous head and neck pain gradually subsided; however, my left side was left numb. I often fell as my left leg involuntarily went out from under me. Later, during the dove season, I fell flat on my face twice while checking hunters with state officers. It was embarrassing and I tried to cover my handicap by explaining, "guess I must have tripped over something!" I would involuntarily drop tools while working with my left hand. I was fearful I would drop my handgun while shooting the left hand position during firearms qualifications. I couldn't remain in any "still" position for extended periods without pain—I would have to move.

All the while another career situation was taking place. My boss, SAC Dan Searcy in Atlanta, one of the best and most supportive gentleman I ever worked under, vacated his position under circumstances I never really understood. The law enforcement leadership in Region 4, in my and many opinions, left with Dan. After almost four decades doing the work I loved so much, I was now tired and battle worn. My physical condition, the fact I knew my most supportive Regional Director, Jim Pullium, was near retirement, and the fact my SAC, Dan Searcy, who held my utmost respect was gone, hastened my retirement. Although I was fed up with the bureaucratic crap, my love of the resource and its preservation remain – it always will.

As recent as one year before my fall at Blowing Rock, I couldn't bear the thoughts of retirement – I didn't ever want it to end. After the fall and experiencing what was taking place at the Regional level, I couldn't "get out fast enough". I recall praying in the wee hours of the morning at home in the den, "Lord, put it all in the right perspective and keep me true to the cause," I asked. At the usual hour, I went to my office and experienced one the most unforgettable happenings of my life. I stood behind my desk looking down at the work I had to do. On the left was a stack of material to read, initial and refer to the file. Centered was a "spike" full of messages and phone calls to return. To the left was stacked work that required lengthy writing regarding employee performance standard updates and appraisals, monthly work assignments and budget reports, etc. The top of my desk was covered with work. Instantly, it was as though I was way above it all. Looking down on it, it all appeared ever so small. I recall thinking, Bailey, it's all crap, insignificant bureaucratic, administrative, stupid, crap. The time has come – your priorities in this life have changed – go home. Go home I did, telling my Clerk, Beverly Moser, I was a little "under the weather" and would return tomorrow. At home, I prayed again, "Thank you Lord, it's over". I've heard many retirees say, "You'll know when it's time to go". I knew my time had come – I looked forward to retirement. I declined the customary retirement party. I knew I couldn't handle it – too many years – too many memories.

After many months of wrestling with my neck and back problems, I decided I needed other opinions. I consulted my neighbor – a chiropractor. He reviewed my medical records and stated, "Ron, I won't touch you." Why I don't know, I decided to consult another chiropractor. Interesting is the fact he was a close friend and went through his chiropractic schooling with my neighbor. His name is Dr. Eric Ewert; his practice is in Garner, N.C. He reviewed my records, x-rayed my spine and after a short while stated, "Ron, I can help you".

"Have you treated a condition like mine before?" I asked.

"Yes, I have, several times and all the treatments were successful," he answered.

That day Eric administered my first treatment. His treatments continued weekly and then monthly. Exactly one year later, all the numbness in my left side had disappeared. I was left with a slight "balance" problem that haunts me yet.

I went to work for the Raleigh Office of the Pinkerton Detective Agency as a contract investigator. I even got a shiny gold badge. The work was certainly different but I enjoyed it. My second year, I received their "Investigator of the Year" award. My time as a "Pinkerton" terminated with our move to our retirement home in the beautiful Blue Ridge Mountains of Virginia.

31
Of Conscience and Stewardship

The words "Honor" or "Character" or perhaps "Integrity" or even "Maturity" may also be appropriate in the title of this story.

During my many years behind a Wildlife Officer's badge, I've taken notice of a particular evolutionary process. Generally speaking, most wildlife law breakers are relatively young. As he (I can't say she as my observations of female violators are limited) grows older and matures (especially spiritually), his poaching activity lessens and in most cases stops. This slow down with age in hunting, and to an extent, fishing activity is true of law abiders as well.

Age brings wisdom and a much different set of values. Not only to the poacher but all of us who are average. Gradually we see all wildlife around us in a much different light. Most see wildlife as "God's creations" the same as man. Their take or harvest attitudes change or modify greatly. The closer they get to eternity, the greater the change.

I've noticed those few who grow older and continue the wanton and illegal taking of wildlife seem to have deep character flaws. I'm forced to wonder what eternity holds for them and if they are aware of the hereafter at all. They are the minority which is fortunate for our wildlife resource.

It is in the Christian Bible's Old Testament we find what may be the earliest stated rule or law of wildlife management – a restriction on take or harvest. It is one of the statutes and judgments composing the Mosaic Law, and decrees that: "6 -- If a bird's nest chance to be before thee in the way in any tree, or on the ground, whether they be young ones, or eggs, and the dam sitting upon the young, or upon the eggs, thou shalt not take the dam with the young; "7 -- But thou shalt in any wise let the dam go, and take the young

371

to thee; that it may be well with thee, and that thou mayest prolong thy days (Dueteronomy 22: 6,7)."

There are at least five accounts of <u>confessing misdeeds </u>(sins) to man found in the Bible. Two in the Old Testament and three in the New Testament.

"I Samuel 15: 24 – And Saul said unto Samuel, I have sinned; for I have transgressed the commandment of the Lord, and thy words: because I feared the people, and obeyed their voice."

"II Samuel 12:13 – And David said unto Nathan, I have sinned against the Lord. And Nathan said unto David, The Lord also hath put away thy sin; thou shalt not die."

"St. Luke 15: 18 & 21 (Parable of the lost son – the words of Christ)

"18 – I will rise and go to my father, and will say unto him, Father, I have sinned against heaven, and before thee."

"21 – And the son said unto him, Father, I have sinned against heaven, and in thy sight, and am no more worthy to be called thy son."

"James 5: 16 – Confess your faults one to another, and pray one for another, that ye may be healed. The effectual fervent prayer of a righteous man availeth much."

Perhaps due whole or in part to the preceding scriptures or others, some doctrines within the Christian faith require the new convert to confess to man as well as God. In any event, some new converts to Christianity feel the need to confess past violations of our fish and game laws to a Fish and Game Official. These matters are what some Fish and Game Agencies call "Conscience Cases".

I'm sure conscience cases can and have resulted from conversion to religions other than Christianity. I know a percentage of these cases have nothing at all to do with a religious conversion, conviction, or belief. The individual, for whatever personal reasons, simply wants to get it off his chest. In any event, "Conscience Cases" are a small part of Wildlife Law Enforcement. They most certainly take place in every state. In most instances, it is the Wildlife Law Enforcement Officer who must deal with them. Needless to say, these cases are ticklish to say the least. They most certainly are not to be laughed at or scoffed. In all instances, the individual who comes forward to confess are undergoing very deep seated and emotional motivations. They are wrestling with their conscience and/or what they believe to be the welfare of their very souls. I certainly admire them. To do what their conscience or religious conviction dictates requires what I call gumption or guts – he-man qualities all too scarce in this day and time. The act is much akin to admitting you're wrong when you are and apologizing to the person you've wronged when the case warrants.

Although I've known several Wildlife Officers in various states who have handled conscience cases, it only occurred once in my career. In this instance, a young man (I'll call) Terry Allen, wrote a letter addressed to: Game Warden, Oxbow Lake Wildlife Management Area, Defiance, Ohio. In his letter,

Terry identified himself, gave his telephone number and detailed directions to his home in a western Defiance County community. His letter highlighted the fact he recently converted to the Christian faith and named a protestant church he joined. He stated his new religion and church doctrine mandated he, as a new convert, "Confess his past transgressions and sins to man as well as God." He asked that a Game Warden call on him at his home so that he could confess to past wildlife law violations. His letter also stated he was prepared to pay any penalty that might be assessed. Reading between the lines, it was obvious this fine young man was dealing with serious soul wrenching matters.

Terry's letter was initially received by the Wildlife Area Manager at Oxbow Lake who referred it to Game Protector, Tim Hood, assigned to Defiance County. Hood brought the letter to me at my home in Montpelier, and stated, "Bailey, if you watched a poacher violate the law, you'd rather let him go home so you could pick him up the next day and put the "B" (meaning, interview the subject and get him to confess) on him rather than apprehend him on the spot just after he violated the law. There's only one Game Warden in this part of the state who can and should handle this – you."

I read Terry's letter, phoned him and made arrangements for Officer Hood and myself to interview him at his home that evening. Later, following the explicit directions in his letter, we arrived at Terry's home and parked our patrol car in a driveway off an alley behind his residence as instructed in his letter. Hood went to the back door and soon returned with Terry who seated himself in the passenger's seat.

With Hood seated in the back seat and me behind the wheel, our interview began (before Miranda Warning). Following the usual introductory amenities, I began by stating, "Terry, I was led to the Lord years ago. I am a back sliding sinner, but nevertheless a believer and I'll be a believer the rest of my days. I have some understanding of what is taking place in your life. I commend you for having the fortitude to follow the teachings of your church and the dictates of your heart and conscience. Now, we'll listen to anything you feel you want to tell us."

At this point, Hood experienced a throat or coughing problem of some sort and politely excused himself from the patrol car. He strolled up and down the alley behind our car as he continued to deal with his apparent throat problem.

Terry's facial expression told me his letter was on the level. This fine young Christian was dead serious. Substantially, he admitted shooting rabbits at night in the headlight illumination of his car on a public road during the closed season. He admitted taking several fur bearing species during the closed trapping season. When I questioned him concerning these occurrences, he couldn't remember a single date that fell within Ohio's two year statute of limitations for wildlife law violations. In other words, his admitted wildlife law violations were not prosecutable.

As Terry told me his story, I recorded his admissions on a single page statement. I attempted to question him concerning others he knew of who had or were at present violating the game laws. From his reaction to this line of questioning, I quickly and in no uncertain terms, ascertained this was the wrong thing to do. Terry wasn't interested in discussing any transgressions except his own.

I asked Terry to read the statement I wrote regarding his admissions. I asked him to tell me if the statement was true and if so, sign it. Terry read it and said it was the truth. Before he signed the statement, I summoned Hood to our patrol car so both Officers could witness his signature.

With the statement procedure completed, I told Terry, "None of the wildlife law violations you've admitted fall within the statute of limitations for Ohio's wildlife laws. Therefore, we can not and will not file any charges against you – you'll pay no penalty. Does this take care of the matter for you?"

"Yes sir, it does," Terry replied. It was obvious he was relieved the matter was over and done.

We both commended Terry again for his straight forwardness and having the guts to do what he thought was right. With the usual parting amenities, we left him walking up his driveway towards his home.

"Not one case – huh, Bailey?" Hood asked as he finished reading Terry's statement.

"Nope, not one case, Tim," I replied.

"And he wouldn't talk about any of his buddies who violate?" Hood asked.

"Nope, I tried to get some information in that respect but he made it clear he was there to talk about himself only," I replied.

"Well Mr. B, I guess we've done our jobs," Hood responded.

"Yeah, I guess we have," I replied thus ending the only "Conscience Case" I personally ever handled.

Years later, working as a Special Agent with the U.S. Fish and Wildlife Service assigned to Pennsylvania, I heard several Pennsylvania Wildlife Officers speak of conscience cases. For whatever reason, Pennsylvania, certainly a state of many cultures and religions, seemed to have more instances of these cases than any other state I worked in or was assigned to during my federal career.

The first PA Officer I heard speak of conscience cases was my boss, Leo Badger, the U.S. Fish and Wildlife Service Senior Resident Agent in charge of PA. Leo was a former Pennsylvania State Wildlife Officer. The conscience cases he handled took place during his tenure as a State Officer.

The next instance I recall involved PA State Wildlife Officer, Ed Gosnell, assigned to Lancaster County. It was said among Ed's peers he was exceptionally talented in handling conscience cases. This was easy to understand as Ed and his wife, Ann, were folks of deep Christian convictions whose lives gave living testimony of their faith. I add, Ed was one of the finest and most highly principled Game Wardens I ever worked with. In retirement, Ed and Ann reside in Addison, Maine where Ed serves as pastor of a protestant church.

On a particular fall day during the waterfowl season of 1976, Ed and I were scheduled to work the goose fields of Southern Lancaster County. Ed took time during the morning to take care of an urgent conscience case. I went on to the goose fields. Later, following his handling the case, Ed joined me and we proceeded on our quest catching "hoofties" (Pennsylvania Wildlife Officer's name for violators). We were very successful in our hooftie quest that afternoon, making several bait and live decoy cases. I recall Ed seemed deeply concerned for the individual involved in the conscience case. I didn't question Ed about the matter but I got the impression he considered the case a very serious matter.

Ed tells of a conscience case involving a young Christian gentleman of a somewhat more sacrificial faith. In this instance the young man confessed to hunting one minute beyond the legal shooting and hunting hours. Ed informed the young man he would not accept a penalty from him -- his one minute error in judgment could be because his watch was a minute off. He further advised the young man, had a Wildlife Officer actually witnessed or caught him, the Officer would not cite him for such a minor violation -- it was too close to call. Ed's judgment satisfied the young gentleman, thus resolving the case.

Ed spoke of another case involving a long time Christian of the same faith. In this case, the gentleman sought Deaconship in the church. Apparently before the title "Deacon" could be bestowed on him, he had to confess his sins to God and man. The gentleman confessed to a relatively minor violation that occurred beyond Pennsylvania's two year statute of limitations. Ed accepted a "token donation" to the PA Game Commission. The case was closed with the gentleman's conscience satisfied and the requirements of his church met.

Another one of Pennsylvania's finest was PA Wildlife Officer John Shutter, also assigned to Lancaster County. John was one of the best and toughest Game Warden's to ever wear the badge. John related an instance in which a wayward hunter contacted him and wanted to confess to a violation. John visited the gentleman; heard his confession and litigated his case under the Pennsylvania Game Commission's "Field Acknowledgment of Guilt" system. (A statute covered system that allows the violator to acknowledge his guilt in the field and simply pay a fixed penalty to the Game Warden. This system is not unique to PA -- several states have similar systems.)

Shortly thereafter, the gentleman contacted Officer Shutter wanting to confess to another violation. Again, John heard his confession and litigated his case under the Field Acknowledgment of Guilt System.

Later, the same thing happened again. This time the violation he committed and confessed to fell outside Pennsylvania's two year statute of limitations. Thus, unable to settle the matter by another Field Acknowledgment of Guilt, the confessor sent a generous contribution to the PA Game Commission.

Still later, this same gentleman contacted John again wanting to confess to another game violation that fell outside the statute of limitations. This time, as John stated, "I felt I had to shut him off. I told him he had confessed enough and I didn't feel it would be necessary for him to confess to any more violations." John didn't hear from him again.

As I write this, John is the Chief of the Law Enforcement Division of the Pennsylvania Game Commission. He told me he receives three or four "Conscience Case" letters each year at his office in Harrisburg. Naturally as Chief, John refers the letters to his field officers to take care of.

I heard conscience case accounts all across our great nation as I worked in the various states as a Special Agent for the U.S. Fish and Wildlife Service. I believe the Ohio and Pennsylvania stories pretty well tell what Conscience Cases are all about and there is no need to tell of others.

The Christian Bible's account of the creation is found in the Book of Genesis. Chapter One: 20-31 – The account of the fifth and sixth day's creation.

"20 -- And God said, Let the waters bring forth abundantly the moving creature that hath life and fowl that may fly above the earth in the open firmament of heaven."

"21 -- And God created great whales, and every living creature that moveth, which the waters brought forth abundantly, after their kind, and every winged fowl after his kind: and God saw that it was good."

"22 -- And God blessed them, saying, Be fruitful and multiply, and fill the waters in the seas, and let fowl multiply in the earth."

"23 -- And the evening and the morning were the fifth day."

"24 -- And God said, Let the earth bring forth the living creature after his kind, cattle, and creeping thing, and beast of the earth after his kind: and it was so."

"25 -- And God made the beast of the earth after his kind, and cattle after their kind, and every thing that creepeth upon the earth after his kind: and God saw that it was good."

"26 -- And God said, Let us make man in our image, after our likeness: and let them have <u>dominion</u> over the fish of the sea, and over the fowl of the air, and over the cattle, and over all the earth, and over every creeping thing that creepeth upon the earth."

"27 -- So God created man in his own image, in the image of God created he him; male and female created he them."

"28 -- And God blessed them, and God said unto them, Be fruitful and multiply, and replenish the earth, and subdue it: and have <u>dominion</u> over the fish of the sea, and over the fowl of the air, and over every living thing that moveth upon the earth."

"29 -- And God said, Behold, I have given you every herb bearing seed, which is upon the face of all the earth, and every tree, in the which is the fruit of a tree yielding seed; to you it shall be for meat."

"30 -- And to every beast of the earth, and to every fowl of the air, and to every thing that creepeth upon the earth, wherein there is life, I have given every green herb for meat: and it was so."

"31 -- And God saw every thing that he had made, and, behold, it was very good. And the evening and morning were the sixth day."

The fact we're charged with the stewardship of all wild creation put here for our benefit and welfare is quite clear. Rest assured, we'll be held accountable for the management and care of this great blessing we've received from our Creator and God above.

To understand our God given wildlife resource, and prayerfully manage it wisely, is to understand a part of Him. This is one of my deepest convictions. Of their life's work, many are asked, "Would you do it all over again?" My answer -- "I'd pray for the honor and the privilege."

For information on other outdoor books

write to:

Lightnin' Ridge Publishing, Box 22,

Bolivar, Missouri 65613